- "No Library is complete without this book – every page astounds. I never wanted it to end." - [Stanley Joseph – Director, Producer, Composer].
- "I could not put it down to take a breath" – [K. Solo].
- "I literally felt I was experiencing the events that have influenced our world to this day. Exhilarating!" – [Gregory James Green – Writer/Director].

BEN HUR II
EXILE

BASED ON THE FIRST CENTURY HISTORICAL ARCHIVES OF THE ROMAN, GREEK AND HEBREW WRITINGS.

"Not to hear one of the parties to a suit in the absence of the other party" [Ex. 23:1]

Flavius Josephus

Queen Berenice

Left Image: First-Hand Witness & Author of "The Roman War with the Jews."
Right Image: Her crown displays the triumph of Rome's Eagle over Judea's sacred symbol.

First Published 2014.
US Library of Congress Registration: TXu 001-890-891.

This work contains references and images controlled by independent sources.

Immense appreciation for permissions granted for limited usage of the copyright works, Images & Services of:

Aberystwyth University, UK. (Images)
Abraham, Nathan. (Translation)
American-Israeli Cooperative Enterprise. (Time-Lines; Images)
Frantz Kantor Productions (Illustrations; Art)
Gordon, Eric Arye. (History)
Greenger, Nurit. (Translation)
Heritage History, WA, USA. (Images)
Jewish Virtual Library Org. (Time-Lines)
Laurie Lamson, Nowwrite. (Literary)
Levin, Alex. Artlevin.com. (Images)
Makarova, Kate. (Images)
Mechon Mamre Org. The English-Hebrew Bible.
Solo, K. (Literary).
Teicher, Robert. (Research).
A Shhhh! Studios Production.

Disclaimer.

The portrayals in this manuscript are derived from independent personal research and interpretations of historical archives by the author and are not representative of any theological or national sectors, groups or persons. This E-Book edition contains instances of explicit historical images and portrayals.

~~~~~~

Also by Joseph D. Shellim.
"PHILISTINE-TO-PALESTINE"
The Modern World's Biggest Deception.
[2015]

~~~~~~

Table of Chapters

ACT III: HOLY WAR

"If I have not craved glory, then glory itself has craved me"

The Decadent Hebrew-Roman Queen Judith Berenice, Grand Daughter of
Herod the Great, Goddess Mistress of Titus.
[Concept Art Frantz Kantor] Source: S2

What 'Really' Happened?

Historys most impacting century remains its most miss-represented. A new appraisal based on
suppressed archives and first-hand witness accounts assesses a long due varied consideration of
this history. Rome's war with the Jews was neither about power nor terrain; nor even against the
Jews per se who otherwise held prominent positions in Rome's institutions. Rome allowed
freedom of belief to all her conquered nations, acquiring a plethora of deities for worship; Rome
accumulated 400 Gods. Yet this war was different from all other wars. The Jews would not 'do as
the Romans do' - they followed laws that Rome called as the Hebrew sorcery:

"So you are the only people who reject my divinity!" (Caligula)
"Gods are Gods - What difference which one!" (Vespasian).

This was a Holy War. It turned history and humanity as no other. Rome's greatest weapon, more so than her military might, was her par excellence in guile and propaganda. Rome allowed no adverse reporting, scrutinizing all writings and killing any who dared her, including prominent Roman philosophers such as Helvidius Priscus. It is why we have a total absence of any Hebrew or Christian writings from the first two centuries. The Dead Sea Scrolls were saved under extraordinary means and became the sole authentic manuscript of this period; all else is questioned by historians.

Here, who won this war, Rome or the Jews, becomes conditional to the question being a retrospective or contemporaneous one. It was a time when Christianity was yet not a religion and Islam centuries away. Here, history itself tilted and the un-expected happened; the victor became vanquished and the utterly vanquished prevailed. According to the Roman archives, Mighty Rome's victory was shrouded in latent defeat, with the Jews' "No Surrender' to the last man and woman on Masada:
"And it seemed to everybody and especially to them that so far from being destruction, it was victory and salvation and happiness to the Jews that they perished along with the Temple." – So writes Rome's most prominent philosopher, Deo Cassius. Vespasian will throw down his victory crown in the Coliseum celebrations; 10,000 Romans will turn sides. Thereafter, the divine emperor realm itself came to a close, conquered by a new religion that became history's biggest and most successful one. Christianity emerged as a Monotheist belief when this was least plausible, emerging out of the belly of anti-Monotheistic Rome.

There is much confusion and contradictions of the first century's reporting, its given history deficient, selective and abounding in non-aligning reports. All such contradictory reporting cannot be equal; it says something is amiss. Rome's war with the Jews began with the Greek Empire in 300 BCE. Alexander, the devoted pupil of Aristotle, enters the Jerusalem Temple with a strange request to the temple priests:
"Translate for me your Torah in the Greek tongue."

The first translation of the Hebrew Bible into another language ('The Septuagint'), will impact humanity more than all of Alexander's war victories. The early Roman Bishops, still under Roman dictates, initially rejected the Hebrew Bible, but the Greeks insisted the Septuagint be canonized. The elite Greek minds upheld Aristotle's 'First Cause' belief, aligning it with the Hebrew 'In the beginning God.' Thereby, Alexander's legacy became the western civilization's transformation to Monotheism - or why we don't worship Jupiter and Zeus today. Therein marks the game changer and the Roman Emperor's angst with the Jews, resulting in history's greatest 'Clash of Beliefs'.

The belief in One God invaded the Roman Empire via the fiery debates of the Jews and the Greek philosophers; it opened new trajectories, including the contribution to Christianity of a Messiah. Here, it was those rebel stiff-neck Jews who alone challenged Mighty Rome, thereby opening the only portal that allowed Christianity to happen; for how can a Messiah emerge without first defending the source that predicted one? Christianity was born out of it:

"Jesus spoke Hebrew, wore Tassels, preached only to Jews, performed sacrifices and had Hebrew writings on his cross" (Acts 26:14).
"Without Judaism there would be no Christianity, and only with Judaism has Christianity a relationship with origin." – (Hans Kung.)

"Certainly, the world without the Jews would have been a radically different place. Humanity might have eventually stumbled upon all the Jewish insights. But we cannot be sure..." - (*Paul Johnson*; author of "A History of The Jews").

This presentation plunges you into that faithful century; how it would be had the Jews succumbed of their belief with Rome. A holy drama lay hidden under the history of this war. It is seen from the first breach of the outermost third wall of the impregnable Jerusalem fortress, the world's largest monument in its time, up to the Holy of Holies, wherein Titus and his lover Berenice entered alone; ripping with his sword first the strangely glittering purple curtain that covered a Hebrew writ in its entry:
"Know before whom you are standing." But Rome knew not of this historical spiritual drama, and came forth with crushing swords. To Rome's bewilderment the Jews were not backing away; they rushed forth to meet the legions with their children on their backs, thrusting into the Roman swords, joyously reciting a war psalm:
"Blessed be the Lord my Rock, who traineth my hands for war."
Perhaps a re-accounting what really happened will turn humanity, even meriting a re-consideration. Thereby, this history is unfolded via a 'Forbidden Love' between a Roman and a Hebrew, betrayers to both their nations and nowhere to turn. When 10,000 Romans turn sides, a 'Forbidden Love' amidst history's greatest destruction will transcend. Deborah Hur, a fiery Nazarite maiden, shouts out from the exile processions:
"Jerusalem will surely be returned - even God cannot change it. For our God's word is of truth?"

"Ben Hur II - Exile" is designed to 'mainstream' the ancient historical texts in a reader-friendly mode. The tedious and complicated archives, biblical references and its charismatic figures come alive with the historical events infused with its emotive dialogue and dramatic action every turn; how it really was based on its historical archives. Fractional dates are rounded; similar names (such as 'Eleazar') are presented as one person. The vast clickable index, time-lines, quotes and archaeological relics act as an ever handy reference almanac and are enhanced with 50 lavish biblical paintings, illustrations and new art works.

"The war between Rome and Jerusalem deserves to be called one of the most important events in world history. If the Temple might still be standing today, the history of the world would be inconceivably different." - (Moses Hess; "Rome and Jerusalem.")

❖

About. As a documentary film writer for 25 years I produced a diverse range of subjects such as Making Movies, W.W.II: The Frank Capra Documents, Deep Space Encounters and biographical films of The Beatles and James Dean. The first century History has always been an underlying intrigue throughout. I took actual historical archives and biblical verses and re-enacted them for today's audiences - to transport, to 'beam you' back to that arena and time. It all began with Berenice's enigmatic final retort to Titus, exposing a hidden core of spirituality in this infamous harlot: "What did you think this war was really all about, my brave mighty warrior?" Thereafter it became complicated. The results are sometimes unconventional, but I believe, historically correct and incumbent. What do you think this war was really all about?

- Joseph Shellim.

BEN HUR II EXILE

PROLOGUES

(Xi) LONDONIUM - 40 AD/CE

In the streaming clouds a distant lone black dot is approaching. Nearing, enlarging, soaring; the most powerful of all birds dominates the heavens alone. To Rome, the majestic eagle was the appropriate emblem of dominion. Above Londonium, a city conquered and Romanized with an adapted ancient Celtic name, the hovering eagle turns its head south; a dark plume of fiery smoke is ascending.

On the ground a war carriage is enveloped in flames, horses are screaming to be freed from their harnesses, and Roman soldiers are fiercely engaged in retrieving their Commander caught within the flaming carriage amidst a raging battle. From beyond the hills, fiery arrows are hurtling. The soldiers pull and tug at their Commander's flaming body in a desperate bid to retrieve him, but the fire is overwhelming and all retreat the raging furnace.

Then one soldier throws himself into the flames, into the carriage cavity, his body igniting instantaneously, yet he manages to throw off his Commander from the burning carriage. A trembling charred hand from the flames reaches out to his Commander, whose life he saved by forfeiting his own.

"Promise me, swear by Rome you will protect my son, my only son. Pledge to me by sacred Jupiteres…"

"You have my oath, Matarian." His Commander rests his right hand on his chest, eyes welling. "By sacred Jovis Diespiter, before our comrades I swear it - with my life will I protect your son. You Matarian, magnificent son of Rome - go in praise of Jupiteres."

The trembling hand wavers, succumbing to the fires. Commander Vespasian turns to his soldiers.

"Erase Londonium. Burn them all as they have our comrade. Heed not for age or sex of these savages." [18]

In the dawn of the next day, amidst the fiery embers, a Briton still yet alive stirs in the heap of burning dead bodies; he crawls out smoldering and bleeding. He confronts naked women on crosses, their breasts cut off and plastered into their mouths; smashed up men are nailed on crosses upside down and decapitated children are strewn about in a great destruction. The young Briton, in his 20's, bushy red beard, tooth ear-rings and tattoos, drops to his knees, screaming in an agony of the horror he confronts.

Vespasian, returning to his Roman base with his triumphant II Augusta Legion, is accounting his comrade's self sacrifice that allowed him to live. A man of humble beginnings and superstitions, Vespasian has the fear of the Roman gods scorched in his mind, and Roman valor seared in his heart. He will retire now from war, he decides, and he will keep his pledge to Matarian. Vespasian yet never saw the significance of his triumph of Londonium's Isle of Wight stronghold, that it would change his life forever; that it would change history forever. Great plumes of fires ascend above Londonium. The eagle in the streaming clouds soars eastward.

(Xii) A ROMAN WAR SCHOOL - 60 AD/CE.

Outside the Roman Metropolis, a hewn stone structure stands in an open field. In Rome's elite war school academy, the War Master pans the fresh faces of his new fourteen year old students. He stands silent and still as a chiseled marble statue, in iron studded sleeveless vest, muscle sculptured arms folded, waiting. There is a table at his side embossed with a Roman eagle; upon it sits a glittering golden sword. Gradually, the students stop shuffling and shifting; a tense pin drop silence develops. The War Master addresses his new students.

"A Roman soldier knows - woe to the conquered. A Roman soldier knows - no glory without the death of the enemy."

The War Master has not altered his statuesque posture, unflinching as three slaves - a man, woman and their terror struck daughter, bound in chains, are hurdled before the class of young war students. He measures the youths' wide eyed reactions of the slaves thrust before them.

"Fear or hesitance before the enemy will see no glory - it is not Roman. Which one of you may achieve this glory… will be decided here and now." He lifts the sword, holding it in both hands before the lads as if it was a sacred item:

"Who thirsts - for GLORY!?"

The slave girl screams, slumping to the floor, burying her face in her mother's protective torso. The students appear agape in shock and fumbling, the golden sword glittering before them. The War Master searches the lads' faces, the golden sword held in folded hands, waiting. None stir; the young girl heaves in terror, slumped on the floor, clasping her mother's feet.

In the rear of the classroom one robust student is jostling his way to the front of the class.

"I… I want it… the glory."

"Your name?"

"Titus. Son of Commander Vespasian. House of Flavian."

The War Master nods, nudging the sword forward. The young lad looks around at the wide eyes students who are frozen still and agape; the slave girl's screams now filling the hall. The lad Titus grasps the sword handed him by his master, grappling with its weight; then he bites his lip nervously and advances to his victims.

The eagle hovering in the skies screeches wildly…

Four years have passed. There is a large figure kneeling on the floor of a balcony, in a mode of fervent beseeching to his gods in the streaming clouds. He rises and bows in devotion, right hand on his heart. Now the fourteen year old lad Titus is transformed into a grown up formidable warrior with a golden sword clutched in his hand, the same awarded him in his youth by Rome's elitist war academy as Rome's most promising student.

He ponders his destiny now, panning the heavens, wincing and searching the streaming clouds: wherefrom will the path to his glory open? Now he hears the winds screaming, then a chanting… voices are emerging in his head. The warrior's suspicious eyes become focused and squinting. The people of Rome are hailing him; a great mass of people are calling out to him:

"Ti-tus! Ti-tus! Ti-tus!" A crazed smirk; his eyes bulge in astonishment as the voices in his head grow stronger. He nods now, waving at his imagined crowds below his balcony.

"They know me… oh great Jupiteres, they know me!?" He is waving at the people, acknowledging the hailing crowds in an empty avenue below.

A thundering boom of lightning emits from the Roman skies. Titus turns from the crowds to the heavens again; ghostly images are hovering above. Now Rome's Divine Emperors appear within the churning clouds; they are calling out to him. Titus is mesmerized of the voices in his mind addressing him from above. Rome's divine emperors now appear in the clouds above his balcony, their hands outstretched from the heavens and inclined to him. They chant in unison.
Augustus, Tiberius, Caligula, Claudius are chanting:
"Glory! The Glory! Glory for Rome! Glorrreee!?

Titus falls on his knees, his right hand pressed to his heart, tears welling. There is a screeching sound behind him; he turns to see a large, powerful eagle with ferocious red eyes perched on his balcony, its mighty talons gripping the iron rim. Titus retreats frozen and awed; an intense eye to eye with the eagle is exchanged. Now, slowly, he begins to understand the message given him from the heavenly abode of the Roman Gods. He nods solemnly at the omen sent to him; accepting; engaging the mighty bird's fastidious gaze into him. Now he understands. Titus imparts a sacred quest to the eagle perched on his balcony:
"The glory. I want it. Tell it to the Gods."
The eagle flaps its mighty wings, ascending, soaring, gliding into the heavens, as if obeying a command. Rome's ghostly divine emperors are prodding the mighty eagle to soar higher… higher into the realm of the Roman Gods; they chant in unison, hands outstretched to the great bird:
"GLORY! THE GLORY! GLORY FOR ROME! GLORRREEE…!?"
Titus' palm grips his golden sword firmly. A menacing warrior's glint emerges in the killer blue eyes.

❖

(Xiii) A ROMAN LIBRARY - 75 AD/CE

The lone man seated in an austere library lays down his feathered quill on the table. He has finished his writing; he rises from his chair, massaging his weary fingers. He is surrounded by an array of scrolls neatly assembled in rows of cylindrical cubicles on the walls. The piercing eyes on the bearded tortured face gaze out the large window of the library hall. His thoughts appear distant now, contemplating in far and deep ponderings. The persona signifies an elite stature and wisdom; the oratory a Shakespeare of his time:

"**WHEREAS**… the war which the Jews made with the Romans have been the greatest of all wars, not only in our times, but, in a manner, of those even that were ever heard of before. Both where cities have fought against cities or nations against nations…"
He holds up a long drop of scrolls in his hands as an offering of his testimony:
"I have submitted, for the sake of the Romans, to translate my books into the Greek tongue, which I formerly composed in the language of my own country. I, Joseph, the son of Matthias, by birth a Hebrew, a priest also, and one who at first fought against the Romans myself, and was forced to be present at what was done afterwards…"
He tosses the scroll on the table:
"I am Flavius Josephus."
In askance; defensively:
"I am the author of the writings of
The Roman War with the Jews…" [16]

ACT 1:

Chapter 1. <u>AN ANCIENT SCROLL</u>

Everyone's Truths Cannot Set Everyone Free.

Century # 1 marks the hinge point between the modern world and the end of the Hebrew biblical period. No century in recorded history incurred greater paradigm altering impacts on humanity. It is a time when the seedling of Christianity was yet not a religion and when Rome's divine emperors had a Jewish problem. Yet this was not a new problem for the Jews; this was the same battle that evolved from their earliest interaction with the nations, its impacts continuing pervasively and unceasing. Here, even simple questions shroud layers of cadence.

Why was Mighty Rome so obsessed over its most miniscule conquered province, one too small to class as a state? How badly were the Jews behaving compared to Rome's other conquered nations - were they poised to invade other lands of the Empire, commit robberies and lawlessness, incite every nation to worship their Hebrew God; or, worst crime of all, did they refuse to pay the correct taxes decreed by Rome? None of these applied. Yet here, two polarized beliefs, irreconcilable as the lion and the lamb, of the unstoppable confronting the immovable, became inevitably engulfed in an existential battle when "Monotheism" - a Greek coined term of a 'One God' Hebrew law emerged as the focus. Monotheism became an affront to Rome's divine emperors. Therein did the Jews became Rome's greatest enemy, a generic historical syndrome seen throughout the divine king realm.

Monotheism was enshrined into the DNA of the Jews as a foremost Hebrew law some 4,000 years ago when the first Hebrew emerged, a law that forbade the Jews from acknowledging divinity of Rome's emperors; it is the second of The Ten Commandments: "Thou shall have no other Gods before me".
It was a command destined to become the theological $E=MC^2$ equation of its times and one far from being a retrospectively designated obvious outcome four thousand years ago. This embolden new thought will become a bigger controversy than Galileo's telescope that changed the centralized and stationary position of a flat Earth. In the ancient world, Monotheism was a premise that contradicted and overturned all of the prevailing belief stabilities; it will cause new reasons for wars, divisions and conflicts; new religions will emerge from it, each proclaiming 'My One God is greater than your One God.' Equally, the faculties of a new judiciary and new pre-modern world sciences will be initiated. And the five large book-size scrolls of the Torah will emerge mysteriously, with no past Hebrew writings ever seen; the Jews will be the only people that spoke and wrote in this language. It is a nation that emerged out of the fiery deserts, a minuscule one that will beguile every other nation they interact with; the Jews will become a controversy in all camps of history.

Monotheism erupted upon the divine king nations with the Greek Septuagint bible in 300 BCE; it is the first translation of the five Hebrew books of Moses into another language. It marks the introduction to the world of an otherwise closed and unknown language outside of the Jews. Hitherto, Abraham, Israel and Moses were unknown figureheads with the nations; these Hebrew Prophets were introduced and contained exclusively in the five Mosaic books; its impacts on the elite Greek minds will alter humanity and history. The Hebrew tongue is a mysterious language that appears to have emerged suddenly and in an already advanced state of literature; the five books of Moses (The Torah/Heb; The Pentateuch/Greek) is the first output of the Hebrew writing. The Greek Septuagint was initiated by Alexander the Great; his request to the Jews of a Greek translation of the Hebrew Bible will become a game changer for religions, the Judiciary, Literature and humanity's early sciences. Its spread was causing widespread intrigue and controversy in the empire, most especially with the Greek philosophers that impacted their Roman conquerors; it also caused fury and angst with Rome's divine emperors and their priestly sectors:

"The issues came to a head over the large number of Gentiles who became converts, or who wanted to become converts, to Judaism"[17]

For the Jews this was a well played drama throughout their history, from Canaan to Egypt, then with Babylon, with the previous Greek Empire, and now with Mighty Rome in the first century. In the year 37, Caligula, the young newly ascended fiery Roman Emperor accuses a Hebrew delegation standing before him:

"So you are the only people who challenge my divinity!"

Rome's most notorious emperor issued a decree to the Jews; his statue of gold must be housed in the temples of all conquered nations and be worshipped with daily sacrifices. The Jews became the only people of the Empire who refused Caligula's commands, as they did historically with all divine emperors and saw great suffering in return. The Jews sent their highest delegates to Caligula, beseeching pardon from the edict, as did the great Caesar grant the Jews. To no avail with this emperor:

"You Jews will worship me in your Temple - in like manner as you do your invisible Hebrew God. My image will be made of your finest gold - else your Temple will become ash and dust. I swear it!"[18]

The Jews moaned: "The one thing that would destroy us is the only demand acceptable for the Romans."
Now, only a miracle could save the Jews from annihilation by Rome's most insane and sadistic ruler; here, a miracle did occur at this time and the Jews were saved. Yet their problem with Rome will not end; it will become compounded with successions of each new divine emperor ascending the throne. And the Jews' legacy of a stiff-neck people, one derived from and decried by the Hebrew God, also flourished as the stigma of this time in the Jews' history:

"And the LORD said unto Moses: 'I have seen this people, and, behold, it is a stiff-necked people. (Ex. 32:9)

Now the Jews stood alone in their confrontation with Rome's divine ordained emperors; here, there was no Moses or David who would confront Mighty Rome. Now, none of the nations understood the true nature of this war and its futuristic implications, and although their curiosity raged of it, none would attend the Jews' plight. Monotheism was yet a lone, controversial Hebrew belief, and almost all conquered nations were contracted into Rome's legions. It is an event that will soon shape the modern world; and the rebel stiff-neck Jews were cast in the front rows of the greatest of all Holy Wars.

This then is an existential battle for the Jews; they will be tested as no other. And they fully understand this and are prepared to engage with history's greatest super power to the last man, woman and child. Equally, all of Rome's divine emperors' credibility was challenged, and all her conquered nations were focused on a new kind of war undertaken by Mighty Rome's most minuscule people.

'There is no Israel without Monotheism; this nation was born in this law and it is Israel' - the Jews decided. Indeed it has been so throughout the Jews' history with the nations, albeit after some spectacular initial failings. Although being a nation of ever contesting groups, the Jews will stand as one in this war with Rome.

In first century Judea the Jewish groups were already immersed in domestic battles resultant from Roman appointed priests controlling their Holy Temple. It was Rome's stratagem of brutal intolerance of the Jews who followed disruptive and disdained laws, wore strange attire, observed restrictive diets, mutilated their male manhood and spoke a language no other nation did. The Jews caused controversy and intrigue, which the Romans promoted as 'sorcery.' The nations found that these Jews had many books of ancient history in the most advanced writings, and none knew how they achieved such books of knowledge before many older and mightier nations; it caused suspicion and disdain.

Now, for three hundred years, the spread of the Greek Septuagint Bible's impacts on the elite sectors of the empire was extending, with over 10% suspected of harboring covert interest in the Hebrew bible or secretly converting. While this created a large osmosis of the Hebrew Bible with the nations, it also became a deadly blow for the Jews. The Roman Emperors were enraged at the affront of one minuscule province's strange laws that showed disrespect of their divine status; for the Jews rejected all forms of the nations' mode of worship with disdain. Such was the history of this people from ancient times:

In 600 BCE, Haman complains to the King of Babylon that one people refused to bow before the king: "The laws of the Hebrews were different from those of all other people." [19]

So the Jews had their own laws which they kept, for these were given them by their Hebrew God via the hand of Moses, and they conflicted with every nation that interacted with this people.

The Jews did with Rome what they always did throughout their history; they responded to the Roman Emperor's edicts that flaunted their laws with fastidious measures of fundamentalist religiosity. And Rome increased her brutality tenfold; this arid land soon ran out of trees to feed Rome's traditional crucifixions with wood. And the Hebrew Monotheism became the Roman Emperor's greatest enemy.

In this most controversial of the empire's conquered lands, amidst the Jews' crises with Rome, internal political and religious battles and deliberations raged between the priestly sectors, including the Sadducees, the Pharisees and the Essenes, how they should respond to such a mighty power that took control of their sacred Temple and flaunted all their laws. In the midst of this turbulent and glowing land of first century Judea, small Jewish groups of Ebionites and Nazarenes were spellbound by the teachings of their Rabbi Yeshua (Yehoshua/Joshua/Jesus of Nazareth). These groups continued a brave following of their teacher even when they faced dire opposition from Rome and from their own kinfolk over differing belief criteria; that some followed their teacher even after he is crucified by the Romans will emerge as a game changer in history's most impacting century.

And concerning the Jews, the issue of the law of Monotheism transcended all else; such was their primal cause and onus in emerging as a nation; the flaunting of their laws constituted a flaunting of their Hebrew God. Monotheism was a law that marked this people from all others wherever they trod and wherever they were driven; theirs was the first game changer for the nations outside of Judea ever since this law first reared itself in the most ancient distant times, even before the Greek and Roman Empires were yet born.

The Source. It began two millenniums before Mighty Rome's Coliseum stood. In the ancient city of Ur in Mesopotamia (later Iraq), its capital the famed Babylon, older than Egypt and considered by many as the cradle of civilization, a radical new thought was sprouting. Here, a disturbing, disorienting and evocative new premise emerged that will overturn the worldly status quo. In the ancient city of Ur emerged a man compelled by strange new thoughts swirling in his mind as he watched his people's dutiful rituals of nature and emperor worship; even as the most devout worshippers performed human sacrifices of their most cherished child as offerings.

This man pondered long; then he concluded that the sun, the oceans, the winds and the thunder were not Gods, neither were the deities who battled each other for supremacy and were worshipped by his people as gods. Then he concluded even more daringly, that his nation's emperor was also not divine, as believed by all others in his nation. Such thoughts were decreed as a blasphemy in the ancient world, when freedom of belief was yet far away from the divine emperor realm.

Thus did one Abraham become a wanted man meriting Capital punishment by the earliest and all-powerful divine king Nimrod of Babylon, the great-grandson of Noah. Abraham became a man pursued, a heretical rebel and subject to the death penalty in his homeland.

The book of Genesis says this Abraham was then confronted by a God who affirmed his new thoughts with a provocative revelation, declaring He was the God of all, even of the sun, the winds, the oceans and the stars; even declaring that only He is God and that there is no other God, thereby sweeping away all other Gods in a single stroke. His newfound God directs the fugitive Abraham to flee his country to a new land: "Now the Lord said unto Abram: 'Get thee out of thy country, and from thy kindred, and from thy father's house, unto the land that I will show thee." [Gen. 12:1]

Thereby, pursued for the 'thought-crime' of Monotheism, Abraham fled his homeland and became the first exiled Hi-Biru ('one who went away') [20]

The source point of the war against the Hebrew Monotheism began with the first Hebrew in the ancient city of Ur. Thereafter, it was made as a contractual divine covenant in Abraham's newfound land. Monotheism became the earliest recorded 'thought-crime'.

Mount Moriah [21].   Canaan means lowland, especially relative to its surrounding hilly terrains. In the ancient Canaanite city of Urusalim, the earliest known name of Jerusalem, a radical new belief was established on the site of a hilltop known as Mount Moriah. Here, a covenant was consummated between a man and his God that will profoundly impact humanity and alter our historical trajectory. Throughout ancient times divine emperors never liked beliefs that opposed their own divinity, especially so the unworldly concept of a God that can never be seen. Abraham's Monotheism was viewed as barbaric, haughty, unacceptable and guilty of disrespect of all other Gods and beliefs; it became the primal cause of the bondage assured to the seed of Abraham.

Four hundred years after Abraham, the Hebrew God will affirm Monotheism as a foremost holy law via the hand of Moses. Deep in the Sinai deserts of Arabia and before a new nation of some three million newly redeemed slaves, the Hebrew God will conduct an open and direct revelation before a new nation and a mixed multitude; the narratives describing such an occurrence make it among the most significant events in the universe that the human mind can imagine. There can be no proof of such an event and there is none; yet it is the source point of Liberty, equal justice for all and a new belief structure and writing emerging for the first time. And this freedom of belief would not come free. Deliverance out of the Egyptian bondage came with stringent new laws for this people; its foremost one was the most controversial of its times: "Thou shall have no other Gods before me". (Ex. 20:3)

It was a strange new law that overturned the prevailing status quo; for the newly freed Hebrew slaves were subjected to many centuries of Egyptian beliefs whereby Gods were plentiful and each controlled their own realm; the God of the underworld ruled where the God of the Sun could not; such was once the way of humanity pervasively and Monotheism was an affront in this ancient realm.

The Hebrews will not succeed initially with such a controversial new command and will go through a rigorous period of some forty years and forty-two stops in the mountainous deserts of Arabia. It is also among humanity's richest periods of acquiring a new future civilization's foundation of belief, liberty and existentialism, of a vast array of humanity's laws and new concepts of a divine creationism. It became set into the hearts and minds of three million newly freed slaves, inherited in the DNA of the following generation when the first assembly of this nation was fully consumed. Monotheism, Liberty and inalienable human rights were born here.

The bondage of Abraham's seed that will eventually be aligned with the mandated law of Monotheism will incur the wrath of the ancient world's divine emperors. The laws also included the earliest forbiddance of human sacrifice, then rampant in this realm; and equal justice for the commoner as the king, also intolerable laws in the divine emperor realm. The Hebrew God forewarned and prophesized it to Abraham in holy writ, when his offspring of Ishmael and Isaac were yet not born, before the arrival of any Hebrews, Israelites or Jews emerged:

"Know for a surety thy seed shall be in bondage." [22]

True: two thousand years later, in the great Coliseum, Rome is celebrating her triumph over Abraham's seed and his invisible Hebrew God. Retrospectively, 'The Roman War with the Jews' - the writings of the historical scribe Flavius Josephus, can appropriately be called 'The Roman War with Monotheism'. Mighty Rome was mightily obsessed with one miniscule province influencing all her conquered nations, for the matter of one unseen God began to corrupt many in the Empire. This was a diabolical new enemy for Rome, and the sorcery of such a heretical new thought was now igniting the angst of Rome's divine emperors.

Cassius Dio, a renowned Roman historian, wrote of its impact:

"The whole earth, one might say, was being stirred over the matter".[23]

(1) THE COLISEUM - 73 AD/CE.

The eagle hovering in the streaming clouds tilts its head south. The eagle begins swooping down in a vertical trajectory, descending towards an egg shaped elliptical structure the size of two large football fields. The Roman Coliseum is packed to its 50,000 capacity on four levels; the massive structure is partly incomplete, sections of its walls stop rising abruptly. The Coliseum was completed in the year 80; its first name, initiated by and honoring the Emperor Vespasian of the Flavian family dynasty, was Amphitheatrum Flavium.

In the year 73 CE, this massive iconic structure opens with the triumphant marking of a nation's destruction and the anointing of a Roman king as divine. The victory of Mighty Rome was never more glorious or richer; the triumph of the Roman Gods is absolute.

The huge arena is surrounded by the coliseum's curved walls, a new iconic design poignantly contrasting other monuments in the Roman metropolis, constructed by the Jews of Judea shipped to Rome as the select few of the world's most skilled builders. [24]

The Jews learned such skills from the Phoenicians and Egyptians and constructed the greatest monument in the ancient world, the Jerusalem Temple, from specifications of engineering marvels and design listed in the Hebrew bible as given by the Hebrew God.

Rome brought the Jewish builders after destroying the Jerusalem Temple; any skills possessed by the conquered Jews became the only saving grace of their lives, their conquerors being adept in measuring the benefits from war spoils prudently. Mighty Rome's Metropolis became a city of marble instead of stone, a mark of grandeur designated by the great Julius Caesar; legend says he became awestruck by the Jerusalem Temple of marble and gold embellishments.

Now thundering Roman trumpets, cymbals and drums are graduating to a great din; a reveling hedonistic circus atmosphere prevails. There is a hum of excitement; the people are privileged to attend Rome's triumphant victory celebrations. Masked Romans are blowing on toy horns, barely naked harlots are soliciting, a senator's wife complains of food drippings from the upper levels.

This day Rome will mark her triumph over the smallest and most controversial province in her vast conquered empire: Judea - a Latinized Judah, formerly Judah and Israel, the ancient kingdom of the Israelites.

Center staged is the Master of Ceremony, the robust carnival attired Speaker Bassus; he welcomes us with shrill, gregarious pride and honor:

"Cari fratelli e sorelle - Rome will not disappoint her people this day!" He dares his audience, smirking in history turning passion.

"This day Rome speaks to the whole world… even unto history!" The Speaker Bassus spreads his arms as he declares open the sacred event of Rome's victory celebrations and its emperor's inauguration of divinity. "Welcome…" Palms flap inviting. "Welcome to the arena!" He bows repeatedly, worshipping, pointing raised hands of devotion toward the Royal Chamber on the second level.

"This day Rome anoints our emperor with the crown of divinity - this day we worship Vespasian!" A din of chanting erupts. "And this day we give glory to Vespasian's son with the crown of victory - we bow before mighty Titus!"

The Emperor Vespasian waves a slight hand palm in response; his ascended Flavian dynasty, immediately adjacent of the royal chamber, rises, waving. The peoples' chanting is unceasing; they roar in unison.

Bassus is flapping his palms, inviting his audience to witness Rome's richest victory celebrations and to account the glory of Rome's war spoils measure for measure, bout by bout. Bearers of large basins of gold coins are parading.

This then is a ringside view that unfolds one of history's most pivotal wars, one incurred by history's mightiest super power against a small province harboring a new world premise and a most disdained one of the ancient world for two thousand years, one the Greeks coined as: 'Mono-theism'; a One God belief. For Rome's Emperors it was the sorcery devised by the Jews, the enemies of the Gods.

In our retrospective ringside view, there is Mighty Rome in the red corner and Judea in the blue corner. Yet such a depiction has less to do with either of the contestants; indeed it is destined to loom larger than both. As we traverse this history, the events will depict Monotheism as a bad career move in ancient times.

The Speaker Bassus assures the massive gathering of the great triumphs and blessings bestowed by the Roman Gods:

"My fellow Romans, what you are about to see has never been seen before! Blood rubies! Sacred sapphires! Gold that makes the eyes to shine! From the ancient kingdom of the Israelites! It is a day foretold by the Gods of Rome!" The raised finger proclaims Rome's justification… "AND by the fallen Hebrew God! Hail Mars! Hail Jupiteres!"
The crowds chant in unison of affirmation.

At one of the Arena's twenty gates, two men and a woman, primitive animal-skin attired foreigners from Rome's most distant conquered island of Briton, are deliberating with the guard to be allowed to enter. The guard examines a parchment with a Roman seal presented by the three foreigners at the gate.
As the Speaker Bassus completes his bowing formalities before Rome's divine Emperor, he turns to address the people; he excites them with wonders never seen in Rome.
"This day you are all witness to the end of a nation, one which stood two thousand years… one even older than Rome!?" Hushes and hisses resound from the crowds.
"Gratis! Gratis! First - a reward from Titus to the most beautiful women of all - Roman! For you, the finest jewels your eyes have ever seen! Hear you are! Here..!"
The women compete in hair pulling fights for the gem stones flung at them. The Speaker Bassus stretches both arms at the Coliseum's tightly packed gathering of spectators, the largest assembly in Rome's history, ushering a display of war spoils entering the arena.
"Citizens! The seal of Alexander the Great! And the famed Queen Bathsheba's crown!"
The people hail the great display of treasures, chanting:
"Glory to Rome! Hail Jupiteres!"
Seated diagonally across from the royal chamber, two Senators in richly Roman toga dress discuss their new emperor.
"He appears not happy. Even in his greatest hour." Senator Marcellus is smirking. [25]
"Word is…" His colleague, Senator Alienus, responds covertly. "The stiff-necks perished without the surrender word." His hand covers his mouth.
For those who served the previous Julio-Claudine Emperor dynasty, this day is not a celebratory event; Nero, the last of the Claudians, committed suicide, to which the Romans responded with joyous satisfaction. This day, Vespasian represents the new Flavians, the less elite Commander of war who ascended the Roman throne after a chaotic period of assassinated candidates that followed Nero's demise. The Flavians now held control of the war legions and the riches of Rome's new conquered wealth from the vast treasury of the Jews; no Roman Emperor held such power and wealth. There is disdain on the faces of the Claudine Senators.
A blast of trumpets prompts the people. The Speaker Bassus directs the peoples' attention as Hebrew slaves hoisting the war spoils appear.
"It is before your eyes! The throne of King Solomon - made from the finest gold and ivory. But Oh! This wondrous throne is empty. No king!?" He empties his palms in the air; hails of laughter from the people resound.

The three foreign Britons at the gate are led by guards to the lower darkened basements of caged slaves. One of the Britons pauses; his gaze is affixed on the tightly packed slaves, his eyes searing in terror. Flashes of Londonium appear before him as he recollects the fires of his homeland and the Roman destruction of his kin; his face in angst, he recalls the burning bodies and decapitated women appearing before him. The guard pushes the three Britons forward. The parading of war spoils continues.

In the Royal Chamber, Titus presents the Queen Bernice with a jeweled broach; it is a Priestly Diadem from the Temple spoils. A Golden Eagle stands atop the Queen's provocative crown, its beak and shining eyes made of ruby red gems pointing to the heavens. The Menorah, symbol of the Jerusalem temple, is clasped as prey under the eagle's feet, clutched by its powerful claws. The Queen Bernice's face dangles droplets of jewels attached to her eye brows; her gown fronts a U-neckline plunging below her navel, exposing swirling coils of gold painted mock pubic tattooing. The queen displays Titus' gift with sensual desire, loving it within her breasts in the sight of Rome; this queen knows of the Roman weakness for lust and how to play them.

A din of chanting and woof's from the Roman men hail the seductive Romanized Hebrew queen; she is voted the star of the day by their wailings; she excites Rome's lusting excesses more than any other. For the Romans, the Hebrew Queen is a gift from their gods; the din of their wailing is insuppressible.

"So that is the harlot Hebrew Queen." Senator Marcellus seethes. "Dare he bring such a woman on this day as his royal escort… even after she was mistress with his own father, the King we now divine!?"[26]

"Hah! First with her brother Agrippa, then with the king we worship this day!" Senator Alienus responds covertly, his face bent. "And now she is seated with his son as a queen before Rome!? The Flavians insult us - we are seen as lower than the Jews!"

The Hebrew King Agrippa, seated a row behind the royal chamber, gazes in askance at Titus fondling the broach on his sister's breasts; his hidden fist stirs in suppressed rage.

"It is said no man can resist her vile." Senator Alienus sways his beer mug, lusting at the brazenly costumed queen. "Ever see a more desirous cunnus - she dishonors Rome so magnificently…"

Titus focuses on the Senators, his menacing eyes peer from behind a jug of wine in his hand; a warrior's smirk understands the Senators' intents.

There is suspicion and dark foreboding submerged in the celebrations; four candidates to the throne were assassinated before Vespasian ascended the throne. Titus must protect his father to assure his own ascension and glory, one that was prophesized by the Gods. And above all, Titus was manically jealous and protective of his Goddess. He lifts Bernice on his shoulders, pointing her to the king; he moves awkwardly, his left hand appears dysfunctional.[27]

Bernice caresses the beak of the eagle on her crown seductively, then she extends her open palm at Titus' father, blowing the emperor a hand kiss. Hailing and woofs resound.

"Does he imagine Rome will allow an incestuous Jewess to the throne?" Senator Marcellus is dismayed by the Flavian politics that harbor Rome's enemy so openly this historic day. "The Gods forgive us - we have yet not recovered the depravity of our last emperors. Now this!?"

"That crown comes from her grandfather King Herod, a true friend of Rome." Senator Alienus confers whispering. "He left her great wealth - mounds of gold, many palaces and security garrisons. Why else will father and son bow before this Hebrew harlot? Betrayers!"

A foreboding drumbeat is blasting. Below the arena grounds in the dimly lit basement of slave quarters, an iron cage is wheeled up the basement ramp, packed with twenty male slaves and paraded in the arena. Three crocodiles are released from an encircling row of cages. As the Roman gladiators direct the kill with spears and shields poised on the snapping reptiles, a bantam weight chanting erupts.

"More boring displays." Senator Marcellus sways face condescendingly. "This is all Rome has become - savages ruled by savages."

A Hebrew wrestles a crocodile, his powerful arms suffocating its large throat; he is cut down by a Gladiator's sword from behind. Wounded, he continues smashing the animal with blows; the spectators roar with laughter, chanting thumbs-down "KILL! KILL!" The Gladiator pierces the slave's back again; a crocodile jolts in a lightning speed, grasping the Hebrew's torso in its jaws, tearing away with a mighty snapping action. A reveling of satisfaction resounds.

In the subterranean basement, a cage packed with women is dragged up the ramp; it rattles and screeches to a standstill, awaiting its turn in a ramp queue. Inside, a young emaciated maiden struggles in her agony, clasping her belly; her woman comrades in the cage are assisting her, wiping off sweat droplets from her face.

The Queen Bernice wins back her desired attention from the savage sporting displays, compelling the Romans to her as she wobbles on Titus' shoulders before the king. She jitters her face, dangling the droplets attached to her eye brows tauntingly at the howling Roman men; their faces sway back and forth from the killings to the brazenly attired queen. She taunts the crowds yelling at them in an ecstasy, tearing out the mock pubic coils from her torso and throwing it before the emperor. The Romans scramble for the glittering coils; the queen screams in her wicked pleasure.

"We'll see about that!" - Senator Marcellus warns. "Such dishonor unto Rome cannot receive honor in return!"

Josephus, the Hebrew scribe in Roman attire and seated behind the Royal chamber, was promised rewards by the new emperor, and this was a most opportune time to collect, the results of his service on display this day. Josephus bows and proceeds towards the subterranean slave quarters.

"Anticipated Flavian treachery!" Senator Alienus angles the Hebrew in welling disdain. "Rome's emperor gets his council from a Hebrew priest and Rome's War Commander is ruled by a Hebrew Harlot. Victory… or mockery?"

The Speaker Bassus points to Rome's most prized war trophy entering the arena, the giant Menorah of gold, lifted precariously by twenty Hebrews and monitored by guards with spears at their sides. [28]

"My fellow Romans, behold this great wonder before you!" The people gasp as the war slaves sway and waver with the enormous weight of glittering gold they carry. "This is a most sacred treasure of their Hebrew God - it will be encircled before you seven times so its blessing shines on all Romans gathered here today." His arms extended: "Be you all blessed!"

For Rome, the Menorah blessing was its one ton weight containing the finest gold, its solid pillars of gold highlighted with delicate filigree; it's worth exceeding the cost of the Coliseum it is paraded in. For the Jews, the Menorah was its oldest national symbol of the Hebrew God, denoting Creation's original light, ushered before the stars appeared in the heavens, a pre-star light, its sacredness established in a fiery desert in holy writ:

'And thou shall make a candlestick of pure gold. Of beaten work shall the candlestick be made, even its base, and its shaft; its cups, its knops, and its flowers, shall be of one piece with it. Of a talent of pure gold shall it be made, with all these vessels'. [Ex. 25/31]

The Speaker proclaims it: "This giant Candelabrum was carved from one single piece of gold! It will never lose its luster!" A brilliant glow flashes on the peoples' faces as the giant Menorah with its seven arms and golden figurine tops extending to the heavens passes by them.

"Let there be light…" The Speaker's raised arm proclaims. "Unto Rome shines the light of the world!"

In the dimly lit subterranean basement chambers beneath the arena, Josephus approaches the Captain guarding the cages of women.

"I have been promised ten slaves by the emperor. I may select one from here."

"These are for the people's sport." The slave Captain sways his face at the Hebrew scribe. "Bring me Titus' orders with his seal or…" He cuts his throat with his fingers, smirking. [29]

"Mercy, mercy!" The caged women scream, extending their hands through the cage bars. "We took no part in the revolt - we are Nazarene, innocent as your own mothers of the charges. Release us we pray you!?" [30]

"You are all the same Hebrew enemy with new names." The Captain negates all hope of the women's cries. "All are guilty of Heresy - all are marked as sacrifice this day for the gods of Rome."

In the opposite rows of cages, the Hebrew men slaves jangle their iron bars fiercely at Josephus. "Traitor! Betrayer! Roman Jew! Jewish Roman! Tfu! Tfu!"

Josephus retreats into a dark protective crevice in the corner of the basement; he crouches in terror of his kinfolk's angst.

Outside the Coliseum, Rome's citizens mock the slaves driven in long rows of cages via the main city avenue leading into the basement chambers.

"Jude! Jude! Roman gods need sacrifices too!" They grab their groins in mocking:

"Jude! Jude! Why you cut off your mentula for!?" [31]

Trumpeters herald the Thanks-Giving Sacrificium. The Speaker Bassus ignites an elaborately decorated furnace with a fire torch; dark purple and red fumes rise to the skies as he announces. "For the Thanks-Giving Sacrificium, Rome offers exotic Hebrew women for Jupiter's blessing." In the arena, twenty women captives are hurtled from a cage in a bordered section before the royal chamber. Three lions are released from their cages; they growl ferociously, tormented by the smell from buckets of blood held before them. The gladiators empty the blood on the women. The two Senators stage a walkout from the sacred ceremony in protest. "Traitors! Savages!" Marcellus sways his closed fist at the Speaker. "Did not Nero forbid human sacrifice to Rome!?" [32] Titus hard stares the two Senators storming out of the ceremony; a gritting in his jaws. "O Vespasian! O Titus!" The women slaves extend their bound hands to the royal chamber. "To the murderers of mothers and children we say… NO SURRENDER!" The crowds boo; the lions jostle amidst the women's defiant screams. In the subterranean basement, guards are dragging the next cage of twenty women marked for sacrifice; the cage is stationed at the ramp queue awaiting its turn. Inside, a young maiden lying in the background of the cage floor emits a scream; a child is being born in the back confines of the iron cage. The young, emaciated mother's companions shield her from the guard's sighting; her tightly wrapped belly is torn of its cloth wrappings which till now hid her full pregnancy. In her labor travails the young maiden manages to acknowledge the defiance of the women's chants in the arena above; her eyes glow in solidarity before her comrades as she grasps their hands. "No surrender… no surrender!?" In the arena above, roars and frenzy of the starved lions reverberate, silencing the reveling din of the focused people. The bound Hebrew women clasp each other screaming, "No surrender" as the beasts mount and drag them down, tearing away limbs and necks; the beasts battle to protect their prey held fastidiously in their jaws. Erotically clad Roman women dancers parade on Gladiator's shoulders as they encircle the killing display; they mimic the slaves' torment with explicit gestures and quivers as a mocking. A drunken Vespasian peers between fingers covering his eyes; the Queen Bernice drops her face in her palms. Titus studies the killing calmly, swallowing from his jug of wine; Rome's great warrior appears unimpressed of an assured slaughtering. Bassus hoists a large basin of gold coins: "By the blessing and gift of Titus - a gold coin for every Roman citizen gathered here this day!" He hurls gold coins around the women's torn corpses. A great din resounds: "Titus! Titus! Titus!" "Let it begin - the divine anointing of our beloved emperor!" The Speaker Bassus kneels with raised hands inclined at the royal chamber, then he turns to welcome their entrance: "See, the Heavenly Beings come…" Two blonde virgins carry platters of leafy crowns, advancing in slow angelic steps toward the emperor's raised dais. They are adorned as divine Heavenly Beings, covered only with white feathered wings attached to their shoulders, their naked bodies sprinkled with silver speckles. The shimmering blonde virgins waver through torn corpses on the ground and bound women dodging the beasts screaming 'NO SURRENDER'. Severed limbs and torsos are strewn across the aisles before the royal chamber. The King holds his palms over his ears, as if to shut off the diminishing 'NO SURRENDER' screams still filtering. Vespasian is assisted to stand by the Heavenly Beings, his left leg is dragging; he groans in a drunken stupor.

"Woe, woe is me! I am being made a God, yet my soul is sickened by their no surrender defiance! These dogs barking at me this day - throw them away from me, shut their cries this day!" He keels over vomiting; maids wipe his mouth.

Now a strange face, in shadow and as yet indiscernible to Vespasian, is seated in close proximity to the emperor; the face is affixed gazing at Vespasian relentlessly. When the drunken emperor winces curiously, when he sees that the strange face starring him fixatedly is of Alexis, the son of Matarian, the offended King smashes his tub of wine on his Royal table. Vespasian gazes back at Alexis, his face wincing. The image of a charred hand extending from the fires of Londonium haunts the tortured tormented emperor: "Swear it you will protect my son, my only son?" - The pointing hand wavers at Vespasian.

When the approaching Blonde Virgins begin placing the Crown of Divinity on his head, he pushes it away, flicking the crown to the ground. [35] There is a great hush of bewilderment in the arena.

The king keels over the Blonde Virgin holding the platter; maids assist to stand him upright. The other Blonde Virgin turns to Titus, standing him opposite his father and begins to place the Crown of Victory on Titus' head in the solemn anointing process. For the Roman masses it is an electrifying moment; but within the underbelly politics of the Flavian family, Vespasian engages his son in a royal chastising.

"You failed to protect Matarian's son…" Vespasian is sneering in a lowly angst. "And Jewish mothers insult me with their last breaths before Rome… victory!?"

"My father commanded me for victory over the Jews and their God - to do whatever I must. I did, my father. See, Judea is no more, and the Hebrew God's glory now rests with Rome. We live this day in glory because you trusted the words of a Hebrew priest… your leg was torn, my arm is broken, such is the price of war, my father. And I stand today before my divine emperor, this is our holy day…our day of glory" Now, Titus wavers; the great warrior pauses destabilized; he winces in a stroke of pain as his palm clasps his forehead. "For all…" He steadies himself. "…All my glory is from you… for you. My father, the Gods of Rome… they have blessed us this day. I worship you." Titus kisses his father's hand, kneeling solemnly. The king turns away unimpressed, focusing again on the man in the opposite chamber, his enflamed eyes addressing Alexis Matarian's challenging gaze.

Alexis begins to leave his seat. He is assisted by two guards, one under each arm, as he is hoisted and being carried off from the great ceremony. Alexis' face is covered on one side by an iron mask which extends to his abdomen, the encased hands appearing as a leper without fingers, the legs also encased in iron castings below the knees. One eye is free of indentation; it winces at the uninhibited reveling. Each movement displays the agony of his existence.

"Alexis, Alexis!" Vespasian bellows in his torment. "My orders were first for your safety - even before my own son! Aah, Jupiteres! Be thou my witness before Matarian?!" Alexis' helpers sway faces at the King; Alexis is unwell; he cannot stay.

Great trumpets herald. The divine anointing begins; the giant, glowing Menorah on the shoulders of twenty slaves encircles around the Arena. Four Roman Priestesses on a raised center dais proclaim a ritual liturgical blessing:

"Hail-Vespasianus-Flavius-Flavian. The Divine Anointed Emissary of Jupiteres." A din of the peoples' response resounds in unison:

"We worship Divine Vespasian! Glory to Jupiteres - Glory to Rome!"

The four Roman Priestesses proclaim a blessing for Titus:

"Hail-Titus-Flavius-Caesar-Vespasianus - glorified for victory unto Rome! JUDEA… CAPTA!!!" The crowds respond with the obligatory chanting:

"We bow before Mighty Titus! Glory to Mars! Glory to Neptune! Glory to Venus!"

In the slave basement cages parked in the dark subterranean ramp queue, a newborn baby's scream mingles in the din of the chanting. A blonde Roman maiden, in Heavenly Being costume, discretely picks up a fallen crown on the arena floor amidst the great chanting. In the cages, the maiden mother's comrades are covertly wrapping up her newborn in torn away clothes, pressing the baby's cheeks on the mother's lips as a last farewell; the mother grapples and heaves in her teary angst to grasp her child again.

In the arena, a Hebrew slave stumbles, his leg quivering by the enormous weight of the golden edifice on his shoulders; the crowds mock in rage. A Gladiator pierces the fallen slave, dragging him to the lions. Menahem, the red bearded leader of the Zealots, chained hand and foot to his neck, approaches a gladiator with gestures inviting a combat; the Jews bang their chained hands together hailing him. Menahem hops on his chained feet comically in the air, drop kicks the Gladiator's knee, mocks and dodges him in a ridiculing, taunting and screaming:

"No Surrender - No Victory!?"

As the Gladiator spins dizzy with his sword swaying aimlessly in the air, Menahem plunges himself into the Gladiator's sword, denying him the kill and succumbing triumphantly. The chained Jews dance and sing hopping on their chained feet, banging their hand chains on the iron bars of their cages. The Romans chant boo's in a rage; the Gladiators set upon the rest of the slaves with a vengeance from the ridicule. Two hand bound Hebrew are hoisted to the top of the Coliseum wall. They are dangled by their feet; they scream 'NO SURRENDER!' as they drop. A focused silence pervades the arena as the wild beast's cages are opened again; the lions feed on the slaves. A child in a purple costume on his father's lap starts to cry amidst the din of the growling beasts.

Amidst the reveling of chants, the skies above Rome sound a thunder and lightning; the crowds continue reveling undaunted. Soon foreboding dark clouds appear in the skies above the Roman metropolis, then a great explosion emits, and a strong downpour of rain pelts the arena. The lions leave off their meals, fleeing into their cages and safe crevices, crouching to hide themselves from the blasts, as if they see what the crowds do not. The downpour washes away debris; the people stumble from their seats in disarray and soon their feet are submerged in gushing torrents; they continue reveling drunken and joyous. Poles supporting the Royal chamber collapse; women and children are whipped and flung from their seats in the gathering power of the torrents. A crocodile emerges from the swelling waters and grasps a Roman child in a purple costume in its jaws. Now a stampede develops for the gates.

"Sisters…" The maiden mother struggles in a slave cage. "This seed I bear is of the house of Hur… may God grant him life… may Israel be returned as God swore unto our fathers."

The blasting rains now pour into the subterranean tunnels, swaying the cage so it is wobbling afloat. The maiden then turns away detached and dreamlike, her gaze appears in a distant time and place. A vision from the past comes before her; her eyes light up. The vision of a hand from a young Roman on his horse extends to her, calling and beseeching; his eyes searing as he waits on her. The maiden's tears well up in a delirious smile of her recalling. The women in the swaying cage crowd closely around her face.

"Sisters!" The maiden mother grasps at her comrades. "Now be you of good courage, be not afraid anymore… for Rome, not Israel, is tested by our God. I see it… I see it… I..?" They sway embracing each other.

In the arena, Titus gapes in pained rage at the people running for their lives; he turns to the skies as if challenging the heavens. His right hand grasps his sword, the left hand sagging awkwardly, as he stumbles over corpses toward the arena's centre. He grins menacingly at the heavens, as a gladiator confronting an opponent, challenging the rains blasting his face, his head gear flying away. His sword aimed at the howling skies, the warrior bellows manically in a powerful rage.

"I am Titus! I triumphed before all! This glory is mine! NOT YOURS!?"

"The rains…" The maiden mother grasps her comrades. "The heavens are shouting! It is for freedom, a light given us from the God of all Gods. Sisters, it is our light in the darkness. I see it now… it is shining on you…and you… and… all of you…"

Titus raises both hands at the skies, bellowing in a manic scream.

"No such thing as an invisible God! No… I entered your holy house… empty! No such thing!?"

The women covertly tear the umbilical by hand as the mother's child is cut asunder; the maiden gasps her final words.

"My son's name… Alexander… ben Hur. My light… in the darkness…"

The women conceal the baby in a pile of garment, setting it outside the back cage floor through its bars; they murmur prayers. The women hold hands over the covered mother and declare their pledge.

"For freedom - our light in the darkness!"

In the waters swelling the arena, wooden vats once holding jewels and a throne bop up floating around Titus; he calls on the fleeing people.

"Fear not! I, Titus, conquered the Jews and their God. I am Rome - I am your protector. I am Titus - I am your savior!?"

On the floor corner of a cage holding slaves, a baby's hand is protruding from under the folds of a bundle of garment; the mother's index finger is entwined within her newborn baby's palm. Josephus discretely covers up the baby's hand and carries off the small bundle.

Now the swelling waters flood into the slave basements in raging torrents, whipping the Roman guards against the walls and sealing the faith of the captive slaves and the animals held in the subterranean cages. In the arena, the slaves hoisting the giant Menorah are wavering by its weight, swaying and staggering.

Titus drops on his knees; he appears struck by an aching. He squats on the ground, pulling at his hair, as if nursing a piercing pain throbbing in his head. He is soaking in the heavy downpour; the menacing warrior's eyes turn challenging at the heavens.[34]

Except for the howling rains storming the Roman Metropolis, there is a prolonged silence, contrasting the great din of the victory celebrations. A blanket of night descends upon Rome.

Beasts in the Arena - A Roman Ritual Sport (Artist: Jean-Léon Gérôme) Source: S7.

(2). THE ROMAN SENATE.

An official report is being proclaimed by the Senate to the House. The Hebrew scribe sits at the rear writing in a scroll; three royal guards stand behind his desk, serving and protecting the Romanized Hebrew. The words 'All Roads Lead to Rome' is bannered on the hall's opulent arch.[35]

"My distinguished Senators of Rome know it well... the empire faces great challenges from rebel nations." The House Speaker Betto is addressing the Senators gathered to hear an official war report of Rome's most celebrated triumph over Judea:

"And of this little Judea... none more treacherous! Little it was, yes, but this was a war like no other. Terrible! Glorious! Holy!?"

The three Britons are brought in and hurdled in a corner of the famed hall of world power. The Ambassadors of Briton have travelled from afar, over many seas and lands to arrive here; they come with the permission granted them to address the Roman assembly once every three years. The House Speaker Betto continues.

"So Rome did what Rome had to do. And Rome is made mightier for it - a 2,000 year treasury the envy of every nation!" He nods of its reasoning. "And good slaves too - with excellent skills. Our great Coliseum is being built by the very hands of the Jews... and their wealth. Rome is made rich! Esteemed senators, you are all made rich! By the order of Titus, a hundred gold coins to each Senator of Rome!" [36]

"Hail Glorious Titus!" The Senators chant in robust satisfaction.

"But be not confused..." The House Speaker becomes forebodingly official. "The Jews despised all that Rome stood for. They disdained and insulted our emperors even when great forbearance was given them to worship their God. This heretic nation must never rise again! Rome forbids a Roman to marry a Jew. Roman law, my comrades?" [37]

"Will the law apply to all Romans..." The Senator Marcellus raises his index finger before his face. "Titus too?"

"If you refer to Titus' royal escort, the Queen, she is a Roman citizen of royal line." The House Speaker Betto assures him.

"Oh?" Senator Marcellus persists; the House now silent and not complicit of his daring. "Then she is not an incestuous Hebrew harlot, from brother to father to son... Rome is not put to shame by her presence here?" Hushes and whispers of alarm resound.

"Dare you! Dare you speak such treachery of one who glorified Rome!?" A stray voice booms from the hall in response to Senator Marcellus' provocative words. "Hail our mighty and glorious Titus!"

The two Senators rise up hoisting their fists in the air defiantly. They stage a walk out, leaving in disdain as they did in the emperor's sacred anointing ceremony.

The Speaker raises his both hands above his head, swaying his face in disbelief. "Huh!" He turns to the Senators. "Great, honorable Romans. Everyone's truth cannot set us all free. In the final count it was not even Roman might - many nations possessed their own powers. Even those Jews who fell screaming in their devilish laughter. No dear comrades. It was... valor." He deliberates each word, pausing of its emphasis.

"Untouchable! Sacred! Roman valor! Bestowed from the Roman Gods!?" He is heaving breathless. "But it seems... not given to all Romans."

A gregarious response of chanting erupts. "Hail Roman valor! Hail Jupiteres!"

"The council will address a petition now." The Speaker nods to the guards standing before the chained Britons: "Bring forward the party of the Britons."

"Great rulers of Rome..." The Briton Ambassador bows before the elite Roman assembly. "We appeal to your mighty Roman hearts. Londonium is destroyed by Rome's fires, 80,000 of our people slaughtered, our youth are taken away as mercenaries... and our daughters made as concubines. We are sent to plead of you - restore our rights, end the brutality, else we all will perish?"

"Nay, my good Senators, nay!" The House Speaker Betto is dismissive of the charges. "This people, with their most hideous warrior queen - Jupiter's curse upon that wretch, consulted their gods by means of human entrails, preferring to worship the balls and arse's of the dead than the glory of Rome!?"

The House responds with a burst of laughter.

"Vespasian did with Jerusalem, a far greater city, the same as was done with Londonium - both were heretics, both were cleansed by fires. Esteemed Senators, there can be only one true divine king in the empire. And Rome has only one living God. Long live Vespasian!"
A hailing and clapping by the assembly; the British delegation is hoisted away.
"And now Honorary Senators, a full war accounting, so you all will see this was Rome's richest... most glorious... most holy victory of all!"
The Speaker pauses as Alexis arrives; his helper lifting him in a chair and settling him beside the royal scribe in the far back end chamber of the hall. Alexis removes the metal covering part of his face, revealing shriveled pinkish skin; onlookers wince. Alexis' unbroken eye is fixed on the scribe making notations.

The Speaker continues, reading from a scroll in triumphant passion.
"Gold Shekels - One Million Talents!" (Estimated as $50 Billion in the modern world).
Silver Shekels - Five Million Talents! Olive oil and vats of Herbs - two hundred shiploads!"[138]
Hisses and whispers arise from the assembly of the astonishing counts; Josephus writes into a scroll as the accounting continues.

(3) A ROMAN BATH HOUSE.

In an opulent steamy bath-house, two maidens are massaging the naked bodies of the two Senators Marcellus and Alienus; the same who murmured and sneered throughout the arena festival against Rome's divine Emperor. Erotic and decadent statues adorn a magnificent spa bath, engraved with the words:

'IT IS ROMAN TO DELIGHT IN THE GIFTS OF THE GODS'.[139]

"Rome must know why we walked out of the Flavian camel dung pouring out of the mouth of Betto."
Senator Marcellus assures, flat on his stomach as the maiden rubs scented oils on his shoulders. "We know why Titus looted the temple of the Jews. The nations also know - they sent delegates to Judea as witnesses."
"Blame Nero for diminishing Rome. Vespasian was following the orders given him by Nero." Oily hands tend Alienus.
"Be not fooled. His son was following Vespasian's orders, not Nero's. We did good letting them know we know of their treachery."
"Some carry strange rumors..." Alienus whispers it. "A Hebrew sorcerer turned the head of Vespasian. A stranger thing I never imagined."
The maidens see Titus entering. His calm smirk belies the warrior's purpose.
"We are now under savages and traitors sitting on Rome's thrones, holding the purse and the legions in their hands - what can be stranger?"
"And what can be more threatening for us, let us work with caution?"

The Flavian Dynasty. Their ascent to the throne followed a period of chaos that was engulfing Rome. A civil war erupted; the city was set alight; some said Nero initiated the fires as a deflection of an impending bankruptcy and many pursued him. Then came Nero's sudden demise; he commits suicide to the widespread joy of the Romans, leaving as his most remembered legacy, 'Nero fiddled as Rome burned'.[140]
The sudden vacancy on the throne resulted in a succession of four hastily ascended and short lived emperors, with the Flavian family earning the royal throne in the merit of a contrived war with Judea and bringing to Rome the vast riches of the Hebrew kingdom. The Flavians now faced many Senators with differing loyalties; they would see to it Vespasian would meet the same faith of the four short lived emperors. But Vespasian and Titus had their own war acquired plans to thwart and beguile such political ambitions.
Alienus gestures Marcellus ears closer to him, away from the maiden's hearing.

"The Flavian plans could not proceed while the Jews spread their vile primitive beliefs against Rome's divine kings… both father and son understood this. Thus they used the Hebrew priest in their propaganda to impress Rome… follow?"

Titus, finger tapping his lips, gestures the maidens remain silent as he sits on a far seat; the maidens, in heaving breaths understand he is not come for a spa bath. Marcellus clarifies further: "Meaning this was not of Nero, but a Flavian father and son conspiracy - a savage breed of devious cunning designed for the battle field, not the throne…"

Titus nods with a thumb down. From behind a penis designed pillar, two sets of mighty hands replace the maiden's tender oily fingers; the maidens back away in trembling. The hands grab the throats of the two Senators sprawled on their stomachs, twisting the Senator's arms across their bent knees. They immerse the Senator's heads into the bath, holding them submerged fastidiously.

The maidens witnessing the assassinations are kneeling head to the ground trembling before Titus. He reclines calmly in a lounge chair, tearing open a red pomegranate and chomping into it with a relish as the two senators wriggle and splash in the spa. Titus explains his position to the pleasure maidens kneeling on the marble floor, his mouth full with redness and dripping.

"Here me, lovely damsels and be not afraid. Did Rome become a mighty empire by allowing treachery to go unpunished?" Titus throws the maidens two gold coins; the submerged Senators battle for their lives in the bath. "Good Romans must glorify their savior." A killer's nodding: "Remember it, hmm?"

When the two Senators cease wriggling fully, Titus accounts his timing calmly, his eyes fixed on the two floating bodies. Finally he nods at his executioners and throws two full pouches at them. They examine a large gold coin curiously; one of the assassins is confused.

"Royal Master, these are… Hebrew coins?" He displays the coin - it shows Hebrew markings.

"You never held a finer piece of gold. Turn it."

The coin's reverse side shows Latin markings: "Judea Capta". The assassin bows.

"Jupiter's glory upon my mighty and generous Master."

"They are now Roman gold coins." Titus nods. "Leave us."

Titus focuses on the two maidens kneeling before him. He grasps both by their manes, dragging them before him on their knees.

"Glorify your savior."

The two Senators' corpses surface limp in the opulent marble bath.

In the Sennett hall, the war spoils accounting continues. In the rear, Josephus is writing into his scroll. The Speaker Betto accounts with hand swaying enthusiasm.

"Gemstones - Rubies, Sapphires and Persian Stones: 600 Basins.

Giant Candelabra: 1 piece.

Thrones, Seats and Tables of Gold: 120 pieces."

Alexis' gaze is affixed on the Hebrew scribe.

"Hebrew slaves brought To Rome - 97,500; 2,500 as circus sport, the rest to serve as skilled laborers. Concubines - 12,000."

When the accounting is concluded, the Senators are greatly impressed; they are leaving the hall each a hundred gold coins richer, a political stratagem of Titus, the victor who controls the spoils.

The Council Chamber is now emptied, except for Alexis and Josephus who alone have remained. Alexis' gaze is relentless on the Hebrew scribe assembling his scrolls and pouches. Alexis leans forward in his seat awkwardly towards Josephus; he addresses the great scribe in a raspy, labored voice.

"Strange destiny, is it not, a Hebrew scribe appointed to write of Rome's victory… and his own nation's destruction?" Alexis smirks at his own irony. There is no response. Alexis leans closer, his questioning becoming more poignant and sarcastically demanding. "Yet, why do Rome's victors throw down their crowns before the people… will the Hebrew scribe's writings tell us?"

Josephus pauses from his diarizing, swaying his face at Alexis' broken condition and his determined enquiry. He looks around at the emptied hall, then he folds his palms on his chest, engaging the battered figure before him.

"Perhaps an honorable warrior does not account victory against women and children - even that it had to happen? And you Alexis, you were diverted to the east to oversee the road works. You were in that fiery hell… you surely remember it?"

Alexis maneuvers to stand precariously. He grasps the scribe's tunic; the metal covered hand shudders. "You did the accounting. What became of her? Tell me - I have not much time?"

"But you must remember it - how can you not? Shall I help you? It was Vespasian, whose life your honorable father Matarian saved in the fires of Londonium… he appointed you Architect of the Road Works. Vespasian gave you Tahrah. You remember Tahrah - the magnificent one?"

"Tahrah!?" The unspoiled eye now searches the clouds churning between the pillars of the balcony, as if a picture is forming. "Yes… Tahrah!?" A faint familiar ethnic melody is emerging in his mind. He appears entranced.

"You Alexis were swept to another road, one very different from the road you made for Rome. You remember…" The scribe's piercing eyes nods pointedly. "Remember?

(4) JUDEA - 66 AD/CE.

Alexis remembers. Six years into the past, he is now a young Roman, one with a wide-eyed honesty and daring charm; he flies into a new land's golden hot winds. He rides in abandon and exhilaration on the highway extending from the coastal town of Caesarea on Tahrah, a noble Arabian mere, an unusual red skinned horse that glows against the searing sun. The terrain is markedly different from the modern Roman Metropolis; palm trees, domestic animals and the Judean hills dot the scene. Alexis rides in joyous abandon on his magnificent Tahrah, a gift from Vespasian marking Alexis' chosen appointment as the Roman Roads Architect of Judea.

There is a construction site in progress on the Megiddo plains, inclined North-West of Jerusalem and stretching towards the Mediterranean coast. Roman and Arabian workers are constructing Judea's gravel roads into a new tarred highway; it is Rome's vast undertaking in the modern world with the discovery volcanic ash solidifies into stone; it is also a stratagem that ensures all roads will lead to Rome more efficiently, transporting Rome's slave labor, taxes and the exotic produce of other lands.

Now the Roman road works become interrupted by a procession of Jews chanting a joyful, gregarious melody as they pass on their journey. The Jews sing in their strange ancient tongue none else can speak, yet there is an attractive rhythm, one discernible before the Roman chagrin and their disdain of the Hebrew tongue no other nation in the empire understood. And these Jews are dressed in provocative attire; the Roman workers stare at the men's tassels dangling at their waists apprehensively, they sneer at the men's coils of hair locks dropping lower than their ears. One of the Jews has his hand strapped with black leather belting; a mark of sorcery, as the Romans saw it.

The Jews are oblivious of the Romans, chanting in their Hebrew psalms with a display of joyous gestures and stomping. When their threading spoils newly laid soft tar, the soldiers cut down several of the Jews, surrounding them in a closed Roman battle formation of raised spears.

A ceremoniously attired man leading the Hebrew procession is stopped with a spear pressed against his chest. The Jews jolt; they stiffen by the razor edged spears held against them. A young maiden from the group attempts to sway the soldier's spear now fixed at the Hebrew's chest; but she is flung aside and thrust to the ground. Florian, a large man who appears ever ready and accustomed to slayings, demands of the Jew.

"Your name and destination?"

"I am Hillel, a humble teacher, these are my students. We travel to a teaching house."

"Then teach me, teacher." Florian twirls his spear on the Jew's chest. "Teach me of your holy books standing on one foot… if you wish to live?"

"What is hateful to you, do not unto others." Hillel totters on one foot. "This is the whole message." The soldier ponders the rapid response, swaying the spear in his hand.

The young maiden rises from her fallen position; she ducks, then pushes the spear off the teacher's chest with a daring, fronting up against the Roman soldier in a challenging stance. With her arms bent aback, she stands in front of the teacher, shielding him with her body protectively and challengingly. In a flash Florian sways the point of his spear; it now rests on the Hebrew maiden's heart, swaying in anticipation of a strike mode. She winces aback, then she returns, determined and pressed on the Roman's sword, wincing, challengingly again, shouting.

"Have you no respect who stands before you!?" The young maiden demands it, undaunted by the spear poised on her chest. Florian smirks; she spits off at him as the Roman grips his spear, swaying it assuredly. She dares him. The spear wavers in the air; the Jews jolt against spears held before them. A tension reigns. Then a hand lowers Florian's spear to the ground.

"Withdraw soldier, let the Hebrews pass. And what… what is the name of the brave one?" There is a stark silence as Alexis pans the Jewess; her naked arms now uncovered of her fallen shawl and still bent aback protecting her teacher. Alexis appears transfixed on the maiden; her defiant almond eyes suppressing a certain inexplicable compelling; she is measuring his next move.

"Please…what be your name?" His gaze is affixed and unwavering.

She focuses on the spear lowered safely to the ground by Alexis' hand.

"I am Deborah. House of Hur. Megiddo." She responds defiantly, an unusually compelling feminine timber; it is un-Roman and of an ancient stirring tongue.

"Rome will not do what is hateful to one with such valor." Alexis dips his head, appearing friendly. "I am Alexander…" She engages him a beat of that name. "House of Matarian. To friends I am Alexis."

The stark silence is broken by Hillel. "There is wisdom and righteousness in all nations."

The gaze of the Roman Road builder remains fastidiously impressed on the Hebrew maiden. She displays disdain of the Romans, pointedly at Florian, as the procession of the Jews begins to withdraw and continue their journey. Alexis' lingering glances remain on the cautiously retreating, sneering maiden.

The departing Jews engage in heated discourse among themselves.

Benjamin: "They made bath houses in Caesarea where men and women go in together with no covering!" Hillel focuses on Deborah questioningly.

Dan: "The same will come to our holy places. We cannot be silent, can we Teacher?"

Young, fiery Boaz, barely 13: "I won't be silent! I will join with the Sicarii!" He hurls his sling stone soaring into the horizon.

"I had the best chance to act." Deborah responds to Hillel's fixed gaze. "The men had spears before them. None on me because… I fell to the floor?"

Hillel sways his face in negation. "But you did have a spear fixed on your heart - and we live now only by a Roman's hand. A strange thing, is it not?"

"But Deborah saved us and our teacher!" The lad Boaz hurls another sling shot in the air. "That Roman made evil eyes on her - I'll show him!"

At the Roman construction site, Alexis picks up a soft leather pouch fallen on the ground; he retreats to a private spot. He finds a parchment with Hebrew markings inside and a rose, pressed and still moist. He appears inspired and moved by this encounter, gripping her purse in his palm, inhaling the rose scent, focusing on the ancient writings. A thought comes to him as he wonders who gave the rose to the maiden. Now he gazes at his workers who are swaying their faces in disdain; Alexis inhales again the scent of the rose clutched in his palm. Florian appears insulted by his Master - he plunges his spear in the earth; it sways to and fro.

'And Moses, Aaron and Hur went up to the top of the hill;
And Aaron and Hur uplift his hands, the one on the one side,
and the other on the other side; and his hands were steady
until the going down of the sun.'
- (Exodus 17/10 / The Dead Sea Scrolls)

"Victory O Lord!" Moses, Hur (Left) and Aaron. (By John Everett Millais)
Source: 6.

(5) CAESAREA IS NOW ROMAN.

Caesarea is the grandiose city-port built by Herod, honoring the name of Caesar. Herod also erected the Hippodrome where chariot races enticed the people, made as a distraction for the conquered hordes.
Now a food trader is roasting meats opposite a Synagogue, attracting crowds of Hellenist and Syrian soldiers. Flaming soot and odors are blasting the main entrance of the synagogue. The offended Jews hurl protests; soon a rowdy altercation develops. The soldiers overturn oil vats and sacrifice birds and pigs on the inverted vat tops at the Synagogue entrance. A soldier tosses a pig's head into the synagogue's window. A fierce battle results. [41]
Soon the town's mayor appears on the scene.
"It is time you Jews realized this is not a Jewish city anymore - Caesarea is now Roman." Aristomy, the town's Mayor, sways his fist at the Jews. "No more will you tell the people what they can eat and when they can work! I gave the order to open a food house for our soldiers. It shall remain open."
Nathan, a Hebrew with a bruised face, states the case of the Roman law. "We were granted Roman Collegia by Caesar - legal rights to follow our laws. Observing our Sabbath is not accounted against the empire's laws?" [42]
"Rome says the people must honor the king with daily sacrifices. You are attacking them for it. This will be reported to Nero himself."
Nathan: "Sell us then the shop which joins the synagogue, then none will be disturbed. We will pay what you ask."
"Aahah! Bribery now!" Aristomy is hissing in disdain. "Will the Jews tempt us by their ill gotten wealth against the empire so openly... do you Jews not understand this is not Hebrew land anymore? Continue the sacrifices. Nero appointed me the town's mayor - let's see what the emperor has to say of you rebels."
A soldier tosses a pig's hoof at Nathan. The Jews' faces are marked with apprehension; of trouble to come.

(6) "RAAL!" ['POISON!']

Simon, a young Hebrew of massive proportions, and Deborah, step back to examine the house he built.
Simon acquired a choice piece of land in the plains of Megiddo; he has toiled for two years building his dream home and now seeks the impression of the only one that matters to him.
Deborah sways her face, frowning; she points at the small front window with dismissing hands. "Bigger!" - She spreads her arms wide.
Simon suddenly jumps; he quickly moves away Deborah with his right hand. He pounds his foot on a large snake near Deborah's feet, pinning it to the ground firmly; she screams in fear. There are drops of perspiration on Simon's wincing face - he has identified the snake as the Horned Viper[43], one of the few highly venomous serpents native to this biblical land. The snake coils itself around Simon's foot, and soon Simon's entire body is entrapped in the snake's length; he is struggling wildly, unable to move his entrapped hands.
Deborah is screaming in panic as she punches her dagger into the snake with no effect; the snake continues extending its grasp, slithering upward of its prey. Simon signals her to back off; his concern for her safety is inspiring, his eyes darting to and fro at Deborah, even as the snake's head is now poised over his face, its fangs protruding in attack mode.

"Raal!?" ['Poison' Heb.]- He warns her; she backs away. Simon rolls over on the ground; he manages to free one hand. He grips the snake with his free hand, struggling to keep its fangs from reaching him. The snake coils tighter its grip around his body; his face now crimson. His fingers squeeze the snake's head as its fangs nears. Simon's grip tightens; his hand and arms shuddering and writhing; the snake's eye pops out of its head. He squeezes harder, his hand veins pumping and swollen; the snake's other eye pops out. The snake's coiling body begins to loosen. He grips the snake's head, his hands tearing it apart from its body. Deborah retreats aghast of the eye-less head of the dead snake on the ground before her, its fangs protruding. Simon kicks off the snake's head; his manner is awkward, sincere, his reddened face pouring in sweat and alarmed at her shuddering. "Fear not any more, all is well now." - He assures.
A foreboding sound of rumbling stirs in the skies. She races into his protective arms; she shudders excessively.

Of Signs and Omens. On the road North-East of The Galilee there is a sudden dimming of the sunlight; the brightness of the sun appears shrouded within a curtain of dark clouds. A rolling thunder erupts, a series of lightning follows, and it flashes across the main highway leaving Judea. The caravans bearing trade goods pause, and people lifting baskets of cargo cover their eyes; they stumble and waver, turning away from the piercing flashes of light.
The glistening rays of light appear focused on one man and pouring down upon his head. The man turns curiously at the lightning, as if compelled. Slowly, he removes his hands from his face, focused, as though the skies are addressing him directly; he dares the shimmering flashes.
His eyes glisten as he gazes un-blinking into the heavens. He staggers disoriented, nodding at the burst of light rays now singularly blasting him from the darkened skies; he trembles, whispering at the clouds, his hand palms gesturing at the heavens. The thunder and lightning ceases abruptly and a still calmness comes. The man's face glows, as if he has received a calling from the heavenly abodes; his hair has turned to silver. The people gaze at him, pointing questioningly in awe and wonder. [44]

(7) RESURRECTING CALIGULA - 37 AD/CE.

A lone horse stands on a magnificently embroidered rug sprawled in the center of the marble floor of the Senate hall.
"Incitatus, my beloved, you shall be my chief consul!"
The new emperor turns to the row of Senators sitting in the back rows of the Sennett hall, his hand outstretched and pointing:
"No, not you foolish Senators - you see not what I see!?" He kisses the face of the horse as tremulous tears of pain well in his eyes. The row of Senators display gestures of disgust; they sway faces at each other. Caligula's beloved horse is adorned with precious Jewels; studs of rubies and emeralds sparkle from its body, a crown sits clumsily on the horse's head and all four hoofs are covered in beaten fine gold. The young effeminate Emperor has his arms around the horse's torso, sniffing tears. Then he pours libations on the horse's head and turns yelling emotively at his horse:
"Incitatus! I appoint you as my royal priest… you are now above this council!" He drops on his knees kissing the horse's hoof. "Forever. I swear it?"
A Senator turns to his comrades whispering:
"Rome's Emperor is insane."

The First Century began with a host of factors contributing to tensions between Rome and the Jews, of two mutually exclusive belief systems avowing their positions in a volatile stand-off. In the 30's there were signs and omens of a revolt in its early imprints; it was ignited by Rome's most notorious one. As Rome's third emperor, Caligula - Gaius Julius Caesar Augustus Germanicus - ascended the throne in the year 37; he soon proclaims himself as divine. [45]

The scenario in the small province of first century Judea is of a miniscule Hebrew kingdom harboring a belief system fully varied from the rest of the empire's nations, yet one established with Rome as bona fide a century before Caligula emerged. In 64 BCE, Julius Caesar declared the Jews were an ancient people with an ancient belief and thereby he granted them freedom to follow their strange rituals; this right was given for the strange particularized religion of the Jews and set in Roman law, known as 'Collegia'.[46]

The 'One God' monotheistic belief of the Jews was a fundamental law commanded by the Hebrew God. It is a foremost Hebrew law, the second of the Ten Commandments given the Israelites at Sinai, one of the two commands that echoed verbally from the fires on the mount, a most fantastic claim in the Hebrew bible; it utterly pierced into the Hebrew minds and hearts throughout their generations.

Monotheism became a most disdained law by the nations, one that contradicted the divine emperor realm throughout the ancient world. While Rome gave its conquered nations religious freedoms to ensure stability within the Empire, this was tolerated with conditional and limited boundaries, requiring reciprocal worship of the Roman Emperors and their Gods. Often these would not satisfy the peculiar laws of the Jews and periodical upheavals and disturbances were commonplace with the Romans.

Historically, the Jews confounded every nation they interacted with. Their Israelite ancestors were embedded with laws that marked them different by their strange diets and dress none could comprehend or align with, and a language no other nation spoke. Prior to Rome's invasion of Arabia, a previous war with the Greek Empire occurred for the same reason of the Hebrew laws. The matter now began to arise again with a fury when Caligula ascended as Divine Emperor in Rome and Herod was the Roman appointed king in Judea.

Caligula ascended after the reign of the emperor Tiberius, under whose reign Jesus of Nazareth is crucified, with many others who indulged in anti-Roman Hebrew beliefs. It was a time of turmoil and tension in Judea, with Rome focused on the Jews who followed laws that disdained and insulted Rome's divine emperors.

Caligula was regarded as an insane and brutal tyrant by the Romans, one whose sadism feasted in watching the condemned being tortured in gruesome measures and forcing parents to witness their children's slaughter as entertainment.

Suspected of a deep self-consuming narcissism and epilepsy, Caligula was infamous for professing incest, bankrupting Rome with his excesses and earning the wrath of the Roman Senate. The Romans found him declaring his favorite horse he adorned with jewels as his chief consul and above the Senate. The conditions faced by the Jews under Caligula became the omen for a forthcoming war:

"Gog-MaGoG!"[47] The Jews warned each other, referring to evil tidings re-emerging.

First, Rome took over the control of the Temple's High Priest. This was intolerable for the Jews who had a complicated, isolated and entrenched history of religious beliefs and rituals; many of the Hebrew laws fundamentally forbade Roman practices, thereby accounting for hard won rights established in Roman law; Caligula flaunted these rights.

Rome, on the verge of bankruptcy, then appointed its own selected High Priests as the controller of the Temple taxes, granting them special incentives; a part of the tax collections would go to the Roman appointed collectors, a traditional Roman stratagem of ensuring compliances, with reward and dire impacts of any refusal. Thus corrupt tax collectors, appointed by the Roman appointed Priests with Roman dictates, sought first to embellish their own purses in exaggerated and corrupt penalty rates, temple robberies, desecrations and massacres. [48]

The final act of revulsion for the Jews was Caligula's demand that his statue of gold be placed in the temple and worshipped with daily sacrifices, as was done by the Jews of their Hebrew God, as was required of all nations in the empire. The Jews, the sole monotheists of this time, refused the command; Caligula threatened to destroy the temple. The Jews sent their delegations of pleading to Caligula, but all were rejected, including the beseeching for mercy by Judea's Roman appointed Priests. Caligula was outraged, seeing the Jews as challenging his decree as no others dared, admonishing them with vitriolic angst:

"You are the great enemies of the gods - the only people in the empire who refuse to recognize my divinity!"[49]

The Jews' pleas were convoluted as a charge of controlling Rome's divine emperors by demanding special privileges. That such charges were rejected by the great Caesar who declared the Jews as an ancient belief and subsisting long before Rome became a power were swept away; the genuine plight of the Jews' long held beliefs and their numerous battles throughout history to secure such rights were ignored. Now Caesar was no more, and Caligula, whose extravagances were bankrupting Rome, made the Jerusalem Temple treasury the focus of his disdain:

"You Jews will adorn my image with the gold you hide in your temple and worship me with the choicest sacrifice daily - or your temple will become as dust. I swear it."

"Gog-MaGoG!" The distraught Jews confirmed it to each other.

This then, the threat made of their holy temple and the defense of their right of belief, became more impacting than all other flaunting of other rights and wealth; it fostered the beginning of the Jews' rebellion. Thus did Caligula put the future subsistence of all futuristic monotheistic beliefs as the #1 enemy of all of Rome's divine emperors, and the stage was set to impact history. The Jews, on the heels of a war with the previous Greek Empire, were again facing a war for the upholding of their laws, now with history's greatest super power.

The Jews were seen as a strange and peculiar people; that they held laws and customs that were condescending and disdaining of all nations of the empire; it contradicted the nation's long held traditional beliefs and honored divine Roman Emperors. Thus did the Jews become a controversy by the laws handed them by their Hebrew God who affirmed their assured bondage with the nations. The Hebrew laws of morals and modesty rendered the Jews to refrain from entertainment and sport, which the Greeks conducted in full nakedness. When the Romans and Greeks celebrated effigies of their deities in feisty drunken processions, hoisting concubines of naked men and women, the Jews turned their faces, covering their eyes with their palms; and they detested the diets and food stalls of the nations.

Caligula commanded his war captain:

"Burn their temple - along with their priests and their families! Their treasury must be housed in my mansion."

Here, only an unanticipated occurrence foiled Caligula's ambitions, while affirming the legitimacy of the Jews' rejection of a crazed Roman Emperor's demands. Herod, the Roman appointed king of Judea, fearing an anticipated Jewish revolt, ignored Caligula's demands. This, and the sudden brutal assassination of Caligula and of his wife and children by his own senators, saved the Jews from annihilation. Herod understood Caligula's demand would have been defended again by the stiff-neck Jews in any wise, as was seen with the previous Greek Empire.

Yet, even after Caligula's demise, the next emperors were also offended by the laws of the Jews that rejected their divine status. The Jews were blamed for causing sorcery against Rome's Emperors; it was an omen of continuing trouble ahead. Monotheism and divine emperors were mutually exclusive paradigms and one had to go; inevitably, the Jews became the prime target of the Roman Emperors that followed. Now, any rights held by the Jews, even those sanctioned into Roman law, were fully disregarded. The freedoms Rome offered to all conquered nations would not apply with the Hebrew belief of the Jews; monotheism was a radical belief system that Rome's emperors saw as blasphemous and heretical. Yet now something far reaching was unfolding.

The First Century is the opening page of a new historical phase that will alter humanity; something was happening here and it was bigger than Rome and the Jews. Henceforth, the Roman war against monotheism will become the standout feature of this period's impacts on history. The Jews are now facing their mightiest enemy, when Mighty Rome's 'All roads lead to Rome' will confront a new kind of adversary that responds with 'All roads lead to one supreme God'. Caligula's demands on the Jews initiated the first bout of this war, one not of terrain or military foes on the battlefield; this was a holy war for both the Jews and Mighty Rome. Now, monotheism and paganism faced each other closely and jostled for their existential prevailing. A theological epiphany was unfolding.

Although the Jews were small and disdained in the ancient world of divine kings, yet they were also seen as significant by their advanced mode of writing and their ancient books of knowledge; they attracted both intrigue and suspicion. And now a great shadow was encroaching; the Greek translated Septuagint Hebrew bible was impacting upon the people of the Empire for three hundred years and it was spreading within the Greek and Roman's most elite sectors. A one supreme creator God was unlike the Gods of Rome, Greece, Babylon and Egypt. Monotheism was set to become the greatest phenomenon impacting humanity. And the lone Jews are going to be targeted to face the full wrath of the Roman Empire.

For the Jews, monotheism was not the belief in one singular entity as the sun or the wind, but the belief of a Living Being Creator, transcendent of and pre-existent of all creation. This was not a pagan-monotheism but a new and different transcendent thought in the ancient world, especially with the Greek philosophers who studied the Septuagint and became highly immersed in it.

The Septuagint's message also posed the ultimate challenge; while the Hebrew bible's output pleased those sectors who desired a Republic, one free of their kings who flaunted the rights of the people, it also resulted in the angst of Rome's divine emperors who cast all blame on the Jews' corruption of the people, which they referred to as the Hebrew sorcery.

This then is the holiest of all holy wars that impacted history and humanity as none other; and the all-powerful Roman Empire had good reason to stir, not from fear of another power, but by the Greek coined term of "monotheism" that was sweeping both Arabia and the lands across the seas since the first translation of the Hebrew bible into the Greek in 300 BCE. [50]

A New Emperor. With Caligula's brutal death by his own people, the Jews now confronted Rome's new Divine Emperor, one who murdered his mother and brother to win his ascension to the throne; one who retained two men as his wives; who castrated the young lad Sporus to make him a woman and also included him as a wife. That Rome had a history of anointing such emperors to their thrones signifies the plight of Rome's conquered nations; especially so those who followed the Hebrew monotheist belief. In response to Rome's problem with the Jews, Nero Claudius Caesar Augustus Germanicus resurrects Caligula's law of "Heresy." [51]

Bust of Emperor Nero

[Capitilona Museum Rome] Source: S8

(8) HERESY.

Nero ruled Rome in 54 to 68 CE. In the year 66, the Commander Vespasian and his son Titus are called upon to serve their Emperor. Titus has arrived from Syria, reporting to his father to hear of new commands from Rome. They are assembled in the Headquarters of Egypt's Roman Prefect Tiberius, a strong ally and political supporter of Vespasian.

A crowd of Arabian men and women are squatted on the grounds outside the Roman base; they wail and lift their children in their arms denoting their plight of poverty. Commander Vespasian peers from the balcony at the commotion.

"What are they protesting for - why do they cease the grain supply to Rome, they are paid well for their labor?"

"Their complaint is whatever Rome pays it takes back in increased taxes." Tiberius, the Roman Prefect of Egypt, explains. "The usual excuse here for bargaining a better reward."

A tribune enters; he holds an official royal scroll on a platter before Vespasian. Titus breaks the royal seal. "Father, it is from Nero!"

Vespasian nods permission to continue reading the message. Titus reads from the royal scroll solemnly: "His Imperial Majesty, Nero-Claudius-Caesar-Augustus-Germanicus."

Vespasian gestures impatiently to skip the formalities.

"To my faithful Commander Vespasianus Augustus, of
the family of the Equestrians and Flavians. I say thus unto you.
The Jews ceased sacrifices for me and did attack a garrison in
Caesarea which was sacrificing birds in my honor. Head me now.
One: Crush this rebellion lest it spreads all over the empire
as the old law of Caesar unto the Jews. I, Divine Nero, now
annul Caesar's law and honor back Caligula's decree of Heresy
upon the Jews.
Two: set up a permanent Roman base in Caesarea.
Three: The Hebrew practices are forbidden; it
is a heresy unto me. Nero demands daily sacrifices from the
Jews - on pain of death."

Titus hand gestures there is more.

"And Four. Bring me one Eleazar's head, son of a Hebrew Priest
who poisons the people against me. It is decreed as Roman law.
I, divine Nero, bids you so by your honor. Fail me not this time."

"Father, fail not Nero this time! Our emperor is granting you the restoring of your honor - you can now secure back Nero's favor, lost when he found you sleeping during one of his song recitals." [52] Titus holds the royal scroll before Vespasian excitedly. "My father, we must heed Nero's calling - it is a sacred path for us. It is an omen from the Gods!"

"Unlike the Jews, there is no rebellion in Egypt other than the grain affair." Tiberius pledges. "Our legions are at your command."

Vespasian paces, gazing at the squatters below. He ponders, then he turns, deciding as a faithful Roman General his emperor's orders. The Commander Vespasian would duly honor the dictates of his emperor concerning the rebel Jews who reject and insult Rome's divine emperors, as would any Roman Commander harboring hidden dreams of ascending the throne.

"Tiberius. Allow the price increase for the grains. Fourteen Million bushels, delivery by the year's end. But no lowering of taxes. Double the taxes of Judea for three years. Secure for me 100,000 Arabian mercenaries - that will please Egypt! Also, secure for me 60,000 elite Romans."

"60,000!?" Tiberius is aghast. "Most honorable General, Caesarea is but one small town and we already have a legion there. This is not a war, just some… Jewish rebels!?"

"This is a people unlike any other." Vespasian's thoughts appear far away. He remembers it well; he lives this day because a noble Roman forfeited his own life in response to such rebellions. "This barbaric religion mocks Rome even more so than did Briton." He turns from the balcony with a stern command. "Tiberius! You must study this peoples' history as you would of any enemy before a war."

Titus approaches Vespasian, lest he forgets his son's place as Rome's worthy and most awarded promising warrior.

"May I suggest father we also alert the Auxiliaries of Commagene. [53] I know these Arabian groups from the Euphrates closely, they hold a deep hatred for the Jews… they will perform their tasks excellently!"

Vespasian again turns to his Egyptian Prefect. Titus appears in frustration his father ignored his good contribution. He paces impatiently with his own thoughts: if only he was in command, Nero would be pleased of his response with the Jews.

"Tiberius!" Vespasian is snarling now. "The reason you don't have this problem here is because this people follow a God none have ever seen, one who forbids honoring any other God. These fanatics attack anyone seen with a statue, even that of our divine emperors - such are the savages Rome finds in these primitive lands. The Jews promote a heresy of our Emperors. And this time I won't fail Nero."

"Titus." Vespasian turns to his impatient son. "Answer the Emperor thus. Give me three weeks in the honor of your decree. And let Nero know I go to Caesarea with my only son."

"Mars shines on us!" Titus revels. "The day of the Flavian glory is nearer - I feel it in my bones and in my hot Roman blood. Hail Mars, the Gods remembered me…us… "

But Tiberius slumps on a chair wearily.

"With respect General, I have had more attachments with the Jews than anyone in this room. Have you considered Nero's judgment well, this people chose war many times to defend their beliefs. These Jews have their ways in Rome and will cause us trouble - remember what end befell Caligula when he made them such orders as Nero does now. And their temple fortress - it is stronger than anything else that stands on the earth… no nation can fell it?"

"Rome has seen such temples before." Titus responds defensively.

"Not like this one…" Tiberius sways his face.

"A Roman does not fear death before the Jews. Better that the Jews fear Rome? All Romans of valor know this truth - no glory without the death of the enemy. Don't you see it - destiny itself calls my father now? See it Tiberius - Rome's glory is given us to crush the Jews… and their invisible God!?"

"And how does Rome crush an invisible God?"

Titus smirks menacingly at Tiberius. "With a most visible Roman God…" He sways Nero's royal scroll in his fist at the war hardy Egyptian Prefect. "That's how Rome does it, Tiberius?"

Vespasian is pleased with his son's determination and resolve. The squatting crowd in the street clang their utensils noisily, waving at Vespasian's balcony, begging and gesturing hunger pangs; they pinch their babies to make them cry louder; they wink and nod at each other.

Titus proceeds to the balcony alone; his thoughts dwell on his own visions of glory, one he alone is destined for, an omen given him by the gods of Rome who came down from their heavenly abode to appoint him. Titus stiffens now; he encounters again the eagle perched on the roof, its powerful fiery red eyes focused on him. His eyes glow as his hand grasps his sword handle impatient and demanding. He affirms his sacred quest again to the bird, its powerful eyes gazing into him:

"I want it…"

(9) A RITUAL BATH

Alexis Matarian, Rome's appointed road builder, is exploring and measuring the terrain to determine the straightest path for his new road; his workers are mixing limestone pebbles.

There is a familiar melodious ethnic chanting emerging from the distant hills. His attention is distracted; he pauses, engaged in the melodious chorus. Alexis mounts on Tahrah and rides away into the winding hills, following the chants, peering from a distance. He sees three women leading a group of children; they sing joyously, dancing and hopping along in rhythmic quick steps. He stiffens when the lead singer appears the same girl who dared his security guard. A curious compulsion emerges; he follows by stealth, moving unseen behind the crevices of the hills. He ignores a wooden sign with a hand denoting "Entry Forbidden". The young maiden Alexis is focused on stops abruptly; Alexis also halts, peering from behind the hills. She proceeds behind a rock, returning holding a baby gazelle in her arms. He watches covertly, his face protruding partially behind a mound, how she squeezes drops from a cactus on the gazelle's trembling wounded foot, nursing it with caresses as her comrades bring water and berries.

As Alexis peers, he wonders what it would be like to talk with a Hebrew maiden, an ancient people with their strange beliefs he learnt of growing up in Rome. When the baby gazelle starts to feed, she nods, setting it free. The group continues on, singing in quick steps, the children's faces also fixed on the maiden - they follow her prompting of the song and feet stomping in robust giggles and chanting. Alexis follows discretely.

He recalls her disdain of the Roman soldiers, as do all people of their conquerors. Yet she was brave before a sword held before her, he recalls, approaching closer. One who tended a wounded animal with such devotion will not see pleasure in war, he imagined. As the procession progress ahead, an image appears before him. She stands unmoved with a spear fixed on her heart; she freely offered her life for another. She is a determined maiden with strong views.

His eyes gaze dreamlike; he is enchanted by the maiden's strides of rejoicing and abandon without any occasion of it; a free spirit dancing in the hills. She would not like a Roman as a friend. He recalls her disdain of his workers and he reminds himself: he is a Roman, an enemy. He retrieves her purse from his saddle, clasping it in his palm, examining the strange Hebrew writings, imagining what it says. Alexis gazes at the baby Gazelle hopping along without fear before the maiden. He nods to himself:

'I would like to know you?' He follows in parallel; advancing nearer covertly.

The group stops and encamps at a wadi, an isolated water pool setting of rockeries affording privacy from the highway routes. Deborah starts to undress. Alexis, hidden behind a hill, sees the naked figure of Deborah bathing, a brief cloth on her bosom her only covering. He turns his face away; then he gazes again in askance; then he turns away again.

Alexis is now distracted by a large snake slithering towards the children. He crawls on all fours, approaching it stealthily with his hand grasping his sword, his gaze alternating between the maiden and the snake. He closes in further; then his sword swiftly detaches the head of the snake. The children scream pointing fingers at the snake's severed head rolled down and now before them. Deborah races to the children; the three women holding their garments against their bodies are looking around. They see no one. "We are not alone." The elder Hebrew woman gazes at the detached head. "This snake is cut clean with the blow of a sword. One who saves us yet disrespects a women's Mikvah.[54] This is not one of our own…"

The snake's head shows an outstretched open mouth, its fangs in attack mode. Deborah retreats aghast and dripping wet, finger pointing, shaking, as if recalling a bad omen. She flees shuddering.

"Go, tend to her - she shakes again." The elder woman says.

In the distance, from behind a shrubbery, Florian winces in disdain at Alexis' devoted gaze of an enemy.

(10) THE ROYAL LIBRARY OF ALEXANDRIA.

Tiberius heeds Vespasian's orders to study the history of the Jews. In the western section of the world's greatest library, one initiated under the pre-Roman Ptolemaic dynasty, two female Librarians read for Tiberius.

"Most honorable Prefect Tiberius, I quote from Apion." Librarian Annia reads from a scroll, a scepter in her hand pointing. "Apion states, many Romans saw the Jerusalem fortress as unconquerable." She changes to a different scroll. "This is also agreed by Tacitus. Both these Roman scribes see the Hebrew's power in three towering walls, which they say reaches the heavens. As well, the Jews made tunnels and water cisterns under the ground that extend up to the mountains, allowing them to withstand long sieges. It says the Greeks conquered the Persians yet they failed against the city of Jerusalem. It is said a God none can see defends this people."

Librarian Livia comes forward.

"Honorable Tiberius, I quote from Tacitus again. Tacitus claims that all other sides of the fortress end sharply in the most treacherous slide of mountains and valleys, even as an abyss looking into hell." She pauses to retrieve a different scroll. "And Hecataeus of Abdera wrote… the Jews' most famed and holy city was called Jerusalem, that is was very strongly fortified. Abdera writes of their teacher Moses… that he gave the Jews new laws that betrayed the royal house of Egypt." She bows, retreating.

Annia approaches again.

"Honorable Tiberius may find this of good interest. Our wise general Pompey the Great was able to capture this temple one hundred years ago, employing good knowledge of their Hebrew customs. Pompey learnt that the Jews' superstitions did not allow them to defend the city on the day of Saturn, which the Jews called their holy Sabbath." She bows, rolling up the scroll; then she engages Tiberius:

"Honorable Tiberius - is Rome preparing for a war with the Jews?"

(11) THE TEMPLE TREASURY.

In a large field of the Megiddo plains, Deborah and her friend Miriam are squatted on the ground examining rows of vegetable shrubs sprouting from the earth; their hands and faces are mud smeared. They empty large jugs of water into containers standing on rocks at a level higher than the ground. The water streams down from the containers into hollow wooden pipes across the field; holes in the pipes are dripping water across the vegetable patch. Since the time of the ancient Israelites, the Jews were an advanced farming people, accumulating their ways in waterless deserts and parched hills; their seasons accounting adept Hebrew calendar being of much assistance.

Alexis is again present, hidden behind a hill as the two maidens work the field checking that the dripping waters feed all its sections. He is focused on the slow dripping water across the field; the arid land now appears moist and productive.

With their field labor concluded, Deborah is riding on her horse, one that is brown with white patches; Miriam sits behind her as they begin their return journey to their village, soiled and muddy. Suddenly, Deborah jolts her horse to a standstill. In the distance a Roman carriage blocks their path. The Romans are smirking, hailing them closer; they display spears and a threatening scorpion machine trajectory, allowing no retreating or fleeing.

Alexis is watching hidden behind a hill, sweat dripping from his face as he considers his own actions as a Roman; he taps his forehead on the stony hill in a dilemma, his hand grappling on the sword at his side, one all Romans carry in conquered lands.

Deborah wraps her shawl tightly, bracing herself and her horse. She gathers Miriam's hands around her, nods at the smirking Romans and proceeds slowly toward them. Her foot nudges her horse's underbelly three times in quick succession; the horse begins to gallop faster, heading directly at the carriage of the Romans. She nudges her foot three times again; the horse is galloping, accelerating in velocity as she nears the Romans in an unstoppable onslaught of crashing. The Romans start to waver, fearing her speeding horse storming upon the Roman carriage, allowing them no time to do anything but to speedily steer away - they leave the road and flee into the hills in disarray. Deborah storms away with Miriam grasping her tightly.

"Hebrew rebels! Hebrew harlots!" The Romans are screaming abuse from their gutted positions off the road; their carriage overturned.

"Rebels yes, harlots no!" Deborah shouts back. Miriam, her hands tightly around her, shouts in Deborah's ears as they ride away.

"Of course you are a rebel! Remember what you told our teacher in school - God was not kind giving Eve such a test? God was not kind!?"

"What is so kind about telling anyone they can eat of all the fruits but only the one with everlasting life - that tree you shall not eat of!?" She waves her hand at the heavens. "Hah! Who can bear such a test!? And why even tell them this!? Not so kind - not so kind!"

"Rebel, rebel! But I know God loves you. So do I."

They flee screaming in the exhilaration of the hot winds.

Alexis nods relieved and smirking of the Hebrew maiden's bravado; he flees also, dipping lowly behind the hills from the Romans sighting him.

The Romans are in heavy labor as they rise up their fallen war carriage.

In Hebron's town square, two Roman soldiers enter the town's rowdy fabric centre. Titus and his soldiers are in wait, hidden and submerged beyond the hills. Rows of cloth sellers display their garments on wooden stalls and tables - they feature headwear, men's tassels, women's shawls, scrolls, tunics and Mezuzahs. [55]

The two Roman soldiers approach a woman at a stall.

"Can you teach me your Hebrew dancing?" He grasps her waist and mimics a dance.

When her husband intervenes, pulling away is wife and pushing off the Roman soldier, the other soldier pulls out a trumpet from his coat and blows on it, creating a loud, piercing signal. The hidden army poised in the hills charges and attacks the town, slaying many men. The soldiers carry off the screaming young women and daughters as prized booty.

Titus nods: "Roman law allows 12 year olds as concubine."[56] He addresses the soldiers from his war carriage. "Your orders are to empty the towns outside their fortress in Jerusalem - easy money for you. Remember that half of all spoils must be delivered to Vespasian within three days - the rest among you. This includes slaves and concubines. So you must know now, all knowledge given me of the enemy becomes your gain. All of Judea is learning what comes from challenging Rome. My father marches on their coastal towns as we do now."

The Roman law for a woman's marriage was 12 years of age; concubines were allowed for men, with the law against adultery only applicable for women; such was concurrent for many nations in this period.

In the region of The Galilee, three Hebrew carriages are stopped by Roman soldiers, headed by Tiberius and a force of sixty Arabian mercenaries. Tama, the leader of the Arabians, finds two scrolls in the carriage; he turns to Tiberius.

"The writings are Hebrew - forbidden!?"[57]

"Forbidden. Burn them." Tiberius affirms.

Tama torches the scrolls. He snatches a talisman from a woman's neckline; she screams, a bloody tear on her neck. The Talisman in Tama's palm shows Hebrew letters. It marks the time this ancient writing became focused on and forever a mark of disdain.

"Hebrew!" Tama shows the torn away amulet to Tiberius. "Now I want to know where their weapons are hidden."

The Hebrew was a language unspoken and unwritten by any other peoples in the empire, as it was throughout the Jews' history with ancient nations like the Canaanites, Egyptians and Babylonians, affirming this nation's aloofness, alone possessing an independent language that emerged suddenly in its surrounds. Even as it accounts as one of the most copious and advanced ancient writings, the Hebrew was known only by the Greek translation of the Septuagint some three hundred years earlier. Many of the Hebrew laws it contained were seen as strange and disrespectful of the nation's deities and beliefs, especially of their divine kings.

Tama conducts a disruptive examination of the Hebrew carriages. When no weapons are found, he takes the hands of one of the Hebrew men and closely examines his finger nails, sniffing it, then, finding blackened mud and oil odors under his nails, smites the Jew. His blade is now against another Jew.

"Your hands carry oils to make fires for war. Where are the others - which way?" When none respond, Tama and his men eliminate the six males; then they collect three young maidens.

"They are of your own region, yet you fight them with a vengeance more than Rome." Tiberius questions Tama. "You destroyed six good slaves. Do this again and its loss will be deducted from your wages."

"Ours is an older war than yours. We fight one enemy now."

"You serve Rome by remembering Rome's orders. Titus was right of you peoples' enmities. But the spoils belong to Vespasian's treasury - else he accounts it from my purse. One more thing… bring the young one to my tent, untouched by your men. A Roman concubine will be better than what awaits the other two."

A whizzing sound; a sling stone on the forehead fells Tama to the ground. The Romans jolt; they take cover, gazing into the distance.

In an inland path behind the hills, six decoy carriages loaded with weapons are racing toward the Jerusalem hills with a determination. Young Boaz grips a sling swaying in the air; he sobs:

"My father! They killed my father - why did they do it!?"

Vespasian and Titus now begin implementing Nero's orders concerning the Jews with a determination. While Titus inflicted attacks on the towns surrounding Jerusalem and collecting wealth, his father Vespasian marches with a heavy laden army of 60,000 elite Roman soldiers massacring other larger towns: Accro, Jotapata, Bet Horon, Joppa and Hebron lay devastated - the town of Gamla in the Golan Heights saw the heaviest battle with over 4,000 Jews killed.

With rewards of looting, Vespasian is a rich man now, more so than in all his life's works; a chest of coins and jewelry is laid out before him in his private mansion. Vespasian and Titus see such actions of collecting wealth from the Jews as their personal wealth acquiring enterprises in addition to assured rewards from Rome.

Titus addresses Vespasian.

"Father, the people confide in me. Word is their Temple holds a strong treasury - one filled for more than a thousand years of Hebrew taxes - their wealth exceeds that of Rome! Father, the Jews took all the gold and treasures of Egypt - it is why they built the strongest fortifications to guard it. It is believed a secret place in their temple contains a giant lamp of gold and a golden box that houses the Ark of their Hebrew God's Covenant." Titus has a glint in his eyes, his excitement overwhelms him. "Imagine it father - this ark is their mark of power, protected by the wings of two golden angels - golden angels from a divine abode!? Surely such belongs with Rome!? And they let none enter their treasury places… my father must let only your son to approach this place. Let this be my reward from my Father. I want it?"

Vespasian caresses a gold coin in his palm; he marvels of its weight and design, how it shines. He nods at his son's earnest pledge.

In a garden patch of his home a young man has a knapsack holding his one year old daughter on his back; a piece of melon is tightly clenched in the child's hand. The child's father works with his dagger; he gently cuts away a rose stem from the bush in the front yard. Now his dagger is gently snipping the thorns from its stem; he blows to smoothen the stem holding the rose.

"Ima told you not to keep Rahel on your back with food in her hand." Amos reminds his father. "You want her to choke again?"

A Ram's horn sounds. His father's eyes are fixed on the hill; a lone man on a horse waits a response of the known code he sounded. The father hands the child and the rose stem to his son and proceeds on his horse to the hill.

Amos' mother and his five children are staring out the window of the house.

"The Sabbath will come soon and he leaves the house now..." Amos questions his mother. "What does Saul want from Abba at such a time!?"

There is a worried look on his mother's face as she gazes at her departing husband. She knows well the code of the short bursts of a Ram's horn; she clutches the rose stem in her hand, clasping her daughter in the other arm.

(12) THE MEGIDDO MARKETPLACE.

Alexis stops before a fruit stall in the busy and rowdy marketplace of Megiddo. He is impressed with the array of fine fruits, grains and the mesmerizing odor of precious perfumed oils. He examines the unusual native Sabra fruit.[58]

"Take any basket for half a shekel." The seller prompts him. "For your soldiers' pleasure under the hot sun?"

Alexis' hand abruptly retreats from the fruit's hairy thorns. His gaze is soon focused on a girl shopping a few stalls ahead. His eyes glow as she nears him.

"I am pleased to see you again." He appears awkward in the strange Hebrew market environment as her large almond eyes challenge him with underlying excitement and confusion of a Roman here. She responds with harshness and disdain.

"Mah!? You... here!?" Deborah is flushed by the Roman's approach; she looks around her in apprehension.

"I came to purchase limestone. You know that I'm a road builder?" He removes a pouch from his belt, extending his hand toward Deborah. "You left this behind..."

Her gaze is fixed on the Roman holding her purse; she is in shock and apprehension, as though he exposed her hidden secrets. Hushes resound; the Jews cast suspicious looks at the maiden; her purse in a Roman's hand. She backs off aghast, retreating and sneering at the Roman's strange gaze of devotion and familiarity.

A Jew prepares to confront Alexis, his hand now about to pull out a dagger, but his comrade withholds him.

"And cause half the town destroyed?"

"The Roman is not here for limestone." The Jew's hand rests on his dagger.

A shrill ram horn sounds. The stall holders begin shutting shop; the people disperse as a swarm and vanish.

Alexis is left alone in a deserted marketplace, a purse in his extended hand. A mesmerized man angling a last glimpse of the fleeing Hebrew maiden; he turns around as he sees now the market place is emptied.

"What happened?"

A Jew on a donkey with a Ram's horn winces at the Roman. "The Sabbath comes!?"

In the outpost of the market, a face is hidden in a hood; Alexis' security guard Florian's hand rests on his sword. Florian now understands why Alexis insisted on riding out into the Jews' market alone to purchase limestone, when it is normally attended to by his workers. His master seeks a maiden of the enemy of Rome; he winces in disdain.

(13) THE SICARII WARRIORS.

Saul rides with a band of Jews he gathered with his Ram's horn code of danger; they ride together on horseback. They slow down as they approach the destroyed town square of Caesarea. The dead bodies are strewn across the streets and piled on its avenues and narrow lanes. Homes are shattered, women's breasts are plastered on the broken windows of the Synagogue and the streets are littered with corpses. Saul, barely 18 years of age, pauses before a fallen body; he whistles a code, gesturing his leader with a hand wave to come closer.

The group's young somber leader dismounts his horse and squats to speak to a fallen mother on the ground, one who is barely alive, her breasts severed and a spear pinning down her gutted chest. Saul gestures again, pointing with his raised eye brows; the dying mother is hiding a child under her knees.

The leader of the Hebrew group of Sicarri warriors holds the hand of the dyeing woman tenderly, his eyes locked on her as he strokes her forehead. He nudges her knees, coaxing her; nodding assuredly.

"It is I, Eleazar, of the Sicarri.[59]

When she finally agrees, he lifts the child from under her knees and hands the child to Saul. Then he approaches her closely.

"This destruction, the blood still flows hot. Their legions went which way - the coastal road?" The dying woman blinks her eyes. Eleazar turns to Saul and nods. Saul kisses the forehead of the woman, shutting her eyes with his palms and murmurs a prayer. His able hand ends her hopeless remaining life swiftly with a Sicarri dagger's throat swipe across a selected vein; the mother succumbs calmly, almost instantly.[60]

A screeching sound signals in the distance - the Sicarii faces turn to a roof where sits a ferocious bird, its powerful eyes focused on fresh flowing blood. The Sicarii pull out their slings and ready for a strike at the eagle on the roof. But Eleazar halts them with hand codes not to attack. Powerful eyes that see all from afar and measuring the strong array of warriors below, the eagle prudently ascends away in flight. Eleazar hand signals his warriors to follow the bird.

The "Aquila." It is the Roman name of the Empire's formidable symbol of dominion and power. The eagle is the bird of Jupiter, the only creature that conquers the heavens above the clouds and glides closest to the sun god. The Aquila is alone able to lift the brave and honored souls of Rome to the glorious abode of the deities. Thereby, the eagle is the ancient divine messenger of the Roman Gods and the deliverer of tidings of omens and of protection in battle. The Aquila is Rome's ensign of war, one accorded to every legion in battle; one most contrasted from the Hebrew dove of peace that brings good tidings.

Eleazar heads his warriors for the Roman coastal highway, following the mighty Aquila soaring in the skies. They storm away in a silent determined fury, unperturbed by the dangers of confronting an elite Roman legion; their eyes stay focused on the gliding bird. They storm away, glistening Sicarii blades clutched in their jaws.

They pause at a vantage point overlooking the Roman legion which has settled down to rest. A Sicarii warrior speaks.

"Too many. There is nothing we can do at this time?"

Eleazar nods; his hand tells his men to stay still. Then he storms away alone towards the Roman legions below; his warriors sway faces at his daring. Saul follows him.

The two Sicarii ride now via the winding dirt tracks of the hinterland hills in parallel to the Roman built coastal highway. They divert and form a loop, pausing unseen when adjacent to the legion's executive carriage.

Eleazar dismounts stealthily, peering through the shrubbery; Saul covers him. When close enough to the open top carriage of Vespasian, he removes two short curved daggers from his garment. He swipes the dagger's serrated edges into a black berry held in his palm; green drops of liquid spurt out. Then he flings the two daggers in a peculiar manner, hoisting from bent elbows upwards with a speed faster than the eye perceives.

The first flying dagger slices into the neck of Vespasian's assistant; the head flops to his side. The second dagger hits Vespasian's lower torso; the General falls off his carriage, landing on the tarred roadway. The rest of the Romans are yet not aware, the assault being of a silent, excellent and assured procedure. Saul kisses his finger in satisfaction of the hit.

Fallen on the ground, Vespasian winces; he is peering behind the shrubs. His dazed vision now has a glimpse of his attacker. Eleazar's stony look, black leather band on his forehead, a close beard and dangling hair locks, stares back emotionless. Blood gushes from a poisoned swollen wound on Vespasian's bosom; the ashen face whitens, then he collapses. The Hebrew vanishes.

(14) DEBORAH HUR HALTED.

She rides the hillside curves with a homespun daring, her uncovered tresses flowing in the hot winds. From a high ridge, Ari and Saul are watching.

"A betrayer." Saul points at the maiden. "Let us make Simon angry."

"Let us protect the village from her…" Ari races down the hills on his horse towards Deborah.

Deborah pauses, turning to see Ari approaching; she understands his determined threatening speed and she flees. There is a prolonged chase, in twists and turns around the hills and inclines of Megiddo, of leaps and strides of abandon. Soon she realizes it is no game when chased by a Sicarii; her confident challenging face now glistens with droplets of sweat, her breath is heaving. She turns for the safety of the dirt tracks she knows so well, relieved now she has freed herself from her Sicarii pursuer; she has finally lost him. She is racing around the dirt track's barren T-junction in a perfect right angle arc; he is no more a shadow behind her. But the adept Sicarii re-emerges; Ari makes a diagonal fast track crossing the T-juncture and corners Deborah's horse, butting her, thrusting her off the road. She is flung off her horse to the ground. Ari grasps Deborah's hair, holding a Sicarri blade to her throat.

"What have you given the Roman spy, speak?"

"He saved our Teacher. I know not why he came back to our village."

"You lie." Ari grips his blade closer into her skin; she is writhing; specs of blood appear on her neckline. "One more time. How does the Roman hold your purse in his hand?"

"I don't know!" She dares his blade, screaming defiantly. "Do what you will… I know no more of him!?"

"Deborah does not lie!" Her friend Miriam appears.

"Betrayer - harlot. But for Simon - tfu?!" - Ari flings Deborah away. Miriam pulls her to safety; they flee, departing from Ari's lingering, accusing gaze.

(15) A HOSPITAL RECOVERY ROOM.

Vespasian is attended by doctors holding a fire torch and blade over a poisoned open wound, one surrounded by a ring of dark green stains. Both his hands are secured by ropes restricting any movements. The Roman Magistrate's envoy arrives; he waves away the doctors, engaging Vespasian determinedly.

"Rome has decided this province must be free of troubles and you must understand fully Rome's orders. I am to report of your advices, especially how goes the road works and Nero's commands trusted to you?"

"If none could vanquish the Jews, I will!?" Vespasian responds screaming in agony. "They tore my leg, I will tear this nation's hearts out so they never rise again!?"

"You are being ridiculed at home for shaming Rome - a single Jew tearing a Roman commander's leg before an entire legion. Yet, Nero has not forgotten your service in Londonium. Nero anointed you the most esteemed rank of Consul for your triumph there. Nero again shows you grace and gives you once more to restore your honor. One more thing. This Judea is known as a most wealthy…"

"Let the Magistrate and the Senate know that I won't fail Rome's treasury?"

"You cannot fail Nero again! Rome has much at stake here and all the nations' eyes are upon us - Rome promises you glory or disaster. The might of Mars shine upon you!"

As the envoy leaves, Vespasian gazes at the ceiling, murmuring to himself.

'One day I will be the richest man in the empire. The Jews are given in my hands.'

His doctors burn a fiery torch into his wound, then a sharp blade descends. As his face wrenches in agony, an image flashes before Vespasian.

He lies on the ground pierced with a Sicarii dagger; he sees the stony gaze of Eleazar behind the bushels, coils of black hair locks swaying about the Hebrew's face; his body begins to shudder violently. As the doctor's blade pierces into his poisoned swollen wound, Vespasian collapses.

(16) SHEKEL OF ISRAEL.

Ari brings a pot of chicken broth and grape juice for Eleazar in his isolated secret cave behind the hills. "The mothers who survived Caesarea sent you food - they say kol kavod and give honor to Eleazar for breaking the Roman Commander's leg. The Romans will find it harder to command killers of Jewish mothers and daughters. Your safety is now my first responsibility. Rome will never find you." Ari serves food.

"Better that you make our people's safety your work now."

"There is news. A problem in Megiddo. A Roman spy and one of our own maidens. The Roman has enticed her, we don't know yet what he knows. You are busy controlling the men, let Saul and I be given permission to use special war laws now to control the people."

"Tell it also to the Teacher Hillel." Eleazar nods. "Tell him why we do this. Be sure of it before your charges upon her - she will find no refuge with her people or with Rome?"

"Understood."

Eleazar tosses a coin at Ari.

"The coin reads…" Ari examines the coin. "Ten Shekels…"

"Turn it."

"The other side says… Shekel of Israel. What is this!?" Ari is agitated, fists clenched and eyes welling in enthusiasm. "The Hebrew stamp covers the stamp of Rome - this will be seen as a declaration of war!?"

Eleazar smiles sardonically. "So what do you think it means when they change the name of our land to Judea to a Roman one - and demand that we worship their king? The coins all Jews hold in their hands will tell us every day Hebrew is forbidden… Israel is no more? Rome wants from us more than war. We must decide our response or we perish."

"Then tell me now, what can be our response against such a force of nations gathered against us? Has our day of light come?" Ari appears tormented. "What is the plan - can there even be one against these brutes!?"

"Hold your blade to your heart." Eleazar bids Ari to pledge. "Go to the temple and send the Roman appointed treasury priest to heaven's door step. Tell the Temple's coin minters they must press the new stamp of Israel on all shekels - they must cover the Roman stamp. The Roman name of Judea must be erased and the Hebrew name of Israel must return. The days of the sons of light and darkness… have begun?"

Ari's eyes light up. "Only from you can I accept such words…" He points his dagger at the skies; the Temple glows in his thoughts. He kisses his dagger in teary devotion, murmuring a prayer:

"Israel's name must return as was sworn to Avraham - peace be unto his name. Israel will be Judea no more. Amen, Amen. From your mouth to heaven's ear."

Ari suddenly jolts in his praying stance; his keen ever ready Sicarii reflex makes him dash behind the hills. A group of ten young Jews are hiding; huddled together. They raise their hands before Ari, whose hand grips his dagger before them, ready to lash out.

"We came to join with you." One of the Jews comes forward, hands raised. Ari examines them for weapons; then he turns to Eleazar.

"They are from the Peace Party - Agrippa's servants of Rome." Ari differs to Eleazar for his decision.

"No, no!? We left our families behind…" The Jew, barely 15, responds. "We are servant to only One God." Ari approaches Eleazar and speaks out of their hearing:

"Keep them here and send one to recruit fifty more?"

"There is only one law Jews don't forsake." Eleazar says, peering into the lads' faces. "One God. Give them Sicarii daggers and war lessons. Also, tell me who protects my family?"

"We hide them as we hide you from the Romans. Be in peace of it."

"No! Their safety must come before mine?"

"Understood."

Shekel of Israel S38a

(17). TITUS SWEARS REVENGE.

Titus' gaze is fixed on Vespasian as he watches his father shuddering in agony, delirious from a green poisoning of his blood; his arms and feet unceremoniously fastened to his bed posts. Titus heaves in labored angst, his eyes consumed in ferocious anger as he watches his warrior father so reduced; he sees his own glory as diminishing as his father lies broken in his first measure against the Jews. Nero will be displeased; the Gods of Rome will be displeased.

A figure emerges from the dark shadowy passage. He whispers it behind Titus provocatively:

"On account of the Jews, Rome mocks your father - only he does not see this now." Aristomy's voice is of sarcasm and taunting as he now infuses his plans on Titus, for he knows well the suppressed ambitions of Vespasian's warrior son. "But I have the way of restoring back the honor of Vespasian… and your own?"

"The Jews will pay for this." Titus warns; his gaze fixed on his father. "Their mothers, their sons and their daughters… lion food in the arena. I swear it."

Aristomy hisses, whispering: "Then deliver the Jew who tore your father's leg as Nero ordered Vespasian - this honor now falls on you, his son? See, your father's intention was honorable in serving Nero, only he never saw a traitor walking among us, one who caused your honorable father's torn leg, one who handed the enemy knowledge of his every movement and location where to find him. Deceit and betrayal to cut down your father!?"

Aristomy now has Titus' unwavering attention; he is focused on him with a warrior's killer instincts, awaiting his further clarification.

"Was it your father's fault for trusting those among us - no, no, not so!" Aristomy consoles Titus. "But as a great warrior who surely understands that such treachery does happen, perhaps you too suspected it? Moan not over your father now but get revenge for Rome and for Vespasian - and for Titus' own honor with Nero. I say to you Nero waits of word of his orders being fulfilled. I beseech the mighty Titus, for if your father's honor falls, your own glory falls too. Hear me, I beg you…" There is deviousness in his smirk. "We must do what must be done - but we blame the Jews for it?" He nods wickedly of his plan. "Come… come now, hear me…"

In Megiddo, Miriam nurses a blade mark on Deborah's throat.

"They rob our women for their concubines. Ari is a Sicarri sworn to defend Israel from the Roman killers. They trust no one, not even the Peace Party."

"That Roman saved our Teacher's life."

"It is how their spies fool us. It is a nation of war that terrorizes and enslaves many with their guile. They have their ways and we have seen their kind before." Miriam washes Deborah's neck. "You are safe now. Only tell me how he got your purse?"

"I don't know how."

"Not even me you trust…" She whispers: "You can tell me? Did you…?"
Deborah flanks Miriam's hand from her neck. Now she understands how her people think of her. She backs away from her closest friend, a deep resentment in her eyes, a torturous pain as she withdraws. She storms away in a fury.

(18) EVERY LOYALTY HAS A PRICE

Florian bows before Vespasian who is recovering from his wound. Vespasian now sits on a seat; his leg is improving and cushioned on a soft stool.
"I summoned you because there are troubling reports of my road builder. I shall trust none but the one I appointed to guard him from all harm."
"Alexis serves our General well and we learn from him the finest skills for Rome's glory."
"His safeguarding comes even before my son. Withhold nothing from me."
"Only his heart is tender and not accustomed to the beautiful maidens of this land. At times, my Master Alexis is known to ride on Tahrah, the horse Vespasian gave to him. Alexis rides in the hills on Tahrah, even into the villages of the Jews."
"How many maidens does he approach?"
"Just the one."
"I see. I should have given him a concubine instead of a horse - it is the Roman thing to do. I see fit to depend on my loyal soldier Florian. You must protect him with your life. Report to me good knowledge of him. Your loyalty will earn your family a reward of honor and a residence in Rome; you will live in honor beside me."
Florian bows and turns to depart; he halts when Vespasian calls him again:
"Also you must rid us of the Hebrew maiden. Alexis must never find out. Dispose of her body so none find it. Swear it?"
Vespasian's inducement of a residence in the choicest centre of Rome and protection for his family has an anticipated effect on Florian; it is an offer that no Roman soldier can resist.
"I swear it." Florian bows with his hand on his heart. Then he retreats.
Florian understood now he has to deliver good reporting to secure the grand future promised him and his family, to even protect Alexis with his life - or lose all if he failed his orders. And thereby Alexis' security guard is compromised; Vespasian, the experienced war commander knows that every loyalty had a price. [61]

At the road works construction site, Florian approaches Alexis. He finds him immersed in the measuring of the new road being made equally parallel of the Roman width and able to contain processions of legions and armor. Alexis is crouched on the ground, dripping in sweat under the searing Arabian sun; he measures different points of the width before its tarring phase.
"There is news Master. More elite Roman Legions have been stationed in Caesarea."
"There is already an army there, what occasions Rome's elite Legions now?" Alexis questions from his crouched position on the ground.
"The Jews made trouble with the Hellenist soldiers. That town has been crushed on Nero's orders so such rebellions do not spread." Florian squats on the ground to inform Alexis. "Religious fanatics practicing sorcery against Rome! Vespasian was brought down by clever means - a flying twisted dagger from behind the hidden hills. Vespasian is in shame. And Titus has sworn revenge - there is rumor he is marching to many towns."
Alexis now pauses from his work, rising with an interest, dusting his uniform; pouring water on his face.
"What of the town of Megiddo? That Jewish procession, that group with the Jewess, what of them?"
"Not good, Master. Titus will search out her kind. Master, that Jew already owes you favor, you saved her once. And I have seen your eyes searching for her. I have done work of her, shall I speak of it?"

"Speak of it." Alexis strokes Tahrah's main, his thoughts far away.

"Her dwelling place is behind the hills of Megiddo. The girl is expert on her horse, a tan horse with white patches. Master, I can bring you the girl for your pleasure?"

"She is everywhere... wherever I look. Even when I shut my eyes..." He gazes into the skies as if envisioning a cherished thought.

"You must be careful, Master."

But Alexis is oblivious to Florian's warning; images appear before him of a maiden with a spear fixed on her heart:

'I am Deborah. House of Hur. Megiddo.'

"Master, the girl is of the enemy... she is forbidden?"

"I must know if her love is promised to another." A far away glow of yearning in his eyes: "I must know... I must!?"

"Master, the Jews insult Rome's divine emperors..."

Alexis turns away. He mounts on Tahrah and races into the hills. Florian considers his master's situation as he dissolves into the distant ancient pathways. He remembers being insulted by Alexis before his workers for a Jew, and he remembers the orders of Vespasian. Florian ponders what forces made an honorable Roman flaunt his nation's commands for a common Jewish enemy.

(19) THE GREEK SEPTUAGINT.

Aristomy, menacing as a serpent, carries a basket of fresh figs as he visits a recuperating Vespasian. He places the basket on the table beside the Commander's bed.

"The figs of Caesarea give strength. But tell me now dear honorable Vespasian, was I not perfectly right to report the Jews' treachery to Nero, will I not be honored for imploring the emperor on my knees, even before they did this treachery to you!?"

"I see. It was you that caused that affair. I wondered what turned Nero - he used to like the Jews. Who did you bribe, the royal butler - or was it his music teacher Beryllus?"[62]

"My mighty commander knows it. Our Gods and priests were insulted ever since Alexander favored their Hebrew writings to be placed in our Greek library.[63]

"Alexander - the famed one! Is that why he was killed by your kind?"

"The great one's mind was twisted by the sorcery of the Jews. Let it not happen to Rome also - I beseech you?

Vespasian is now focused on Aristomy's strange words. Aristomy is relating to an event that happened three hundred years ago in the Greek Empire.

The Roman war with the Jews becomes clearer only by a historical enumeration what lead to it. It is one that followed an ancient repetitive history with all nations that interacted with the Jews. Rome's obsession with the Jews was not unique; the previous Greek Empire, the Babylonians, the Assyrians and the Egyptians affirm this as a historically generic syndrome. Its cause is best seen with one pivotal event that made the Jews a worldly anomaly that continued unabated in the Roman Empire.

The Septuagint, a term evolved from the Latin *Septuaginta*, is generally translated as 70, a reference of the Hebrew scribes called upon to translate for the first time the Hebrew Scriptures into the Greek in 300 BCE, some 350 years prior to the reign of Nero, when the Greek Empire was the power ruling Arabia. Historians refer to this work as an extraordinary event in the world's history:

"Its chief value lies in the fact that it is a version of a Hebrew text earlier by about a millennium than the earliest dated Hebrew manuscript extant. It is, moreover, a pioneering work; there was probably no precedent in the world's history for a series of translations from one language into another on so extensive a scale." - (H. St. J. Thakeray) [64]

Prior to the Septuagint, the Hebrew was a closed language to the nations. The figureheads Abraham and Moses were not seen in any other writings; only in recent times have relics been uncovered and affirming biblical emblems such as 'House of David; Jerusalem; Israel; Hebrew' as real history. The Greek Septuagint Bible marks an epochal historical triggering, one that exposed for the first time what was under-laid but not known before by the nations concerning the strange Hebrew beliefs, and set in a language none of the nations spoke.

The Greek-Hebrew interaction that created this monumental work merits a most important placement in history, for its infusion of belief provisions, the opening of historical trajectories and its output of new depictions of the knowledge status of its time. It produced a disdain and intrigue position between the Jews and the Greeks that would stream down to the nations across the seas.

The first recorded Hebrew figure confronted the first recorded divine king in Ur, Babylon, ushering an assured history of conflict from its inception; one that again reared with the divine kings from across the seas. Abraham's conflict with Nimrod is the same with the Hebrew seed and the Greek and Roman divine emperors. Monotheism was at the core of all holy wars with the Jews; and now Aristomy well represented the traits of a deep disdain by those loyal to their divine emperors and the Greek religion.

Aristomy: "Hear me, Vespasian! We cannot let their Hebrew God make us as forgotten as was done to all other nations - none survived this peoples' mischief." Now the Greek Mayor impresses upon Vespasian, his Roman Commander, the deep variance of the Hebrew belief. "The Jews are the enemies of our gods and divine kings - Rome's too. Yours too. It is us or them?"

Vespasian, a superstitious man from his early days, ponders on Aristomy's words, caressing a fig fruit in his hand.

It was the Greek emperors who assumed themselves as divine immediately prior to the Roman Empire and fostered the war against monotheism that culminated in the Roman war with the Jews; it was the Greeks who brought the Hebrew bible to the Romans; and it was the Greeks who initiated the name Palestine upon Judea. [65]

The Greeks also introduced alphabetical writings to the nations across the sea; they acquired this from the Jews via Arabian channels.[66] It was also a Romanized Greek Jew whose teaching amalgamated Christianity as a new religion. The Septuagint marks the first alphabetical book the elite Greek minds confronted, its depictions contrasting all else; it will alter humanity, history and the universe.

The notion of a holy war is nowhere better allocated than the animosity displayed by the ancient nations of divine emperors and the Jews; all who interacted with this people wanted the Hebrew laws abolished, and all is traceable to one foremost law coined by the Greeks as "Monotheism" - a One God belief. The Greek input in the success of Monotheism as a worldly premise is thereby substantial and pivotal. Contrastingly, the Greeks also fostered the Roman war with the Jews. This was not a battle against one minuscule group of Jews, but with a thought crime that was a bigger paradigm.

The Greek War against Monotheism. In 160 BCE, prior to Rome's invasion of Arabia, the Syrian-based Greek Seleucid Emperor Antiochus IV Epiphanes sought to destroy the Hebrew Monotheism beliefs that contradicted his divinity; Epiphanes stood for 'mad one' by his vile deeds. More than Caligula and all others, Antiochus can be singled out as one who had a fanatical hatred for all things Hebrew, when the Jews became the first people that rejected the ancient Greek religion of multi-deities and divine emperors; it caused a devastating outcome. As with Caligula, Antiochus was the first who used his divine status in demanding the abolition of the Hebrew belief on penalty of death, ordering a statue of Zeus in the temple, and conducting desecrations, vilifications and terrible acts of cruelty.

Antiochus also changed the name of Jerusalem to Zeus Olympius, a stratagem the Romans would later emulate as expressing a nation's existential negation. Antiochus imposed intolerable demands and forbiddances on the Jews; he appointed Hellenistic priests in the temple, forbade the Sabbath, had thousands of Jews massacred and deported thousands to Greece. Two globally impacting paradigms resulted by the enforced Greek exile of Jews.

First, the migration of the Jews to Greece infused historical and religious impacts, with the osmosis of knowledge transfer that shaped the emerging modern world's beliefs. All major Greek philosophers and teachers studied and debated the new controversial and provocative Septuagint Bible, namely the five books of Moses (The Torah), a Hebrew scripture that fully negated the premise of divine emperors and its Greek gods. The Septuagint infuriated the Greek divine emperors, as was seen with ancient Egypt and Babylon. Again, the Jews braced for a holy war against Hellenist Assyria, then history's greatest super power, one greater than all that Alexander accumulated.

The other result was the inevitable rebellion of the Jews in 166 BCE under the leadership of the Maccabees against the Greek emperors who sought to negate all things Hebrew. When the Jews prevailed with astonishing results by a far lesser priestly force in a war, the Seleucid Greeks never forgot or forgave it, harboring a lingering disdain they would later transfer to Rome in the fostering of a continuing holy war.

The Jewish victory was seen as miraculous by the Jews, ordaining the festival known as Hanukah - the notion of light extending to the heavens in the Menorah emblem of Israel; the Greek royalty and its priestly sectors saw it as an insult to their kings and ancient beliefs.

The bondage for the Jews assured in the Hebrew scriptures offers no alternatives of its reasoning other than the most primal and foundational precept introduced by Abraham, one all divine emperors were specifically obsessed with. Thus did Monotheism, the Abrahamic equation of 'One God' become the enemy of all divine kings.

Under Antiochus's rule, the forcefully transferred exile of Jews to the Greek empire anticipated the great Jewish revolt and the Roman exile for the same reason; it also resulted in generations of Greek Jews that would trigger historical impacts on the first century's contributions to the world at large; including of Christianity ushered by such an exiled Jew.

During the three centuries prior to the Roman war with the Jews, the Greek philosophy and science inclined sectors, in opposition to its self-appointed divine rulers, developed an intimate focus in the Hebrew bible; and it began to annoy the Greek Emperors. Antiochus represented a growing sector of a Greek priestly class that embodied a deep disdain of Monotheism. Yet, this Hebrew law was not becoming conquered; instead it was going to conquer both the Greek and Roman Empires. Saul of Tarsus, a 5th generation Jew resultant from the Greek exile, and a Roman citizen when the Greeks were conquered, emerged in a backdrop of the Septuagint's pre-existing influence. Monotheism will prevail over mighty Rome via Christianity.

Aristomy continues imploring Vespasian earnestly:

"Our king Antiochus understood the Jews' deep hatred of our beliefs. Both Caligula and Nero also understood this. Vespasian must also understand why the Jews tore your leg - their message is Rome will not stand."

Vespasian nods smirking. He ponders Aristomy's words and the Greek Mayor's bold design of turning the Emperor Nero's mind with bribery; it caused the massacre in Caesarea and turned Nero's sights against the Jews he once favored; Aristomy's deeds was also the subsequent cause of Vespasian's shame of a wounded leg. Aristomy offers Vespasian another fig fruit.

Alexander the Great in the Jerusalem Temple. [Artist: Sebastiano Conca, 1764] Source: S9

Alexander the Great. The Septuagint bible's translation is believed to be initiated by Alexander, who gave the Jews many privileges and was highly impressed by their ancient beliefs and historical writings that predated the Greek. Although he never lived to witness his quest, dying suddenly, the monumental work was conducted by his successor King Ptolemy.[67]

Alexander gave autonomy of self-rule and religious freedom to the Jews; this would cease soon after his demise, as was seen with Caligula who flaunted Caesar's granting of religious freedom to the Jews - so did the Greeks do after Alexander's death.

Alexander's departure from the later Greek Emperors can best be applied to his mentor Aristotle, one whose philosophy more aligned with the Hebrew belief of monotheism. Yet the Hebrew bible's translation by the Greeks, more so than any other cause, initiated the Hebrew Scriptures to become a worldly treatise and the most known of all theological writings.[131] And it was happening under the most implausible historical scenario; that none of the nations spoke Hebrew is a factor signifying the Septuagint's importance of the Hebrew bible's spread.

A retrospective assessment says the Septuagint marks a greater impact on humanity than all the war victories of Alexander; its influence being also a strong factor for the emerging Christianity's acceptance of the Hebrew bible, one that almost never happened, again signifying this translation's poignancy in history. While the Jews fully mastered the Greek language, the Greeks spoke no Hebrew; King Ptolemy pledges to the Jews:

"Write for me in our Greek tongue which you know well, the Pentateuch of Moshe your Teacher."[68]

Legend has it, and stated by both Josephus and Philo of Alexandria, that seventy Hebrew scribes were contracted by the King Ptolemy to perform the enormous task of the Septuagint's translation, each scribe placed in separate chambers, without being told of the other translators - this to see if the Hebrew God would put in the heart of each one to translate the same as all the others would do.

Ptolemy pledged further to the Temple Priest to release all Jewish prisoners held in Egypt, requesting 70 priests be sent, six from each tribe who are expert in the Hebrew law. A formal contractual agreement was undertaken to comply with the monumental task; the Greeks who were determined to achieve this quest at any cost, as though driven by a strange compulsion, provided enormous facilities to the Jews:

Living quarters for the 70 Hebrew Priests, their families and working assistants; for this was an undertaking of many decades and none would return back alive.

Each Priest will carry three scrolls of the Hebrew bible - 210 scrolls authenticated by the High Priest; it indicates 100's of scrolls were housed in the Temple Genizah (storehouse of religious documents), which would have been consumed in the fires of Rome's war with the Jews; the Dead Sea Scrolls are among its saved portions.

Ptolemy accepted the working academy to be housed separately from the Library of Egypt, with security guarantees the priests will be free to practice their Hebrew faith.

New Greek words emerged in the world's lexicon; the term 'Pentateuch' (From the Latin *septum* meaning seven, plus-*gint?* meaning "times ten"; or 70) is a Greek translation for the name given to the five Mosaic books ('The Torah'). The term 'Jew' is also a Greek derived one, as are the terms Bible, Genesis, Arabia and Arab. The Septuagint translation initially produced only the five books of Moses; it continued in later years by other scribes to include the Prophetic Hebrew books of Kings, Isaiah, the Psalms and Jeremiah, indicating the Greek penchant for more.

Maimonides, the Jewish sage and scientist of the 12th Century, the author of 'A Guide for the Perplexed', explains the importance of the Greek influence on the modern world. He writes that the elite Greek minds were even superior to the opinions of Hebrew prophets such as Ezekiel in matters of the sciences and the natural world, and that Aristotle's views were also monotheistic. Essentially, Maimonides expressed that the elite Greek sectors, ruled by fanatical self-assumed divine rulers, were not of a true pagan people.

The Greek philosophers began their spiritual pondering independently, as did a pagan family's son Abraham who inspired the Hebrew monotheistic. Here there is a thread of alignment; both nations arrived at one common premise prior to any interaction that ushered an underlying unity of minds within otherwise irreconcilable surrounds of division and war. Aristotle, the mentor of Alexander, upheld his premise of 'The First Cause' - of a supreme force in the beginning, thus aligning with Genesis' opening words of 'In the Beginning God.'[69]

The ancient world's Masters of Philosophy, Geometry, Music Notes and Earth Maps aligned with a host of pivotal factors in the Hebrew Septuagint Bible:

That 'Change' marks the only attribute of Infinity:

Aristotle: "That which moves without being moved, that which changes without being changed."
[Aristotle's Natural Philosophy; 'The Unmoved Mover or Prime Mover']

Hebrew: "I am the Lord I have not changed" [Malachi, 3:6]

That all of creation is the work of one Supreme Creator:

Aristotle: "That there must be an immortal, unchanging being, ultimately responsible for all wholeness and orderliness in the sensible world."

Hebrew: "I am the LORD and there is none else, there is no God beside me." [Isaiah 45:5]

That everything contained in the universe never existed before the Universe's Creation:

Aristotle: "It is clear then that there is neither place, nor void, nor time, outside the heaven. Hence whatever is there is of such a nature as not to occupy any place; or does time age it" [First Cause Philosophy]

Hebrew: "In the Beginning God" [Gen.1:1]. Namely, once nothing else except God existed.

The Septuagint Impacts. The Hebrew bible's dispersion to the world at large began with the enforced exile of the Jews to the Greek lands, one prior to the Roman one that drove the Jews to the European continent. It is the historical background that most substantially impacted what evolved as the new theology of the West, in its sectors of science, philosophy, the judiciary, the Hebrew moral and ethical laws and its high literary merit, culminating in new belief provisions that contradicted all that the ancient world previously held. The globalization of the Hebrew bible was initiated by the Greek recognition of the Septuagint and its absorbing by the Christian bible.

Josephus, under the Roman dictates, emphasizes the merits of the Septuagint to the world at large; he writes:

"I would therefore boldly maintain that the Jews have introduced to the rest of the world a very large number of beautiful ideas. What higher justice than obedience to the laws?"

The osmosis of manifold new paradigms, the beautiful new ideas referred to by Josephus, resulted from the first translation of the Hebrew bible into the Greek. Creationism became an early proto-science and one of the new paradigms introduced to the elite Greek minds. This was a new rendering of the world's origins that contrasted all prevailing beliefs, especially those held by the Greeks and Romans. A sole Creator-based Creationism that emerged in an intelligent protocol contrasted the warring deities of the ancient world; it marked the first pre-science premise of cause and effect from a pre-universe source, as apposed one that is self-created by other components within the universe, such as the deities of the sun and the oceans.

The Felling of Zeus. The Greek thinkers eventually accepted that their mythical panorama of deities were false and used as political ruling tools; they eventually saw the Hebrew Scriptures as the more credible, much to the chagrin of the Greek kings and their priests. Here, even Christianity would have faltered without enshrining monotheism as its foundation. The Greeks who had aligned their 'First Cause' belief with the Septuagint bible three hundred years earlier would have desisted, marking their variance from the Romans; Christianity aligned itself with the Septuagint.

Monotheism faced great opposing forces. Rome's propaganda schemes and its brutal force will forbid any promotion that rejected its divine emperor belief with appropriate precautionary measures, appointing its writers to promote Rome and forbade any from promoting an anti-Roman philosophy; the Hebrew scribe Flavius Josephus was one such imprisoned writer. Rome's rejection of the Hebrew monotheism and the Jews' rejection of Rome's reciprocity requirement of worshiping its emperors were mutually exclusive paradigms. A holy war was inevitable. Soon after the Septuagint impacts, a submerged chasm emerged within the belief sectors; many of the bravest and most profound Greek philosophers rose to challenge the divine emperor platform by promoting a more inclusive ruling mode, and many were killed for it. [70]

The Greek emperors ensured that all blame for the division of belief will fall on the Jews and their Septuagint sorcery; it became a historical deflection syndrome of the divine king nations that battled with the Jews; and this mode will be used by Rome who emulated numerous deeds of the Greek Emperors. Concurrently with the Jewish war, Rome's forces were causing great destructions with the Druids and Celtic peoples, and merging their sacred deities with that of Rome. While Rome allowed all conquered nations to continue their own faith, it also required reciprocal reverence of the Roman deities; its aim to minimize discordances and gradually form a common Roman belief alliance in the empire. The Jews mark the one people who will challenge Rome and thereby became the sole defenders of monotheism. The Romans were wise in their conquering stratagems and propaganda but possessed no Godly impacting moral or ethical laws, and held brute power as their mark of glory.

Now an important interaction of knowledge and belief was occurring here that would impact Mighty Rome, then Christianity and the modern world. The Septuagint exposed a new, different set of law-based knowledge; its derivative imprints impacted the first century war and beyond, thus its accounting is incumbent as a major contribution that shaped the Jews' defense against Rome and altering the empire. Here, within the core of Rome's war with the Jews, history's under-belly was turning, impacting humanity's future as never before. Zeus and Jupiter's pillars were shuddering with cracks and will soon fall away from history; and Rome's Emperors will increase their destruction of all things Hebrew to turn this tide.

Vespasian and Aristomy's deliberations of the Greek and Roman positions continue as a weapon of kin solidarity against the Jews. The cause of the sudden death of Alexander remains suspiciously unknown and Vespasian responds wryly to the Greek Mayor:

"Perhaps your priests feared Zeus was losing to the idea of an invisible God - and lo! Alexander dies very suddenly, most unexpectedly! But Rome's might is seen by all who challenge her. The Jews know this well."

"Tell me my mighty Commander…" Aristomy draws nearer, reminding the Roman General with challenging sarcasm: "Did the Jews not beguile your greatest king - did not Caesar allow them rights to shame us? See, all the nations honor Rome's kings - except the Jews. Why is that?"

Vespasian is again handed food for thought by the Greek whose outstretched hand bears another fig fruit. Vespasian responds to Aristomy with prudent Roman practicality:

"Indeed it is a strange and lonely belief that cannot stand. One unseen God who controls all peoples and nations - where peasant slaves and divine kings are of the same value. Bah! Such is folly - such is futile in the real world. Yet the Jews show no interest in invading the territory of other nations and pay their taxes handsomely, even more so than the Greeks. And sacrifice to an unseen God is not seen as one against the gods of Rome. We both know how they have beguiled our people, yet there is also wisdom in these Jews. The Greeks don't like such competition - one unseen God opposes your belief, hmmm? Rome sees it differently - it takes many gods to make all things. Caesar only allowed them a God unseen because it posed no threat to Rome."

But Aristomy dismisses Vespasian's unseen God response.

"Yes, that is also how the Jews want us to see it. It is a clever idea. After all, an unseen God cannot offend any emperor, nor can any army fight an unseen God. That's how they catch you, my dear wounded and honorable Commander of many victories of Rome - that is how they tore your leg. Their killers were, as you said… unseen!?"

"See, I have their writings as part of my treasury, one brought to Rome by the Greeks." Vespasian offers. "I found good wisdom in it, even much sorcery in their knowledge. It is true the Jews have chosen to become our enemies by their writing and beliefs. They reject our divine emperors." [71]

Aristomy interjects: "The Jews will work for your downfall and will not abandon the sorcery of their laws. Believe it!"

"Yet I have examined their writings and I have wondered who showed these Jews all they know - even to know of the first man's name!?" Vespasian appears in distant thoughts. "If only they gave up their terrible laws that insult our emperors, Rome would grant the Jews generosity. But you Aristomy would not like that, hmmm?"

Aristomy: "I have shown you that this people will not surrender their laws. The Greek Emperors could not achieve this, nor could any other nation. Rome will fail in this also."

"Rome is not as the Greek Empire. Rome does not fail." Vespasian chews on the fruit. "Rome has her ways." He leans closer and whispers it. "I intend to find such a way?"

In the first century, the conquered Greeks were impacting Rome against the Jews with strong anti-Hebrew fostering, jostling for priority place among Rome's institutions. Josephus writes of Nero being instigated by the Greeks as the cause of the Roman war with the Jews. [72]

The Greeks had one winning stratagem that would please Rome's Emperors. In this politically charged juncture of divine kings and their fundamental priestly hierarchy that saw their status being diminished, the Hebrew Monotheism was promoted as the #1 enemy of the Greek and Roman emperors. There appeared no exit or retreat facilities for the Jews against the targeting of their most primal law.

Aristomy continues to turn Vespasian. "The Greek kings saw how they hate our ways and that they will not change… they take and do not share. None in the world speak their tongue…even as they speak all others. They gain from all nations."

Vespasian: "I will gain from the Jews. So will Rome."

Aristomy: "Their Hebrew God is a jealous God - the Jews will corrupt your people against Rome's Gods same as was done with the Greek gods. Our people do not offer to the gods anymore…like the Jews they secretly mock the Greek gods. As a surety this will also befall Rome. Tell me now, will an honorable Roman as Vespasian not be shaken of it?"

Vespasian ponders the Greek's warnings silently and in askance:

"Rome's gods are also jealous and the Gods of Rome know I already paid a price." He points to his wounded leg. "My leg will heal and I will repay the Jews. Remember it."

Aristomy smirks. "I know that you will save Rome… and all of your kin."

The conquered Greeks offered their kin Romans impressions of a dire past history of Hellenist wars with the Jews, especially of the later kings of the Seleucid Dynasty, one that broke away after Alexander's death and formed a powerful force that ruled from Syria. The Seleucid Dynasty kings also assumed divine status and avowedly disdained Monotheism before the Romans conquered Arabia, as seen with the War of the Maccabees and the Greek king Antiochus in 164 BCE.

Aristomy: "Only know this, Vespasian, all are rebels, trust none of them. Their Peace Party and Agrippa… secretly they disdain all things Roman!"

Vespasian responds: "All nations have their rebels. I saw this in Briton and in Germania - even in Rome. Of a surety the coward rebels who pierced me and fled into the hills will pay. Titus is attending to it and Agrippa and the Peace Party are assisting Rome."

Aristomy: "No other way with this nation of rebels - many have tried and many have failed. Surely Vespasian knows of this truth, as does Rome's Emperor!?"

They gaze at each other in a heavy silence.

Outside of Vespasian's window, a Bedouin worker tending the gardens is stealthily eavesdropping.

The predicament of monotheism, historically traumatic for the Jews, now became the dominant obsession of this century, when many belief systems were losing credibility in their ancient mythical religions and thereby igniting the wrath of the ruling divine emperors. All blame fell on the Jews as the carrier of the monotheism strain, one seen as a barbaric, heretical and a suspicious belief that threatened the empire's historical traditions. The Jews' invisible God, one none could see or war against with sword or mighty legions became the enemy; therein lay the assured bondage of the Jews.

Monotheism became the most ferocious adversary and by subsequence the negative adopted legacy against the Jews. A most validated prediction made to Abraham in holy writ was unfolding.

The Greek and Roman kings forbade the Hebrew ritual requirements as antennae marks of monotheism and ridiculed the strange Hebrew dietary laws, the dress rituals and especially circumcision. Here, not even Christianity could impress the Greeks and Romans to forgo swine and shellfish consumption or to mutilate their manhood. Thus far, the science-inclined Greeks did not yet indulge in the Hebrew spiritual facet of the laws; forbiddance of human sacrifice, women's rights and animal rights laws were yet distant and of low priority, awaiting the advent of Christianity to fully impact and spread such laws upon the world stage.

Aristomy pokes his finger in the air as an emphasis for Vespasian:

"I have seen other nations sacrifice their most cherished child on their high alters for their beliefs - yet they honor Rome. Is belief only for the Jews!?"

"You twist my words. Caesar saw none else who worshipped one unseen God - he accounted this belief older than Rome, not newly made to challenge Rome. The Great Caesar saw their belief as strange but also, it appeared to him, as sincere."

"Sincere!?" - Aristomy screams in a hissing rage of negation. "Hear me well Vespasian and allow me to tell you of their sorcery and how they control their people! Do not believe the Jews when they say their Ark is lost - they have hidden it away with great cunning… Babylon, Persia and our Greek fathers were all unable to find this Ark of magic and sorcery…"[73] Vespasian is focused now, recalling his son's earnest quest of the Temple treasury. "So the Jews returned, spreading their ways against all others, hoarding wealth by sacrificial rituals to control all… and hiding behind a hidden never-seen God. So clever they are! And know this Vespasian…" He approaches closer, as if imparting precious, hidden knowledge. "Hear me well! Capture their Ark and the Hebrews fall - our Philistine brethren knew this well." He nods, implying his wisdom.

"Control is different from robbery Aristomy, all nations conduct sacrifice and we all protect our wealth - don't you?" Vespasian now becomes the stern powerful Roman, placing the Greek before him as the conquered and inferior; reminding that Rome rules:

"Rome employs many excellent Jewish minds for controlling our wealth and in tax collections, and they understand well the war spoils belong to Rome. Why do the Jews concern you so much, is it their strange laws… or is it their wealth?"

An underlying tension prevails with the Greek Mayor's deliberation with the Roman Commander. Aristomy affirms to Vespasian the holy war against Monotheism:

"We are your kin, and in this war Zeus, the father of the Greek gods, stands with Jupiter. It is us or them, a battle of both our divine honors! Nero understood me well - he has forbidden all things Hebrew. Nero also knows of their wealth, two thousand years of hidden treasuries… surely you also know what it means for Rome's glory… and your own when you become emperor…?" Aristomy nods at his own insight.

Suddenly, Vespasian appears distraught; he begins to moan in agony from his wound.

"I should not disturb your rest with such troubling matters now, but I will say this…" Aristomy raises his hands to the heavens, his eyes filled with a distant foreboding:

"When the great discus of Zeus hails down from the Heavens, then Vespasian, then you will be witness to my words!"

"Zeus is no more - Jupiter rules. You have your own past issues with the Jews. But leave Judea to me, as did Nero. Rome has her ways…"

Aristomy: "Si vis pacem para bellum… if Rome seeks peace, Rome must prepare for war!"

Vespasian's poisoned body begins writhing; a vision of Eleazar behind the shrubbery comes to him as he lies pierced and fallen on the ground. Two doctors come rushing in to his rescue. The Greek Aristomy withdraws; he has impressed his dark foreboding on the Roman General.

The Bedouin at the window proceeds to a tree in the corner of the gardens. Ari hides behind the tree, dressed in Arabian garb, receiving the message.

"Aristomy poisons the well. He wants your temple treasures. He convinced Nero."

Ari nods and quickly departs from the Roman security zone.

(20). AN OBSESSED ROMAN.

Alexis is stalking covertly in the hills of Megiddo; he winces in the searing hot sun. Suddenly, he confronts an animal peering at him; it is a Gazelle, native to this land, its demeanor curious and unthreatening. In the distance, Deborah is feeding carrots to baby gazelles.

She spots the Roman covertly stalking her from behind the hills. She flees in breathless terror, dodging him, hiding behind tree to tree, attempting to reach her tan horse with white patches. Her horse is yet a distance too far to flee safely from the Roman. She crouches behind an olive branch, hiding and trembling, recalling now Miriam's warning of the Romans, how they beguile and capture women for their concubines; she recalls how her family fell. Now she faces this Roman stalker with no protection.

Alexis retreats behind a hilly mound, realizing the Hebrew maiden has spotted him. He leans against the stone, hidden in his pain of exposed guilt, unable to decide his next move, ashamed now of the Hebrew maiden seeing him as a Roman stalker.

Florian's warning comes to him. "Master, the girl is of the enemy… she is forbidden?"

He maneuvers himself crouching down stealthily to a squatting position; his eyes shut, unable to decide what to do.

"Master, you must be careful…" - His security guard's good advice fills his mind.

He must turn away from this quest; he must throw away her purse. But his hand grasping her purse shows a withered squashed rose; he is unable to fling it away. He is heaving; nudging his head on the stony hill. He cannot turn away from her.

Deborah, unable to remain in the vicinity of a Roman stalker hiding behind the hill, decides to make a run for it. She pokes out her face to test the area; she sees no one; there is only a Gazelle in the distance gazing at her curiously. Will she also be lost at the hands of a Roman, the last remnant of her family; she begins to shudder? She braces, gathering her breath; then she races towards her horse in the distance, a dagger clasped in her trembling hand.

"Wait, please!" The Roman addresses her. "No need to fear. I bring important news for you!"

Deborah is racing away, alarmed by the Roman's calls to her, that he is approaching toward her. She increases her pace towards her horse. A baby gazelle leaves its carrot feed and chases after her.

"You must stay away from Caesarea. Also, no Hebrew teachings. Only till things quiet down…you hear me?"

Recalling Miriam's warning, Deborah displays her dagger in hand before her; it glistens in the noon sun. Now she dares him, confronting the Roman, brandishing her dagger from behind her horse with an abandon; she hides her trembling.

"Hear me, please!" He continues approaching. "Nero has issued harsh new decrees on the Jews on pain of death. You must be careful now?"

Deborah raises her dagger, pointing it at the Roman to and fro as a warning not to approach closer. Alexis winces pleadingly at the dagger wavering in her hand. After a tense silence the Roman pauses, he nods, his opened palms raised in a surrender gesture, retreating slowly in response of her dagger and her resolute refusal to engage with him. He mounts his horse, preparing to leave. "That… that is all I have to say…"

Deborah, behind her horse, focuses to see the Roman is not armed; she becomes curious now, yelling at him.

"Why does a Roman risk his life to save Jews, it is the second time!?"

"I don't know why… as yet." His answer increases her curiosity.

"You don't know why? What kind of an answer is that!?" She peeks from behind her horse, the dagger in her trembling hand. "What is its meaning?"

"I have not had time to think about it. I just…?" He winces helplessly.

"You need to think about this!? You have already caused me trouble with my people. You are a Roman spy - this is its meaning! And I don't need to think about it!?"

They stare at each other in uncertainty; she is flushed by the Roman's intense gaze; she dashes away on her horse.

"Wait, please?" His outstretched hand holds her purse.

The news of Vespasian's wounding now makes all the towns of Judea as marked for terror and destruction with a Roman vengeance. Eleazar is now a wanted criminal with the offering of a handsome bounty. The town squares display large signs in Greek and Aramaic for the wanted Sicarii leader and a punitive double tax is levied on the Jews. Now the massacring of the Jews as an example to any who may attack a Roman commander is expressed by displays of crucifixions in the towns. The strung bodies are left till the victims' suffering is endured for days and only skeletons remain, as a warning to all Jews who challenge Rome.

Scrolls of the Torah are burned in the town squares and the Romans commit acts of desecration, urinating on scrolls and on those strung on crosses. Only the Jews within the Jerusalem Fortress city, defended by a 6,000 strong Roman legion and three impregnable stone walls are spared. King Agrippa II, grandson of Herod and brother of the Queen Bernice, is given Vespasian's orders to locate the Sicarii leader and his supporters before any ceasing of Rome's brutal killings can be negotiated, a Roman stratagem of using conquered nation's own assets as its weapon; Agrippa was given no choice of refusal.

Rome's great guile will be in its use of propaganda. Vespasian begins studying the Hebrew Scriptures earnestly; he will begin to know his enemy. Vespasian will appoint a team of writers to shape his persona and present the Jews as the enemy.

The attempted barring of the Hebrew practices was initiated after Nero's edicts. Yet the Hebrew did not cease as the primal written and spoken language of the Jews in Judea and would continue into the Second Century, ending in 200 CE; thereafter this ancient language that caused great controversy in the world's camps will enter a mode of dormancy.

The Aramaic and the Greek were the secondary languages the Jews spoke with the nations, with foreigners and in trade, for Aramaic was a generic language in this region; it became so when Persia conquered Babylon and decreed the Aramaic to become the main language in Arabia. The emerging Greeks will later impress their language as the primal one in all their conquered lands. The Jews learnt these languages during their exiles in Babylon and the Greek lands. The Hebrew will yet remain the primal language of the Jews in Judea throughout the first century.[74]

The language and Script of the Dead Sea Scrolls accounts for 80% Hebrew; both the Greek and Aramaic, which became generic in the entire Arabian region, begin gradually occupying portions of the Jews' lexicon during exiles and foreign invasions since the Babylon invasion of 586 BCE. The Israelites spoke Aramaic with the ancient Egyptians who knew no Hebrew; portions of an Aramaic passage transliterated into Hebrew are contained in the Passover Hebrew liturgy tracing events in ancient Egypt.[75]

After the Hebrew was banned by the Roman Emperor Hadrian in the 2nd century, this language's biblical translations into other languages yet made the Hebrew bible humanity's most widespread of scriptures. The resurrection of the Hebrew language will again occur after 2,000 years, led by an exile returnee named Eliezar ben Yehuda (1858-1922). No language is known to return after a dormant period of more than 100 years, marking the Hebrew as a hardy language with a strong core.

The Jerusalem Fortress. On a high ridge overlooking Jerusalem in the far horizon, the faces of Eleazar and the Sicarii warriors rise, peering over the hill's edges; they measure the land from hidden vantage points. The Sicarii warriors are embarking on their own daring plan against Rome, led by their leader Eleazar, Rome's most wanted fugitive.

Saul engages the somber Eleazar who says little, whose eyes are focused on the towering walls that surround the holy city in the distant horizon, sealing her in an amber haze of protective hewn stone. The Sicarii warriors gaze with yearning at the Jerusalem fortress, the refuge of the Jews when enemies invade, now controlled by their mightiest foe.

"When the fortress is in our hands again the people will be protected from this enemy of Israel." Saul attempts to learn of Eleazar's undisclosed mission. "When we are behind the wall and the Romans outside, Jerusalem will defend us. It is why you turned from the towns which Rome is tearing down… it is why Eleazar comes to Jerusalem…"

"The Romans know the strength of our walls." Eleazar answers without shifting his gaze from the fortress. "Dry foods and water… our most important weapon. Spread this code to all the towns so none die from hunger or thirst."

"The siege - what Rome does best?

Eleazar's gaze shifts to a black patch gliding above the temple.

"But we are outside the siege walls?" Saul follows Eleazar's focused eyes.

"See the bird flying above the Bet Hamikdash ['Holy House']… our journey brings us closer to our destiny…"

Their eyes follow the arc of the eagle's flight till it disappears in the distant haze.

(21). SAUL OF TARSUS

In a darkened basement dungeon in Caesarea, a barefoot figure is draped in soiled dress. He stares out the small window of his prison cell; he can see rows of Jews being nailed on crosses in the outer courtyards. His lips murmur in prayer, the long uncut finger nails tracing his small window bars. For Rome, even a Jew from outside Judea and granted Roman citizenship becomes an enemy of the empire when found guilty of anti-Roman beliefs, as were numerous Roman non-Jewish citizens. [76]

The imprisoned Jew, a Pharisee who once castigated his fellow Jews for their diminishing of the Hebrew laws to please Rome, now gazes through his small window bars. He had told how it is faith, not the law, that saves; but Rome harkened to neither.

In the skies above something dark appears; an eagle is gliding across the streaming clouds. Saul's eyes are fixed on the bird; his eyes are piercing and glowing, his breathing heaving. He appears distraught and agitated; he is swaying his face in negation, whispering:

"No… no… no!" His face winces and shudders, screaming at the bird: "NO!?"

The eagle is descending swiftly towards the earth, as if its powerful eyes have detected a prey. The imprisoned man sways his face in his angst, as if he understood the bird's mission:

"No…no…no!?"

(22). A MEGIDDO CEMETERY

In the hinterland of Megiddo, outside the town's village, Deborah sits in a cemetery plot, cleaning a tomb stone with cloth and water. Alexis appears from behind the hills, approaching cautiously. He gazes at the Hebrew maiden squatted in the dry muddy ground. She cleans the Hebrew and Greek writing on the stone's epitaph, her legs wrapped around the tombstone, pausing to kiss the cold stone as she cleans it of any gathered dust; she pauses to examine the sparkling stone and kisses it again, hugging the stone with a devotion. The name on the tombstone she attends jolts Alexis; he nears closer.

"Who is Alexander ben Hur?" He is focused on the tomb's epitaph.

"Huh! You follow me again - you didn't go away?!" She races behind a tree.

"What is this name to you?" Alexis lays a flower stem by the grave.

"My brother, peace be unto his soul, lies here. Left on your Roman cross to die slowly. This day is his anniversary." She rushes to the grave, hugging and protecting the tomb from the Roman. "Why does a Roman visit a Hebrew grave?"

"A brother… with a Greek name?" He remains focused on the tomb name. "Is there any Greek in you?"

"Mah!? Roman fool! Have you not heard of the great Alexander? Our priests named their sons by this name. Don't you know Alexander showed respect to the Jews - he ordered our holy book to be in the Greek tongue? We don't forget such things." [77]

"Yes, yes… I know of this book!? We call it the Septuaginta - the Work of the Seventy. I know it well?" He appears enthusiastic to talk of other things.

"What is your purpose here?" She looks around the cemetery in fear.

"To warn you." His gaze into her eyes is intense and devoted, nearing her with emotive enthusiasm. "Nero brought back Caligula's Heresy decree, do you understand this law? Sacrifice for Nero is now a royal decree for Jews. You must be careful?"

"We have seen your kind before." She turns from his lingering and waiting gaze. She cleans her brother's tomb; he waits on her intensely. "Alexander never told Jews to worship him, as does your mad kings. My brother chose to die instead." She turns to him abruptly, both hands outstretched behind her, challenging. "And so would I!?"

"Yes, I believe you would. You must also know that Rome's emperors don't like books that forbid worshiping them."

"You must also know Israel does not like emperors who want to be worshipped!?" Her stance is challenging; Alexis gestures his acknowledgement. She turns away, continuing to clean her brother's tomb, taunting him with disdain. "Go make your kings learn from Alexander… whose name you hold… don't you know, a name means a lot?"

He is again focused on the name on the tombstone. "I know now you can never forget my name after this day. It may be why I am here."

"Dare you say such a thing - you are mad as your kings! I came here to mourn for my brother, not his killers. This name for me is of a Jew, not of a Roman."

"Don't you know… a name means a lot?" He reminds her.

"Your name to me is Roman spy. Looking for secrets because you saved us once?"

"I am not a spy. I give you my word of it."

"Hah! The word of one who's been spying on me? We Jews are not fools?"

"True, I have searched you many days. But you must know… I was compelled to see you again!? My word to you now is from my honor. Also from my heart. I am not a spy. You must believe this?"

Shaken by the Roman's intense gaze, she turns away, hoisting her shawl over her head. She is admonishing him now. "You must not look at a woman you don't know so strongly."

"Yes, you are right, yet… I do want to know you." He nods, dipping head, retreating backwards. "Truly?" He is departing, his gaze fixed on the maiden. "I say it by my honor…" he stumbles retreating, a boyish pleading in his eyes. "I am not a spy. I'm here of my own doing… as you said, just a mad Roman." He departs on Tahrah, his face inclined aback on her from afar.

She turns away cleaning the headstone, her hands polishing her brother's name more vigorously; she is murmuring in her native tongue.

In his gymnasium, Titus is practicing combat fencing as part of his daily ritual; he plunges sword before a hanging slab of wood as Aristomy arrives before him.

"Vespasian's hands are tied by an oath given to one who saved his life… in his battles in Londonium. But surely no oath can apply to one who betrays Rome?"

"My father honors his pledge made to a Roman of great valor, one who surrendered his life for his Commander." Titus is threatening, making his sword to sway before Aristomy's words.

"Yes, great valor by a Roman, one who saved your honorable father's life. Yet I ask, how then did the Jews know of your father's precise location, striking when the legions were far at rest?"

Titus pauses. "What are you saying - speak!?" His sword now rests on Aristomy's chest.

"The Jews know well how to suck away any Roman weakness… they send their beautiful ones to beguile our men of power. Does the mighty Titus not know this truth with his own father?" Aristomy winces of the point of the sword on his midriff. "I…I have seen even the great Nero humbled by a Jew wife!?" He smirks, spitting out his words in terror. "It is the reason I came to you. There is none else to turn to but mighty Titus?"

Titus' eyes harden. "Speak clearly. What are you saying?"

"Eleazar." Aristomy nods; then he assumes a tremulous and hypnotizing demeanor. "The son of a Hebrew priest… his father also a priest of the temple, one who tore your father's leg. He knows of the Ark's location… and this… this is the greatest prize you can give to Rome. This ark was seen by all nations as the most worthy treasure the world has known. It belongs with Rome. Remember it when you have him, my future divine king?"

Titus disengages his sword; he is in deep thought: "What is this Ark?"

"None are allowed near it!" Aristomy gives Titus alluring details. "It is said to be guarded by the wings of two golden angels in their holy of holies - where none can enter on penalty of death. Let Titus enter and live. Let Titus bring this Ark to Rome. You are the anointed one for both Zeus and Jupiteres. This glory belongs to you!?"

"Then…" Titus' eyes glow. "I will do it. I want it."

The Ark of the Covenant The conquered Greeks had brought with them the Septuagint Bible to Rome which recorded the Ark's structure and its significance. The Holy House within the temple, also known as the Holy of Holies, derives its title by virtue of being a resting place for the Ark, a golden box containing the two original stone tablets of The Ten Commandments that was molded in the Arabian deserts on the Mount of Sinai; and five books that is known as the Torah. The Ark houses the original and first Hebrew bible written by the hand of Moses and dictated by the God of the Israelites in a desert. The Ark's five scrolls mark the first time the Hebrew writing appears, in a strange mode of abstract letters that did not contain faces of animals and mythological deities.

The Greeks, after studying the Hebrew writings given them in the Septuagint Bible, saw the Ark as the fruit of knowledge of good and bad, protected by the angelic Cherubim's golden wings, and that the Hebrew God commanded the Jews to build such a temple as a sanctuary to protect the Holy Ark:

'And let them make Me a sanctuary, that I may dwell among them'. [Ex. 25-8]

Moses and Joshua in the Tabernacle. (By James Tissot) Source: S10.

For the Jews this was their most holy possession and held as the mark of their sacred laws from Sinai; it became 'The Ark of the Testimony' as the symbol of a covenant of the acceptance of the laws made with the Hebrew God.

For the Romans this Ark would represent the mark of their victory over the Jews and their Hebrew God, thus a most desired and wondrous item in their quest of war spoils.

In the cemetery of Megiddo, Deborah sits alone, hands clasped around her brother's tombstone in prayer and murmuring. Suddenly a black eagle swoops down on her; Deborah screams in terror, ducking her head behind the tombstone.

Alexis, who is now a short distance retreated, hears her screams; he turns racing to her on Tahrah. As the eagle darts and screeches, swooping down again to attack Deborah, Alexis pushes her aback, swaying his sword at the bird crashing upon her. The eagle ascends away into the clouds screeching wildly, missing Deborah's head closely.

Deborah is shaking in fear, staring at the Roman in disbelief, a hint of reluctant gratitude in her trembling. Alexis brings her his flask of water. There are blood and scratch marks on her forehead. Alexis looks around and finds a cactus plant; he crushes its juice out in his fist and attempts to dab her wound. She shuns him, looking around in fear; her hand covertly nearing her dagger. He tends her tenderly, respectfully; he now sees an opportunity to talk to her, of things he longed to say.

"Tell me. Can you truly worship a God you never see?"

"We don't worship killers of women and children as gods as you Romans do."

"I have yet not learnt to worship anyone - perhaps I will one day. I too lost my father by a war. I'm a Road builder, not a warrior?"

"Huh! Whatever Rome does is for Rome! You make new smooth roads only to conquer more nations faster. Rome freely crucifies and enslaves the innocent, with no pardon by the Jubilee year." Deborah points at the image of an eagle on Alexis' dress, turning away in disdain. "Rome is an abomination of God's sacred laws." [78]

"You have laws of freedom, but no freedom? Rome follows the law of dominion - does your own holy book not say… 'Go and have dominion of all the world'? It is also Rome's belief of freedom in a harsh world and they lay their lives for it. Rome knows of no other road to glory… is there one?"

She turns her face admonishingly. "One must give their own lives before causing the death of an innocent. That is our first law… that is true glory!?" She hand kisses the name on her brother's tombstone, bringing her hand to her lips.

"Your God also knows about the stranger in a strange land. Can you consider it… will you?"

She jolts, moving away from him, shocked by the Roman's words, gripping her dagger again. "Those who throw away their babies to die if they are not enough beautiful cannot know love of the stranger." She turns to her brother's stone, shaken in her anguish. "Mine was a princely family in Judea that hearkened to God's sacred laws - and all was destroyed by Rome. My brother was all I had left, God's glory be upon him! You Romans know desire, but not love and true honor. Leave me now!?" She turns away her face gesturing, warning him not to approach her; she is trembling, a knife held in her hand again.

Alexis appears struck by her anguish and shaking; her bruised head now slumped on the tombstone. Now the daring Hebrew appeared as a wounded sparrow, needing his protection, he decides. He looks around, then he approaches towards her as if drawn by a compulsion.

"I meant no harm. And this stranger before you wants to know of this unseen God… and your sacred laws… in my heart I have thought about it, but never said it to anyone. You must believe me?"

A group of mourners are passing. Deborah ducks, not to be seen with a Roman; her hand behind her holding a knife, gesturing that he leaves.

"If I'm seen with you again I will be killed. You also. Leave now!?"

"Then we both have the same problem…" Alexis is now in a state of enthrall and yearning, gazing at her with his emotions swirling within him. He grasps her hand impulsively; her dagger drops.

"Huh! Dare my brother's killers touch me?!" She is in a terror; she struggles fiercely to free herself.

"I cannot leave by those words…" Alexis' grip of her hand is measured so not to cause her more pain than is required. Hebrew mourners pass in the distance; he beseeches her with imploring words.

"See, my life is in your hand now, if you but hear me?" He holds her hand pressed on his chest now; he too is trembling. "See, this stranger before you has the same name as your bother… and we sit by his grave this day with your hand on my heart… does it not mean anything to you? It does to me!? Do you not see… it is an omen for us!?" His gaze is intense and welling with devotion.

She kicks; she attempts to bite his hand; his hand remains unflinching at her disposal; then he sets her hand free.

"Wherever I look I see only you… even when I shut my eyes!? All else is become ugly to me…? And I know now… something has happened to me!?" His eyes are pleading of her. "Can one who saves an injured animal have no heart for a stranger's truth? Look at me… look at this stranger before you?"

"Such talk is forbidden!?" She raises her dagger at him, trembling, pulling from him, retreating. "Do not touch me again… Roman murderer of my people!?"

"But I murdered no one… and I'm not a spy… your holy book tells you to love the stranger… are you not different from the Romans? It was I who slew that snake… I was compelled to follow you. But I… I never knew you were going to bathe…"

"You!? It was you!?" Her eyes pierce him aghast in shock and embarrassment; she winces, shunning him. "You spy even in women's baths - don't you know it, men cannot enter a woman's Mikvah!?[79] You Romans have no respect of women! Leave me - if I scream you will die!?"

"Dare I not even save a child from a snake? Now promise this stranger you will refrain from violating Nero's decrees - just for a short time. I ask no more of you?"

"I see only my brother's blood on your face…" She defies him.

His gaze is without any anger from her words, displaying a strange devotion. There is the sound of a thud, a hard blow from behind, and Alexis slumps to the ground, blood streaming from back of his head. He lies on the ground unconscious before her brother's grave. As she releases her hand from his grasp, Deborah is in sobs of confusion, shuddering, her face distorting in fear. She turns away, racing to her brother's tombstone. She sobs, focused on the epitaph engraving:

Alexander Ben Hur. Born 3810 - Died 3825. [80]

(23). THE MISSION.

Eleazar and his band of Hebrew warriors are storming on horseback through the winding hill tracks. They stop in an isolated cave hideout in a hidden retreat. The soldiers are handed dates, berries and water. As they consume their feed sitting on rockery, Eleazar addresses his Sicarii warriors.

"It is time that you know of our mission." His calm, measured gaze compels their devoted attention.

"First… the cost. In this mission all our sacred laws will be set aside and we will be committing sins. Those who cannot accept… those who are newlywed… and those who have fear in their hearts … let them turn and leave now." The warriors turn to each other unsure. "Even transgressions will be set aside. Even it will be brother against brother…son against father…" The new recruits from the Peace Party turn to each other unsure. A Sicarii, teary and pleading, rises to leave the Group; they all nod at him in a grace of understanding; then they turn to Eleazar again devotedly; they will remain whatever be the cost. They wait on his every word.

"In this mission…we abide only by one law. Our right to our freedom of belief. When we achieve this right, then, only then will we again uphold our God's laws. Till this time comes we will sin, and when we are taken to pay for it - we will pay its price. No other way for Israel. Even our teacher Moshe knew this - thousands of our kin were killed on his orders before Sinai on account of Dathan and Korach[81]. We now battle for our belief as did our forefathers of old. Israel hearkens to One God only." He pans their faces, then the calm man of few words displays another demeanor; he bellows in the thunderous demand of a savage warrior:

"WHAT SAY YOU!?"

The warriors rise up shouting, their eyes glowing fiercely, fixed on Eleazar:

"WITH YOU! WITH YOU! WITH YOU!"

Again he pans their faces, measuring each one. Then he nods; he approaches closer and sits before them, gesturing they come closer. The warriors surround Eleazar tight and close; he looks all around, insuring they are alone. Then he speaks calmly and slowly, ensuring their full understanding of their mission.

"When we pass the Carmel hills, we ride past Megiddo - the Romans won't travel outside their new roads. We head then to Shiloh - there is a receiving party there. The Roman legions have taken possession of the fortress and sit there safe by its mighty walls." The Sicarii faces are fixed and measuring every word now; Eleazar gazes into their eyes: "They won't expect us in the holy city, or that any will challenge them in Jerusalem's fortress." He rises now standing before them… "We will!?" He ascends atop a raised rockery; arms stretched at the heavens. He declares it in a fiery, thundering outburst:

"We will not live without our beliefs! We will not worship images of Roman brutes! We will not sacrifice unto them! And we will equally confront those Jews who do so! Jerusalem… our sworn mission! SELAH!?"

The Sicarri warriors rise, shouting in unison: "Jerusalem!" They raise their Sicarii daggers to their foreheads, kissing it, then pointing their daggers toward the distant glow of Jerusalem's temple. Their eyes glisten in their darkened cave hideout as they recite a war psalm in a fierce chorus:

"Blessed be the Lord my Rock, who traineth my hands for war, and my fingers for battle; my loving kindness, and my fortress, my high tower, and my deliverer; my shield; and He in whom I take refuge… [82]

As the Sicarii men chant their solemn pledge, Eleazar stiffens as he sees a lone man emerge in a bone tunic in the distance, staring at him fastidiously. The man is smiling, speaking calmly in a whispering, his finger pointing, swaying his face.

"This war before us… it is not about your mission."

The strange man vanishes.

Eleazar's gaze is far away; he is intensely focused at the fortress in the horizon, questioningly, whether his daring plans would succeed, or will he bring even greater calamity for his people. His weary gaze reflected the heavy burden he harbored, the lone thoughts he yet could not share with anyone.

(24). QUEEN BERNICE AND KING AGRIPPA.

In his mansion in Caesarea, Vespasian's wound is tended by a physician; he has gained strength and is improving. A guard announces visitors.

"Queen Bernice!? Bring my golden robe, and make sure she is seated close to my side. Bring red wine and black grapes, feisty servings, and my treasure case. The Queen adores fiery gem stones."

King Agrippa and the brazenly attired Queen enter; they are escorted by their own security guards who stand at the entrance and do not enter with the Hebrew Queen and her Roman appointed brother, King Agrippa, as a display of respect of Vespasian.

"Greetings to the king and queen. Oh! Most wondrous Bernice, your visit is a gift from the gods."

"How is my sweet war hero - trouble with the Jews again?"

"You are welcome to stay with us." King Agrippa offers. "At least till your wound recovers."

"Grateful Agrippa, but it is here I belong now. My son battles the last refuge of the rebels. It is not a simple battle - they hide expertly in caves and tunnels. But I am already better seeing you Bernice - had I known you were coming I would not see you with empty hands."

"My dear Vespasian, you are my true and precious jewel. But even that my wealth has surpassed Nero, yet I am still a queen poor for being unloved and far from the splendors of Rome. But we are here for another purpose, my mighty general." She approaches him closer, stroking his shoulders, whispering seductively:

"Agrippa and I were made witness in the case of one Saul of Tarsus, a Greek nobleman and a Roman citizen, but now a prisoner in the dark dungeons of Caesarea. You my treasured hero must know, the Governor Festus has concluded there is no truth to the charge of sedition, he has indeed done nothing against Caesar, nor is he guilty of creating disturbances as charged in Jerusalem."

"The gods of Rome would make it a crime to leave Bernice unloved and far from Rome."

"Hear me then my Commander. Now this Saul has chosen to be tried in Rome, being a Roman Citizen. Of course, this should be granted him of his right - it is Roman law?"

"I understand he is also a relative of yours."

"Oh, torture me not anymore my faithful General." She rests her face on his chest. "You surely know as I do, if this Saul was languishing in a Roman dungeon two years, he could not have any part in the charges against Rome, could he, my brave Adonis?" Her eyes appeal to him in alluring decadence. "How can we ever doubt each other?

"If he was in prison, if no heresy against Rome, then Agrippa is welcome to him. I too have news, will you stay?"

"Oh, thank you my magnificent warrior!" She sprinkles powders from a tiny jar into his fire torch; fumes crackle. "Agrippa can vouch of the wonders I made for him. Inhale the fumes and wait for me. Your powers will soon return."

"My sister is a true Goddess. I have been restored by her - and so will you, dear Vespasian."

"Agrippa, your peace party must separate from the Jews who revolt against Rome. Plant for me spies among the Jews. Honor Rome as Rome honors you." Vespasian uncovers his robe and points at his poisoned wounded leg - a large, shriveled cavity of missing flesh appears on his upper thigh. "Bring me this devil's head!?" The sustained gaze of warning reminds Judea's Roman appointed King Agrippa II who rules Jerusalem.

Nero's commands to Vespasian are now heavy laden on him by the Greek Aristomy's warning about the Jews. His demeanor is now of a Roman commander; he ponders in silence, his gaze fixed on the desirous departing queen. Tiberius approaches Vespasian, presenting him a scroll of deed:

"Your stamp will confirm your approval - the Jewish prisoner will be judged in Rome."

Vespasian slams his ring on the scroll; the retreating queen nods in her captivating alluring gratitude. Vespasian turns to Tiberius lowly when the queen is departed:

"I will not fail Nero's orders. Roman justice…" He gestures a thumb down hand sign: "In Rome?" Tiberius nods his understanding. Therein the fate of Saul of Tarsus is sealed.

(25). DEBORAH AND THE MOON.

In a garden patch in Megiddo Deborah sits alone, gazing at the moon. Images of a Roman slumped on the ground with a bloodied head storm her mind. His words come to her:

"I'm not a spy… you have my word."

She gazes at the moon, her friend of old; she searches for answers to the hidden thoughts she cannot dispel or express to anyone else. Her face is imploring, questioning, as the words of a Roman come again to her.

"This Roman seeks more than your forgiveness…"

Her brother's tombstone appears before her:

Alexander Ben Hur. Born 3810 - Died 3825.

She gazes at the moon and whispers it, sobbing and shaking.

"Forgive me?"

The moon light shimmers on her face, then it hides behind the clouds. Deborah flees away.

At Alexis' construction base, the road workers are in chagrin of his attention for a maiden of the enemy. They sit with jugs of beer around a fire under a starry Judean night. They discuss the events of their days of labors before Florian.

"Why is he so maddened for an enemy?" A drunken road worker speaks. "If we remain silent, we may be seen as traitors. Florian, bring us the maiden so we won't be questioned by Titus and die on crosses, what say you?"

"Hold your tongues." Florian dismisses their drunken outbursts. "Be warned my orders come from Vespasian himself."

The drunken worker approaches Florian. "We serve a twenty five year term, the price of a Roman citizen or a slave forever… many of us will not live to the end of our service. But we are allowed conquered maidens - so why oppose us our rights? Inform Titus of a Jew loving traitor among us - or by Jupiter I will!?"
An enraged Florian lifts up the road worker and bear hugs him, so his eyes and tongue hang out and he is ready to die in Florian's killer grip. The other soldiers beseech Florian to spare their comrade. Florian releases his deadly grip and tosses the soldier in their midst. The soldiers back away from Florian's rage.

(26). THE MESSENGER.

A Tribune brings a message to Vespasian. The Queen Bernice sits at the Commander's side; she inhales from a coil attached to a pot of incense.
"Titus has captured a war general, one who was found to also be a Hebrew priest. He is one among 250 other Hebrews. Now the Priest lays surrounded in the hills of Jotapata in the Galilee, in the hollow of its fortified caves. Titus sees the captured priest as a sorcerer and seeks your orders. Titus also enquires of his father's wound."
"No, wait!" Bernice inclines in the general's ear. "This priest must be accounted a war asset to be taken alive. There is much to learn from him… you must entice him!?"
"I will question this Priest myself in the light of the Palace balcony, bring him in haste. Bring also my son with him."
She strokes Vespasian's hand approvingly; he has made his orders in accordance of her own plans with Rome. The Hebrew queen's smoke from her pot of gold swirls; she exhales in satisfaction.
In Rome, Flavius Clement, from the Flavian family, suffers the death penalty when he underwent circumcision and married a Jewess named Domitilla.[83]

(27). A STRANGE TURNING.

A mystical entrance denotes history is about to turn. In the hills of Jotapata, Roman soldiers surround a cave's entrance. A disheveled war torn Hebrew in chains emerges out of the dark tunnel; the face becomes discernible as it approaches the light. The eagle hovering above the hills screeches, hopping and bopping its head wildly, its powerful red eyes focused on the figure emerging from the cave.
The Hebrew in chains appears a strange one before the Romans, one bearing an unruly beard, swaying side locks and a full head cap. There is a black frontal pouch on his forehead and his left arm is strapped in black leather coils; sparkling blue tassels dangle at his waist.
"A sorcerer!" A Roman soldier points at the Hebrew.
Tiberius, standing beside Titus, approaches the Hebrew cautiously:
"Your name?"
"I am Yosef…Ben Matityahu." The strange figure engages Titus with his piercing eyes, as if he recognizes Vespasian's son.
"What be your story - war with Rome?" Tiberius demands.
"Once a priest. Then I was ordered to disrobe my priestly garments and take sword in hand." The piercing eyes smile sardonically; he speaks in an eloquent Greek tongue, compelling the Romans' attention. "I led an army stationed in the caves of Jotapata… the mission given me was to engage the Romans outside Jerusalem… to hinder them away from the holy city? I engaged you 47 days and nights. Then, destiny made a strange turning… and here I am before you… as was given me to see will come…" His eyes glow; he knows hidden things.
"It is a strange site." Tiberius backs away. "Looks like a Hebrew… speaks like a Greek Master."
"A Hebrew sorcerer." Titus is focused on the Hebrew. "Bring him."

(28). SCROLL OF HANANIAH.

In his secret hide-out in Shiloh, a scroll arrives for Eleazar from his father Ananias the priest, via a Hebrew messenger. He retreats alone to a palm tree to read in private the scroll of Ananias his father:

"..Our people are being crucified in all our
towns. 800 last Sabbath. We will be the Peace
Party for a compromise or we perish. Your father
also begs you to fulfill your duties to Ruth and
your family - leave them not alone at such a
time. Finally, I must tell you this is the
opinion of Rav Yochanan ben Zakkai." [84]

Eleazar responds to his father with his own scroll via the hand of the messenger:
"My father, the only way to avoid another massacre is to avenge the one in Caesarea. Collaborators with this enemy will be the Sicarii's enemy. Ruth must know I have never been a better father and husband. Tell it also to my children - especially
to Amos."
Eleazar slams his fist on a tree. A vision of his twelve year old son appears to him. "Father, why do the Romans hate us?" The studious, intense lad seeks to know. "Why do they want to kill us - did we do bad things?"
"It was told by God to Abraham, as a surety we will be in bondage." Eleazar whispers to himself. "Fear not my son."
Suddenly, Eleazar is again confronted by the man in a tunic before him.
"This war before us… it is not about Rome."
Eleazar remembers the massacre in Caesarea; he smirks in disdain of the strange man's contradicting words.
"Not of Rome?" He smirks in disdain.

(29). A HEBREW PRIEST'S ORACLE.

The black eagle is now perched on the roof of Vespasian's balcony; and dark streaming clouds begin to swirl above. The Hebrew figure stands before Vespasian and Bernice in chains; Titus and his Captains are also present. A sudden swish of wind swirls all about him with each stride as he is hurled before Vespasian. The soldiers back away with swords raised in ready mode. There is a long silent pause of beholding the Hebrew before them; then the man speaks with a sudden boldness before Vespasian.
"YOU!?" The Hebrew raises his chained hand, pointing his finger at Vespasian, his eyes searing. Titus readies his sword before the Hebrew's hand in protection of his father from the pointing finger. A faint thunder emits from the skies; the soldiers move aback, holding on to their head gear against a wind gush which carries the strange man's every word. The Hebrew priest now appears in a trance; only the whites of his eyes are seen. All faces are locked on the strange Hebrew figure in their midst; all sense that something strange is about to happen.
"You… Vespasian!? You must know for a surety the finger of heaven points to you. The kingdom at hand… shall be yours!? It came to me in the caves of Jotapata, where I lay 47 days and nights… it came to me from the God of my forefathers!?"
Then, facing heaven with his hands raised, his manner is changed to a solemn demeanor of murmurings, as if talking now only to his God:

"Since it pleased thee who had created the Hebrew nation, even to suppress them when they go astray, I willingly give my hands to the Romans thou has sent me to, and I declare openly before all of them, I do not go over as a deserter of my people - but as a priestly delegate from my God." The Hebrew drops on his knees; hands enjoined. The Romans are frozen in silence, confused by the strange Hebrew's words.

Then Bernice approaches the strange Hebrew as he kneels in supplication to his God; his head bent; for she compelled Vespasian to do this deed; to bring the captured Hebrew to him instead of crucifying this warrior priest; she must now redeem herself.

"What fires come from those oracles… savior or betrayer?" She encircles about him, opening her jar of powders. "Be still now. I will measure your truth for Vespasian, my own savior."

Bernice takes Josephus' hand against her ear and listens. The soldiers sway in the howling winds, in wait of the Queen's assessment of the Hebrew, for none could determine his nature. The priest's hand remains steady in the Queen's hand. Bernice turns to the gathering and points at Vespasian, her goddess-like figure displaying the queen's fames sensual power; it beguiled many great ones in her net. Her skin glows; her strides evocative and captivating. Titus appears compelled by the queen as she addresses the soldiers.

"Hearken to me all! Vespasian is now raised to divine glory by the words of a Hebrew priest. This is not a treachery of the king… yet this Hebrew priest's finger points to the next divine Emperor of Rome… as a surety of its coming! Be you now all its witness…be you without fear and vouch now your divine emperor to be!?"

Bernice pans the gathering of soldiers, then she nods in approval, compelling all to her verdict; now the queen Bernice compels all to her, including a mesmerized Titus. Her hand turns, swaying to Vespasian; she bows before Vespasian in solemn devotion; she nods in affirmation of the newly declared one in the oracle of a Hebrew priest. Titus and the soldiers turn in unison to their General, all on single bended knees, their right hands pointing in a unified worshipping mode at Vespasian.

But Vespasian is cautious of the Hebrew's evocative proclamations. "You have also good reason to save yourself?"

"O Vespasian, you are now Caesar and Emperor all in one, both you and…" The priest's pointing finger now sways to Titus. "And this your son…" The Eagle screeches; Titus' eyes begin to glow. "Know it O Vespasian, you are not only lord over me now, but over all of the land and the sea and of all mankind. And be you the judge of my words to come true or not?!" The Hebrew's stance is bold and daring; his gaze challenging.

"Yet you failed to protect your own people?" Vespasian deliberates.

"I plainly foretold it to the people in the caves of Jotapata - that they would be taken on the forty-seventh day. And that I would surely be caught alive by the Romans. But they doubted me, not wanting to know of such tidings. Yet here I am before you now?!"

"Let me enquire of you and consult on my own." The experienced war Commander is not easily beguiled. "I shall not set this Hebrew free before then."

Bernice is caressing Vespasian's neck, measuring his son's lusting gaze. She challenges him back, kissing Vespasian's ears; taunting Titus.

"And this your son…" Titus murmurs back, reminding her with a warrior's demanding eyes, his fist taping his chest.

"Mine…" She grins wickedly, the lips expressing her words without sound; she nibbles his father's ear, clasping her arms around him. "Mine…mine?"

Titus taps his fist on his chest. Then he pauses; her devious eyes captivate the great warrior to a motionless submission; Titus appears mesmerized, beseeching and lusting of his father's mistress. They measure each other. He nods at the queen; she turns away caressing his father, taunting Titus wickedly. The great warrior is a captured prey in her net. She taunts him wickedly.

(30). ELEAZAR ANOINTS LAD BOAZ.

Eleazar is reclined on the edge of a hill overlooking the Galilee. He is scraping smooth the stem of a rose in his hands with a glistening dagger, spitting on the tender stem, softening it, blowing on it and shaving it rounded and smooth.

Ari arrives on his horse, laden with a blind-folded passenger. An agent of the Peace Party has requested a meeting with the Sicarii leader and a secret location was chosen, one that does not disclose the hidden Sicarii base.

Ari unfolds the man. There is a pot of water, fresh fruit and bread laid out before Peretz, a noble Jewish figure who holds a high office in the Roman protected Peace Party group that controls the Temple. They sit in long heavy silence before each other; then they exchange greetings.

"Shalom Eleazar, brave and strong leader of the Sicarii."

"Shalom. Now speak."

"I bring you the word of the Peace Party and of Gischala and Giora."

Eleazar is sarcastic: "Also of Agrippa and Vespasian…and Nero?"

"Hear me please." He points with clutched fingers like he is feeding grains to a bird, each item of his reasoning measured and weighed. "They say, all say it, together as one they say it… that the war you engage in is not with Rome but with us… the people of Israel." He pauses to impress that his words are registered; then he continues, swaying his clutched fingers foreword as if feeding more grain. "We have worked hard to negotiate with the Romans for any means to survive under our occupation." He turns to Ari, nodding, swaying face as a convincing. "We did so even when we had no choices, you understand me?" He turns again to Eleazar. "But now Rome will see all of us as conspirators who could not stop rebel groups such as you - what do we do, you tell me? Is the Sicarii not one of Israel - of course he is, and so are your faithful men!?" He slaps his chest. "We say to Eleazar, all three with one voice, the groups of the Peace Party, and of Gischala, and of Giora… you must cease your war with Rome!?"

Eleazar continues working on the rose stem, spitting, blowing on it. Peretz continues:

"You know it well, as we do… the Sicarii can't fight such a mighty force. So hear me now Eleazar, heed our words as we plead and demand of you… the Sicarii must work with us, not against us? Three groups against one - it says you must cease." His open hand palm waits, anticipating complete agreement. "Israel says cease, Eleazar - three against one!?"

"I will give you two more." Eleazar turns from shaving the rose stem. "Rav Yochanan ben Zakkai… and my own father. Five against one?"

"You must hear me well…" Peretz sighs, swaying his face in a condescending frustration. "You are the son of a priest of Israel, you know the laws when the multitude supports how we must turn, even when our sage Rav Yochnan vouches it!?"

"You also know the laws… you shall not follow a corrupt…blinded…cowardly multitude…to drink bitter waters. [Ex. 23:2].

They engage each other. Peretz nods, acknowledging Eleazar's own masterly of the Hebrew laws; he now also understands his mission will not succeed.

"You will call the Rav of Israel as corrupt - is it not an evil thought? Tell me now son of a priest of Israel, will you put in danger all of your people - will you also use the laws of our God to suit yourself - and do so in the name of our God, that you will be Israel's savior by destroying her!?"

"I say this to Rome's Peace Party." Eleazar responds with a menacing; he lays down the rose stem. "Israel is forbidden the worship of other gods… even in the face of death. You know Israel's laws and Rome's laws. You know, without the second command from Har Sinai we have no laws and we will have no God. We will become as them. It is the Sicarii answer to all five of you?"

Peretz rises to leave, nodding in suppressed fury of Eleazar's rejection. "There is too much at stake now - more than you will ever know."

"On that we can agree." Eleazar turns to shaving the rose with a Sicarii blade. "More than you will ever know…"

Ari dips his head respectfully, then begins to bind Peretz's eyes and hands as they ride away on one horse. At the Sicarii base, the lad Boaz stands before Eleazar - he has been waiting patiently with a youth's fiery tension for an audience. The lad turns to the skies, retreating out of Eleazar's range to display his feat; Eleazar pauses with an understanding of the lad's display before him. Boaz gestures at the sky; a large black bird is gliding in the streaming clouds. Boaz begins whirling his sling in the air so it becomes invisible except for its whizzing gust. The lad is whizzing his sling faster now, awaiting a crevice in the wind flow. Then he releases the stone with a gentle measured twist of his finger - it soars perfectly towards the path of the eagle in the sky.

Eleazar and Boaz wince, swaying as they follow the stone; it closely misses its mark, the eagle glides into the heavens unhurt. Boaz turns to Eleazar in tears.

"My Teacher says 13 years is a man. I am a man this day - I will join!?"

"Then…" Eleazar's gaze has a glint of softness, perhaps recalling his own son of similar age. "Then you will teach the Sicarii sons how to stop the Roman Commanders who order fiery machines on Israel. You will teach them to do as David did with Goliath." He applies spit to his thumb and presses it on the lad's forehead in an anointing mode. "And as did Samuel with David, you are now anointed a Sicarii warrior with a mission…"

Young Boaz bows retreating; he whirls his sling in a joyous display of tears as he inclines his face to Eleazar, shouting.

"I am a Sicarii now…?" Eleazar nods affirming it. The lad glows in tears and joy.

Suddenly a wild screeching; they both turn to the heavens. The mighty eagle hovers, encircling the Sicarii base in the streaming clouds.

Eleazar is in distant thoughts - he recalls the words of an Essene monk:

"This war before us… it is not about your mission."

In the Megiddo village, a Roman's words come again to Deborah as she flees in the dark night; the words she cannot cease recalling come haunting in the winds.

"Who is Alexander Ben Hur?" She pauses abruptly in fright; she looks behind, suspicious, as if being followed. Is someone there…watching her; she is suspicious.

"I know now you can never forget my name…" The voice echoes in her mind again.

There is a rustling noise; she halts abruptly at what she beholds in the path before her. She nears cautiously; a gazelle is on the ground, its body torn away and disemboweled by an eagle pecking away its prey. Her hand trembles as she grips her dagger.

"Is there any Greek in you…?" A Roman's question resounds in her mind.

The moonlight appears from behind the clouds; it shimmers on her face, as if following her. The eagle pauses tearing its dead prey; it turns, its blood red eyes engaging her threateningly; then it abruptly ascends, vanishing into the dark night. Deborah backs away in a horror, recalling an eagle that terrorized her - and a Roman coming to her rescue.

She wraps her shawl around her as a protection, fleeing into the hills, racing to her village, turning behind her shoulders she is not being pursued by a Roman enemy. Or her own people. She pauses as she turns to check again; shuddering and trembling in the howling winds, a knife grasped tightly in her hand.

The searing eyes of a Roman come before her.

"I know now…" His words emerge challenging her. "You can never forget my name…"

She flees.

[END OF ACT 1]

King Agrippa and Queen Berenice attending the Roman Trial of St. Paul. Source: S11.

BEN HUR II EXILE

ACT II: A FORBIDDEN LOVE

(31). THE DARKEST FORCE.

On a windy hill on the outskirts of the Megiddo plains, the teacher Hillel has arranged a meeting with a Sicarii member. Hillel, a peace advocating pacifist of high order is transferring a political stance to the Jews' most intransigent warrior group, one that opposes any form of alliance with Rome. Eleazar has sent his most trusted personal agent, assuring confidence of such a significant secret meeting between the honored teacher and the Sicarii warriors.

"There is a time for all things." - Hillel justifies his reason for such a meeting. "If Nero does not annul his Heresy law upon Judea, we will stand with the Sicarii."

"Eleazar's mission will be stronger by your blessing." Ari honors the teacher, bowing his face. "Any more?"

"Yes." The teacher nods; his eyes shut and distant. "Eleazar must know this pledge will apply only in this instant. Otherwise, all remains the same as before."

"Understood."

"And the Flavians… the darkest force before us."

"Understood." Ari dips his head; he kisses the teacher's hand and departs.

(32). THE COVENANT.

Vespasian visits a prison in the late hours of the night; he is seated before the captured Hebrew priest in his prison cell. Two guards bearing torches are in attendance. In the dungeon darkness the torch fires shimmer on Vespasian's silhouetted face as he addresses the priest.

"I don't sleep any more. Something bothers me. Your God made you a covenant, yet you say he will forsake Israel and raise me up. Either your God is a liar… or else your oracles are false?"

"Neither." The Hebrew assures.

"Then you will read for me of this covenant. You are expert in both the Greek and the Hebrew tongues…" Vespasian's gaze is focused on the scribe, as if searching him for hidden powers of a sorcerer. "See, I brought for you your Hebrew writings." A guard lays a scroll before the scribe. "Explain to me how both can be true, your God's covenant and your own words to me. Read?"

Moving closer to the light of the torch, the Hebrew priest roles the pages of the scroll; then he reads for Vespasian from a specific section, its location he knows well.

"…And when Abram was ninety years old and nine, the Lord appeared to Abram."

"How strange…" Vespasian is sardonic. "So an invisible God can appear to one Abraham yet be unseen by all others?"

"…and said unto him: "I am God Almighty; walk before Me, and be thou wholehearted and I will make My covenant between Me and thee, and will multiply thee exceedingly."

"Multiply? Exceedingly? Never happened." Vespasian suppresses a smirking, swaying face in negation. "Continue."

"…And Abram fell on his face; and God talked with him saying:

'As for Me, behold, My covenant is with thee, and thou shalt be the father of a multitude of nations'."

"What multitude… where… when!?" Vespasian demands in disdain.

One of the two guards raises eye brows in ridicule of the priest's words, also smirking of the Hebrew scribe.

"…And I will establish My covenant between Me and thee and thy seed after thee throughout their generations for an everlasting covenant."

The other tall guard is intensely focused and moved by Josephus' words.

"Everlasting covenant… or a heresy against Rome, one which brought you to this dungeon?" A war commander's threatening tone emerges. "Did you think such tricks of sorcery will make me spare your life? You account me a fool?"

'…And I will give unto thee, and to thy seed after thee, the land of thy sojourning, all the land of Canaan, for an everlasting possession; and I will be their God."

"Was this covenant not made as a lie when Babylon crushed Jerusalem - where was your God's ever-lasting covenant then!?" Vespasian speaks with fury now. "Why then do you still trust the empty words you read to me - even as you see I may crush Israel again?"

One guard sniggers and smirks; the tall guard contrasting him.

"…And God said unto Abraham" The scribe's voice becomes tremulous. "And as for thee, thou shall keep My covenant, thou, and thy seed after thee throughout their generations…"

"How come your Moses can see an invisible God and all else not… do the Jews imagine mighty Rome to be made of fools?"

"He who fashioned the eyes makes us to see…" The priest answers. "He who implanted the ear makes us to hear…or not?"

"Hear me well, Hebrew Priest. Judea will fall in a heap, Israel will never rise again. It is a false covenant. Your own oracle is far wiser. Know that such guile will not save your life. Go now and wait your end - soon it will come!"

Josephus bows, then he lays the scroll on the tall guard's arms, retreating in chains. Vespasian now understands the strange determination of the Jews and their covenant; one that they held throughout their generations of old and in many existential battles with mighty nations. He ponders how this small people in a minuscule land returned, when many other mighty empires did not. As the guard shuts the priest's prison door, Vespasian ponders the Jews' strong belief with Rome's own. The torch fires flicker on Vespasian's face as he murmurs to himself:

"You people took the land of Canaan and slaughtered many… our Philistine kin told us of your doings. How then can you point now at Rome?" The torch fires flicker on Vespasian's face as he mutters at the guards:

"A foolish, primitive people. After all, Gods are Gods…what difference which one!?"

Vespasian's face is distorted.

The Hebrew Canaanites were one of the nine national groups of the Canaanite kingdom. The Hebrew people were born and incepted in this land; they knew not any other land as their own. Vespasian's charge of the Israelites invading a foreign land has dubious validity. Despite that their forefather Abraham was born in an adjacent city, all of the children of Abraham, Isaac and Jacob were born and raised as Canaanites, including the twelve sons of Jacob that constituted the Twelve Tribes of Israel and his one daughter Dinah, one the prince of the Canaanite groups will marry. The Hebrew people were thus original Canaanite inhabitants and had inter-marriages, water wells, land purchases and commercial dealings like all Canaanite inhabitants; they were a renowned part of the Canaanite peoples. The Hebrews became called as the Israelites when Jacob's name was changed to Israel; thus the twelve Canaanite sons of Jacob became the twelve tribes of Israel, a Canaanite people.

The Book of Exodus accounts that the Israelites became captive slaves in Egypt; it was fostered by a sore regional famine that drove them there to purchase grains. The Nile never runs dry; the law land of Egypt was the only land in the region unaffected by the famine. The Israelites were drawn there by strange means that resulted in bondage and became captive slaves by the Egyptian Pharaoh.

When freedom from the Egyptian bondage came via the hand of Moses, the grown and exceedingly multiplied twelve Canaanite tribes of Israel now numbered as three million. The Israelites knew only one destination - the return to their homeland whence they came from, the land they were created in. Canaan was Israel's Promised Land.

On their return from Egypt, their entry was denied them by six of the eight Canaanite groups aligned with Egypt as vassal kingdoms; news of the destruction of Egypt at the hands of the Israelites had reached Canaan. When a peace offer by Joshua was refused, mandated in the Hebrew laws before undertaking a war, it signified the Canaanite's ancient form of genocide; the banishment from the land. A domestic war resulted, one that saw the Hebrew Canaanites as the victor, and the name of the land was later changed to Israel.

The surviving Non-Hebrew Canaanites, among them two groups who sided with Joshua, became fully absorbed as national Israelite inhabitants:

"The Jebusites dwell with the children of Judah in Jerusalem until this day"

[Book of Joshua 15: 63]

The Israelites and the other Canaanite groups managed well, conducting trade and commerce facilities. Seven centuries after the Israelites returned, the Jebusites will sell a high ground hilltop to King David for a vast measure of gold and silver and a guarantee of protection and security in the Kingdom established by King David. Thus did King David purchase the hill which was the sight of Mount Moriah, wherein David established Israel's capital of Jerusalem. The remnant Canaanites, including the Jebusites, are known to have lived as inhabitants of Israel under King Solomon:

"Then Solomon began to build the house of the LORD at Jerusalem in Mount Moriah, where The LORD appeared unto David his father; for which provision had been made in the Place of David, in the threshing floor of Ornan the Jebusite." [2 Chronicles, Ch 3:1].

Later, in 740 BCE, when the Assyrian ruler Sargon II invaded Israel, its entire Northern population, including those Canaanite groups who became embedded as the Israelites, also containing the remnant Philistines conquered by King David, became exiled as Jews; these became known as The Ten Lost Tribes of Israel. Thus the surviving Hebrews of the Southern Kingdom of Judah became known as the only known active and living Canaanites. The scattering of The Lost Tribes of Israel across the nations constitute that none can account them anymore, where or who these may be; yet these are prophesized to return to their land in the future.

The Jews are not known to have ever invaded or occupied another peoples' lands in all their history, despite the many invasions and exiles that dispersed this people throughout the nations; the Jews never took of those lands and sought always only to return to their own homeland.

The Hebrew bible uniquely forbids the Jews of taking a single cubit of land of another people or nation, even when such an occasion prevails itself, setting it in holy writ:

"Take ye good heed unto yourselves therefore; contend not with them; for I will not give you of their land, no, not so much as for the sole of the foot to tread on" (Duet. 2/4 & 2/9)

(33). THE KING IS DEAD.

Romans, Hellenist and Arabian mobs are chanting in the streets:
"THE KING IS DEAD - LONG LIVE THE NEW KING".

The chanting rages in Egypt and Judea and soon spreads over the vast Roman Empire. As Tiberius brings Titus the news he pauses from his daily combat practice incumbent on all Romans.
"Good news for the Flavians. The Julio-Claudiane reign has finally come to its end. Nero is dead."
As Tiberius speaks, Titus gazes at the streaming clouds; a glint appears in his eyes as he focuses on an eagle soaring in the heavens: is this the sign of his own glory? He recalls the chants from the Roman gods and the omen given him:
"Glory! Glory! The Gloreee!"
In her mansion's private domain, the Queen Bernice is mixing strange incense to mellow Vespasian as the news is brought to him. Bernice mixes strange incense from India; the Romans became enthralled with such powders of spices for enhancements of foods and aromas from this ancient land of the east. The art of incense burning, smoking and sniffing predated the use of tobacco which later spread via ancient Persia and the Americas. The queen has set her plans for Vespasian; she expects him; she has her plans.
He enters appearing in awe and fear of the news. He recalls his meeting with Josephus; he recalls the oracle giver's predictions and how soon it materialized. Vespasian gazes unsure and questioning at Bernice for her impressions. She is sniggering wickedly at him, as if she understands his thoughts. She raises her pot of intoxicating fumes, the mesmerizing eyes reminding him; she is pointing her finger at the Commander who would be Rome's divine emperor. Now she is emulating the Hebrew oracle giver's stance:
"YOU!" She screams in dramatic alluring. "You must know for a surety - the finger of heaven points to you! To you, Vespasian, YOU-YOU-YOU!?"
"And it comes from the mouth of that Hebrew sorcerer - an enemy of Rome?" He wraps a cover over his shoulders and turns away in disbelief. "So soon it comes… so soon, the Hebrew priest must surely be a sorcerer!?" Vespasian's eyes are agape in confusion. "Yet… he favors me…the enemy of Rome favored me before all, did he not!?"
Bernice sways her face in negation. "It was I who favored you… so soon you forget?"
"If this Hebrew's light favors me, I shall not forget those who stand by me… they shall ascend with me in Rome."
"Tell me now, my would be emperor of Rome - who made you see the light in the darkness?"
"Yes, yes, true!? It was your advice that made me turn from crucifying this Hebrew priest as an enemy of Rome! It was you, my precious queen!"
"You are before a Goddess…" She blows her fumes at him. "Can you not smell the glory, my divine, divine and divine emperor!?"
"Yet… this people and their belief worry me…"
"Do the Jews not pay their due taxes on time?" - She taunts in sarcasm.
"It is their terrible one God belief. Many in the empire have been lost to it. They spread their sorcery against me wherever they go. How does one respond to a people that rejects Rome's divine emperors - even when their own priests says so. How - tell me!?"
"Do you even know what Israel means? One who strived with the Lord and prevailed. This is a stiff-neck people - words given them by their God. Because they pursued truth more than others. You must entice them, my clever emperor… give them something that pleases their minds - just like their God did for them. You must rise up the Hebrew priest…you must entice him?"

"Entice them?" He is accounting her words intensely now. He hurriedly dresses and races out of the Queen's boudoir. "Entice them…?" He murmurs; then he pauses, turning to Bernice. "You people… you know things. I love you… and I fear you!"

She exhales smoke, turning away, moving languidly in triumphant measure.

In a secret location of the Judean hills, Ari approaches Eleazar with the news.

"The depraved one of the Romans, one who proclaimed himself divine… is dead. Perchance the next one will be less insane and annul Rome's evil laws against us?"

Eleazar jolts; he sees again the man in a tunic in the corner staring him, swaying his face in negation of Ari's words in a strange resolute confidence. Eleazar now recalls the teacher Hillel's message: 'The Flavians… the darkest force before us'.

"With their emperor dead they will be in chaos for some time." Ari is eager to know Eleazar's thoughts.

"Tell me now, has the darkness turned to light for us?"

Eleazar turns away gazing at the churning clouds, in contemplation of Hillel's warning of the Flavians, if it be darkness or a light. His thoughts are far away, the somber face appears both of a warrior and a sensitive father, a savage killer and a loving demeanor; his eyes engulfed in defiance and the foreboding possibilities ahead.

There is confusion in the people; there is a smirking Essene monk and a devoted teacher's warning. But Eleazar's face regains his determined posture; there is no confusion which way the Jews must stand. There will be no surrender of Israel's beliefs. He turns to his intense, persistent and most trusted Sicarii warrior.

"No light without freedom. And it always comes after the darkness."

"But…"

"Go now. Talk again with Shimon."

"We are all in terror inside… just as you are. And I am with you no matter what comes. All of us…"

"Simon. Go!?"

Eleazar is in deep thoughts as signs and omens flare before him. He recalls again:

Hillel: "The Flavians… the darkest force before us."

The Essene: This war… it is not about your mission… or about Rome."

Eleazar whispers it to himself:

"There is nothing without our freedom. There can be no Israel with Rome… and no Rome with Israel." He understands this as a surety. Yet the stranger's words come:

"This war is not about Rome".

Eleazar sways his face in calm, deathly negation of his path with Rome:

"No surrender!?"

(34). SOME THINGS ARE WORTH DYEING FOR.

In the Megiddo hinterland, Simon steps back from his newly completed home to view the new large window he made. He nods to himself in satisfaction; she will be pleased. He works his chores lifting crates of olives, piling them on a caravan. As he works moving olive crates, he recalls Deborah convincing him away from joining the Sicarii forces, as his comrades have been courting him for a long time.

"Simon… some things are worth living for."

He recalls his response to her. "Some things are worth dying for." He recalls how she frowned upon him, how his words became a silent, unspoken wedge between them.

Now Simon's two comrades Ari and Saul arrive; they appear determined with an emergency.

"Your brethren are calling you - how can you grow olives at such a time!?" Saul asks as Simon loads heavy crates on a caravan, shifting and adjusting them in a neat symmetry.

"We must defend the Temple and the nation now." Ari joins beseeching: "You are our strongest - how can you not understand we need you - will those given strength among us sit calm and silent when evil sits on our doors?"

Simon does not take their bait; he remains silent of Ari's charges, hoping the wedge that distanced him from Deborah will pass away. But the Sicarii are a hardy breed and Simon's physical power is no match for this group of warriors' cunning. The Sicarii are infused with an ancient stiff necked resoluteness inculcated in wars with many nations - the ancient Egyptians, the Philistines, the Midianites, with Babylon and the Greek Empire; and now with Rome, their greatest opponent. The Sicarii warriors understand how to strike at Simon's soft parts just as they do in tossing their daggers and slings at an enemy with a precision not seen elsewhere. Ari continues:

"Feel free from the pledge you gave her, it is no longer valid. She has betrayed you and her people for the brutes that are killing us… for those who send spies among us."

Now Saul advances the attack stratagem dangerously. "And there is word she has mingled already. There is more than they show us…"

Enraged, Simon grasps Saul, holding his neck in one hand and his feet in the other, swaying him in the air, about to cause Saul great damage.

"He is bone of your bone!" Ari shouts loudly. "Flesh of your flesh!" One who would freely give his life for you!? Hear me! There is word of the largest cargo of war machines and new legions from across the seas - all are bound for Caesarea. Maybe even for the holy city… can any Jew not remember Babylon!?"

Simon pauses with Saul wavering horizontally in the air; he hard stares Ari. "Who gave you this information, a Roman spy?"

"The most trusted one we have…"

Simon releases Saul who is tottering in the air, tossing him on the ground.

Ari: "You know who…"

Eleazar's face rises from behind a hilltop ridge in the outskirts of Jerusalem. Except for Ari, none know the Sicarii's location; neither the Jews nor the Romans are yet aware that the Sicarii have advanced closer to their mission's destination.

Jerusalem is eerily quiet, its temple silhouette against the heavens appear motionless. Roman soldiers walk calmly in her streets by the Jews; all know none will dare to attack the Roman stronghold in the Jerusalem fortress.

Eleazar gazes, panning the fortress walls in the distance, as if studying its impregnable defenses - the same that defended his nation, but now defending it defends the Roman enemy. The Sicarii warriors surround him, waiting on his word in excitement and trepidation.

"We will prevail." Dan says.

"Israel will prevail." Eleazar mutters to himself.

"Jerusalem is our refuge. The only blessing from Herod."

"There is also another Herod made for us."

Dan appears confused. Eleazar turns to Ari and Saul as they arrive with news of Simon. Eleazar is focused on Ari, waiting on his report of Judea's strong man.

Ari nods. "He is starting to break."

Saul nods: "Amen, Amen!"

"Give Ari and Saul food and drink." Eleazar turns to Dan. "Also give their horses."

"Who is starting to break?" Dan questions, confused; he gets no response.

(35). A STRANGER IN A STRANGE LAND.

In the Megiddo village, Alexis awakes in the strangeness of a Hebrew house. Hillel stands in the background. Deborah's face hovers over him as she nurses his head wound.
"The face that is always before me…" He gazes at her in wondrous joy.
"Thank God you look well. I am Hillel, a humble teacher whose life you saved.
"How long have I been here?" His hand reaches for his wounded head.
"A full day and night." Deborah answers. "I told our teacher how you saved the children from the snake."
"And that I'm a Roman spy - a stranger in your land?"
Deborah appears embarrassed; the teacher comes to her aid.
"There is no stranger here, only an honored guest before us."
"Who hit me - from behind, surely?"
"Dear man, tragically, there was a great error and confusion. Someone imagined you came to attack Deborah - what with the sad news we have in so many of our towns. He knew not you had saved us."
Alexis' eyes are fixed on Deborah as Hillel explains. "We prayed for your forgiveness and your recovery - we are in sorrow and forever in your debt. Forgive us, we plead you?"
"Be not concerned of it - the matter is now before me. Tell it also to the one who struck me - from behind."
"The Lord bless you for it!" Hillel's eyes are closed; he appears far away. "There is a festive occasion, the birth of a new male child. You must come as our honored guest. Rest now, Deborah will bring you food and drink and tend your wound."
The lingering glances between Alexis and Deborah are broken by a piercing wailing of women. Deborah dashes out; Alexis peers from the window. Six Hebrew men lie on the ground, their throats slit by Tamar's blade. The lad Boaz, sling around his shoulder, turns from his fallen father to his wailing mother and Boaz's younger brother huddled together:
"I got him, Imma! I avenged my father!"
Young Boaz gazes at a Roman jacket in the window; he appears confused, his reddened face heaving in tears.
The people appear suspicious, murmuring:
"Is there not a Roman spy planted in our midst?" They gaze at each other.
A Hebrew remarks: "What Jew can trust a Roman?"
Another whispers: "Shhh! The teacher welcomed him here. He blessed him also."

(36). VESPASIAN ANOINTS A HEBREW SCRIBE.

The Hebrew priest is brought out from his prison cell. Josephus, in chains, stands before Vespasian and his son Titus in the Commander's private mansion in Caesarea.
"Nero is dead… compelled to kill himself!" Vespasian is excited before the priest. "Now Rome calls me, perchance to offer me the throne, as you prophesized? Perhaps then there is a way I can also give you life in return - does this interest you, my good priest? If your visions be true I can protect you, even give you glory along with me." He limps to the priest, offering his hand. "Come now, let us go hand in hand in your own visions. I will bestow on you garments of splendor, precious gifts and a concubine for your pleasures. Also, I will release you as a free man and protect you from your people. Tell me again your priestly Hebrew name?"
"I am Yosef… ben Matityahu."

"Come, my son will take over my position here and anoint you with an honorable Roman name. I will put my own name upon you. You are now… Titus Flavius Josephus. And tell me now before I depart for Rome, what have you more to say, you Hebrews have prophesies, you know hidden things?"

"Know it as I do of a surety. Vespasian will ascend as Emperor over all successors." The Priest's hand then sways away from Vespasian. "And this your son, he too shall ascend in his father's footsteps of his own glory… he will see all his desires fulfilled." His eyes pierce into Titus' eyes; Titus' eyes are glistening. Vespasian re-directs the priest's attention to him. "Priest of Judea, I speak now for Rome. Since you possess such eloquent speech and you are also expert in the writings of both your native tongue and our own, I will appoint you as my royal scribe. Then you will honor Rome and also me, as I honor you this day. I will surely require a good mouth to set my destiny - do you follow my meaning, Priest of oracles? Go now. Guards, remove his shackles."

Therein the Hebrew Priest's Hebrew name is set to become Latinized with the new Roman one of Flavius Josephus - aligned with the Flavian family of Vespasian and assured with a royal appointment and residence in Rome's security portion to protect him; also, to keep him in close watch.

Financial rewards and status appointments are entrenched Roman stratagems of inheriting the loyalty of a previous enemy; this was a successful maneuver, one also displayed by the Roman appointed King Herod who gave generous privileges to the Roman appointed Temple priests and to Jewish tax collectors.

Roman writers like Tacitus, Suetonius and Pliney the Elder speak suspiciously lauding of Vespasian and Titus, a syndrome also seen in Josephus' later writings, where any negative reporting of Rome or Vespasian is forbidden, its perpetrators eliminated. [85] While Pliney's 'Natural Histories' was dedicated to Vespasian and Titus, many Roman citizens were charged with promoting 'un-Roman' writings and killed; the pro-republic writer Helvetius Priscus was executed when his philosophies were deemed adverse of Rome's divine emperors. [86]

In Rome's heady politics of guile and deception, an emperor's ascension rested on propaganda as the governing merit, more so than even the required elements of ruthless might and accumulated wealth. No Roman, Greek or Jew could write or speak their minds freely without consequences; all had to pass the careful approval of Vespasian, and anything negative was destroyed. The Dead Sea Scrolls will be saved from Rome only by undertaking the most dangerous scheming endeavors; all other Hebrew writing was destroyed.

Josephus bows and leaves. Given freedom, security and rewards, with specified conditions, the newly appointed Roman Scribe now understands the strange turning of his life; that the path of his destiny is not in his hands anymore. The Hebrew priest now understands how mighty Rome became the world's greatest power; that Rome measures her war spoils prudently; that Rome has her ways.

Now alone by themselves, Vespasian turns to Titus.

"My son. Both our destinies now hang before us as a talisman swaying to and fro. Know it well now only a complete Roman victory will make your father ascend to the throne." He limps toward the statue of Jupiter. "And victory over the Hebrews is made our only path - their own priest has said it. So do whatever you must my son, and give me a victory over the Jews… and of their unseen, hidden Hebrew God that seeks to shame all our divine emperors, to rob every glory we dream of as sacred."

"Father, he is of the enemy, yet you ask me to anoint him with a Royal Roman name, even our own family name. How so, my father?"

"It is because he glorified our name before all. We will give this Hebrew our full protection, a residence of honor close to my own and the pleasures of Rome's finest concubines… and wealth and stature. He will be my scribe! My son must know it is the victor not the vanquished that will decide history. We must turn this Hebrew and make him as the enemy of the Jews - not of Rome. We must…" He utters the words of Queen Bernice: "Entice him?"

"My father, how can Rome trust Jews, this people hold a belief that opposes all of Rome's divine kings?" Titus holds his sword before his father. "Yet my arm is ready to serve in my father's will."

Vespasian sways his face in negation. "My son must know the sword alone will not suffice with the Jews." His warrior son's face winces; he appears confused. "But father, what other way can anyone conquer such a belief, one that resisted every offer and went to war with many nations for many years. Father, this people will not change their ways?"

"There is another way to conquer the Jews' belief…" Vespasian engages his son's confusion; Titus waits on his father.

"What other way can change their belief?"

"Another belief."

"Another belief?"

"When the fanatical ones are eliminated, we must entice the rest. Such is the merit of a true divine emperor of Rome. Your own also."

"None have succeeded with the Jews, my father. This is a stiff-necked people of old who understand only the sword."

"In this you will need the help of the Jews. Remember it."

Titus appears confounded. "Help from… the Jews!?"

"Roman guile… for Hebrew guile?" Vespasian nods at his son.

Titus begins to ponder now, as if enlightened by his father with a new understanding. He nods; placing back his sword.

Behind a curtain, from the boudoir of Vespasian, Bernice is watching covertly, a smoking coil clasped in her hand. She has secured Vespasian as already assuming himself as an emperor, and that he understands it is her direction that guided his path of ascending the throne. Bernice's fingers dip into a small pot; she rubs incense paste back of her ears, on her neck and her belly and her toes; she inhales the sweet mesmerizing smell on her glistening skin, nodding approval as she prepares her snare. She knows her power before all men and she knows the weakness of the Romans.

Vespasian holds a scepter above Titus' head:

"Swear it by your father and by Jupiter to achieve this victory, else take your leave now from this glory."

Bernice smirks as Titus falls on his knees before his father; his hand pressed on his heart.

"Let hell befall me if I fail my father or Rome. I won't fail you. This glory is mine… I want it?"

Bernice also understands Vespasian must go to Rome to secure his throne. In this he will need the voices of support from Rome's foremost minds and scribes; and what better than a Hebrew priest to affirm it, making his war with the Jews a required blessing for Rome and his own ascension to the throne? Bernice understands Titus must be left in Judea, that a victory of war and the wealth of the Jews must be used as the instrument of Vespasian's ascension. And Bernice knows of Titus' own dreams of glory; and of his own Roman lusting of her. She knows all of Titus' desires must be fulfilled. She smells her fingers nodding; planning; smoking from her Arabian pipe.

Vespasian continues his final condition to his son.

"Also, while I am in Rome you will protect the road builder, son of Matarian. This I swore unto his father by Jupiteres, and Jupiter watches us now."

Bernice now also understands the pledge that haunts Vespasian concerning his friend Matarian's son. She inclines herself on his bed languidly, waiting for one who will be Rome's divine emperor. And of course, she will be Queen of Rome and the Goddess of Rome's emperor, with her own desires to fulfill, as yet undisclosed and shrouded in confounding the Romans and her own people.

'Another belief?' She murmurs to herself. "Does the world turn by men - or was Eve the final supreme act of creation, the one who changed all men's path?' Bernice waits on her prey. 'Who made Adam turn?' She squirms devilishly, forming her own path of glory on Vespasian's bed. 'Who else can turn Mighty Rome?" She exhales. "I'll give you another belief!' She smirks wickedly, leaving the boudoir curtain half open; waiting her prey.

Vespasian retreats from Titus kneeling before him.

"Lastly my son, know that if you fail we will both perish. We have greater enemies in Rome than in Judea…"

As Vespasian leaves limping, entering his private domain, its curtain half open, Titus sees Bernice lying in his father's opulent bed; he will be her next prey when his father leaves. Titus stirs in a lust filled envy at her sight and is consumed with desire for the Hebrew Queen, the strong gush of magical incense swirling out. He envies the sordid and intriguing relation his father cherishes with the wealthy, powerful and most desirous queen. He heaves in wanton agony for her; he murmurs gazing at the curtains his father draws closed:

"I want it."

She smirks wickedly, gazing from crevices and slits.

"I want it…" The killer blue eyes glow in angst. She exhales her smoke.

A figure now emerges crouching out of a dark hallway from behind Titus. Aristomy lays his hand on his shoulder and whispers it:

"You will not be disobeying your honorable father. The traitor who controls our road works… we will make the Jews deal with him for us. Your hands will be clean!?" Aristomy rubs his palms clean in the air. "You will hold only honor before Rome and thereby your own glory will be realized. Even all your desires will be fulfilled, as the Hebrew priest prophesized it…this Hebrew woman will become your joy, only yours and of none else?"

Titus nods approving.

"Come. Titus must know more."

(37). YOU SHALL LOVE THE STRANGER.

In Megiddo, Deborah brings Alexis an elaborate platter of exotic foods, desert fruits, freshly baked bread and golden grape juice. He rests on a bed; his eyes focused on her every movement. Now he engages her when they are alone again.

"Your holy book says… 'Therefore you shall love the stranger".[87]

She ponders on the familiar Hebrew law coming from a Roman.

"Such a law, in truth, can only apply to one as I am, not one of your own." He extends his hand to her.

"Your own God has said it?"

"I brought you food." She is dismayed and flushed by his words from the Hebrew writings. "Return now my purse?"

"First, explain to me your poem. What does Halle…luyah mean?"

She turns to flee; he grasps her hand tenderly, as he did in the cemetery of Megiddo. She panics, looking around if anyone in the village will see such a sight, of a Roman holding the hand of a Hebrew maiden, alone and none else as witness. Again the Roman holds the Hebrew maiden's hand clasped in his, with a gaze of devotion she never experienced in her village life; she appears breathless and unsure now of the Roman she tends.

"I have read your Hebrew psalms - this word Halle-luyah is always there. Have you heard of a Roman poem?"

She could do no more than sway her face in negation.

"Listen…" He holds on to her hand; it is shuddering. "Listen…" He recites to her:

> "Set now the wine and the dice
> and let one who goes without care
> of tomorrow know it…
> for the end calls all, saying,
> 'I will come, I will come,
> so love to-day, love today,
> for none know what the morrow brings."

"Such words I have not heard." She pulls away her hand that is shaking tremulously in his. "But our sages say there is wisdom in all nations. I seek forgiveness of your wound."

"This stranger seeks more than your forgiveness…?"

"There is nothing more to seek for us. Release my hand?"

She flees from him, flushed and embarrassed. Outside, Deborah confronts Simon. The towering giant is frozen and appears lost for words before her.

"The window… fixed." His words come out awkwardly. She flees him also.

Alexis drifts into a deep sleep. He dreams of a garden patch of roses. She comes to him; she enters his arms and rests her face on his chest; he is in a blissful trance. Then Florian's ominous warning comes to him: "She is of the enemy. This love is forbidden."

Alexis awakes in a jolt. He sees Simon standing outside in the doorway. Simon stares in silent angst; then he storms away. Alexis is dripping in sweat; he looks around the strange Hebrew setting that surrounds him. There is a Menorah in a corner of the room; tassels hang from a post and parchments are attached on every doorway; an enchanting smell of baked bread permeates. He ponders what force compelled him to this strange place in the home of the Jews, the sworn enemy of his people. He ponders his life's destiny and purpose now; soon he will enter a point of accounting his actions with his people. Alexis' head throbs.

(38). THE PHILISTINE'S KIN.

The Sicarii warriors have been stationed in their hidden enclave on a high hilly terrain for three weeks. They have sustained themselves on meager food and water rations and growing weary and impatient, yet they maintain their alertness throughout. Ari approaches Eleazar, who is squatted resting against a rock; he shaves a rose stem smooth.

"The Sicarii wait on your word while each day the Romans kill many of our people. The men worry for their families. How long?"

"Good." He continues shaving the rose stem. "Let them be made worried and angry - it will help them with the Romans."

"They are angry now, they are ready."

Eleazar rests the rose stem and smiles at Ari. "Understand what is ahead of us. Israel has never faced a mightier force. No nation has. Rome knows nothing more than it does war and she plans everything and practices each day. How did Rome conquer mighty empires… the Greeks? Babylon? Hannibal? Could Israel do such - no nation can?"

Eleazar turns to the heavens, wincing as though he is tracking something; Ari measures Eleazar's words intensely. "Rome's war machines are made for dominion, they faced many nations before, but none prevailed against them. Israel is a small nation." He smiles as he delivers his ominous warnings. "Rome spends more time preparing for war than we Jews do praying." Eleazar, sensing Ari's tension, hands him his flask of water as a calming pause. Ari sways his face and continues in his deliberation.

"The fortress is also a mighty force like none other. Their war machines won't break our walls, not even by the strongest cedar."

"They know this."

There is a long silence.

"Wood can break wood." Eleazar elaborates. "Iron can break… stone?" A pause of silence. Ari deliberates again.

"King David conquered the Philistines in Gaza." Ari counters with growing agitation. "They too had irons!?"

"Now we face the Philistine's kin from the other side of the sea. And they come back mightier than before and are not lacking in knowledge of war. Rome seeks her honor for her kin. Rome's emperors do not want to lose the glory of their thrones."

"We pay them double taxes, we have never invaded another nation, never robbed others… what else do they want from us!?" Ari screams in fury. "What more!?"

Eleazar states his position calmly. "From the Pharaohs of Misrayim to Babylon, then with the Greeks - all wanted us destroyed. But they would all love us if we only worship their divine kings in our holy Temple and offer daily sacrifices for their Roman gods. What else can Rome want from us, to enlarge their armies or their conquered lands - do they need such? No, we are as a grain of sand to them." Eleazar laughs mocking at the situation he describes.

"What then is your secret plan - which you will tell no one and you don't need our opinion, even when you know we are with you whatever comes?

"We must battle their irons with something much softer."

"Softer? Like roses from the Sharon, is that your plan!?" Ari is agitated.

"Oil."

"Oil?" Ari is incredulous. "Oil!? If I'm your right hand, then you must tell me your meaning!?"

"There is a meeting with the Zealots tomorrow night. Menahem will explain the plan."

"Menahem!?" Ari's eyes light up with the additional surprise. "I see that much has happened since you sent me to deal with Simon. Are the Zealots with us, tell me now?!"

"Come tonight. Now take a crate of dates for our men and give them water."

Eleazar turns his face to the skies. Ari's ever suspicious eyes follow his gaze.

A lone majestic eagle is gliding in the clouds; the eagle turns its head south.

Below, a flotilla of Roman ships queue up at a port in Caesarea as new war machines are being unloaded. The workers appear small before massive platforms on huge wooden wheels; the wheels extend taller than the soldiers.

'You must entice him!' Vespasian begins to hearken to Bernice's advice. He removes the Nomos, the Latin term for a book of Holy Scriptures which he keeps secured in his private treasure chest. He begins to read from the pages of the Greek Septuagint with renewed interest. And he devises meetings with Josephus, questioning him, to learn how the Jews uphold their laws and beliefs that are so different from all others. Vespasian must learn from a Hebrew Priest how to entice the Jews.

That night, Vespasian is immersed in his private bath and attended by female maidens rubbing oils on his body. He summons Josephus. When the Hebrew priest arrives in the steamy, marble bathhouse of opulent decadence, Vespasian addresses the priest now with his Roman name and in Roman dress.

"Remove your cloths and act like a Roman." He nods to one of the maidens; she begins to undress the Hebrew priest.

"If there is only one God over all, why does your God favor the Jews among all others, tell me?"

"No favor is given the Jews, they are left small in both number and land. All are equal under the law, the mighty as the meek."

"So you account Rome's Emperor as equal to any peasant?"

"The Hebrew laws say a righteous Roman is better than a bad Jew."

"Righteous!? What nonsense talk is that!? The mighty earn their merit by their velour - the meek expect it for naught. How can these be equal!?"

"Merit, for the Jews, is accounted by sacred laws given by God."

"It was I who saved you from death, not any Hebrew God's laws. Remember it?"

Vespasian leaves the steamy waters while the maidens dress him. He hails the security guard at the door and three young concubines are brought in.

"Spoil yourself with Roman law, Hebrew priest. I bring for you Rome's most desired maidens. Keep them for a month, they are yours if they meet your liking. Roman hospitality - gifts from the mighty Gods of Rome, the only gods who can benefit you now. Remember it?"

The concubines enter the bath; they draw closer, clinging to the Hebrew priest. One kisses the priest's hand enticingly.

The Romanized Hebrew priest will succumb to the enticing gifts of the Roman gods and get married to an alluring Egyptian maiden of irresistible beauty, one who not a Jewish and forbidden to a Hebrew priest. It is Vespasian's gift and the Hebrew scribe has no choice of it; Vespasian saved his life and he must be made to remember it. He now understands his position, a captive with both the Romans and the Jews, accounted as a betrayer and traitor; his life is always hanging on his Roman master's word.

Unlike his people of Judea, Josephus did not agree to die by his nation's laws. Vespasian's captive Hebrew Scribe will give the only historical writings as a first-hand witness of the Roman war with the Jews and account the greatest destruction in history. And every verse in his copious writings will be subject to approval by the Flavian family. Vespasian's stratagem, one instigated by the Hebrew Queen and assisted by an elite Hebrew priest of great stature, is showing merit.

In that same night, Aristomy has come to Titus' residence. Titus is seated before a table with the fire of a torch lamp on his silhouetted face, his fist tapping the table, the killer eyes glowing impatient; he grasps a jug of wine sitting on his lap, swallowing to its final drops. Such is the demeanor when a passion of lust stirs in the veins of one who is promised all his desires will be fulfilled, and he wants it. As Aristomy enters, Titus bangs his fist; he grits his teeth and snarls at him.

"Will this tiny peasant people challenge Rome and break my own glory, as you tell me? Or will I live to see my own father also take away all my desires. Speak!?"

"Never!" Aristomy bows in fear. "You are destined by the Gods for the same Roman divinity of Caligula, one who saw Rome's truths when Caesar did not. You are Rome's glorious son who will conquer the Hebrew God."

"And you have a snake's tongue! What more is in your mouth for me?"

"You must know both our gods' truth, for we are kin. And the Gods say Rome waits to anoint your divinity, to bestow upon Titus unimaginable wealth and power, you heard it even from the Hebrew God's priest, did you not? Yes, certainly you did hear it."

"My desire is the throne my father seeks and the woman he holds." Titus screams, banging his fist again; his eyes reddened in teary angst. "The throne and the woman - I want it?"

Aristomy bows again, then he confronts Titus. "The throne is closer to you now than before, it is empty. You will be Rome's savior. But first, two must be confronted. The one who threw a blade in your father, a Roman Commander, will be revenged. As well, you must deal with Rome's betrayer - for he is worse than the one who defends his Hebrew nation. Even a Roman can be crucified for betrayal and treachery of Rome. Does Titus understand my meaning?"

"You are a fool. I swore to my father no harm will come to Matarian's son. I won't do it."

"You won't have to. Allow me to speak and judge me how you will of it. I am in your hands?"

"Speak."

"The Jews. We make them do it all for us." His eyes glow with devious cunning. "We blame the Jews. They will do the needful with the one who pierced your father, to remove his shame. And there are Jews who will take care of Rome's betrayer… for a price. I will make sure your hands remain clean!?" He wipes his hand in the air. "Clean hands for Titus, your road will be freed to ascend. Then Rome will hand you all your desires to be fulfilled. The throne and the queen?"

"How - speak more?"

"See, I do this now before you with my life in your hands. See, I bring it before Titus…"

Aristomy places a small container covered with black cloth on the table before Titus. He unveils the container and opens its top to reveal a black, sealed royal case.

(39). CIRCUMCISION AND CRUCIFIXIONS.

In the Megiddo village, a young Hebrew lad, barely 15 and dressed in ceremonial attire, is seated on an ornate high-back chair in a hall where a 2,000 year old ritual is taking place. Hands from the crowded room lay a newborn child on his lap; chants of jubilation and rhythmic hand clapping resound. It is the celebration of the covenant, of a new born Hebrew male child, the mark of the covenant made with Abraham, the very first Hebrew.

It is also a day of foreboding in Judea, where the contrast of birth and death in this land again becomes poignant and stark. While Megiddo celebrates a new life, another town in Judea is contrasted by death and destruction.

At the entrance straight into Caesarea, the two side paths of the highway are lined with rows of crucifixions. The newborn child sways in his young apprehensive father's arm. There is a hum of joyous excitement in the hall.

Alexis approaches Hillel's school hall where the celebration is in progress. Hillel welcomes Alexis by his side as an honored guest to witness the event of circumcision. The school is packed with the Jews of Megiddo, with Bedouin and Arabian guests in the ceremony. Deborah and her friend Miriam stand arm in arm in the crowd.

"Offeh!" Miriam sighs towards Alexis, a Roman in their midst. "A spy from paradise comes."

"Teacher invited him."

The young man seated on the ornate chair holds the baby in his trembling arms, flanked by a densely packed crowd around him. As Hillel sharpens his blade above the baby's miniscule torso, amidst rising chants and devotional choruses, Deborah's gestures soothe the wincing, astonished face of Alexis as he beholds what is about to happen. A small shining blade moves with the surety of an experienced hand amidst a focused silence; Hillel's finger feeds a lick of wine into the baby's mouth, then a snip and scream is followed by a rowdy burst of prayer chants, gulps of strong drink and songs and dances.

A Jew grasps Alexis' hand, pulling him outside to the fields, inviting him to join in the Leaps of Joy dance, dragging him away.

On the highway before Caesarea Jews are being nailed to crosses; hands are pierced with the thuds of hammers on large iron nails.

In Megiddo, the men are locked together by their arms, moving in quick steps of a dance to a vigorous chanting. The dance steps graduate faster; the feet of every alternate man leaves the ground. They urge Alexis to lift up his feet from the ground, and soon Alexis and every alternate man is flying horizontally in the air, whizzing around in a circle. Then each is released and flung; Alexis lands in the far fields on the grass in delirious sweats of joy. Deborah races to Alexis lying on the grass.

"Praised-Be-The-Lord. That is its meaning. Return now my purse?"

"Do you love the man Simon?" He asks breathlessly: "Have you promised him?"

"Nothing to do with a Roman!" She backs, appearing caught off guard. "My purse!?"

"Then you are not in love with him. And it has much to do with this Roman?" There is the same devotional intensity in him; his outstretched hand is pleading her fervently. "We can go any place you want... even a new road?"

"New road!?" Deborah expresses shock and bewilderment of his empty hand held out to her; she stomps her foot on the ground. "This! This is my road, mad Roman!?"

"Our road?" His eyes are filled in wondrous excitement, his hand held towards her. "I know of no other road but ours?"

Deborah cups her mouth speechless, pointing at the ground. "My road is here!" She demands, stomping the ground. "My purse!?"

The hand of the Roman beacons, waiting on her. "Away from..."

The reveling ceases abruptly; Alexis and Deborah turn to confront Florian.

"Master, it is an order from Titus. I am to escort you to him for urgent matters. Come my honorable commander, come now with me in haste...?"

Alexis sees the frozen faces of the Jews; Roman soldiers appear in the distance.

"Here is your purse." He turns to Deborah. "I kept your poetry and left for you something in return - it belonged to my mother. Let it be as you have said is its meaning... Halle...luyah. Praise be the Lord?"

As Alexis leaves with Florian, Deborah opens her purse and is in trepidation what she finds. A sparkling blue stone is in her trembling palm; a blue heart shaped sapphire glows. A Jew casts a disdainful gaze; Miriam comes to her side.

"Halleluyah! Where is Simon, I don't see him?"

"He wanted me to see his house again. I did not go. My heart is still in moaning."

"The heart in your hand… is of a Roman!?"

Caesarea. In the Roman controlled base of Caesarea, the Town Square is littered with slaughtered bodies and destruction; masses of Hebrews are lined up in chains and surrounded by Roman soldiers. A great wailing fills the air.

(40). THE STRANGE LAWS OF THE JEWS.

The king is dead, suspected of being assassinated, and a fire rages in Rome, where chaos reigns. In Judea, Vespasian and Titus begin upholding the decrees left by Nero concerning the Jews with unbound determination. It is now the perceived road to glory for the Flavians, one of assuring victory for those who conquer Rome's greatest enemy and securing of the Temple wealth of the Jews to secure the throne. Although hated, Nero's orders concerning the Jews remains his legacy; it now becomes a widespread understanding by the Romans governing Judea, and an opportune time for Roman appointed Captains and Prefects to acquire private wealth; they understand any measures against the Jews will not result in punishments.

There is a disturbance in the holy city; a crowd of Jews address the new Roman Governor of Jerusalem, Gessius Florus, a Greek from Asia Minor who favored the Hellenists with solidarity by his own fierce disdain of the Jews, and renowned for his obsession of acquiring personal wealth. The Jews charge Florus of failing to report their complaint to Rome concerning the desecration of their rights in Caesarea, having paid him a large fee for this purpose. [88]

Eleazar and his warriors are watching the upheaval from a subterranean tunnel under the fortress. Florus addresses the Jews of his price.

"What you ask is not a small thing. To report your case to a magistrate in Rome of the matter in Caesarea will cost Judea twenty talents. Get it, Jews?"

"Twenty talents!?" The Jews are incredulous of the enormous price demanded of them. "Such a sum is unheard of!" The Jews wail rebelliously; they charge Florus of stealing from the temple treasury and aiding the Hellenists against them. "You seek to fill your own purse. We already pay you double the taxes required by Rome. Give us justice under Roman law, else we can make known your deeds to all."

"Robber of Rome!" The Jews chant loudly in the temple square. "You are a robber of the Temple treasury and of Rome!"

The Jews parade with bowls; they shout their charges in a ridiculing of Florus before all:

"Mercy, mercy! We beg for Florus! Let it be known Florus needs twenty talents for his own purse to report our case - else no Roman justice - no Roman law!"

Large crowds gather; there is a commotion. Florus, watching his ridicule before the Romans and Jews becomes so enraged he orders his soldiers to attack the Jews. There is a massacre - over 6,000 Jews fall; children are also cut down. Florus and his soldiers enter the temple treasury and take six basins of gold coins.

The Sicarii warriors urge Eleazar for action of the massacre of their kin. "We must save our people?! See, they kill even the Peace Party who side with Rome."

But Eleazar is calm and unmoved.

"The days of darkness and light are upon us." Ari declares.

"The Peace Party and all of Israel must learn…" Eleazar responds calmly to the Jews' beseeching him. "They must fully understand there can be no peace treaty with this enemy. Else Israel's bondage will not cease."

Eleazar turns away from the massacre. The Sicarii warriors he leaves behind voice their fury as the slaughter continues.

"He leaves us…" A Hebrew warrior watches their departing leader; they question his departure. "Maybe he has no plan for Israel?"

Another Hebrew, bloodied and battered: "As for me and my family, we will give our lives before sacrificing to Rome."

"All of us will give our lives!" The other Warriors shout out.

"Eleazar knows this." Ari responds, gazing at the departing Sicarii leader. "He knows why Rome appoints the likes of Florus… he knows what we face more than any other… he is more with us now than ever before."

As Ari speaks, Saul gestures his faces in an alarm, drawing aback, signaling a suspicious figure appearing; it is a Roman soldier who left his comrades and veered away.

"Who goes there - a Roman?" Saul draws his sword.

"No more…no more…" The soldier staggers, swaying his face in a foreboding.

But Ari is ever ready; he tosses a dagger before the Roman could reach Saul. The Roman's face sways in disbelief, then he drops with a blade inserted deep in his throat.

Saul races to the fallen soldier, dagger in hand, grasping his head to see if he is still alive, to find from him his story for approaching.

"No more…" The Roman soldier gasps, his blood gushing out his throat. "I am Gentis… of Londonium… what they do to you they did also to us… I will join you… let me join you… I beg you?" The soldier's head flops in Saul's hand; he lays dead.

Saul is shaken; he lays him down with tenderness; he kisses the dead soldier's forehead. He gestures to the other Jews; they come forth reluctantly, lifting the dead body and placing it behind a distance away in a ditch where many corpses of Jews lay in a mound. Saul approaches a silent, apprehensive Ari.

"Not your fault. You did not know."

"I was not thinking of myself. I was unsure just like you… I had to act."

"I would have done the same." Saul consoles Ari.

As Eleazar turns into a dark tunnel, his son's image comes before him. Amos is reading from a scroll, his face swaying; his finger pointedly at a portion of the scripture in his hand.

"Father, Abraham was told of this bondage even before Israel was born." Eleazar pauses as Amos urges him. "My Father, how can one be punished before they are born?"

Eleazar ponders his son's question and appears unsure how to answer him; he is hesitant. "It… it was told about the future, of things to come. Never fear my son, whatever our God, Blessed be His name, gives us is good."

Eleazar turns away again into another tunnel in the subterranean maze, pondering his son's question, murmuring to himself: "How can one be punished before they are born?"

"You have no answer for your son…" The man in a tunic is in the distance, staring at him, holding a torch of fire. "But you will… in its due time."

The man before Eleazar vanishes; his son Amos vanishes. Eleazar is in deep contemplation as he turns from Jerusalem and retreats deeper into a dark tunnel.

The Sicarii warriors watch helpless as Florus, sword in hand, pushes his soldiers to slay the Jews, bellowing:

"Kill them! Kill them!? I hate them! I hate Jews! Hear me Jews - I drink the blood of swine for breakfast!"

The strange laws of the Jews made their dress and diets varied from all other nations. Swine meat consumption was an important and cherished food of Roman cuisine, and its forbiddance by the Jews a major source of irritation; it became the chief mark of ridicule. It was seen as an emotive and curious affront to the Romans, one that would not be stemmed by any reasoning or forbearance. The Romans mocked the Jews with pig organs and pig blood, desecrating the Jews' strong aversions fostered by a mysterious law in the Hebrew bible.

The swine meat forbiddance is based on anatomical structures listed in the Hebrew Scriptures denoting which animals are allowed and which forbidden. The Hebrew bible gives two chief criteria applying which animals can be consumed: only those animals with split hooves and which chew their food in slow grinding [masticate]; a variation from the carnivorous tearing by claws and sharp protruding teeth. The pig is singled out in the Mosaic scriptures as unique among all the earth's millions of creatures: it is the only domesticated animal that has split moves but does not chew its food, thus highlighted to avoid its confusion by the pig's unique attribute of only one of the two required traits.

It is a mysterious law because such knowledge could not plausibly be possessed by mankind; its mystery stems from one animal being singled out as possessing a unique trait without the requirement of first examining all the millions of creatures upon the earth and how this was derived at. The cadence of knowledge of hidden things inherent in this law only increased the hatred and suspicion toward the sorcery of the Jews: none could negate this laws' veracity, inciting the Romans and Greeks as if they were specifically targeted by the Jews.

And for the Jews, such a law, as well other dietary laws which forbid consumption of shellfish, the mixing of meat and milk, and the restriction of all manner of work on the Sabbath, not only incurred a commercial and sustenance handicap, but marked them as being different from all others. Such laws rendered the devout Jews restricted from performing basic comradeship and pleasures of dining with non-Jews and was perceived as an insult, earning them hostility. Other Hebrew laws such as 'To love the stranger' [Duet. 10:19] and 'Not to wrong the stranger in speech or trade' [Ex. 22:20], left the Jews forever on an oxymoronic balancing act of assured bondage and awe.

(41). A TOWN CRIER.

Alexis is escorted by Florian as they ride out of Megiddo. Deborah and Miriam watch from a hillside in the distance as the two are departing.

"What will happen to him?" Deborah asks her wise friend.

"If he's a spy he will be fine. Otherwise…"

"Otherwise?"

"I don't trust his Roman security guard." She turns to Deborah, whose eyes are focused on Alexis. They hurl rumors and defenses at each other.

"You must know there is talk in the village of a Roman and a Jewish maiden."

"No talk of a Roman saving our Teacher?" Deborah counters.

"His Roman law marks all Jews as enemies…"

"…And the children he saved from a snake?"

"…One who disrespects the women's Mikvah."

"…Our Teacher blessed him and made him as a guest of honor."

Deborah appears in distant thoughts. Strange words come to her she cannot utter loud; they come pounding her mind. The Roman with his hand extended calls her:

'A new road…?' His hand waits on her. 'Our road?'

"What are you thinking now? Come on, we have work to do in the village." Miriam turns away, swaying her face in frustration.

Deborah remains, tarrying, monitoring the departing Alexis. Then she falls on her knees; she wails at the heavens in tears:

"I'm sorry?"

Strange words she cannot stop come to her again:

"This Roman seeks more than your forgiveness…"

"Forgive me?" She beseeches her God in angst and guilt.

"What does Helle-luya mean…?"

She shudders, looking around, then she hides behind the hills, fearing her people may hear her thoughts. She flees.

(42). SOME BELIEFS CAN BE DANGEROUS.

As Alexis and Florian approach Caesarea, they ride through rows of crucified Jews either side of the road. Alexis pans the dead, side stepping corpses on the tarred road he built. The crosses display long dead and dying bodies too forgone to rescue, their bones starting to show; wild birds are pecking out their flesh. Florian is worried by the silent, suppressed fury he perceives in Alexis and what awaits them ahead with Titus.

A Town Crier appears in the midst of the Jews hung on crosses.

"HEAR YOU ALL, HEAR!" A Town Crier is chanting in the midst of the Jews hung on crosses. "The emperor has decreed it! All Hebrew is forbidden. Jupiter shall be worshipped and honored - or heresy falls - on pain of death. It is decreed - it is Roman law before all. Hear you all Jews, hear you - give glory to Rome - and live!"

"I saw many torn apart by beasts at the circus and my countrymen reveled in it." Alexis tells Florian. "I saw no glory there."

"Master, my heart trembles of this meeting. I beg you, hold inside your words before Titus."

Alexis, noticing a man still alive on a cross and whispering for help, takes a flask from his saddle and brings it to him.

"Not for me..." The face on the cross pleads. "My wife, my children... give to them, save them... I beg you?"

"You!! Stop that - get away!" The Town Crier rushes at Alexis in a rage. "Who is this Jew loving Roman come here?"

The Town Crier plunges a spear into the Jew on the cross. Alexis rushes at the Crier in a furious attack mode; but Florian bear hugs and drags Alexis away.

"Roman traitors belong up there with the Jews." - The Town Crier's sword points at Alexis. Other guards appear.

"My master, I beseech you, I am made responsible for your safety. Stop! Cease now, let us not perish here on crosses like the Jews."

"What made us as beasts to kill the weak as our glory?" Alexis, clasped in Florian's powerful grip, screams at the Town Crier. "DO BEASTS HAVE GLORY!?" - He screams in his fury.

The pierced Hebrew on the cross raises his eyes to Alexis. There is a feeble nod of gratitude, then his head drops as he succumbs.

Florian pulls away his master, fearful of the encounter ahead of them in Caesarea. Florian is aware of Titus' deeds from the legendary stories by those who graduated from Rome's most elite war school...

The fourteen year old lad Titus grasps the sword given him by his War Master and approaches the three captive slaves before him. He slashes them repeatedly in an uncontrolled fury, long after they are disemboweled, axing their remains with his sword, screaming in a manic mode and unable to cease.

Then the War Master and the other students prevail upon him. They gaze at the blood smeared heaving lad in awe. The young Titus' tortured face quivers, teary droplets stream down his killer blue eyes as he stammers:

"The g'glory... I w'want it...?"

"The golden sword is yours" The War Master nods. "We honor Titus."

Alexis and Florian have arrived at the town square of Caesarea. The lad Titus, who was honored to become a mighty warrior and prophesized to have all his desires fulfilled, now stands in an ornate open-top war carriage. A red stone is studded to his ear and the tattoo of an eagle's head is etched on his right arm; he grasps a glistening sword of gold in his hand. Two barely clothed concubines sit beside his feet in his carriage floor. Titus and his carriage are surrounded by Roman guards. Titus pans the Jews hurdled in the town's centre, encircled by Rome's soldiers; rows of empty crosses stand in the background.

"Jews, hear me. A decree has been issued against your treason. You all wish to live, but…" He sways his face in a mocking disappointment. "We must honor Nero's orders, hmm?"

He glows triumphantly; now his glory is at hand, its path opened before him. Now it is his time to prove himself, as he did as a lad in war school and became honored with a golden sword. He pans the chained Jews and the soldiers waiting on him; his fingers caressing the handle of his golden sword.

Titus nods at the executioner and puts up two fingers and a thumb down, a code for two hundred to be crucified. The soldiers round up and drag the chained Hebrew men to the centre, amidst wailings from the women and children. Titus focuses on the women screaming for their husbands to be spared. He points at the women, nods at the executioner with a thumb down again.

Titus grasps the two concubines in his carriage by their manes, their hair in his fists, his face above the open top carriage monitoring the Jews bound in chains and their women wailing. He smirks menacing; he shudders as the wailing women are slain before their husbands struggling in iron chains and spears before them. He thrusts the concubines away from him, heaving in a manic satisfaction.

"DIE SCUM, DIE!" He screams in a rage. "Give me Eleazar, the one who pierced my father, else no one lives!? Caesarea is made a Roman base - this city is to be cleansed of Jews - for Romans!" He turns to the executioners. "Leave them up till all flesh leaves their bones. And put up a reward for the one called Eleazar. Dead or alive." He screams at the Jews. "Hear me Jews who choose life - as did one of your wise Hebrew priest - the reward for Eleazar can be yours too. Yours to choose, hmm!?"

The executioners approach the bound men; two executioners tend to each Jew. They slam the men with a heavy baton on their heads, ceasing the victims from jostling and struggling. Then they place the men on crosses that are piled on the ground. One executioner holds down the hands steady on the horizontal beam of the cross, the other pierces a large nail between the wrist and the elbow, between two hand bones, a point that won't loosen when the body drags down by its weight. Bulbous hammers pound the large nails three times and driven deep into the beams; fresh blood sprays on the executioner's hooded faces. Should the victims struggle or scream again, they are pounded on the head. Then both leg ankles are nailed to the vertical beam of the cross to cease their wriggling all about. The Roman crucifixion process is a silent procedure.

The crosses are then stood upright and inserted into pre-dug holes in the earth; a hammer thuds down the vertical beam. The Jews are crucified this way in well rehearsed expedient process by sets of two soldiers, enabling rows of many crucifixions in a single day. The standing crosses with hung bodies are left for many days in town squares to be seen as a warning for all who challenge Rome. The young Hebrew maidens are dragged away and hurled before the eager soldiers as prizes; the dead are swept up and dropped in a large mass burial ditch.

The crosses are re-used due to the lack of trees in this region. Crucifixion was primarily used for betrayers, those prophesying beliefs which contradicted or maligned Rome and as an instigation to acquire rebels protected by the people.

Titus now turns from the crucifixion process as Florian bows before him, presenting his master Alexis as Titus commanded him. Guards are examining them for weapons and removing their swords. Alexis pans the destruction in suppressed detached rage; Titus smirks at his disdain.

"Look who's here! Our pretty-pretty road builder - he has been busy elsewhere. We are pleased to see you again." He pats Alexis' horse. "Magnificent! Yet you travel without a concubine - what manner of Roman is this, hmm!?" The concubines giggle. There is an awkward silence. Titus now becomes menacingly serious as he approaches Alexis closely.

"Nero is dead. Vespasian is called to Rome. My father has placed all power in me. And you road builder, you serve Rome by serving me. Compri?"

"I became aware of Nero's death by the rejoicing of the people. Does it not mean Nero's orders are also done away with?

"Not so. They are set into Roman law and will be honored. There are two orders for you." He points to his caravan, dismissing the concubines. "In private audience…"

"Pay good heed to my words." Titus engages Alexis inside the caravan. "One: the road works must be expedited four fold, able to withstand crossings in and out of Judea. Three hundred Arabian workers will be added to your charge. New legions and heavy armory will arrive. Such knowledge is for your ears only. Two…"

A commotion interrupts Titus.

"Roman brutes - devil brutes you are! Sons of demons!" A Jew screams hysterically in the background "Murderers of children and women!" Titus extends a thumb-down sign; the one who is screaming at the Romans has his head slain to silence by the guards.

Titus sways his face at the slain Jew. "See, they become insane by their heresy."

"Smash their brains out, then charge them as being brain damaged?" Alexis nods in sarcasm.

Titus focuses on Alexis threateningly; then he begins to laugh, unable to suppress a devilish yelling, nodding, pointing finger at Alexis; his eyes welling in tears.

"Ha-ha! You are learning how Rome does it, pretty road builder!" He composes himself, becoming menacingly serious again. "Hear me now - the laughter is over. My father is upon his divinity. And I…" He beats his chest with his fist. "..I am prophesized to turn this destiny. We turn with Rome or we are broken by Rome. We must all make our choices. Life or…?" He points at the Jews on crosses.

"Your second order?"

"We Romans are sexual beings and love is our gifts from the Gods. Rome surely understands you well. Rome has no issue who a Roman beds with… woman, man, Roman, Greek, Briton, Arabian… even a Jew. My father is with a Jewess - the same was with King Herod and Agrippa. Nero also." A sarcastic nodding smirk comes: "Rome's pretty road builder must know, Rome loves the stranger too?" He brings his face closer up to Alexis. "But I remind you one Roman to another…" Suddenly, a shrill manic scream: "WE ARE ALL OF ONE ROAD FOR ROME!" He bangs his fist on the carriage window. "YOU FOLLOW!?"

"Am I guilty of poor workmanship?" Alexis responds unmoved.

"A Roman has no need for guilt. It's a Roman world - and Rome guides all our roads now. Yours too… don't you know it, Road Builder? Only be not confused, Rome is the true light of the nations - not those wretched ones on crosses!? ROME!? And here, I am Rome? Don't you know it, I am prophesied to be Rome's savior… anointed by all the Gods. Vouched by Roman Gods and the Hebrew God?" He moves closer to Alexis' face again in a threatening posture. "Hear me and hear Rome's truth. Rome finds an invisible God a suspicious thing. We Romans from old times prefer a divine king we can see, the truth of flesh and blood. Is that a crime? An unseen God can pierce you from behind the hills, then - vanish away, hmm?"

"Your second order?"

Titus whispers it in a growl, as if it appeared to him a wondrous secret being departed. "Secure for Vespasian the hidden location of this Hebrew Ark. It is the only prize to satisfy Rome's lust and restore honor to my father. You know the designs of such temples and monuments and where it can be hidden."

"Does Rome need another trophy in the circus? Rome has seen enough spoils to satisfy all her lusting. Romans do not know of any such Hebrew Ark and they care not for it - give them wine and beasts tearing up bound slaves instead?"

"Get it… I want it?"

"Glory to you, but this never worked when Babylon destroyed this temple. The Jews returned?" They stare at each other in a tense silence.

"Have you forgotten, Nero commanded us to end the Jews' rebellion and their heresy of our Gods and emperors - yours is to serve Rome, pretty boy? Nor will there be any return this time. I am Titus - a Roman. Is Rome not the Greek and Babylon's ruler, hmm?"

"Tell me, mighty Titus. Do the Jews not follow Rome's laws? Yes they do and they would serve Rome even better if allowed them their ancient beliefs…what is Rome's issue then with such a small nation of old?"

Titus sways his face menacingly. "As long as these Jews insult Rome's emperors before the nations, the both cannot be. I desire this Ark paraded in a Roman circus in honor of Rome's gods… and as a warning to others in the empire. Tell me now, can I trust you in this sacred task - or will you bore me with more of this region's camel drops?"

"I have never been to Jerusalem. How should I know of this Ark's location."

"No one knows, no one will talk, they allow none in their temple's secret places. They have hidden it away and you Alexis must unlock their secrets. Play no games with me anymore - I gave you a soft task, no war, and you know why?" He nods smirking. "Soft task, pretty road builder?"

"I asked no favors. Your father appointed me in the work I chose."

"So choose - mingle with them, dress like them, even smell like them. Go, fill all your desires with any you choose - it is given you!? But you are a son of Rome and Rome orders you to seek this Ark. Follow my orders - or will you spend more of my time as a Jew loving betrayer of Rome?"

The screams and wailings of Jews being dragged and nailed on crosses interrupt the discussion again. Alexis peeks outside the curtain of the carriage.

"I will have Rome's orders when I speak with Vespasian - he gave me my appointment in Judea…"

Titus sways his face. "My father is called to Rome. I give orders in Judea." He waits impatiently, challenging.

"You want me to dishonor Caesar - even when Judea's king Herod ignored Caligula's insane law of heresy!?"

"Insane law? Is that so?" Titus grips his sword and holds it against Alexis' chest in a menacing fury. "Then learn how Rome holds her power in these savage lands…" Titus kicks open his carriage door and races to the captive screaming Jews. He slays two Hebrew women wailing at the feet of their husbands, piercing them repeatedly after they lay dead. He staggers back to Alexis with a dripping bloody sword and heaving with a dire message.

"Tell me Alexis…" He wipes his sword deliberately slow. "Insane law… or my duty to destroy Rome's enemies? ALL of them? Any place I CHOOSE? Any ONE I choose?" He brings his blood soaked finger to his mouth, sucking on it, smirking, glaring at Alexis calmly; waiting.

Alexis and Titus exchange challenging gazes at each other; Florian winces in trepidation. Then…

"I will do what I can to fulfill your two orders." Alexis responds to the ultimatum and its consequences should he fail Titus. "The road works - and I will find all I can about this relic of the Ark. In honor of your circus amusements. Will that be all from the one who will be Rome's savior?"

Titus has a wicked smile of triumph. "You love her dearly, hmm?" Titus wipes his bloody sword, flicking blood in the air as he speaks. "But Mars shines for me, and Rome's truth is before us. You see…" He points at the dead Jews. "Some beliefs can be dangerous." He gestures at the Jews being nailed and their women screaming. "Belief - the easiest emotion to exploit. For the common people it is as a divine truth, for the wise as a guile to secure loyalty, and for Rome's rulers… it is useful? And I…" He heaves in a menacing determined focus into Alexis' eyes. "I intend to use it against Rome's enemies. Rome understands about beliefs in all nations, once it takes hold, they follow as the sheep. I will give them a belief. A Roman one?

"If you have finished with me, I will depart." Titus and Alexis are locked in silent challenge.

"You leave when I dismiss you." Titus sways his face, smirking. "Now I have something for you. Something to save your favorite Jews. Come, tonight I shall wait for you. Tonight we dine as true Romans, with Roman maidens feeding us - pomegranate wine and red meat - food for the gods - and red Roman men."A crazed smirk. "Dismissed for now?" He wipes entrails from his sword; a crazed smirk at Alexis.

Florian bows, pulling away Alexis. Florian now understands Alexis is able to risk all and forfeit his life for a Jewess; and that he has a hidden disdain of his own nation. He wonders to himself if Alexis is a betrayer, the common response to one displaying a variant view from other Romans. Florian ponders of Alexis' mother if she was a Jew, for many Greeks and Romans had such offspring. Florian ponders why Vespasian cared for Alexis so strongly, and why his son shows such disdain - was the son jealous of it?

(43). BETHLEHEM - A HOUSE DESTROYED.

South of Jerusalem, Aristomy enters the quiet town square of Bethlehem; he is followed by Roman soldiers. He stops before the houses and shops and conducts disrupting searches.

"Jews!" He shouts. "Nero has ordered all your sorcery forbidden! On pain of death. You have been warned - no more emblems of sorcery on your doors, garments or heads. From tomorrow such houses will be burned down!"

"But Nero is dead, my Master…" - a soldier offers.

"Nero's orders are sealed as Roman law. I have seen the royal scroll."

In a deserted hill, Ari approaches Eleazar in searing angst and anger.

"The Roman devils are going town to town, killing and burning - they attack the weak, they know Jerusalem is safe from her walls."

Eleazar sways his face in negation. "Jerusalem is being weakened from any outside attack. First they destroy the white of the egg that holds the yoke, then the center. Such is Rome's design of destruction."

Ari appears in shock of Eleazar's words, staring him in disbelief.

"Now you must stop your work of town watching." Eleazar orders him. "Go and talk to Simon - get him to me if you say you have softened him. Go now!"

(44). A NAZERITE VILLAGE.

Deborah's usual route home is now a new tarred highway. She pauses, searching the new surrounds. In the distance, Roman soldiers appear; they wave her to stop, advancing with a lusting. Her trembling hand moves to the handle of a blade hidden in her dress. An intuition tells her to look for an alternate path. Then she spots a Gazelle in the distant dirt track; she races away following it. The Romans give chase; then they soon abandon their pursuit, fearing to venture the dirt tracks outside their new roads.

The gazelle leads Deborah to a small village tucked away in a hidden location. She enters its gate, breathless from the Roman pursuit. Inside she finds a girl drawing water from a well.

"This is a Nasserite village. Are you lost? Drink water, come with me."

Ari and Saul again approach Simon. They find him on the front porch of his newly built home; they approach him cautiously. He appears forlorn, his face reddened and anxious and staring at the ground. They bring with them gifts of cooked foods and grape juice; they lay the pots on his porch.

"From my mother's hand. Know now my brother, there is no shortage of fine Hebrew maidens for a prince such as you." Ari says. "It is what Eleazar answered me when he saw me grieving for your pain."

"There is none in the land better than you" Saul enjoins. "We are with you all the way and with our lives. Be free from all your pain we beg our brother, for you have been saved from an unworthy woman who knew not your worth. This is a blessing, not a curse."

Simon moves towards a palm tree, gripping its two main branches and tearing it from its roots. His comrades move away, unable to withstand his wrath and power. He uses the tree as a battering ram, tearing away the walls and rooms. When the house is collapsed in a pile, he screams so loud, a horse begins to neigh in fear, then it shudders and faints by the wrath of his screams; Saul attends his horse.

"With a Roman spy!" He tosses the tree on the shattered house and bellows in agony. "How can she find love in those who want to destroy us - how!?" His eyes are red in fury, his large muscled arms raised to the heavens shining in perspiration.

"Selah! He is with us now." Ari nudges Saul, whispering. "And I know how we must deal with the one who betrayed Simon… and her people."

"I know how we must deal with the Roman spy." Saul assures him.

As they return to their base, the lad Boaz appears before them. His face is inclined at the skies, his hand churning a sling in the air. He lets go. The stone soars toward an eagle gliding in its cross-path. The stone misses its target, now by a closer margin. He turns to Ari and Saul.

"I'm a man now - a Sicarii like you. Ask Eleazar."

"Sicarii don't miss." - Ari reminds the lad.

(45). INFILTRATE THE JEWESS.

Alexis attends Titus' invitation. Erotically clad Roman maidens serve food and wine.

"If this ark is found, will this war with the Jews be over?"

"Surely you know Rome's laws are honored by all… all but the Jews. They imagine an unseen God allows them to disrespect all our divine emperors. They imagine an unseen God won't offend anyone, very clever of them. Rome will end their treacherous game."

"What treacherous game do you mean - this has been their belief before Rome was born? So I see this is not about any relic you desire, nor did Nero mention any such Ark - yet you say I must follow his royal commands. I will speak as a road builder. The Jews are excellent in building works - imagine now a great monument in Rome, or even of honoring your father, built by the hands of the Jews. Perhaps they will honor Vespasian by naming their children after him, as they did with Alexander?"

"And have my father also assassinated?" Titus smashes a jug to the floor. "Rome is disgusted of their laws - every nation in the empire is. Invisible Gods do not exist - Rome does!? Our road builder must understand fully this is a war for our beliefs - sacred Jupiter or death - so choose your God, road worker?" He pulls a maiden on his lap. "I show him a path to glory, the most beautiful of women, but his Roman manhood is weakened by a peasant Jewess. Here…" He throws a silver coin at Alexis. "They have covered the Roman name of Judea with the name of Israel. The bastards hate us!"

The coin is embossed with the words:

'FOR THE FREEDOM OF ZION' and 'JUDEA SHEKEL'. It covers the face of Rome's Emperor.

"Every mother loves her child and all people love their heritage. Judea is a Roman name taken from the Greeks. Israel is Hebrew. If the Jews are allowed to keep their beliefs, we can ask in return other works of them, like a great temple in Rome - glory to Vespasian, Glory to Titus. But you say this is not about any Ark but the old beliefs of this people. Caesar never saw it that way?"

"What has blinded you, don't you love Rome's women anymore? Look here Alexis…" He exposes the breasts of the pleasure maiden sitting on his knees. "Ever see more desirous meat than Roman?"

"The Jews are part of the empire, and they have rights under Roman law. The disruption of the law will only cause other nations to question the rights Rome gave them. Other nations will also rebel. I have said my piece. I will take my leave now." The concubines clutch onto Alexis; enticing him not to leave.

"Not yet… I told you I have something for you? An opportunity to test your Jews, a means to grant them pardon of the dog that tore my father's leg. I - only I, not you, can offer Rome's pardon for this people!?" Titus places a black case before Alexis. "Get this to the house of Eleazar. No one else must get hold of it. Do not open the royal seal. You know how to get this to him."

"Rome has conquered many nations with many beliefs… all are tolerated, except this one small province. Why is mighty Rome so worried by the Jews? And is this you give me truly your Roman peace offer?

A menacing smirk comes on Titus' face, a deep chagrin suppressing his killer gaze. He slams the royal case in Alexis' hands:

"Infiltrate the Jewess - for Pax Romani!?"

(46). THE TEMPLE OF JUPITER.

A drunken Titus is now alone in his dining room; the concubines have been dismissed and Alexis given his leave with a black case in his hands. Titus winces and staggers as his imagination soars, a tendency developed as a lad in war school. He again hears voices in his head.

From Rome, Vespasian communicates with his son Titus in Judea via an 'astral' exchange, for he was a suspicious one from an ancient village, also possessing dark powers from his Gods. Titus sees a vision hovering; his father is before Jupiter's image, engulfed in a bubbling, frothing green mist. Titus is awed.

"My son." Vespasian communicates from across the seas in Rome to his son in Judea. "A new Temple shall arise here to glorify our Gods. Jupiter, the God of the skies, will send you the power of Mars… the God of War, the protection against all who ever challenge Rome." A Roman sword of fire, the symbol of the might of Mars, hovers above Vespasian.

Titus gazes in awe of the voices and images rising in his mind; it is before him now.

"And see, I have already made sacrifices to Neptune, God of the sea and the brother of Jupiter…" Titus now sees a bearded giant holding a Tri-star lance emerging out of the bubbling oceans.

"And the vestal virgins, the pure ones, they have sprinkled sacred waters on our temple's foundation stone…" Dancing vestal maidens with leafy crowns now appear around his father.

"My son - Jupiter's temple shall rise on Capitolina Hill, the highest point in Rome." Vespasian stands before Jupiter. "All the omens say we, the Flavians, are appointed by Rome's gods to prevail over the Hebrews. Bring me their treasury, their works of gold and their Hebrew Ark to display before Rome - tear out the land and find it. This Ark is the source of the Jews' power - our Philistine brothers knew of it… the Greeks also know of it…"

Titus' drunken eyes wince as he now focuses on a vision of his father retreating, turning, approaching Bernice; she sits on a Roman throne at the raised marble platform of the hall of Vespasian's royal abode. Titus lusts after Bernice's decadent attire; his desire for the Queen is all consuming and there is no forbearance of his father anymore. He wants her more than his life. If love and desire are the foods given by the Roman gods, then his father's mistress will fulfill all his desires, as foretold by the Hebrew oracle giver. Bernice will surely accept this of him, she secretly waits for him; Titus convinces himself, for she knows the Roman doctrines of love as no other. He gazes at the queen in wanton desire.

Bernice engages Titus tauntingly, languidly; she knows him as a beast of desire, that he wants her now more than his father ever could. Bernice raises her feet before Vespasian; he kneels before her. She smirks at Titus, her foot in his father's palms, her finger pointing at herself, nodding, indicating her dominance. She taunts the lusting Titus in askance as his father adores her feet; she is heaving in ecstasy.

"Have you forgotten?" Titus screams in rage. "The oracle said all my desires shall be fulfilled - you both heard it before all!?" Titus taps his fist on his chest in fury. "My desires, what are my desires, have you all so soon forgotten the words of the oracle given you… and upon me!?" Titus staggers drunkenly to his father's empty chair. As the image of his father worshiping Bernice flashes before him, as Bernice taunts him by her manner of deliberated ecstasy, he screams aloud, his sword hoisted in the air, both hands grasping it:

"My desires - where is it - show me!? Show me!? Let me show you…"

His raised sword crashes down, slashing the chair before him till it crumbles in broken piles. "My desires - where is it - is it here!?" He continues slashing his sword into the purple drapes on the window. "Or here!?" Then he nears his father's bedroom, his sword breaking up the opulent bed to shreds, declaring his ascendency in a rage:

"Hear me, my father… you were only made a bridge to me, only a stepping stone. Your time has passed. Therefore the oracle rested on me… ON ME!? Hear me now, my father. Bernice is my desire, she is mine. NOT YOURS!?"

The drunken, fiery eyes wince. Bernice taunts Titus, a wicked challenging laugh as his father worships her feet. Titus pounds his fists to his chest, staggering aimlessly in tears; he hugs his golden sword close to his chest; his jowls trembling. Then he staggers in an uncontrolled delirium, stumbling, falling to the ground on his head with a thud in a drunken stupor, his face immersed in his stomach's outpouring; unmoving and stilled.

Bernice is smirking devilishly and triumphantly.

"Rome… mine… mine."

(47). THE JEWISH REVOLT BEGINS.

Following the massacre of Caesarea, the mayor Aristomy has moved residence to the outskirts of Jerusalem, a more protected and safer place; it is now Rome's strategic prized fortress and heavily secured with Roman legions. The Jerusalem Fortress is the most protected and largest monument on the face of the Earth. The two infiltrating Sicarii have a strong hand with then as they now venture into this impregnable fortress guarded at every entrance by the Roman legions.

Simon, Saul and Ari have entered the fortress via a secret submerged tunnel. They approach Aristomy's mansion in the dark of night. Simon disables three guards, then he blows open the iron bars of a window with his fist. Saul and Ari climb inside stealthily, confident with Simon covering the house from outside. Ari's Sicarii dagger first pierces Aristomy's throat, pinning him to a wooden beam; Aristomy sees the slaying of his entire household, in silence, blood gushing from his throat. Ari ends his struggles with a hand jab on the embedded dagger. The three Sicarii then pour combustible oil on the slain bodies and the walls. Saul throws down a torch and a great fire lights up the night.

The assassination of the Roman mayor marks the initiation of Eleazar's revenge of the massacre in Caesarea. And that Simon has joined with the Sicarri.

In the same night of Aristomy's elimination, in the hillsides surrounding Jerusalem's fortress, dark silhouettes of Sicarii warriors are descending down into craters hidden in the hill tops; the craters lead into secret dark subterranean tunnels under the fortress grounds. They proceed via the pathways lit by their comrades bearing torches of fire; weapons are handed out to the incoming warriors. The Sicarii leader's mission is daring and bold, one the Romans will not anticipate.

Ari and Saul now proceeded elsewhere from Eleazar's temple mission, as was their pledge to revenge the Roman spy who betrayed Israel. A Sicarii pledge cannot be made falsely; vows are holy, the third law in The Ten Commandments. The great revolt of the Jews against Mighty Rome, the darkest force Israel faces, has begun.

In the Nasserite village, Deborah is fare-welled by the girl and her father.

"You are not a stranger here" The girl hands Deborah a flask of water and a pouch containing bread and sun-dried fruit. "Come again."

"You gave a stranger shelter when death was all around and nowhere to turn."

"The Lord loves the stranger and commanded us to do so also." Her father has parting words. "When danger comes, and it surely will, our salvation will be across the Jordan. We have been foretold of it."

Deborah removes the blue sapphire from her purse. "You see this stone… keep it for your daughter, I beg you?"

"O no my child, this is not what is meant by love of the stranger. True love is for naught. See, like you, I too come from the tribe of Judah…"

"Oh!? But…" Deborah is bewildered and awed the man knows of her family tribe. "But how did you know?"

The father turns to the skies, his hands raised and extended:

"And Moses said unto the children of Israel… 'See, the LORD hath called by name Bezalel the son of Uri, the son of Hur, of the tribe of Judah. And He hath filled him with the spirit of God, in wisdom, in understanding, and in knowledge, and in all manner of workmanship. And to devise skilful works, to work in gold, and in silver, and in brass, and in cutting of stones for setting, and in carving of wood, to work in all manner of skilful workmanship." [Ex. 35/30].

The man's eyes are smiling; assuring her. "I know it as my own forefathers who carried this tribe's name. I shall always remember it, of my name and yours. Hur is the first of artisans who worked with his hand to create wondrous things - such gifts are given me also, yet in far smaller measure. Hur also held up the hand of Moses in his last days to keep it steady when war came. Hur is a goodly name of Israel, my child - fear not, wear it with honor?"

"Then…" Deborah is in tears now, understanding she is before a man of great wisdom and skills. "Then make me of this an amulet, for you are a worker of silver and gold and you understand such shining stones." She places the stone in his palm. "Let the grace of your hands fashion this stone for me, however you decide. Make it a sacred thing - else I fear it will fall in the hands of killers."

"Oh!" The girl gazes at the stone. "It is shaped like a heart and it shines like the color of the Heavens! Abba, how can such a thing be made more beautiful?"

As Deborah mounts her horse and rides away, the girl's father holds the stone clasped in his palm. He whispers to himself Deborah's words.

"Make it a sacred thing…"

In a dungeon of Caesarea, a disheveled man in the dim prison cell gazes out his small barred window, entranced in prayer and visions. Suddenly, his prison door swings open and a guard with a heavy rung of keys addresses him.

"By the order of Vespasian, the court in Rome will judge you as you requested. Arise now and face your destiny - you leave tonight by sea. You owe this favor to the Queen Bernice. [89]

(48). THE DANCE OF BERNICE.

As dusk falls in the hills of the Galilee, Titus arrives in his war chariot at Bernice's Palace. Bernice's guards bow; they move away for the great warrior. Inside, the maids bow; they escort Titus to the queen's private domain of provocative Hebrew-Roman lush décor of wealth. He finds Bernice in a focused attention of a golden pot set on a high stand.

Bernice pours herbs and incense powders into the pot, stirring with her fingers, then raising handfuls and releasing it back into the mix; a swish of fumes crackle as the pot heats from a small fire below it. Titus gestures for the maids to leave.

"My father bestowed his legacy unto me. I am now heir apparent. But more than any kingdom I desire the queen Bernice."

Her fingers continue mixing her powders; her back to him. "Did your father not tell you why I left him?"

"Father wanted your wealth. I want you."

Bernice turns around, measuring Titus' proposal. She leans on a draped marble pillar in a measured pose, a slit in her provocatively sparse evening gown revealing traps of hidden beauty. She approaches the enticed warrior with sensual, inciting whispers.

"I want also. I want… Queen of Rome?"

"Why then am I here before you, most desirable glorious Queen - am I not the road to Rome?"

"I never trusted your father." She blows fire into her golden pot; fumes swirl. "Why then should I trust his son?"

"You vouched the Hebrew priest's oracle before all. The oracle giver said all my desires will be fulfilled. You are my only desire. Hear me wondrous queen, I beg you. Now I am but a blood stained brute, but with a Goddess as you by my side... together we shall ascend the steps of glory as one. I need only to prevail over a colony of Hebrew peasants. My destiny is assured. Be my queen... in Rome?"

"Did you imagine I would not know a man's desire for me? Before your own father you lusted on me... and he desired me more than any other." The blackened paint around her eyes make her gaze glowing, piercing into him with hidden secret things. She approaches closer, blowing her fumes of incense at him... "I expected you?"

"Then you know I desire you more than life?"

She nears the great warrior with the golden pot raised in her hands.

"It is forbidden to mix such magical herbs and incense as I have." Her closed eyes are focused distant. "And it is forbidden to raise the powers of such powders with urine, lest one becomes overwhelmed." Her eyes open; she engages him now. "But this law is only due for the temple. Be still now. I will measure your truth in the fumes of pure frankincense. First, I must shut your eyes... to open your mind?" She lays a cloth over Titus' face.

Bernice oscillates around the warrior, his face now covered with a dark purple cloth. She kneels on a rug before him, laying down her pot on the floor. She tugs at a tassel and the curtains drop down around them amidst swirling incense fumes.

"Does the mighty warrior understand...?" She whispers it. "He has to win... else I lose queen of Rome? If yes, then my truth will be opened to you."

"Give me your truth. You have mine." A blind-folded Titus answers.

Under the dropped curtains, Bernice now covers her own face in a veil.

"Now I will reveal my truth to you." She uncovers Titus face. "Open your eyes." Titus sees a veil that is partially covering Bernice's face, showing him only the right side of her half face profile: a Roman eagle in black onyx dangles as an ornamental droplet on her cheek, fastened from her right eye brow by a golden thread. The Roman ensign sways on the uncovered half side of her face.

"The Jews are small in number, less than a tenth of Rome..." She presents only her half face to Titus; inclined tauntingly. "But know who you are dealing with... peasants you say... victory assured?" Bernice now slowly turns her face posture around, then removing the veil, displaying now the left half profile of her face to him; it bears a droplet of the Menorah, the symbol of Judea's temple.

"Look now at my other side" The Hebrew symbol attached to her eye brow now sways on the right side of her face. "What do you see? Might... or mind? Rome excels in her valor and her power and her magnificent brutality... all the world has seen it. Whereas the Jews, so small in number, yet mighty in their minds and history... can prevail Rome! Have you never considered it, my great warrior?" She sways the eagle and the Menorah on her face tauntingly, then she passes to him the pot of fumes.

"This!" He raises his fist and strong arm, swaying it. "The language of might is here, my precious queen, in these arms, to serve you?"

"Aah, yes! The mighty eagle towers over all. Yet the eagle cannot miss, for he is soon spent... then even the sparrow goes by him with no fear. But I see both faces of the coin!? Now, some history lessons for my mighty warrior..."

She claps her hand three times; exotic music emerges. Bernice rises, initiating her dance to provocative music beats, her exotic movements aligned to the history lessons inclined at Titus. She raises both hands, gesturing fingers tauntingly at him.

"The Jews have large books of the most supreme writings of their history... made before Rome was yet born. They survived many nations like Rome..." She leaps on the table in a taunting stance, accounting...

"Canaan? Egyptus? Phoenicia? And Sumeria?" She sways on each name. "The Amorites? And what of the Hittites? The Medianites? The Moabites? And the Jebusites? What of the Philistines and their mighty stone god Dagon...?"

Bernice pauses to inhale; she blows fumes on Titus; he nods acknowledging her history lessons." What of Babylonia? And Persia? And the Hellenists? Do you not see the Jews were tested before all those mighty nations... for the same reason Rome tests them now? But where are all of those nations today?" She draws away from his lusting reach. "Where are they - tell me!?"

"Wondrous Queen. I am not another nation. I am Titus?"

"And where would Titus be should the Jews prevail, as they did with the Greek empire before you? It can happen again, mighty warrior. UNLESS!?" She pauses to inhale. "You heed me now!" She commands him. "Even as your father heeded me and waited on MY vouching of a Hebrew priest!? Play me not for your own glory young warrior, for I hold all your desires in my hand." She unfolds her open palm before the great warrior. "It was I who made your father keep the priest alive…I made your desires to be accounted? And I expected you to come to me!?" She sways her face, dangling the conflicting droplets before Titus. "You amaze me. How can you be inclined for and against two opposing nations?"

"I learnt well from Rome. I go where the road leads me. Now all your roads lead here… to me. Incline now to my words of truth, even as your father harkened to me, even as did King Agrippa, my own brother" A wicked, daring sneer. "You too hearken now to a Goddess before you. For a Goddess is always behind the emperor, glorifying him as only a Goddess can… fulfilling all his desires. Can one be mighty and not know of this truth?"

"Why then am I here before you? Let me glorify you this night, to honor you… to worship you?" Titus extends his hand to her, revealing a blood red ruby the size of an onion in his open palm.

Bernice approaches closer, entranced by the red over-sized stone offering glittering in Titus' open palm. She grasps the red ruby and holds it closely to her breasts, as if savoring its powers in a vile ecstasy. Her hand holds up the fuming pot in a triumph, the other hand pressing the red stone on her breast.

"If I have not craved glory… then glory itself has craved me!"

She approaches closer, her foot raised; she dangles her slipper at Titus seductively, letting it fall away on the rug before him.

"I am already a queen and my treasury is full of fiery stones. From you I want more. Much more…"

She performs a perfect waist bend towards the floor, then she rolls up her sheer folds of fabric to reveal an ankle, a naked knee, then a silky white thigh. Titus drops on his knees mesmerized and lusting. She stamps her painted foot on Titus' bosom. On her toe is a ring with a Roman seal.

"Make this your seal of glory, the place for your stone. Choose your destiny well my great warrior, for this is the true battle field…" She waits on him, naked foot on his bosom.

"Agreed. In Rome my Goddess shall be my queen." He removes one of her sandals from her foot. "This shall be the token of it - we each keep one sandal. It shall be our covenant - never to break." Titus slides her sandal in his coat, then he prostrates to kiss his Goddess' naked foot, as once his father did. The great warrior worships the ring on Bernice's toe.

"Rome… Rome…" As the warrior mounts her in his uncontrolled lusting, Bernice shuts her eyes, screaming. "MINE! MIIIINE…!?"

The massive red ruby bounces in her raised palm. Incense fumes swirl.

(49). ELEAZAR'S REVENGE.

The lad Boaz brings a coded message to Menahem. "Eleazar says the dinner table is ready for the guests." Menahem nods.

In the dark of the night, via a maze of underground tunnels, the Sicarii warriors have successfully entered the temple fortress undetected. And they have disguised themselves as the Peace Party, dressed in the white dress attire known to Rome as obedient non-combatants. Menahem examines their decoy white tunics as they thrust forth in the subterranean pathways. The figures in white emerge as ghosts out of the tunnels in the dark breaking dawn. Eleazar guides them with nods and hand sways of his attack plan.

As the sun rises, the Sicarri warriors mingle with the Roman soldiers and the Peace Party Jews, using this decoy in moving freely among the unsuspecting Romans and Jews.

Thereby, the Romans start dropping with lightning quick jabs of daggers; protruding then hidden in the Sicarri garments. The Romans fall without a notion of who was doing the killings or from where it comes. The Sicarii daggers move too swiftly for the naked eye, piercing, then hidden swiftly again, that none see any weapons; they see only Roman soldiers falling.

While the Romans assist their fallen, not knowing who the assassins are, there is a rush of the hidden and ready groups of Sicarii warriors that have mingled among the Jews, charging from four sides upon the dazed and bewildered Roman soldiers. The Sicarii warriors massacre the entire Roman legion of 6000, inflicting poisonous jabs from their daggers till the late evening; they collect a bounty of Roman war weaponry, including golden swords, shields, spears, batons and knives.

The Sicarii warriors now face another formidable battle; they confront the Jews of two opposing groups with different agendas than the Sicarii's unyielding intolerance of Rome. The forces of Gischala and Giora have barred the Sicarii way, surrounding the temple with armed war-ready Jews, thereby posing a dilemma for the Sicarii; for the Jews are forbidden to carry irons of war within the holy temple vicinity. But the Sicarii, now emboldened by their elimination of any Roman protection, see this as their choice opportunity of succeeding the two opposing groups.

Now the Sicarii warriors understand Eleazar's warning of all laws will be set aside till their freedom of belief is achieved - even they must now battle their kin by such an oath. They charge in hot fury upon their brethren, even profaning the temple laws where irons of war are forbidden.

A great slaughtering of Jews by Jews gives the Sicarii a decisive win. There is the blood of their kin on the Sicarii swords as their hands rise proclaiming their victory. The Sicarii thereby win the control of the temple fortress from Rome and from their Jewish foes. Many of Sicarii look at each daunted and guilt ridden; they know they have committed grievous transgressions before their Holy Temple.

The Sicarii mission to oust the Romans from Judea continues. Outside the Jerusalem fortress on the highway along the Galilee, Alexis' road works camp is quiet this night. Saul and Ari are covertly approaching between Alexis' workers and their weapons storage, thereby separating them apart. They signal a code and a dozen Sicarii warriors storm. Alexis' entire drunken group of workers is slain before any opportunity to arm themselves.

"This road leads to Jerusalem!" Ari's blood stained dagger rises in his hand "Not to Rome!"

Saul, who searches the slain, sways his face in disappointment.

"He is not among the dead - the Roman spy lives."

(50). HOUSE OF HILLEL.

News of the capture of the temple fortress by a rebel Jewish group and the great massacre of the Roman legions headed by Rome's most wanted fugitive spreads as a wildfire among the Jews and the Romans. There is trepidation and a certain satisfaction with the Jews. They whisper to each other:

"The holy city is returned to us. Blessed be Eleazar."

"Amen, Amen!"

As Alexis rides toward Megiddo, a sealed royal case in his saddle, he ponders the demands of Titus to cease the war with the Jews. He recalls Titus' words:

"We must all make our choices…"

"A means to grant Rome's pardon…"

"Infiltrate the Jewess for Pax Romani…"

Alexis wonders if he is a mad Roman, as Deborah once applied to him, and if his quest to save the Jews by a dangerous balancing with his nation and the Jews will bear fruit, for he is suspected of being a traitor by both. He arrives at the house of Hillel with eyes darting for the owner of a white horse with brown patches; he looks every which way for their eyes to engage an instant.

Inside Hillel's house, a meeting of Megiddo's men is in process; Simon is also present. There is an abrupt pause of silence as Alexis enters and declares his opening words:

"I am not proud to be a Roman anymore."

"We know about Caesarea." Hillel pours water for Alexis, a tradition of welcome in this region. "We try to keep such news from the women and children. The first lesson is not to show panic in the village - it produced ill deeds and errors."

"Does Israel need lessons from a Roman?" Simon's gaze is not welcoming; he now knows of his quest for Deborah.

"Perhaps you should safeguard yourself now Alexis, for you have done enough for us. The Passover festival is at hand and there is no place to go other than Jerusalem."

"Oh no! Jerusalem is the last place to think of! Eleazar has taken over the temple and issued a challenge of war. Roman legions and new war machines will arrive…"

There is a tense pause amidst hisses and whispers of new war machines.

"So how is a Roman not proud to be a Roman anymore - who gave him such knowledge for the enemy?" Simon is suspicious of Rome's new legions arriving.

"Titus summoned me. He ordered I hasten the road works fourfold to carry heavy weapons. Fleets of shiploads will come."

A pause of silence. Then whispers erupt from the Jews:

"The brutes will destroy us all" - "Our towns, our families will be slaughtered."

"Those who lie make sure their evidence is far away." Gilad, Simon's comrade, sneers. "No Roman ships come."

"If they come or not…" Simon now shows interest in Alexis' words, aligning it with the warning of Ari and Saul. "Your Roman forces cannot breach Jerusalem's walls."

"Then you have no idea of Rome's new machines." Alexis answers. "Rome was not sleeping while you tended your olive groves. Rome has been busy conquering nations such as yours. Hear me." Alexis turns to the gathering. "Jerusalem's walls will be crushed like the olives you trample upon - no force can stop Rome. I saw great evils by Titus… daughters taken before fathers, children's limbs torn before their mothers, your men strung on crosses to die slowly. Great evils that made me ashamed to be a Roman - it is why I am here - to talk to you all."

Hillel is ashen faced and aghast at Alexis' report. "We have no other place to go. The Passover festival approaches and all Jews will go to the temple, as they have for a thousand years."

"Oh no! That is the last place to go now? Rome's legions will surely come there."

"A million will fill the temple grounds." Hillel responds. "It cannot be stopped…"

"Then you have to make some compromises first. Otherwise…"

"No compromises with Jerusalem… or our beliefs." Simon anticipates him.

"Painful compromises…" Alexis sways his face. "Regretfully."

Deborah, in a back room, watches covertly through a curtain.

"What do you mean by painful compromises?" Hillel asks.

Deborah is enjoined by Miriam; they eaves-drop the discussion.

"I have a plan. You all can decide its value." Alexis pauses, he struggles with his words: "Give Rome the Ark as a gesture. And tell Rome you will remove Eleazar from Jerusalem and deliver him… this is the man who destroyed a Roman legion and many Jews. This act of remorse can save your nation from Rome's anger - I believe it strongly?"

A heavy silence falls; faces turn and wince in revulsion of Alexis' suggestion.

Simon stiffens at Alexis. "A better plan would be to remove Rome from our Land. We know of the Roman reward for Eleazar. You are a confused Roman - tell Rome our belief is our own affair and the Ark is not for trading or bartering."

"Negotiate with Rome!?" Alexis implores. "The Ark can be as just a loan, to please Rome's ego, it can be returned to you eventually. This can save many lives?"

The Jews again respond with a heavy silence.

Hillel lays his hand on Alexis' shoulder; his vision pierces deeply into the Roman.

"Alexis, your intention is honorable, but no Jew would think in such a manner. And the Ark has not been seen since the Babylon destruction."

"Babylon did not find this Ark. Rome believes it is hidden in Jerusalem and some know its secret location. At this hour, no small compromises will suffice. You have to offer Rome something of great value to turn the situation facing your people from an assured destruction. Yes, an assured destruction, as many mightier nations have seen. If you know this Ark's location, then I beg you, use this knowledge to save your nation?"

"It is a devious Roman thing he brings us. Let me smite him!" Simon approaches Alexis. Hillel sways a negating finger; Simon slams his fist on the table. Hillel again responds to Alexis.

"Alexis, this will be difficult for you to understand. The location of the Ark is unknown, and if its true location was known it would not be negotiable."

"Even if it means saving your nation, is this what your laws tell you? I have studied your writings - even your Sabbath can be cast aside in a crises. This relic, sacred as it may be, cannot be greater than your nation's survival? Your strange laws oppose Rome before all the nations and Rome will not sit idle… the Hebrew nation will be erased… as happened with so many other nations greater than yours… how do you not see this!?"

Alexis turns to approach Simon's towering presence.

"The Jews will be sacrificed to make Vespasian a king, and his son thirsts for revenge to serve his own glory. Rome will appoint Roman masters over you - even in your temples. This nation's very survival rests on your decisions… so think well?"

"Israel has seen your kind before." Simon smirks.

"No, you have not seen this kind before. No nation equaled Rome in power. Rome is already passing new laws allowing mixed marriages… so their soldiers can make concubines of your Hebrew women in foreign lands. How don't you see it that Rome will end your nation's future!? Pay no heed of me or my life now - consider only my words and your own saving?"

A silent pause holds again.

Hillel approaches Alexis; his vision focused on him, his outstretched arm a signal to the others to hear. All move aback in silent waiting of the Teacher.

"You risked your life many times for us." Hillel is nodding; he now begins to heed the words of Alexis, offering disclosure of unspoken and hidden things before all. "I can tell you only the truth now." His focus appears far away. "Our King Solomon saw such days to come. He saw it from his father King David's time… how the Philistines from across the sea invaded the land and took the Holy Ark. So Solomon made that none will know of the Ark's location anymore. Some of our sages believed it may be on the top of a high mountain - we do not know which one. Jeremiah pointed us to the Mount of Nebo, where Moses last stood - "Naha-be" the high place and the pupil of the eye." The teacher points his hands to his eyes. "For the Babylonians who sought this Holy Ark…" He smiles in his knowing of hidden things. "There was only a decoy, and even that they never found. Such was the wisdom of King Solomon."

"I don't believe what I hear from our teacher this day! You are talking to a Roman who has a different belief from ours." Simon is in angst; he does not want any more said to Alexis of the temple's provisions; but Hillel, understanding what the nations face in this hour, offers more; his gaze is distant again now, his hand stemming Simon.

"Israel's kings saw that many invaders will come to destroy and build their own temples here. Some say the King Josiah sealed the Holy Ark forever under Jerusalem, under its own earth, believing it the safest place."

"What ever you say to this spy will tempt them to tear Jerusalem apart to find the Ark!?" Simon turns from Hillel to Alexis. "This is our land and we don't bow to your insane kings. We never did with any nation before. Ask the Greeks!?"

"Bless you Simon" Miriam's eyes are searing of Simon's words; she hand kisses him from behind the curtain.

"And that is why your position is so dangerous!" Alexis responds to Simon.

"Tell me strong man, will your sages and farmers prevail Rome's elite warriors? Or will your darts of oil stop Rome's war machines, able to fly huge boulders 2000 cubits? Will your walls stand against Battering Rams with iron heads the size of this house? Or the unaccountable legions and mercenaries from across the empire? For how long? Remember that Rome never retreats before complete victory?"

Simon smirks unmoved; Alexis deliberates:

"Know thy enemy well, for all the nations oblige Rome with sacrifices, except one, Rome's smallest province. I say to you - nay, I plead of you, to all of you, trade your shekels for your nation, for your children, your women and your aged. You are a wise people - your wealth will soon come back to you. Give Rome no excuse now, it's what a good war general would do. Survive - and make no rebellion with Rome?"

Miriam gazes disapproving at Deborah, whose eyes are fixed only on Alexis.

"Rebellion!?" Simon smirks disdainfully. "Is that what you Romans call it? Denial of our beliefs, all the lives sacrificed for 2000 years of wars… just a rebellion of primitive conquered peasants?" He grasps a silver cup on the table; a fierce gaze fixed on Alexis.

"Are you so confused what this war is about… Jews rebelling to give up their gold coins? Rebellious Jews refusing worship of Rome's depraved ones? Spoken like a Roman. Glory to you! But we've seen this before and…" He crushes the silver cup in his palm. "I'll give you rebellion!" He tosses the crushed cup at Alexis.

"I give you the truth of your situation." Alexis responds, a crushed cup in his palm. "The truth… as I see it?"

"Roman truth? Do you imagine this war is about gold shekels and old relics?" He smirks disdainfully. "This is only about Israel's truth before Rome, before all nations… even before our God? We have defended our right of belief with mighty empires before. You Romans are confused about Israel, just as the others were?" He is heaving, emanating a fury in the hall; all are frozen by Simon's words and formidable power as he moves closer to Alexis, who remains steadfast and un-moved.

Suddenly, the door swings open; three Hebrew men stand at the entrance. They appear as savage desert warriors; their gazes fixed on Simon. The leader nods, blinking at Simon. Simon wavers. He hard stares Alexis; there is an intense interaction with Hillel. Simon walks to the door; he pauses and turns to Alexis who holds a crushed cup in his palm.

"We Jews are not used to being saved by Romans."

"Sicarri?!" Miriam, behind a curtain, is aghast. She appears shaken of the Sicarii warriors approaching the house of the teacher Hillel, risking the village safety should Rome find out of their presence here. A tension reigns what Simon will do.

"I'll show you rebellion. I know what I must do now." Simon sways his face at Hillel, then he storms out.

"Wait… hear me!?" Alexis implores him in vain as Simon storms out the house of Hillel. Simon follows the Sicarii into the night.

Behind the curtain, Miriam is sobbing. "Be you blessed Simon!" She fears the loss of the village protector, while being in solidarity of his actions. She nudges Deborah, sobbing and whispering. "The Roman is not a full shekel, telling Jews to forsake God's Holy Ark to the Roman devils! Heaven forbid this evil thought."

"Maybe he sees what we do not…" Deborah responds.

"Mah?! What is there to see!? They want to destroy our beliefs and rob our land?" Miriam whispers admonishingly. "They bring houses of harlots to our holy city, they murder their new born babies created in God's image and they display our people to die on crosses before us? They do great abominations and evils everywhere they go, then they ridicule us for not eating the swine! But oh! Forgive me I beg you… who knows these Roman killers more than you!?"

"Shhh! I want to listen." Deborah's eyes are affixed on Alexis. They both watch covertly as Alexis appears shaken after his deliberations that made Simon storm out; the gathering has now left. Alexis turns to Hillel; the two are now alone. Deborah's eyes are affixed on him as he struggles to disclose his intentions; he has more to say.

"Nero brought back Caligula's insane law. It is a calamity for this small nation and your strange laws. Rome calls it the decree of Heresy. I have a bad feeling of it."

Deborah now recalls his words of warning when he first pursued her: 'Rome has issued new laws…on pain of death'. She now understands Rome's Heresy decree, what it means for her people. She trusts her teacher Hillel, and she also understands the pain in Miriam and in Simon's anger and suspicion of Rome. Yet now she cannot understand her own confusions stirring within her; he seemed sincere even to her teacher. She recalls his solemn pledge:

"I am not a spy… it is my word of honor to you."

She stares in askance as Miriam's words emerge:

"Be you blessed Simon!"

Her sight is fixed on the Roman.

Alexis appears awkward now: "I have a bad feeling of it."

Hillel knows there is more he wants to say.

(51). SAVE US ELEAZAR!

Thousands of Roman soldiers and Jews lay dead on the vast temple foregrounds. Eleazar stands between the temple pillars, a Sicarii dagger raised in each hand. The Sicarii leader proclaims his thunderous address in a blood stained Roman uniform.

"Hear me Israel!" The people gather before him, filling the massive courtyard now strewn with death. "Our freedom of belief began by our forefathers on this very ground." He slams his foot on the ground. "Here - on Mount Moriah! IT WILL NOT END HERE!?"

A din of hailing resounds from the Jews.

"We Jews have never robbed another peoples' land - we have no such plans. Our God forbade us not to take a single cubit of land outside the borders given us via Moshe, peace be unto his great holy name, and such is written in our holy Torah for all to see. This is our land - we will not live in terror in our own land. We follow our own God given beliefs in our land - we do not follow the Roman beliefs here! Here me Israel. Blood for blood - death for death! Israel lives only by One God of Israel. This be our answer to Rome…"

He stirs them, screaming thunderously, demanding of them:

"NO… SURRENDER!?"

"NO… SURRENDER!" The people chant. "SAVE US ELEAZAR!"

"Israel makes sacrifice only to the God of Israel… All sacrifice to Rome is forbidden from this day!"

"Amen-Amen! Save us Eleazar! Be you our Savior!"

A Peace Party Jew is crouched bloodied and wounded in the far back of the temple's outermost wall. It is a marketplace area of rowdy robust stalls competing with exchange rates of foreign monies into Hebrew half shekels, a ritual derived from a law commanded in the Hebrew bible, with the sum and mode of temple contribution made an exacting command: half shekel from each for the Temple, no more - no less. The Money Changers sell the exacting half shekel coins in exchange of all foreign coins from the nations. Now the money changer's market lays desolate and shut for business in this war. The wounded Peace Party Jew covertly whispers his disdain of Eleazar to a Money Changer:

"He stirs up the people by their devout worship of one God. Who does he imagine he is - Moses - King David?" He smirks with disdain.

"He has massacred their entire legion; even he killed our own people where bloodshed is forbidden." The Money Changer sways his face in apprehension. "And the forbidding of sacrifice is a declaration of war. All the nations will be watching. Rome will not let it pass. God help us!"

Temple Sacrifice. The practice of sacrifice as a means of worship was a historical and global trait throughout humanity. A time-line shows this was a ritual practiced by all nations. The book of Genesis says sacrifice existed with the first recorded human family. In historical comparisons, Israel's sacrificial laws were reasonable and mild: animal sacrifice was forbidden in Israel for wanton crimes; these were subject to penalties listed in the Hebrew bible laws. All sacrifice was conditional to accidental sins, guilt offerings and thanksgiving, and limited to a specific list of life forms. All sacrifice was to be conducted only at this one temple, not in the home or elsewhere; thereby, the sacrificial ritual was reduced by some 90% with a single command, and gradually weaned off the people from what was a historically embedded human trait. The sacrifice ritual became annulled for the Jews in the absence of the temple and cannot be performed anywhere else. Henceforth, devout prayer, repentance and charity became its replacement, enacted with prayer by directives such as:

'Accept, please Lord, the sacrifice of my lips.' [Psalm 119].

For the scribe Flavius Josephus, the event of Eleazar's great rebellion, especially his forbiddance of sacrifice for Rome in the Holy Temple, was a major turning point of the war. He writes of it:

"This! It is by this man, it is by this arrogant deed that turned our destiny to cause what happens hereafter… what had to happen."

The people are chanting:

"Save us Eleazar! Be you our savior. Amen-Amen!"

(52). ALL ROADS LEAD TO ROME. [90]

In Rome, a large wooden cage on wheels is thrust forward in an enclosed isolated compound. The cage is packed with tightly packed Hebrew slaves. Guards open the cage's small shutter door and pull out three slaves, dragging their chained bodies to the center. Another guard reads their names and the charges against them aloud from labels of wood droplets attached to each slave's necks:

"Gavriel - Caesarea - Pharisee - Crime: Heresy."

"Achinoam - Caesarea - Pharisee - Crime: Heresy."

"Saulos - Cilicia, Tarsus - Pharisee - Crime: Heresy."

From a window of a Tower on the wall a Roman Captain leans out; his outstretched hand makes a thumb down sign.

Three detached heads roll on the ground by the instant action of an executioner's heavy sword. Elderly slaves come forward to move away the decapitated heads and bodies. The cage's shutter opens and three more Hebrew slaves are thrust forward. [91]

The War Room of Titus. In Caesarea's Roman base a Tribune, bleeding and tattered, enters Titus' war room in Caesarea. He delivers the somber news in panting of fear and sobs:

"My Commander. Bad tidings from Jerusalem. Six thousand Romans… massacred in open daylight… by the same bandit you seek. Eleazar has forbidden all sacrifices to Rome… any Jews collaborating with the Peace Party were also cut down. The Syrian armies ran away terrified when confronting the Sicarri. The Temple Fortress… is in Eleazar's hands."

"That Syrian Commander." Titus sways his sword in a vulgar gesture: "My sword up his coward ass."

"Mighty Commander, the Jews attacked us deceitfully, wearing the white garment of the Peace Party."

There is shock on Titus' face of the Tribune's words; his jowls tremble in fury. He recalls now Bernice's warning:

"Some history lessons for my mighty warrior…"

Titus paces, then he turns to his Captains who stand in fear of his fury; they await his terrible response. A torturous war now appears on the horizon, many Romans will die in securing again the indestructible and impregnable Jerusalem fortress now in the hands of the Jews.

"Remember how they attacked my father - waiting, hidden like snakes behind rocks!" Titus addresses his Captains. "The Jews are a small primitive group of peasants, less than a tenth of us. It is the reason they use such guile and deceit in war. What has now become of Rome's legions that we fear them?" He pans his captains' faces waiting on his words in silence. "We must confront these treacherous ones in the open light of day as Romans - not as the cowards who flee from them. And as my father swore to Nero, I swear it now before all of you. It will take less than three weeks to destroy these devilish rebels."

"Master, these Jews don't let us take prisoners, they fight to the death, each taking many with them." A Captain comes forward. "They die dancing and singing…"

Titus commands his captains in fiery angst, pounding his fist on the war table:

"Good. I don't intend taking any as prisoners. Summon the forces! The legions from Caesarea and Syria - assemble all the Arabian mercenaries. Turn to me the legions from Cyprus and Briton" He pauses, then he remembers, his face smeared in perspiration:

"Get me also the road builder and the Hebrew Scribe - they were given orders to fill. You must know now, for your ears only. I ordered shiploads of heavy armor supply which will arrive soon - new war machines never seen in this region - to tear up the Jews and their land for all time."

Titus turns aside to Tiberius in a lowered voice.

"Now the dog that pierced my father is also at hand. This is war. My war… my glory. I want it?"

The Temple Fortress. Eleazar sways a blood drenched Roman sword before the people:

"Make this your sword of Gideon!"[92] He sways his Sicarii dagger in his other hand, stirring the people to frenzy, referring to their biblical kin who battled their enemies in the past and saved Israel. "And make this the blade of Deborah - as did Israel's saviors after Joshua! We scream to our God with all your might and all our soul!?"

"Amen! Amen!" The aged and the young, the feeble and the strong, hail.

"Bless you Eleazar - be you our Savior! Tear away the Roman enemy from our land as did Gideon - as did Deborah!"

The people shout as one, hands extended to the heavens.

The House of Hillel. Alexis is now alone with the teacher. He appears tense, pausing awkwardly, oscillating around the teacher as if withholding something. Deborah and Miriam are peering covertly from behind the curtains.

"Will you see the Jews risk their nation for the law of a festival?"

"All laws can be put aside to save lives. But one."

"But one?"

"Yes Alexis, but one." Hillel's eyes follow Alexis as he moves around, pausing and halting and gathering his words. The teacher Hillel's sight is fixed on him in intense focus, as if sensing a lingering long held matter will be exposed; he waits patiently.

"You will risk your land, your people, your Temple… everything for your… but-one-God belief?"

"This has been our lot with many nations."

"Yes, I know of it, and I, err… you see… I am given freedom now to act and dress as one of you… in the quest of the Ark, an order from Titus, one I was compelled to accept… can you understand me?"

The teacher focuses on him in patient attention, nodding.

"But I…I…" Alexis looks around; a sense of awkward emotions fill him as he pans the strange Hebrew symbols in the room - the candles, the silver cups, a Menorah, the shelves heaving with the weight of Hebrew scrolls, the pouches affixed on the door posts. "You must know of it now… you must!?" He appears unsure, as if struggling to say something.

"What is it… tell it, Alexis?"

Deborah is focused on Alexis through slits in the curtain; her eyes are agape with emotion; Miriam measures her focus in apprehension.

"Now I also know what I must do… you must make me one of you… an equal of you." He turns to the teacher in urgency. "I will become a Jew! You must do this for me. You must!?"

There is a long pause of silence between them; Alexis waits on the teacher; heaving.

"Miriam." Deborah hides her teary eyes. "Did you hear it?"

Hillel responds cautiously. "Rome has forbidden circumcision. I cannot cause your death."

"No one will suspect a Roman dressed as a Jew…to be a Jew!" Alexis assures the teacher. "Now I am hated by my people, yet I have found my calling. I have thought of it deeply and I cannot lie to my heart anymore. You must do this for me… whatever be its cost!?"

Miriam questions Deborah. "Have you yet not understood why the Roman keeps visiting us? You are so young and so foolish."

"Is that all you see, Miriam?"

Hillel offers a deflection of Alexis' strange request. "This is not a safe time to be a Jew. Wait, we must let the danger pass."

"Israel is surely inviting disaster with Rome… yet I will stand with her at this time?" He grasps the Teacher's hand. "And there is not another time for me!?

The teacher peers eye to eye into Alexis; a prolonged silence holds. Then Hillel speaks in a serious tone; officially; pointing finger at the Roman.

"Three times you risked your life for Jews. Now you risk your life to become a Jew. I will prepare for you. Come tonight."

"Miriam, is our teacher also so young and foolish?" Deborah winces; tears streaming down her cheeks.

"I will not hear of such betrayal - Romans cannot be made as Jews!" Miriam turns away unimpressed.

"Our own teacher said it… it is just as Ruth did three times…" Deborah's hand reaches out to Miriam as she quotes the Hebrew scriptures of the thrice made pledges required of an intending convert, her voice breaking, her eyes moistened red and dreamy:

"For whither thou go, I will go… and where thou lodgest, I will lodge… thy people shall be my people and thy God my God. What more will you want from him - tell me!?" [93]

"The stranger in that room is a Roman - a traitor." Miriam points her hand accusingly.

"Was not Ruth the Moabite also a stranger, one from an enemy's camp?" Deborah responds earnestly to turn Miriam's uncompromising stand. "A Moabite, not one of us, yet one who's seed gave us King David… to bring us our savior. If our own teacher sees it how don't you see it?" Deborah's emotions stir; she flees away from Miriam and runs across the fields in the village.

She runs far into the hills, panting and heaving in sobs. She is alone now, exhausted and gazing at a full moon, her secret friend. Deborah is shaken as she realizes Alexis' true intent and of her own strange stirrings; guilt and shame overwhelm her as tears flow, as she gazes at the Moon for help.

She looks around that she is alone; then she begins beseeching and imploring the full silver disc in the sky; she whispers her hidden thoughts to the Moon.

"You are wise… you see everything… you know from old times…even more than us all. I am a Jew, from the House of Hur, Megiddo - you know me… for I know you since I was small. See… he is a Roman, one who worships killers. It is abomination… an abomination!?"

Suddenly, a tremulous female voice echoes from the moon:

"Is it an abomination to forsake one's life, life, ife…?"

Deborah is in fright - she backs away; stiffened in shock and pressing against a tree.

Then a male voice echoes, enjoining the female voice:

"To forsake one's life… for the love of a stranger… is it an abomination?"

Deborah is in fear; her senses are confused; she is hearing her own mind's words. Then she pauses, pondering on the Moon's challenging response. She is grasping her hair, shutting her ears from the mysterious words echoing. She begins to withdraw, retreating from the strange voices she imagined coming from the Moon. She steadies herself, recalling now how her own life was saved, that was not an abomination. She turns, deliberating with the Moon again.

"True, true, you see all from above, you know it, how he risked his life for me, a stranger to him. But this Roman…" She looks around that none hear her talking to the Moon; she whispers it. "He makes roads to murder the innocent… and my people are sworn to the God of righteousness… you must surely know about the God of… the Holy One of Israel, the God of my forefathers. The God who created you!?"

Now a male voice echoes from the Moon:

"Where a repentant sinner stands… even the most righteous cannot…" [94]

Then a soothing female voice enjoins:

"Therefore the Lord loveth the stranger…strang…ger…" [95]

Streaming clouds cover the Moon; lights shimmer on Deborah's face. Her eyes glow in a crazed delirium as she nods in agreement with the Moon. Now she knows what she must do. Her eyes glow; she is in tears of joy, as if a new understanding comes to her. She is leaping and hopping, dancing alone in the hills of Megiddo, and pointing at the Moon in an abandoned flight.

Miriam appears, hand covering her mouth; she is in disbelief at Deborah's joyful revelry. Deborah becomes frozen still, unable to withstand Miriam's appearance now; her face is turned to the streaming clouds.

"Oh yes, they sent a charming Roman spy to catch you. So tell me, how hardened has your soul become that you will think of love with the killers of your own people?"

"Who did he kill?"

"He serves Rome who kills our people…how can you ask such a thing!?"

"I know he saved our teacher's life…" Deborah retreats, backing away. Miriam stomps toward Deborah who has retreated behind a tree and hiding from Miriam's presence. Now she is sobbing and laughing behind a tall palm tree, the Moon light shimmering and passing on her face; she is shuddering and heaving in sobs. Seeing Deborah's shaken state, Miriam now attempts to calm her, wiping her tears.

"You are shaking! Be not so excited. Israel will survive the evils we heard this day. And Simon will return to you… he will always protect you from the Romans… and that stranger among us."

"Why does our Lord command us to love the stranger?" Deborah is laughing deliriously amidst a hail of tears pouring down her face.

Miriam is aghast, retreating from Deborah's question; she cups her ears and flees.

Deborah is trembling in tears against the tree, the moonlight exposing guilt and defiance in her glowing eyes. A Roman's words come to her:

"*I know now you can never forget my name…*"

Deep in the dark winding hills of the Megiddo plains, Simon is storming in a fury; he is dressed in Arabian attire. He knows what he must do now.

A Roman War Room. In the early dawn, Tiberius appears before Titus concerning the preparations and accounting of war legions commanded to him. A banner on the wall reads:
'ALL ROADS LEAD TO ROME'.

The wall of the war room is featured with a display of Roman shields, each marking a conquered nation:
CARPATHIA - ITALIA - MACEDONIA - ARMENIA - HISPANIA - GAUL - ACHAEA - CORSICA - GERMANIA - BELGICA - ILLYRICUM - CYPRUS - HANNIBAL - SARDINIA - CECILIA - ARABIA - AEGYPTUS - MESOPOTAMIA - BABYLONIA - NUMIDIA - SYRIA - NORTHERN AFRIKANIA - MAURITANIA - IDUMEA - BRITANNIA - WALES - MOAB - LEBANON - JUDEA.

Tiberius reports to Titus:
"The 18th and 3rd Augusta Legions will arrive soon. The 12th Legion will arrive from our Syrian Legate, and the 23rd and the 24th Legions will come from west of the Euphrates. Egypt is commissioned to secure 100,000 Arabian Mercenaries, as your honorable father ordered. Also, 10,000 Britons will arrive from Cypress, as you ordered." Tiberius spreads an ancient map on the Table. "These are the towns that are secured: Caesarea, Jotapata, Jericho, the Galilee, Accra, Gamla, Bethel, Tyre, Gilboa, Samaria and Hebron. The Jews have caged themselves in their Jerusalem fortress, making the task simpler."

He waits now in a foreboding to get a vital response from Titus, one that will lead Rome's legions to a point of no return. They face each other in a long silence. Titus knows what he must do now. He brings his sword on the map; its point rests on Jerusalem.

"We march… to Jerusalem."

Titus' face is distorted.

This night, Hillel is awoken by a knock on his door.

"Forgive me disturbing our teacher so late. I fear for Deborah. You must know of it…" Miriam has a head cover; she tightly grasps her shawl around her neck.

"She thinks our teacher accepts a Roman murderer… she does not remember Simon, who you know builds a house and waits on her…"

After a long pause of silence, Hillel nods; his eyes shut as he responds.

"And they said… we will call the damsel and enquire at her mouth." [96]

Miriam is confused; she waits for further words.

"If our forefather Isaac, the son of Abraham and Rebecca's parents, had to wait on her answer, must we not also do the same - tell me?"

"But…" Miriam becomes anxious. "He is a Roman!?"

Hillel quoted the earliest recording honoring a woman's right of refusal of a marriage proposal. Miriam accepted Isaac's proposal, and thereby did the nation of his son Jacob (Israel) emerged by it.

"Such is our laws we are tested by, they are not as those the nations follow. The maiden has the right of refusal and we must enquire of her mouth. Simon knows this."

"How can you not understand Simon's pain… she made him believe her?" Miriam turns away abruptly; she storms away in distress.

(53). A PLEDGE EVEN GOD CANNOT CHANGE.

There is a quickening of pace in the Megiddo village as two Hebrew messengers storm in on horseback.

Faces of foreboding grip the people as they gather in the town square to hear of the messenger's reporting. Alexis is watching from his room's window.

"There is news. Tyre, Gilboa, Samaria, Gamla and the Galilee have fallen. Those who survived are fleeing to the Temple fortress. There is more. The Romans are assembling a war council in Caesarea. Eleazar's message is the oil and weapons are the only works allowed, and the Passover is due - the dry Matzo works also must not cease."

The people nod and sway, grimacing; there is an understanding and acceptance, one gathered in the Jews' hearts and minds from their history's imprints of such foreboding news.

Alexis' attention turns to men lifting war weapons; they are collecting large baskets of firebrands and transporting them to carriages covered up with decoy layers of Passover foods.

In closed sheds behind the rear of the village, Hebrew women are making primitive Molotov cocktails; they fill jars with combustible oil, affixing the bulbs on sticks and darts.

A young lad with a sling in his hand races to Alexis with a Sabra fruit, a native food of this land; it is the same lad Alexis saved from a snake. The fruit is prickly; Alexis pulls away from it, his finger embedded with its fine, hairy thorns. The lad shows him how to open the fruit correctly. Alexis fakes great pain of a thorn embedded in his finger; he appeals to the lad, holding his finger as if in pain.

"Pokey outside, but soft and sweet inside?"

"Can you bring Deborah to help me?" The lad grins; racing away.

Deborah approaches; now their glances linger too long searching each other's eyes with an abandoning. She holds Alexis' hand and dislodges a thorn, bringing him instant relief.

"Your uniform is washed clean. I will attend to your wound now to see how it heals." She takes hold of his head in her hands, examining his wound.

"Titus bid me to deliver a message to Eleazar." He whispers.

She stares at him surprised; suspicious and unsure of his strange words.

"It may save much destruction and many lives if his offer is accepted." He gazes into her eyes affirming it.

"We must stop this war from happening!?"

"You cannot approach Eleazar."

"I must!? And no one else must know of it. Tell me how?"

She gazes into his eyes long, then she nods, accounting him as sincere. "You ask of me to have great trust in you. I give you it. If it saves lives I can deliver it to his wife. She will come to pick up her children."

"First…" He holds her hand to him. "Tell me you don't see your brother's blood on my face anymore… so I may stay here?" His gaze of devotion is fixed on her, awaiting her response. "I have no other place I wish to be now?"

"You have no other place to go to. Our teacher saw an honored guest in you. He blessed you. You must forget my words spoken in pain. Then I saw you only as the Roman killers of my family."

"I understand. I have forgotten it. So I have good reason to change such a future again of my nation upon your people." He covertly hands her the royal case; she looks around, then she hides it in her dress. "Don't be seen with this. Tell me now, where will you go if war comes and this town is not safe for you?"

"Tell me now, where will you go when Rome becomes not safe for you?"

They gaze into each other; he has no answer for her. She nudges Alexis' hand as he ponders her question. "Pella!" She prompts him. "It lies on the other side of the Jordan!?"

"Abandon Jerusalem? Rome's way is to leave nothing her enemies can return to."

"No! Israel will surely be returned to her land… it is a pledge even God cannot change." She leans forward to impress her words with the same defiance he recalled with his security guard. "For our God's word is of truth!?" She inclines her face defiantly. "Israel's destiny is not in Rome's hands…"

He is mesmerized by her confidence in her God. He takes her hand to his heart - it trembles; he is calming her wild reaction, he feels her fear.

"My destiny is in these hands."

A blacksmith in the distance is sharpening blades of daggers and swords piled up as war armory. Another Hebrew whispers in his ears.

"How is it war comes and a Roman sits in our center?"

The blacksmith's face turns to Deborah and Alexis; he nods, returning his arms to stroking the blades of iron, its sparks flying with a piercing noise.

Alexis tests Deborah. "But if you have such sure faith in your God, then why flee from Jerusalem to Pella?"

"For life!?" His question is annoying to her; she pulls away her hand. "We are forbidden to rely on miracles. And till I return to Jerusalem…" Her hand on her heart. "I will keep the holy city inside me - why do you say such a thing!?"

"My wish is to be there with you."

She flees, her tears welling.

In the hinterland roads surrounding Jerusalem's towns, throngs of Jews in the hillside tracks are proceeding with their families towards the safety of the fortress; they carry food baggage and children over their shoulders. There is a foreboding with the Jews as they move with their families to Jerusalem's high hills.

(54). SHEIK DANAK.

In an isolated Bedouin village, Simon approaches a large white house; he is dressed in Arabian attire. As he approaches the house, Simon's towering presence and renown makes the guards back away as a precaution. Simon opens his dress to display he is unarmed. Three guards lead Simon to the Bedouin leader; he sits on piles of rugs, his hand flicking measured drops of amber beads strung on a chain. Simon dips his head and speaks.

"Can a Jew buy information for 500 Shekels of fine gold?"

"Our hearts bleed from the insanity of the Jews."

'It is a deposit. If your information is not a betrayal, another 1000 pieces will…"

"None in Arabia has your daring. This time you are alone and no one here thinks you will survive to pay them later."

"We don't ask for help in battle - only signs from outside if a siege is upon us - nothing more?"

"You have not measured your enemy well. They have stationed bases in our village. We want no trouble here now. This war is of Rome and the Jews alone. We have not challenged mighty Rome as you Jews did."

"With Rome we are all alone."

"Everyone prefers alone to the cross. As you leave you will see the sign of the Romans. You will know why you are now alone."

"Israel is always alone… in our God's hand."

"One thing I will give you. Come closer." Simon inclines his ear to the Sheik's mouth. "It is happening. Think well how your people must turn. We did."

"You know us from old. We cannot live by Rome's demands on our beliefs."

"That is the battle of your gods - it is not for our village."

Simon leaves empty handed, understanding now Israel is again alone on the edge of a precipice. Outside the house, he sees the ensign of the Roman eagle affixed in the centre of the village square; the powerful bird on a tower confronts him ominously.

A young Arabian lad gives Simon chase, panting; calling him as he nears.

"I will do it - I will spy for you."

"You need money?"

"No money. My heart tells me to do this. I hate the black eagle in our village."

"You will become a man with a good heart. But Sheik Danak is right - you cannot risk your people's lives to save us Jews now."

There is a distress call from a ram's horn coming from behind the hills. Simon stiffens by the Hebrew code of urgency and races into the hills. He is met by Saul and Ari.

"Eleazar's wife." Saul is in tears; swaying his face in pain. "His five children and his mother."

"Late at night." Ari eyes display intense anger. "While they lay sleeping! I cannot face Eleazar anymore."

"How did they find his house?" Simon asks.

"How do you think?!" Ari's rage intensifies. "Their spy was seen in the village with her, both whispering in Megiddo. He knows our weapon making places. He beguiled the girl and our teacher. Would you dealt with him before."

"A black box they delivered was empty, but for stones and grass." Saul explains further. "Once they knew the house, six Roman soldiers came at night…"

"I was in charge of Eleazar's security. I must resign." Ari offers.

Simon and Saul sway their faces in disagreement. Suddenly, Ari stiffens. A repetitive thud under their feet emerges. Ari presses his ear to the ground. He turns to Simon in panic:

"That Roman spy warned us of it. It is happening!?"

The thuds graduate stronger. Saul and Ari jolt, gazing at one another, then at Simon.

"It was the Roman spy." Simon is in a fury. "Or else…"

"It was Titus!?" Saul corrects Simon.

"There was one more." Ari offers one he slew with his household. "One who prevailed with turning Nero. The destruction in Caesarea - let us not forget it."

"It is happening…" Saul says, as their feet are vibrating. "Rome is Israel's enemy." They nod at each other. The sounds of foreboding distant thuds are approaching stronger.

"I never imagined Rome would attack the Fortress. Yet it is happening." Ari confirms from his squatted position on the ground. "Can Simon not know what we all must do now…?

(55). ESSENE MONKS.

In the Qumran mountain ranges south of Jericho, dirt tracks lead to an intricate maze of caves and living quarters of an isolated Hebrew monk-like group. The Essenes are gathered to hear an address by a tall bearded man in a bone tunic, his eyes searing.

"We have been given the evil report - they are marching to Jerusalem. We will go and put our case before Eleazar. We shall return with the sacred writings, God willing."

The evil report has reached all of the towns of Judea. Swarms of Jews are fleeing in haste to the safety of the fortress via the hinterland routes.

The thuds of marching war precessions are graduating stronger.

(56) ROME'S GREATEST ENEMY.

The Romans were a highly superstitious people from their early beginnings in the region of Latium before they became a mighty empire. The early Romans held beliefs in a pantheon of deities, each with specific attributes of powers and personalities. The early Roman successes in wars inculcated a strong belief in the power of their gods.

The Romans saw that the deities they worshipped can bring them success; they held thanksgiving sacrifices of both animals and humans. And the Romans freely integrated other gods of their conquered nations, most especially of the Greeks, deeming the conquering and gathering of more Gods as war possessions that will enrich Rome with greater powers. As well it was a prudent Roman stratagem in affording Rome better control of their conquered nations. Rome encouraged and accumulated a vast and enticing display of decadent celebratory art and sculptured works, with little reservations of modesty, using explicit sexuality as a Thanksgiving ritual to their vast collection of gods. Almost all doctrines of Roman were in direct opposition of the Hebrew laws, with inevitable consequences.

Roman Decadence Art before its Bacchus Deity [Thomas Couture] Source: S27

The Gods of Rome. Jupiteres was Rome's head of all Gods, armed with hurling arrows of thunderbolts; his wife was Juno, God of women, with the pomegranate of fertility in her hand. Mars was the second most powerful God, bestowing might in war. Venus was the God of love and beauty, Minerva the God of wisdom, and Diana appears only at night for she is the moon God. Vulcan was the God of the dark underworld who caused volcanoes to erupt. The most favored God was Bacchus, the giver of wine and delights of sensuality, thus sexual pleasure was a gift from the Roman gods.

The Romans amassed power and loyalty accepting the gods of their conquered nations: Isis, the Egyptian God; Mithras, the Persian God of light; Pan, the Greek God who is half man and half goat, and the Greek Hercules was welcomed as a Roman God of strength.

Ares e Afrodite. Cupid confronts Venus and Mars in the act of adultery.

While such in-gathering of gods found cohesion among the conquered nations, one proviso caused a war with the Jews: Rome's reciprocal requirement of a conquered nation also having to worship the Roman Gods. While such a demand was reasonable because it asked the same of all other conquered nations, it was a deathly blow to the Jews. Judea's Hebrew belief which rejected such a reciprocity requirement was unacceptable to Rome's divine emperors, and the Jews soon learnt this was not an attack on their dietary and dress laws, but that the real culprit was elsewhere.

The matter became critical for the Jews and Rome's anointed divine emperors. Mighty Rome's glory and power could be diminished before the nations by the Jews' rejection of divine kings, while the Hebrew belief would vanish by any accommodation of the Roman demand. The real culprit for Rome's Emperors was the Jews' most fundamental Hebrew law from its inception with Abraham. Rome's Emperors became obsessed with the negation of Monotheism; and Rome saw the destruction and annihilation of the stiff-neck Jews' holy city and their Hebrew beliefs as the only way to succeed in this quest. The Jews understood their problem with the nations of old.

Before the advent of sciences, nature driven polytheism was humanity's pervasive state of beliefs; and for the same reason, such was not an unintelligent reality but a reasonable one, all things considered. In Abraham's time, Nimrod, the primal ancient king and the great-grandson of Noah, was endeavoring to conquer the sun God with a united, conquered humanity of the generations amassed in constructing the Tower of Babel. This construction, which soared into the clouds of heaven, involved many decades and spent lives; eventually a stone brick became more precious than the human lifting it, and its news would have been known to all in the region, also with Abraham's family.

Abraham's father Terah is believed to be a builder of statues for the Royal house of the king, and Nimrod was focused on seeking the power of everlasting life by conquering all other Gods, including the sun God whose abode was beyond the clouds. Such aspirations of eternal life also became the obsession with the Egyptian Pharaohs, as seen in the Book of the Dead.

Despite the Adam and Eve story appearing as legend or metaphorical to many, it impacted the historical psyche. In the Hebrew bible, Eve won the fruit of knowledge of good and evil, one that rendered mankind as the superior life form and given a divine portfolio to have dominion of all the Earth; it is vindicated. But the fruit of everlasting life Eve did not partake of; the Genesis writing thus indicates that this source of everlasting life does exist somewhere, somehow; as did the fruit of superior knowledge given to mankind, rendering a belief of life after death.

Such were also the pervasive ancient beliefs of humanity held in the early periods which sought everlasting life via chanting, sacrifices and other means of occultism. Nimrod sought to begat everlasting life by conquering the Gods. Akin to mankind's conquering of the mysteries of the heavenly outer limits, Nimrod, master of all conquered nations, did believe himself as a God, one who could conquer all other Gods.

As the stars were not understood prior to telescopes, the flat earth conclusion of our ancient ancestors was also a reasonably intelligent one. So too that the actions of nature upon the Earth were seen as controlled by various mythical deities - the Gods were angry when thunder appeared in the heavens; it too was a reasonably intelligent conclusion for its time; thus the ancients also assumed other life forms abounded in the dark unbounded deep abodes of the heavens. Yet in Babylon a new thought was set to overturn the calm of the divine emperor status quo: while it impacted a certain potential truth and logic to the people, it became the enemy of the divine kings. Monotheism became the first recorded 'Thought Crime' and remains so in the modern world, splitting humanity's discourse with a legitimate potential reasoning of only two possibilities of the unknown origins of all things.

Monotheism, a term devised by the Greeks when they landed in Arabia, and an indicator of its premise being unknown to the peoples across the seas, refers to 'One God' or 'Single God'. The Hebrew Monotheism premise was varied from a belief in one singular deity such as the Sun, a Mono-Paganism which some historians have aligned it with. Zoroastrianism, a beautifully reasoned belief, aligned closest to Monotheism when it emerged in the 6th Century, although it contained a Godhead with attached agents. [97]

The Hebrew Monotheism law was anew, allowing nothing in creation as aligned with the one unseen and never fully known God. In the Hebrew paradigm the closest between two points was when there is nothing in between:

"Unto thee it was shown, that thou mightiest know that the LORD, He is God; there is none else beside Him." (Duet. 4: 35)

The Hebrew laws were highly advanced and stringent for its time, mandating equity of rights for all and stood on their own merits as a divinely ordained belief; these laws were specific, as opposed philosophical; elaborately enumerated and many emerging for the first time upon humanity, becoming almost exclusively enshrined in the world's judiciary. Aside from the Hebrew God as the originator, none of the Hebrew laws were attached to their prophet's names: there was God with nothing else as equivalent; thus 'In the beginning God' [Gen.1/1] - and only thereafter there was everything else; 'And God created the heavens and the earth' [Gen.1/2'].

The Hebrew Monotheism was affirmed as foremost by an invisible God. It is the longest and most worded command of all; it also forbade the worshipping of any other Gods assumed by the nations, requiring this law to be simple, pure and holy, and equally incumbent on all humanity in a universal mode that gave none special privilege:

"Thou shalt have no other gods before Me. Thou shalt not make unto thee a graven image, or any manner of likeness, of anything that is in heaven above, or that is in the earth beneath, or that is in the water under the earth; thou shalt not bow down unto them, nor serve them." [Ex. 20:2].

The law against images is limited to worship only ['bow down to serve them'). Such a law, by a God never seen, was a most radical thought in the ancient divine king world, difficult to accept, isolationist in design, disruptive and challenging. Such anti-establishment laws, accepted by the Jews as a covenant with the Hebrew God, were in a manner also forcefully thrust upon the Hebrews. Namely, 613 laws were handed down to the Israelites in an unchartered desert, in a pre-compass terrain, with the prospect of starvation hovering accept by the will of this unseen Hebrew God. Here, many Israelites were initially not able to wholly assume the premise of Monotheism and they incurred some renowned failures, as with building the Golden Calf to appease Egypt and flee from the deserts. The eventual success of such a premise cost a whole generation being consumed in its fastidiously monitored study and wonderings in the deserts, in 42 stops in the period of forty years. Many of the laws handed down were inexplicable:

"And thou shalt bind them for a sign upon thy hand, and they shall be for frontlets between thine eyes." [Duet. 6/8]

The Israelites thus gathered before Moses morning to night in unending queues in the deserts, seeking explanations of the large array of laws handed down. These explanations became the 'Oral Law of Moses' and he became known to the Jews as 'Our teacher' and the 'Law Giver'. Moses incurred many battles with the stiff-neck Hebrew rebels, as described in the Hebrew narratives, even after witnessing great and awesome miracles:

"And it came to pass on the morrow that Moses sat to judge the people; and the people stood about Moses from the morning unto the evening. And when Moses' father-in-law saw all that he did to the people, he said: 'what is this thing that thou doest to the people? Why sittest thou thyself alone, and all the people stand about thee from morning unto even?" [Ex. 18/13]

'The Law of Delegation' was activated by a non-Hebrew Prophet, Moses' father-in-law Jetro (Yitro). It became one of the 613 Commandments after Moses conferred with his God in the Tent of the Meeting and it was approved, so says the Hebrew narratives. The sages thereafter declared:

"There is wisdom and righteousness in all nations."

Eventually, the desert journey produced the required results whereby the next offspring generation acquired the laws as ingrained forever in their hearts and minds. The forty year sojourn of the Hebrews remains a pivotal period in human history, an epiphany which resulted in the Hebrew Bible and a nation that cast a great imprint on civilization. It holds as one of the most impacting largess of knowledge and laws ever embedded into one group, encompassing a 3,000 year history of humanity since creation, and laws covering every aspect of existence for the future generations of mankind.

Often some laws contradict the new generation preferences, including by some Jews; this is especially true of the heavy punishments accompanying its transgressions such as stoning. Some of these laws are a testing by balancing these with other laws of forbearances, and the punishments are exchangeable to the period's generation; a historical Time-Line shows Israel used such means to become the first nation to abolish capital punishments; thus the law becomes a testing to measure one's intent of kindness or cruelty.

God was now directly introduced to humanity and thereafter all will change by its output. The Greeks were the first people from across the seas to acknowledge the Hebrew merits, and will extend this to the western world via Christianity.

As with the Israelites under Moses, such a plethora of new laws, derived under such conditions, could not be seen as reasonably acceptable to humanity wherever the Jews trod; it was especially not acceptable to the divine kings of the ancient world. The most primal Hebrew law of Monotheism was fully embedded in the Israelites' psyches and was inseparable; it became the bondage predicted to Abraham.

The law of Monotheism happened some 4,000 years ago in the absence of modern sciences. It was ushered via Abraham as in a stirring from a vivid dream's vision not experienced in one's actual reality, and by a limitation of any other reasoning available for the emergence of such a new envisioning, one that challenged the status quo of all existing beliefs, its source mysterious; its impact anew. The 'One God' law was later affirmed in the Hebrew bible via Moses. Monotheism, Creationism and the Judiciary were introduced to humanity and rendered with a challenging literary sweep that remains un-diminished.

Like Einstein, Galileo and other such thinkers that changed our universe, Abraham would have been immersed in deep rumination when a new jolting 'Eureka!' construct appeared in his mind. By his deep ponderings, Abraham would have been the perfect vessel for the ushering of Monotheism as a game changer, one outside of the ancient world's mindset, and one not to be confused with today's retrospective views of Monotheism as an obvious premise 4,000 years ago. This was the E=MC2 of its time; its impact and reach will be historically pervasive as no other thought.

Just as Abraham would have appeared as a radical heretic in Babylon, so the Jews were seen as different and suspicious by all nations they interacted with; for none but the Jews yet knew of this invisible God and spoke a language not shared by other nations. Here, the *'hi-biru'* [Apiru] - an ancient sound of the Hebrew as appearing in an Egyptian Stele more than 3,000 years old. [98] It refers to a new people entering the historical radar some 3,400 years ago.

One man, his wife, father and nephew Lot, were made to flee from the land of Ur in Babylon, as was one Galileo imprisoned and held as a heretic in the medieval world.

Just as surely as a spherical earth was unfathomable in the pre-science world, Monotheism was not in humanity's mindset before Abraham appeared: it was a radical and blasphemous premise in the ancient realm; a heresy in the Greek and Roman reigns. Monotheism's negation of the long held beliefs of mythical deities would have caused disorientation and angst in its time, akin to the formidable scenario of one confronting the disintegration or rebuffing of his entrenched ancient beliefs; for these were equally as genuine of all later periods: they sacrificed their cherished assets and possessions in a crises, even embracing human sacrifice, hoping for saving graces by their celebrated religious ceremonies conducted with devotion.

And in the First Century, the Jews were now confronting history's greatest power, one obsessed with Monotheism's negation; it was again a time of the oft repeated historical bondage assured to the Jews as a surety.

Eleazar's Dream. In a cave of the Galilee hills a shrouded secretive hideout is camouflaged with desert shrubbery. Eleazar sleeps on a stone bed on a mattress of dry leaves; he tosses and turns, heaving by the images that storm in his dreaming.

A man stands before an array of statues of various deities in his father's workshop; human torsos with faces of beasts gaze down at him. He pans the sacred foreboding statues his father Terah[99] made with skilled devoted hands for the Emperor Nimrod, the ancient king who ruled as supreme and divine in the kingdom of Shinar which is Mesopotamia (Iraq). Nimrod, according to the Hebrew writings, was the great grandson of Noah, one who rebelled against God with the Tower of Babel; one who sought to conquer all Gods in the heavens and thereby become supreme with everlasting life.

The man confronting the foreboding statues in his father's workshop raises an axe with both his hands. Then, in a frenzy of fury he smashes the heads off the statues. They each come down in a loud bursting of destruction, stone images which cannot move, hear or speak, smash and fall to the ground. Such a legend from the Midrash becomes an apt description of the period of our ancient mindset. Monotheism was born here, in this place and this time.[100]

Eleazar awakens from his dream in a jolt. He staggers to the front of his secret abode. Two Sicarii warriors guard his location; all is calm and quiet. Eleazar is panting and heaving, his face dripping in sweat.

A New Capital Crime. Monotheism became the factor of the Roman Emperor's disdain and revulsion, a term later refined as treason, heresy, blasphemy and made as a Capital crime; and it will conclude in history's most impacting holy war. The Roman war with the Jewish rebels was thus only about one singular factor; both contestants of this conflict understood the true reason of their war. The bondage assured to Abraham, affirmed in numerous wars with the nations of old, is now happening again in the First Century. And since the Jews are forbidden to depend on miracles, they prepared their meager defenses against their greatest foe, while praying, hoping and debating their woeful plight.

The thuds of Rome's march of might are vibrating the ground, becoming ever stronger.

(57). SOMETHING IS HAPPENING.

In an enclave of the Megiddo hills, moonlight and shadows shimmer on the faces of Hillel and Alexis. They proceed inside a torch-lit cave that leads to a sunken pool of water surrounded by rockery designed as seating.

Alexis: "Why is there such harsh bondage all places?"

"Before Adam and Eve were placed in their Garden of Eden, the cows roamed happy, nothing bothered them." Hillel responds. "They had plenty of the cleanest grass to eat in their paradise…all was beautiful for a long time."

Alexis, sitting on a stone, watches Hillel undress fully before him and then immerse himself in the pool of water.

"Then one day the cows looked up and saw a lion on the mountain…" Hillel sub-merges his body and re-emerges head above the water for breath three times. "But the lion could not eat of the grass… and it became hungry. See, all was made with plus and minus…heaven and earth…light and darkness…day and night…good and bad….how else can we be tested to know good from bad? So our forefather Avraham was tested ten times."

Then Hillel leaves the pool and nods at Alexis. Alexis removes his clothing fully and emulates the teacher's ritual actions. He asks of Hillel again:

"So we are only good when tested in the harshest ways… else we are not good?"

"The cow is not good because it cannot eat the lion…the lion is not bad because it cannot eat of the grass. Can you see another message here?"

You are saying Adam and Eve were tested not to eat of the forbidden fruit…and they fell by it?"

"The higher the test the greater the reward…those who fall lowest fell from the highest abode of the heavens."

"What does it all mean?"

"To be a Jew is to know there is but one God. Even to give your life for it."

"One God. Your nation saw this light long ago. The Greeks brought this to Rome as mono-theism. I have no issue of one God - it is a most reasonable truth."

"It is my sacred honor to prepare your road on this path of truth so you will prevail when tested. We make this ritual of emersion as a cleansing of mind and spirit. You can dress again now. You have chosen your road."

"My road turned when I first set eyes on Deborah. She showed me your greatest law and the most testing… to love the stranger."

"You saved her life. And mine. Two strangers before you."

"She did. I see her now standing before you…" He points his index finger to the air above him. "With a spear fixed on her heart. I turn now with a people who honor their God with such valor."

"In truth, our God was always your God. Your soul is returning, not turning, to the same one God."

"Your words heal my spirit." Alexis grasps Hillel's hand. "I know now the path I shall always walk."

A sudden ear shattering boom echoes in the distance; the thuds of approaching cymbals and drums resound. Alexis appears stiffened; Hillel smiles calmly.

"You are to be inscribed in the nation of Israel. Also, of the bondage assured to Israel's seed as a surety." Hillel is nodding and smiling reassuringly in the midst of the ground vibrating under him. "Something is happening now…"

Something is happening. It will alter the future path of humanity, acting as a fulcrum hinge point between two worlds, the ancient and the modern one it evolved into.

In her mansion, the Queen Bernice stirs her pot of incense powders; she pauses as the distant din of drums echo. She races to her balcony; she shudders, clasping her arms protectively around her.

Josephus is assembling his bag of scrolls, his quills and inks; he has been given orders to report to Titus; he knows what is going to happen.

In the Megiddo plains, Deborah pauses on a white horse with brown patches; she tightens her shawl under her neckline and races away into the paths of the hills she knows well.

Simon, dressed in Arabian attire, turns as his horse jolts from the vibrating ground; he nods acknowledging, then he storms away. He knows what he must do now.

And Saul and Ari's faces rise from a hill top peering.

"It is happening…" Saul's face has a foreboding. "Our families are behind the walls."

"Our orders are we have to work from outside." Ari reminds what they must do now.

Alexis turns to the full moon above him and recalls for Hillel:

"She also showed me that a name means a lot."

Hillel is smiling and bouncing by the approaching thuds on the floor, amidst an ear shattering burst of a foreboding symphony of crashing war drums and trumpets:

"What is your mother's name?"

A heavy pantry cabinet sways; it wobbles violently, then it crashes down to the floor.

(58). ROME'S MARCH OF MIGHT.

As the dawn breaks, Mighty Rome's war processions have burst forth like a gigantic caterpillar heaving through the cobbled stone grounds of the ancient towns of Judea. The Hebrew scribe Josephus is now embedded in Rome's march of might, to account history's greatest super power marching to the calamitous destination of the famed holy city of Jerusalem.

Josephus stands in a royal open top carriage, his scroll in hand, as he accounts the protocols of the procession of unsurpassed power, of one mighty force that alone ruled the world, and now challenged by one small lone nation. As he writes, Josephus tells what he beholds of history's most terrible holy war, one that will alter both history and humanity:

"The passing through of each town takes up the entire day and night. Such is the great mass of men and machines in the towns they pass."

The war processions from Caesarea contain Titus' 10th Legion, the 12th and 15th Legions and the 3rd Augusta and 18th Legions; each legion is fronted by their raised ensigns and numbers. They march with the numerous recruited auxiliaries from Briton, Ghoul, Germania and Cyprus, and their Arabian mercenaries and laborers; they march with their beasts of burden; the trumpet and drum bearers; and the largess of the world's most formidable new war machines.

The faces of the Jews are marked with disdain and fear, and awe and wonder as the processions of terrifying war machines pass. The Jews peep from their windows and roof tops, and throngs line the town's edges. Mothers cling to babies; food stalls are dislodged from the legion's paths and domestic lambs, donkeys and chickens run amok. The Jews assure each other:

"God will help us!"

"Be not afraid!"

"None can breach the fortress walls!"

As the only first hand witness, Josephus accounts the measure and the threading route of Rome's march of might:

"From their base of Caesarea's coastline, and proceeding south to Joppa, then turning inland, the pomp and excellence of this mighty power passing through Judea's towns shakes the grounds and hearts of its peoples. A double drum beat pounds the ears and feet of the Jews of Rome's legions approaching in the distance."

Behind the hills, in parallel to the Legions marching, swarms of Jews are proceeding covertly through Samaria, Judea, Parea and the Galilee - they are heading to the safety of the Jerusalem fortress.

Josephus describes the strict protocols of Rome's march of might:

"As the armies march through Bet El toward Jerusalem, they proceed in the strictest order, their steps and movements in the most excellent accord of their strong drum beatings. A foreboding assembly of bands and a passing show of might heralds to all that Rome's war has begun."

Josephus accounts the Roman divisions:

"First march the archers, footmen and horsemen - these to prevent any sudden pelting or ambush from the Jews. Next to these follow ten out of every hundred to measure out a camp. After them are those who make the road level, so the army might not be in distress or tired with their marching. Behind these come the carriages of Titus' army."

The beasts of burden, which are the heavy laden animals, are pulling the monster war machines mounted on massive wooden wheels:

"Next come the mules that carry the heavy war engines for sieges implements. In the front moves the Torsion Ballista, developed by Alexander the Great, a machine which can be placed on embankments and able to hurl massive rocks great distances against defensive walls. Every group of 100 soldiers is allocated one Ballista."

Josephus explains the particular usage of each war machine as they pass:

"This is the Oneger, a Roman machine so named for its kick of a wild ass action; this machine acts as a catapult which throws out inflammable projectiles into defensive towers. It is a most feared machine and usually followed with the Legion's final onslaught. Then follows the Scorpion machines, each given to groups of ten soldiers, these being the most accurate against approaching enemy forces."

Massive tree logs with iron belting wraps and heads of ferocious Ram heads pass:

"Then follows a separate procession of the most formidable Battering Rams - they cause any defensive wall to be shattered, allowing entry into the enemy's strongholds. These monster machines have iron sculpted heads of charging Rams, hence its name. Roman law made any defenders who failed to surrender before the first Ram touched the wall to be denied any rights thereafter. A gold crown, called the 'Corona Muralis' is awarded to the first man who captures the wall of an enemy city, seen here on several heads of the marching soldiers; they account the fall of all nations that Rome prevailed upon."

The Aquila, a golden eagle with wings raised and towering above its body, as in a swooping attack action on its prey, with red beak and claws, and mounted on a silver staff, is lifted before each legion. Josephus:

"Then come the showcasing of the Aquila, Rome's sacred ensign - the eagle, the strongest of all birds, which to Rome was the sign of dominion. They shall conquer all against whom they march - true indeed! Finally, the trumpeters and the main army in their squadrons and battalions, six men in depth, are followed at last by a centurion."

Now the enlisted Mercenaries and Red cages with young concubines pass:

"As for the servants, they all follow the footmen and lead the baggage of the soldiers, borne by the mules and other beasts of burden.

Behind all the legions comes the multitude of the war contracted mercenaries. The bright red carriages house the Roman concubines of pleasure women."

(59). A COVENANTAL RITUAL.

In a troubled night in Megiddo there is urgency in the town. With the news of Rome's march to Jerusalem, the people are hastening into the hills and the town is being deserted. Hillel and Alexis are alone in a small room in the teacher's house; there is a large ornamental chair, a water basin, a wine flask and a leather pouch set on a table. Hillel now directs Alexis to be seated in the large ornamental chair in urgency. He hastily serves Alexis a full cup of strong wine, gesturing he finish the drink. Hillel addresses Alexis amidst a din of wailing in the background.

"Three days you will be in pain, highest on the third day. Thereafter, you shall be bound to One God according to the Law of Moses, our teacher. What say you?"

"I say… Let there be light."

Alexis is reclined in the chair. As a short blade hovers in Hillel's hand, Alexis shuts his eyes and lets his mind wander. A vision comes to him. Deborah appears from within a misty stream of sparks of light, reaching out to him, hands outstretched; an immense glow comes to his face. Then Simon appears in the mist; the massive man is approaching with a threatening fury. Deborah races to stand before Alexis; her arms bent aback protecting him. Simon hard stares them, then he turns away. Deborah stairs in empathy as he fades away, then she turns to Alexis, taking his hand and leading him into the stream of sparks.

Hillel holds a cup of wine; a short blade in his other hand. He recites a covenantal priestly blessing before administering the circumcision ritual that will transform a Roman into a Jew:

"The Lord bless thee and keep thee.

The Lord make his face to shine upon thee
and be gracious unto thee…"[101]

Behind the hills. Deborah is cautiously returning to Megiddo; she is careful to avoid the Roman tarred highway this time. As she maneuvers the inner paths toward the Nasserite village, Deborah halts abruptly as she confronts Ari and Saul emerging from behind a shrubbery; their demeanor appears threatening. Seeing the two dismounted from their horses, Deborah makes a dash, riding past them in a flash. But as she turns the curved gravel track, she is flung off her horse when she hits a thin white ribbon that is not discernible by the eye of a rider; an entrapment prepared by her cunning pursuers. The two Sicarii calmly gaze at their captured prey; she lies fallen on the ground. Saul binds her hands and feet, securing her to a tree; Ari declares the charges against Deborah bat Hur, a Hebrew maiden from Megiddo who once stood before a Roman spear to protect her teacher:
"Betrayer of your people.
Murderer of Eleazar's family.
Harlot of Israel's enemy."
Saul expresses with uncertainty: "God help us if Simon finds out."
"The nation's faith before us marks our actions now…" Ari assures.
The two Sicarries descend upon the bound Deborah with daggers held in their jaws.

(60). MOUNT SCOPUS.

Mount Scopus is one of seven hills that form the city of Jerusalem. Its Hebrew name of 'Har Ha'Tzofim' is derived from the Latin 'Mountain of the Scope's Watchers'; so named by the Romans for its strategic location offering an excellent vantage point of the city.
Rome's March of Might concludes its journey through Judea's towns at dusk and her war legions have arrived at the outskirts of Jerusalem's fortress. Titus' own 10th Legion, the 12th and 15th Legions and the 3rd. Augusta and 18th Legion come to a halt before the holy city. Tiberius hastens before Titus:
"Mighty General, the Jews call this place as Mount Scopus. We are north of the Jerusalem Fortress - from here you will see the entire land. Tomorrow, your own Julius Caesar Legion will march in from Jericho and camp on the Mount of Olives, east of the city. Glory to Titus! Victory to Rome!"
As two nations face each other before a war, Titus pans the massive towering fortress before him. A soft rain begins. From atop the high towers, distant silhouette faces eye Titus as he sways aback in suppressed awe and angst of the mighty outermost wall. He gazes long at the fortress, panning the towering monstrosity ahead of him and the detail of its excellent symmetries. He pans the delegates secured in safe points, who have journeyed to witness this war. Titus grins; then he raises his golden sword in the air in a manic scream:
"DIE ISRAEL, DIE! DIE AS ALL WHO CHALLENGED ROME?!"
There is no response from the other side. The rains increase; the army becomes drained awaiting its orders. An eerie silence holds.

(61). MESSAGE ON A DONKEY.

That night, in a rain-drenched Jerusalem, a donkey enters Titus' camp. Around its neck dangles a twinkling bell and a parchment of Hebrew writing.
Tiberius enters Titus' tent with the parchment in hand, disrupting the General's nightly sessions with Bernice. Tiberius proclaims the reading of the message in a trembling, as Titus' face hovers above his Goddess, receiving the urgent report:
"It is a message that came on a donkey's neck from the enemy. It was translated by the Hebrew scribe. It says…
'Thus sayeth the Lord God of Israel:

I shall make Jerusalem as a burden unto the nations.'

A long pause of silence follows. Then Titus disengages from atop Bernice; his eyes a crazed fury. He stumbles out of his tent of swirling incense fumes, fully naked and soaking in the rain, his gaze filled in a manic terror. He approaches the animal, raising his right hand into the nightly storming heavens. His sword descends with a swift power on the donkey's neckline, slicing its head clean with one swoop. The donkey's severed head rolls to his feet, its bells twinkling.

He staggers aback dripping wet, blood sprayed on his naked body. He is heaving in labored breathing; drunken red eyes affixed on the towers. Then with both hands holding his golden sword, he slashes open the donkey with repeated gusts of blows. His soldiers stand frozen silent in the howling rains.

"The Jews have accepted Rome's challenge of war." Bernice covers Titus' nakedness with a robe. "That is the message on the donkey."

Titus nods at the towers, affirming the Jews' message to him. Blood from the severed donkey's head flows ominously towards his naked feet.

"Yes, this is it." Titus concurs; his eyes inflamed. He jolts aback, his golden sword rising, pointing at the largest monument on the face of the earth:

"Yes to Israel, this is it." Titus' face is distorted. "Holy… war…"

Hebrew silhouettes sway in the dark on the wall towers; in their midst is the shadowy, stony gaze of Eleazar.

END OF ACT II

HISTORY'S GREATEST SUPER POWER.

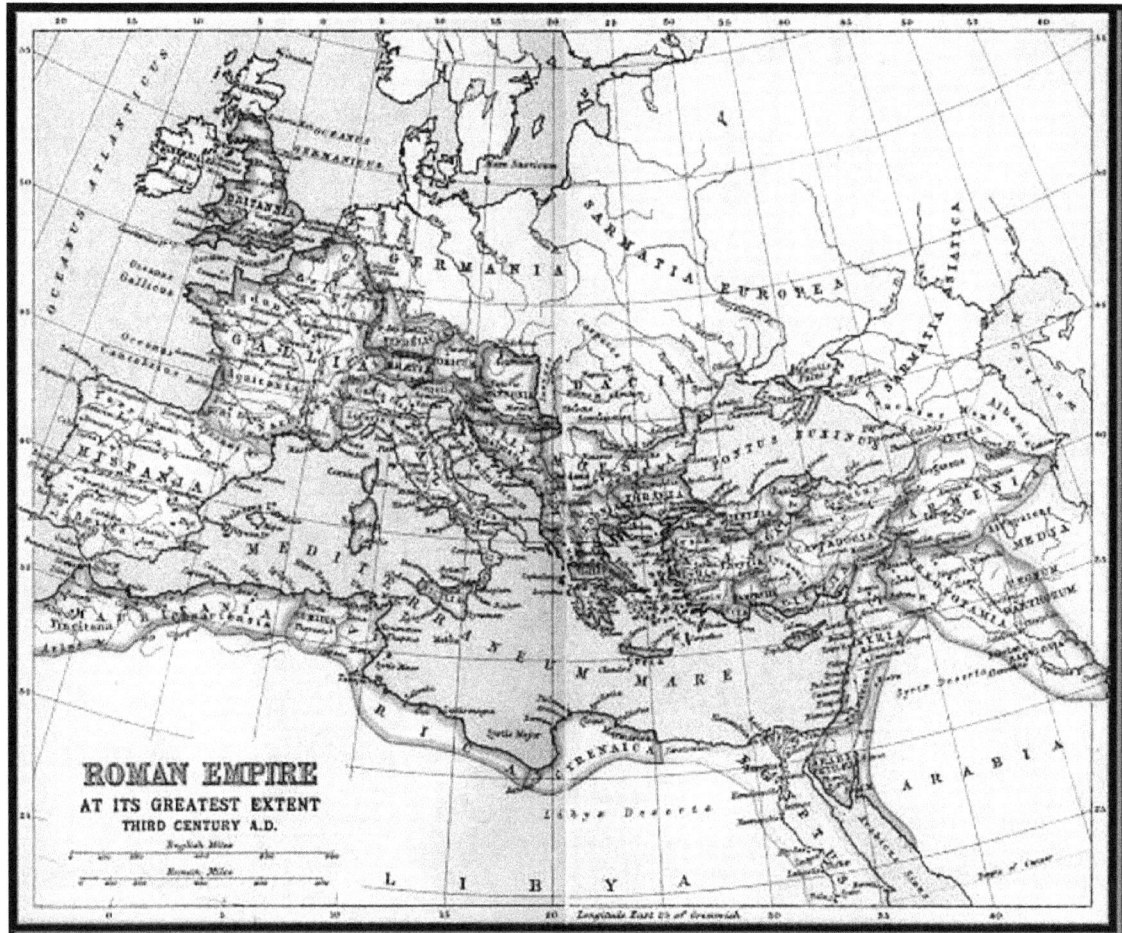

The Roman Empire. Source: S5

_____

- *"A snake or scorpion never injured anyone in Jerusalem."*
- *"The Land of Israel sits at the centre of the world and Jerusalem sits at the centre of the Land of Israel."*
- *"In the merit of Jerusalem I split the sea for them."*

_____

'And let them make Me a sanctuary that I may dwell among them' [Ex.25:8]

King Solomon directing his Temple builders. Source: S12.

Jerusalem - Origins of the Name.

• The hill city was called Salem and refers to the place that became Jerusalem and its Temple site. It is also the place where Adam was sent after his expulsion from the Garden of Eden.

• After Noah's flood destroyed the hill city, his son Shem started the first Academy of Study and was crowned King of Righteousness ("Malchi-Tzedek").

• Abraham studied in Shem's Academy wherein he received knowledge of God.

• Abraham offered his son for sacrifice in nearby Mount Moriah before a Covenant was exchanged with his new found God.

• Abraham added the word 'Yiru' ["Awe"], connecting this with Salem and the name Yerusalem (Jerusalem) was born.

• Adam lived all his life on Earth in Jerusalem.

[Tradional/Metaphorical/Legend] [102]

Jerusalem Fortress, 70 CE - N.E. Aspect. Source: S14.

Territory of Ancient of Israel

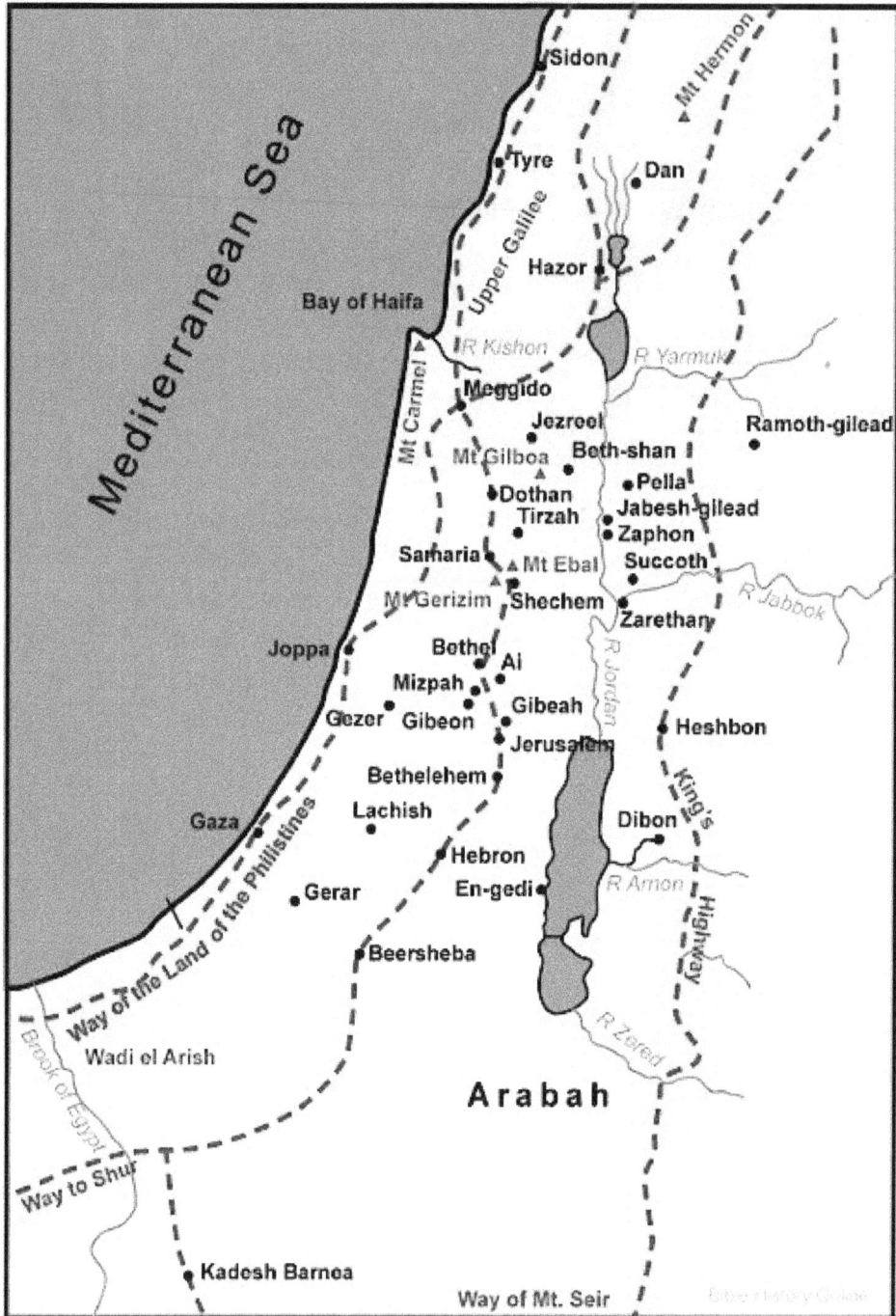

Mediterranean Sea

Sidon

Tyre

Dan

Mt Hermon

Upper Galilee

Hazor

Bay of Haifa

R Kishon

R Yarmuk

Mt Carmel

Meggido

Jezreel

Ramoth-gilead

Mt Gilboa

Beth-shan

Dothan

Pella

Tirzah

Jabesh-gilead

Zaphon

Samaria

Mt Ebal

Succoth

Mt Gerizim

Shechem

Zarethan

R Jabbok

Joppa

Bethel

Ai

R Jordan

Mizpah

Gezer

Gibeon

Gibeah

Heshbon

Jerusalem

Bethelehem

Lachish

Dibon

Gaza

Way of the Land of the Philistines

Hebron

En-gedi

R Arnon

King's

Gerar

Highway

Beersheba

Brook of Egypt

Wadi el Arish

R Zered

Arabah

Way to Shur

Kadesh Barnea

Way of Mt. Seir

"Whoever has not seen Jerusalem in its splendor has never seen a fine city" - *Josephus Opener.*

Jerusalem at first Sight 1:30-1:80

Artist Alex Levin Source: S13.

BEN HUR II EXILE

THE ROMAN WAR WITH THE JEWS

ACT III

"HOLY WAR"

TEMPLE LOCATION.

Mount **Moriah** is the name of the elongated north-south stretch of land lying between The Kidron Valley and the "Hagai" Valley, between Mount Zion to the west and the Mount of Olives to the east. [105]

'**Then Solomon** began to build the house of the LORD at Jerusalem in Mount Moriah, where [the LORD] appeared unto David his father; for which provision had been made in the place of David, in the threshing floor of Ornan the Jebusite'. — [2 Chronicles Chapter 3] [104]

"**For he saw The Walls** were so firm, that it would be hard to overcome them; and that the valley before the walls was terrible; and that the temple, which was within that valley, was itself encompassed with a very strong wall, insomuch that if the city were taken, that temple would be a second place of refuge for the enemy to retire to. (War Bk1:7)

Eleazar Ben Jair. "A priest named Eleazar, incensed at Roman high-handedness, led a movement to stop offering the customary temple sacrifices on behalf of the emperor. A very bold young man who was Captain of the Temple — Eleazar, son of the high-priest Hananiah — moved that no gift or sacrifice was to be permitted during the service of worship. And this set the foundation for the war with Rome. For, on this pretext, even the sacrifice for Nero was eliminated. Hence it came about that the war was so long protracted and the Jews drained the cup of irretrievable disaster. - *Josephus, 20:409*

Herod's Refurbished Temple in the Time of Flavius Josephus; 70 CE

The Massive Wide Temple Stairs [Reconstruction model of Jerusalem Temple] Source: S15

"The view of Jerusalem is the history of the world; it is more, it is the history of earth and of heaven." - Benjamin Disraeli.

The Temple Fortress.

The 450 acre city-sized fortress, measured from its rear backend, displays the following inner structures:

1. The farthermost raised Holy of Holies.
2. The Temple.
3. Massive gold and bronze Temple door.
4. Massive wide stairs leading to the Temple.
5. A hundred and sixty Massive pillars measuring 30 feet (10 Meters) circumferences.
6. The Overpass Bridge; a hundred and twenty cubits tall (15 stories).
7. The Massive Centre Courts: vast, open courtyards of smoothly surfaced stone slabs, each court the size of 20 football fields.
8. The First Wall - nearest the Temple.
9. Herod's Palace.
10. The Antonia Towers.
11. King David's Tomb.
12. The Second Wall.
13. Sloam's Pool; a Ritual cleansing, massive marble basin of fifty feet length.

14. The Perfume Factory.
15. The Rose Gardens.
16. The Sheep Pool Market.
17. Third [Outermost] Wall.
18. Two and three story dwellings tightly woven throughout the alleys and lanes.
19. A series of periodical exits behind each wall signifies a maze of deep, dark tunnels stretching underground across the fortress and beyond.
20. The Money Changers' stalls stand abandoned before Rome's Legions.
21. A Water Ditch [a man-made lake] appears before the wall; razor sharp blades dot the water surface; wooden buckets of flaming torches and protruding Sicarii daggers warn of underlying entrapments.

"And darkness was upon the face of the deep." (Gen. 1:2)

(62) HOLY WAR - APRIL 70 AD/CE - DAWN.

Rome's Legions stand before the outermost third wall of the Jerusalem fortress. Two contestants face each other in this confrontation, one which allows no exit features or compromise for either contestant. Now Rome is a mighty eagle, panting and heaving in quickened breaths, its fiery bloody eyes focused on its prey: Rome is set to destroy one miniscule group of bandits and primitive peasants assuming a right to alter the Roman world's status quo. Above the highest wall on earth, the faces of Jews line the towers; they gaze at the greatest super power amassed before them. In the distance stands a temple harboring the core of the

Hebrew law of Monotheism; therein is what stirred Mighty Rome, as it did all nations of the divine emperor realm.

Titus, Tiberius and Josephus are stationed on Mount Scopus, a raised northern plateau affording them a grand vista of the 450 acre city-sized fortress. Delegates from the Empire have come to witness this war from safe distant hill tops. The stiff-necked Jews have become an affront to all of Mighty Rome's divine emperors, and not without immense impact for Rome's other conquered nations and the right of their own beliefs. That one small province has alone challenged Rome's Heresy decree, rejecting Rome's forbiddance of their Hebrew monotheistic belief, made all of Rome's conquered nations focused on this unusual war, one not of might or terrain, yet one destined to become history's most impacting; it will become history and humanity's ultimate game changer. The Holy War syndrome began in Jerusalem in the year 70 CE.
The Roman Historian Casius Dio writes of the nations' reactions:
"The whole earth, one might say, was being stirred over the matter."

The legions appear as a swarm of locusts surrounding the tallest structure in the world; they occupy the entire terrain stretching to the distant hills across the Fortress. The outermost front wall of the Fortress casts a shadow covering more than half the Roman armies. The Jews gaze from the wall tops - 120 cubits high, at the unending legions below, arrayed in formidable armory with their new monster war machines in the midst of each legion.
That Rome was more than another brute force is now displayed before all; a dedicated, disciplined, majestically choreographed and fastidiously organized assembly of her power is showcased before a poignant juncture, outside the towering stone walls of the Jerusalem fortress. Rome's legions stand in sparkling costumes and armory, with their ensign banners displaying each legion's numbered signatures. Each article of Rome's forces is accounted, every action is measured, and all is rehearsed and ready. Perfectly symmetrical square blocks made of hundred soldiers each stand before the outermost third wall of the Jerusalem fortress; they cover the horizon east to west and extend to the northern hills opposite the fortress.

Atop the wall, the lad Boaz removes his sling from his shoulder; he squats to collect a smooth rounded stone from under him; he stands on a box containing a large stock of such boulders. He loads the stone and begins whirling his sling; he is focused on Tiberius, the Roman Captain some 2,000 cubits (Elbow to palm length) away from atop the tower. The stone whirls in ever increasing radius, a faint and formidable wind lashing sound; the people back away, fleeing to secured places in protection of the Roman response. The lad turns to Eleazar awaiting permission to launch. Eleazar sways his face in negation at the enthusiastic inexperienced lad. The lad drops the stone back into the box under his feet in angst and frustration.
The Jews again focus on the power amassed before them; crouched atop the wall, faces agape in fear and defiance.
Eleazar has a smirk; he calls to the lad Boaz with hand gestures.
"I could have hit their second in command?" The Lad winces.
"I know you could. But I have bigger plans for you. Always wait for my signals."
They turn to focus on the power assembled before them. The thirteen year old lad is becoming a man too quickly; Eleazar nods at him tenderly, then he hands him two berries.
"Raal!?" Boaz knows what it is.
Eleazar nods. "Treat it carefully…don't put it near your mouth. I will show you how to use it on your stone."
Behind the walled fortress city, over a million Jews are packed here for the Passover festival, one that introduced to humanity the premise of Liberty; the larger than usual gathering this year seeks also protection from an existential onslaught. Included here are Jews from other land and Greeks and Romans who came in solidarity against Rome.

The Jews have numerously faced such battles before; now they scatter about in preparation of a war with the mightiest force, one that felled all other nations and mighty empires. The Jews tightly fill the entire single and double story dwellings and commercial cavities behind the walls. Armed with war insights derived from their own history, the Jews understand their hopeless stakes and the inevitable conclusion of this war.

Vespasian has made his son understand the importance of this war for Rome and the Flavian dynasty's future. Titus stands still and silent, panning the fortress in suppressed awe, as a gladiator measuring and sizing up his opponent before battle. The two contestants face each other in a measured stand-off; all future monotheistic belief systems are on a precipice; it is a holy war for both these contestants and also, retrospectively, humanity's unfolding derivative history.

The Jews assemble makeshift fortifications in strategic crevices and behind shields made of tree barks; they have equipped themselves with clever village produced weapons and those captured and stolen from Rome. They are armed with daggers, firebrands, slings, fire torches, javelins, stones, spears and buckets of oil - and a small dose of ingenuity before history's most awesome power. The defenders behind the wall appear somber and purpose united, communicating orders in few words and gestures. They are seen as prepared, resigned and braced for war - one in defense of their strange Hebrew belief every empire of divine kings found barbaric and intolerable; and the Jews equally saw the same of their invaders from across the seas. Behind the wall, priestly groups are chanting war psalms of blessings before battle, and women are handing out foods and drinks to the defenders; youth groups are rehearsing sling rotations in the centre courts.

Those Jews arriving late are blocked from entering the fortress safety by the legions. They turn away fleeing for the northern hills opposite the fortress; those caught are strung on rows of crosses in the sight of the Jewish defenders on the wall towers; rows of crosses appear.

Finally, after sizing and panning the enemy, Titus nods, retreating to his war carriage, smirking menacingly at the Jews starring back at him defiantly from atop the walls.

"I promised my father a short war." Titus addresses Tiberius. "Josephus will ride with us and impart all knowledge he possesses of the enemy."

"Will the mighty Titus not afford even small forbearance to prevent this war, as did the great Caesar?" The scribe attempts to sway Titus' unrelenting focus of war; his deliberations are conditioned; he was not saved from death by any measure of benevolence; he was made to understand his orders that Vespasian must appear as Rome's light unto the nations and the rebel Jews as the dark forces of this war. [105] Josephus has few outlets to maneuver before Titus; he has no friends in Rome or Judea anymore; his deliberations are couched; saving the holy Temple is presented by the Hebrew scribe to Titus as a mark of Rome's glory:

"Let Titus now see the terror and wonder before us, see how the holy city's walls reach to the heavens - has any eye seen such works of holiness and beauty upon the earth as fit to destroy!?"

"Great Jupiter!" Tiberius is awe struck by the fortress. "Did I not tell you so truthfully? That wall would measure thirty of Hannibal's elephants high... those stones, the weight of a hundred elephants! Higher than the pyramids. Who made all this?"

"Speak, scribe." Titus orders, focused on the wall.

"The temple's raised location was chosen wisely by the Hebrew king David. He conquered the Philistines, then he purchased part of this hilltop from the Jebusites and established Jerusalem as the nation's Capital. The Temple Fortress will serve Rome as no other city's monuments." Josephus points at the wall top. "See those walls - they scale 110 cubits high. And that lake before the wall - it makes moving Rome's heavy weapons an insurmountable task. Titus must consider a negotiation to save the Temple as Rome's glory."[106]

Children wave hands from the tower tops; parents pull them away in disdain of the Romans.

"I see why this people have been so bold. They imagine this city's design undefeatable." Titus remains focused on the wall.

"For the Jews it is the most sacred place in God's creation."

"I have seen sacred places of Rome's enemies before." Titus retorts.

Josephus deliberates. "The city is not to be desecrated. Here was Abraham tested before his God, here was the belief in one God born."

"And for the Jews, one God is the Hebrew God. How convenient. But for Romans the mark of sacredness is Rome, and Judea is part of the Roman Empire. Remember it."

"That is why I appeal to the mighty Titus - let this great Temple serve Rome." Josephus continues his imploring.

Behind the Fortress, as the Roman side measures their war plans, the Jews prepare their own responses. In dark underground tunnels below the fortress, Menahem, the red bearded warrior of the Zealot group, directs male youth carrying buckets of oil; they proceed deep into a dark subterranean cavity directly below the grounds of the Romans.

Josephus continues his deliberations before Titus.

"Mighty general, the Jews can be convinced to accept Rome's terms, only they are held hostage by bandits who murder any one seen talking of the surrender of their beliefs."

Tiberius sways his face. "What purpose when they are a conquered nation, why do they not then respect Rome's divine king?" - He sees the futility of resistance to Rome.

In the underground tunnels, Menahem now directs female youth holding rabbits in their arms to follow the male youth.

"The Hebrew will worship only one God." Josephus responds. "In this they will all stand as one."

"How barbaric not to honor man's greatness." Tiberius is unimpressed.

"Rome believes in one God too. The emperor." Titus reminds, while he pans the walls, as if searching how best to proceed against such an impressive structure.

The scribe points out Rome's past history with the Jews to Tiberius. "When Caesar saw these works and learnt of our laws and history, did he see us as barbaric? Did the Jews not pay their taxes, even more than any other nation, or did they plan war when they had freedom of belief - tell it now in truth who showed more respect than the Jews to Rome?"

"Now I am Caesar. The Jews disrespect Rome's Gods." Titus speaks pointing at the wall. "And I see four suitable entry points. "Tiberius, we build four bridges across these lakes. Order 100 trees of strong wood cut down. Scribe, tell us who made these works?"

On the top of the Northern hills behind the Legions in the rear, male youth pop out of holes in the ground. They spread distances apart and pour oil from their buckets into rows of trenches prepared as their own response; the oil gushes down the slopes towards the rear legions' feet.

Josephus continues to deliberate before Titus, hoping to grasp any opportunity in preventing Titus of any thought of destroying the sacred Temple.

"These massive stones were cut, hoisted and brought from the Jerusalem hills by a secret knowledge. The Israelites learnt it from their labors in Egypt." He points at one tremendously large brick. "Those bricks measure from ten tons up to a hundred tons and some are more than 400 tons. Those walls are twenty cubits thick - they sit so closely pressed not even wind and water can pass between them. The walls cannot be breached!"

Titus smirks. "Tiberius, does Rome have a problem breaching walls?"

"One week - two days each wall." Tiberius clarifies Rome's war abilities. "Our Hebrew scribe is yet to see Rome's new machines."

"I was a soldier too and I once dwelled in this Temple." Josephus turns to Titus. "My accurate reporting is now the only honor left me. This I pledged to Vespasian. And you Titus, you also witnessed my pledge before your father."

"Let the scribe amuse us. Continue."

"Look there!" Their faces turn skyward as Josephus points at a massive bridge resting on an array of giant pillars. "That over-pass bridge - nothing higher in the world. Anyone looking down becomes faint in dizziness and unable to see the bottom."

Josephus now points them to the connective bridge standing on the tall pillars. "160 of these mighty pillars, each made from one block of marble, support that bridge, each pillar's width of three men holding stretched arms to encircle." Josephus stretches out his arms repeatedly three times to display and impress his descriptions. "Cannot the mighty Titus see the benefit of leaving such a Temple untouched for Rome's glory - and your own glory!?" A pause of silence follows the viewing of the overpass bridge; their faces skyward. "This place was made indestructible by Herod - his works were appointed by Rome - for you?"
"This is surely a place of glory." Tiberius appears awed. "It must be saved for Rome!?"
But Titus appears in his own distant thoughts.

On the hill tops behind the standing Legions, female youth pop out of exit holes in the grounds. The rabbits held in their arms wear head rings with cabbage pieces dangling over their faces; and bags of combustible oil are tied to the rabbits' bellies and on their backs. A young Jewess sobs, kissing the rabbit in her arms, then releasing it reluctantly. On their release, the rabbits gallop down the slopes chasing the food before their noses; they race swiftly towards the Roman armies below the hills. The male youth sway their hands, a code for the sobbing females to return down the tunnels they came from.
Josephus continues to impress Titus not to target the temple.
"..And the temple's white marble and gold overlays become a blinding light by its reflection of the sun on an attacking army. Those roofs are overlaid with gold spikes to prevent soldiers climbing over and to prevent any soiling by bird droppings - the place is sacred!?"
"Gold spikes?" Titus nods at Tiberius. "The Jews have been paying a tax to this temple for a thousand years - do you see why this place is so well protected, Tiberius?"
"Your father ordered me to study their books." Tiberius gives his own reasons for the temple's preservation. "This temple's strange design was given them by their Hebrew God. I have seen many wonders Titus, but nothing like this…"
"There will be a greater wonder. In Rome! Live to see it, Tiberius."
"Bless such a dream." Josephus offers. "I can bring you the finest Jewish builders to make a wondrous design in Rome."
Tiberius gestures approval to Titus of Josephus' offer. But Titus is resolutely single-minded, eyeing the fortress in disdain.
"And leave this affront to Rome shining in our faces, shaming our Gods and emperors by their barbaric laws?! How will a Roman ever pray before Jupiter - how shall a Roman honor his divine emperor when the Jews insult us every day before all by this Temple's protection!?" He turns to Tiberius, poking his finger into his chest. "I, Titus, will show you how!" He nods to the Captains of the terrifying war machines; groups of soldiers begin moving massive containers on giant wooden wheels closer to the fortress.
The Jews watch with dread, pointing from the towers:
"Look! Monster machines come to the holy city!"
"They want to kill us all and take our land!"
"We must not lose faith - our God is our truth."
The Jews spit and hurl eggs and refuse at the Roman soldiers. A soldier assembling war machines is hit by a sling stone; children on the towers poke tongues mocking the Romans.
"I don't trust those Jews." Tiberius warns. "They may attack us to interrupt the siege works."
"We do the attacking, Tiberius. Soften them up with a taste of what will be coming before entrapment phase. I assure you they will be silenced."
The Jews point at the war machines being assembled:
"The empires who wanted to kill us are no more."
"Now we face a power mightier than any other!"
"Greater than Babylon and Greece!"
A Jewish warrior smirks at the fearful Jews: "Be strong. No surrender - never give up even when your head is in the lion's jaws."

The Jews brace abruptly; they assume a defiant determined front as they gaze at the swarms of legions. They chorus loudly: "No Surrender!"

(63). ATTACK PHASE 1: THE ROMAN CATAPULT.

Catapulta! [Edward Poynter] Source: S17.

Tiberius raises his hand, giving Rome's coded signal to the catapult machine captain, initiating the first shot of the war. Boulder-carrying missiles from hundreds of catapults cross the horizon; they land 1000 cubits behind the wall. When the dust from its destructive force finally clears, craters emerge in the ground with a heap of broken bodies in the vicinity of each boulder's hits.

A mother fleeing with her two children clasped to her hands has her head blown off, her headless body falls amidst a great wailing. The Jews gaze silently in shock. Then they quickly remove the dead bodies speedily and return in haste to their war positions. They cover their eyes with their fingers in a quick prayer, grasp their daggers and focus on the enemy ready for battle.

"They return so eagerly to die and they have all gathered in one place for me. I will make Jerusalem their prison and their graveyard." Titus turns his fist up at the Jews as they defiantly station themselves for war undaunted. "No walls of stone will hinder me… I am Titus?!" He beats his chest with his fist; children wave back from the towers.

"Tell me scribe" Titus asks. "Why are all non-Jews forbidden entry beyond a point of this temple?"

"Not just non-Jews, everyone."

"Everyone…?" Titus questions in ridicule.

On the far hills behind the Roman armies, the Jews now respond to Rome's initiation of the war. Hebrew youth are whizzing slings loaded with fiery balls in ever increasing circles. In a code of counts in their joint symmetry mode, one acquired in the ancient Israelite tradition of battle, an array of fiery balls sling out from the hill tops in high trajectories. The fire balls land on the oil soaked grounds under the rear Roman army's feet, causing a sweeping fire. Now the combustible oil bags attached to the backs and bellies of the rabbits explode amidst the soldiers, setting the rear legions ablaze. It causes the front and back sections of the armies to race towards each other; many Roman soldiers fall in the surprise rear attack and the chaos of exploding fires. The Jews see the Romans in pandemonium, ceasing their attacks, lifting burnt Roman corpses.

"Every one?" Titus now stares the scribe in a demanding tone. "Are the Jews also forbidden entry - have you, a Priest, not been inside?"

"Everyone - Jews and priests as well. None but the High Priest enters the Holy House and this only once a year. None at any other time. I could never enter."

"Preposterous!" Titus challenges.

"Perchance the high priest dies inside; therefore he goes in with a rope tied to his waist so others can pull out his body. None else will enter this place!?"

Tiberius nods affirming. "It is in their ancient books."

"Very clever." Titus smirks disdainfully. "Scare the superstitious peasants with such nonsense… for the protection of your gold. Clever Jews."

"Not just clever. It is a command from the Hebrew God."

Tiberius gestures agreement.

Suddenly, hearing a commotion of screams, Titus turns toward his soldiers; he winces curiously. He notices the legions all face the other way instead of the temple; they march towards the opposite foothills. And Titus is confused at their odd formation of disarray.

"There was a rear attack on the legions, but we will prevail." A war captain reports to Titus.

Suddenly, the legions turn again, rushing now toward the temple instead of standing their ground awaiting orders. Fires are exploding behind them, the soldiers are screaming, many are ablaze and Roman armor is aflame. The rear legions are also racing towards the Roman forces, abandoning their war positions - one that incurs a death penalty under Roman war rules.[107]

Another Captain appears before Titus: "Fires… explosions in the rear! The soldiers had nowhere to turn. They have not disobeyed - the fires came rushing on them from behind."

The Captain hands Tiberius the remains of a rabbit with torn exploded bags tied on its body. Titus stares at the disemboweled torn rabbit; he turns in a menacing rage and begins beating his sword on the ground. Tiberius races to console him.

"The Jews sent fires on our legions from hidden places in the hills." The Captain pleads. "They had to abandon their positions to escape the fires - be not angry with them?"

"That is how the dogs attacked my father - from hidden places!"

"We must abandon the sealing of the Fortress exits" Tiberius advises. "The Jews made underground tunnels which serve them as roads. They can enter and leave from any part of the land, even under the mountains. They move now under our feet."

Titus jolts, focusing in disbelief at the ground he stands on. He stares at Tiberius, then at the Jewish children on the towers waving at him as a diversionary mode. Titus sways his sword in a rage, screaming:
"Up your Hebrew asses, Jews!"
The 'Cease Battle' trumpet sounds; screaming, burning soldiers are carried away. Rome's legions retire for the day with many war machines left burning. Titus screams - he flings the disheveled rabbit now in Tiberius' hand with a stroke of his sword, barely missing an ashen faced Tiberius' hand. He gazes at the grounds, pondering what the Jews are doing under the earth beneath him this moment; he beats the ground with his sword repeatedly - all retreat from his fury.
Bernice's words come to Titus:
"Know who you are dealing with, my mighty young warrior…"

The trapped Jews who were unable to enter the fortress now rush from behind rocks and hurry up the hills to safety. The youth with the slings on the hill tops vanish into the holes they popped out of.
The delegates are swaying fingers in the air, acknowledging the first bout of the war a win for the Jews. A silent moonless night descends on the fortress.

(64). ONLY THE ONE YOU TRUST CAN CHEAT YOU.

In the hinterland of Megiddo, Deborah is bound limbs and mouth and tied against a tree. Her two Hebrew captors sit by a campfire, deciding how to dispose of the Jewess who betrayed her people. She stares at her captors defiantly, understanding well their thoughts.
"No choice with this traitor who poisons our wells… one who sold out Eleazar's family." Saul affirms his position to Ari while he straddles three horses to a tree.
"We take the body to the village for burial." Ari nods. "We make it appear like the Romans did it - we found her on the Roman roads, no?"
She gazes at them in defiant knowing understanding.
Behind the dark shrubs, a stealth hand extends and cuts loose the three horses. Saul feels a sword on his back as a hand grip-locks his chin. But Ari is already set upon Deborah, his trained ever ready Sicarii dagger held tightly on her neck again; a tension prevails as Ari's blade presses into Deborah's skin.
"Simon won't believe this Roman killed her…?" Alexis also brings his blade to Saul's neck. "You will have to take me too - or release her and go your way in peace - what say you?"
"No peace with a Roman spy…" Ari craftily hoists his elbow, tossing a Sicarii dagger aimed at Alexis' neck as he talks. But Alexis shields himself by raising Saul's head gripped in his hand, so Ari's dagger lands on Saul's heart. Alexis' sword flings, hitting Ari's shoulder - he flees bleeding into the night on foot; his horse now scattered away.
Alexis cuts loose Deborah's ropes. She grabs Saul's knife from his dead body on the ground; she is moving away from the Roman.
"Why did you return?" She is backing away, the knife grasped in her trembling hand; a red mark on her neck. "You got what you wanted…?"
"Only Titus got what he wanted." Alexis, mounted on his horse, waits on her, his hand extending that she come to him. But Deborah is retreating in a horror, turning away in rejection of him, cupping her ears with her hands. She is swaying her face and moving further away. Alexis looks around if Ari still lurks, his outstretched hand waiting on Deborah.
"Better I die by my peoples' hand than be saved by you again!?" She screams in anger. "Away from me… all hope is gone now - gone!?"
"My hope never left me." He sways his face with his hand outstretched to her; his welling eyes the same pleading gaze she knew well. He waits, hand extended.
"God forgive me! I caused a family's killing by trusting a Roman…"

Alexis now understands her pain of guilt and shame, one he too shared by the works of Titus and Aristomy; he knows of the unbearable burden he caused on her.

"Your cause was to save, not to kill." His gaze is relentless, his outstretched hand challenging her with a strange and unwavering display of his truth. "Come…?"

She is turning away disbelieving. "All trust… gone…?" She retreats. "How foolish… a Jew trusting a Roman…"

"They say only the one you trust can cheat you?" He waits on her; she sways her face from his challenging words. She readies to flee from him now.

Suddenly she pauses abruptly; jolting, recalling; his words challenge her who is the betrayer; hidden thoughts sprouting a truth invade her mind. She turns to face him one last time, gazing at his waiting eyes again, the hand outstretched to her. A flash emerges in her mind: the smirking face of Titus; the words of Alexis before Hillel and Simon; the words of Ruth from her Hebrew scriptures blast her mind. She stomps her foot on the ground as if doing so most reluctantly; she drops her knife and races to him in an abandon; sobbing, screaming and pounding her hands on his chest.

"But my heart still says you are not a spy!? My heart says you trusted Titus to save us! But why? Why, Roman fool!? How could you do such a thing, trusting a killer like Titus?!"

He winces, shutting his eyes in pain, hapless with no words. She is screaming and shuddering in her torment.

"I am your only fool now. Move back!" She pushes him aback on his horse's saddle. "Lay your coat between us. You don't know the way in this night." She mounts on Tahrah, seated ahead of him, his coat between them. She covers her head tightly with her shawl, looking around, measuring her path.

"You told me you were not a warrior, but no single Roman can take two Sicarri."

"I had the advantage of surprise."

"My peoples' surprise… a Roman who keeps saving Jews - who can blame them for not trusting a Roman!" She turns into an exit track and comes to a clearing. He is enchanted with the picturesque setting of the place; the moon is hovering above the hills in the distance. As they dismount and rest under a palm tree, she gazes teary eyed at her secret friend in the streaming clouds.

"God forgive us." She shakes her face. "But the Sicarri won't forgive Saul's death. We can camp here tonight and decide at dawn."

"I fear for your pain and the position I left you in." He speaks with pain, beseeching her. "I must meet with Simon. He must know that Eleazar lost his family because I was betrayed. I must meet him, to tell him, I was the foolish one to trust Titus and cause you this danger."

"I too fear for you if you approach Simon. Be warned he will not believe you. But this I know, he will believe our teacher." She cups her mouth in sobs, shaking. "My own people account me a betrayer! No place is safe now."

"We are safe together."

"You have destroyed my life. Yours too, Roman fool… no place is safe anymore!?"

He removes his coat and approaches her. She stiffens. He lays his coat on her shoulders and retreats to a distant corner.

"Why would a Roman want to be a Jew… are you mad?"

"I will remain one even if you don't marry me."

"You are mad!" She jolts startled. "A Roman and a Jew - where will a Jew go with a Roman - where shall a Roman go with a Hebrew?"

"I have no place to go. I will be with you. Forever". He gazes at her helpless.

"Shhh! No place in the world for such a thing. Sleep. Don't speak anymore."

She covers with his Roman coat; her hand resting on her dagger. He crouches in the night's cold crispness, his eyes darting about in the night's shadows - he is looking for a revenge attack from Ari. The moon hides behind the clouds.

(65). AND ISRAEL WAS ENTANGLED IN THE LAND.

The sun rises. In the golden dawn of Jerusalem, Titus sits alone on a hill facing the fortress walls. He is gazing at the wall in deep concentration. Tiberius joins him.

"All forces must target one brick." Titus is focused on the wall as he speaks. "We abandon all exits for one single brick - one very large brick. When we have our breach, it will be big enough - the only entry required for the armies to enter." He nods in a fierce angst. "We use the size of those bricks to serve us - not the enemy."

"These walls are bigger than any city's gate. We had three plans. None as wise as yours. The hand of Jupiter surely shines on you."

"AND the hand of the Hebrew God? I gave you orders for bridges on four points?" He is focused on the wall.

"Done." Tiberius affirms.

Titus turns from the wall and engages Tiberius eye to eye.

"Then… the matter is settled. Have the priests ready the sacred maidens."

(66). THE ANGELS OF VENUS.

From the top of the fortress tower, Eleazar pans the legions before the fortress and the rows of formidable armory stationed between every six rows of soldiers; his face pans the legions from the extreme left to the right of the horizon, and its depth stretching to the hills as far as the eye can see. Four new wooden bridges now stand over the lake; Rome's Legions are ready to cross over and take position before the outermost wall. Eleazar understands the Roman determination and their abilities to do what other nations would not. His eyes are affixed on every movement of the legions.

The two sides have yet not engaged each other in physical combat; the Romans are aware of the Sicarii ability to prevail in a close confrontation and rely on Rome's superiority of war machines and their overwhelming numbers.

Titus is on a hill focused on a particular brick. He nods at Tiberius and the legions begin moving over the four bridges toward the outermost third wall. Eleazar signals Boaz to remain atop the wall; he retreats, descending, dangling on a rope to his base in a subterranean tunnel.

A rumbling sound. Behind the wall, the Jews brace as a faint repetitive thud is increasing in a pattern. They press their ears to the heaving ground. The patterned thuds increase in intensity; the ground is vibrating and shaking the Jews in their secured positions. Mothers holding large jugs of water begin to totter; they grab their children and place them in protected enclaves.

"Climb the tower and measure the machine." Eleazar directs the lad Boaz, whose face already searches for his orders from the wall top. "Report to me its distance and lifters."

The towers are lined with Jews focused on the oncoming sight.

Three golden haired Roman maidens, clothed only in white feathers and adorned as Venus Angels with leafy crowns, ride on white horses; they turn to the legions in unison, pointing their silver spears at the armies, stirring their desire for blood and treasure. They chant Jupiter's blessing:

"Victrixa! Erosa! Blessings upon you of Venus! She will hail the power of Mars for you! Hail Holy and mighty Jupiteres! Glory to Rome - Rome will not fail!"

As the Venus Angels disperse, a bulbous edifice approaches in the distance. As it nears, a formidable chorus of heave-ho chants emerges, rising to a great din. Then its size becomes realized to the Jews on the towers.

"300 cubits! 100 Lifters. Maybe more!" Boaz shouts his report to Eleazar.

The Jews on the towers gaze dropped jaws and transfixed at the approaching calamity; they jerk and bounce, gripping the walls to steady them. Mothers cling to their children clasped tightly in their arms.

"We chose north of the Jaffa Gate as the first target point." Tiberius confers with Titus. "Mars must shine upon us now - it is the strongest wall Rome has ever faced. It is a decisive moment."

A massive black log, wrapped with iron belting and fronted with a ferocious Ram's head the size of an elephant, is hoisted by a 100 soldiers either side; it is Rome's new war machine, of a size and power that has never been seen or tested in war as yet. Vespasian made sure his son must prevail in this war and sent him Rome's most powerful new machines. The legions are stationed ready behind the Ram; they cover the hills as far as the eye can see.

The Jews gaze motionless at the approaching monster machine and the swarms of armies covering the horizon.

In the Nasserite Village. The girl's father impresses the point of a small knife on a mark etched on the blue heart shaped stone; he gently taps it. Flecks of blue dust flare out; his daughter gives a cry of anguish. Her father blows off the blue dust from the heart and examines it closer. He gives his daughter a nod of satisfaction, then continues, making more taps along the markings. Then, ever so gently, he dislodges the marked section with a gentle flick. He puts away the dislodged pieces of sapphire aside and examines the stone. Now, on one front of the stone, there are hollow pathways between rows of arms, extending upward from its center, as if the seven arms on the stone are reaching out to the high heavenly abode. A design is starting to form. His daughter's eyes light up.

(67). ATTACK PHASE 11: THE MIGHTY BATTERING RAM.

A trumpet blast brings the Ram to a jolting halt, feet screeching and twisting to cause the enormous log to come to rest before the outermost wall. A silence holds as the Rammers gather breath from exhaustion; they drink gulps of water from mugs of helper soldiers. The delegates from the nations in the far hills sway their faces with thumbs down signs, many are rubbing snuff in their palms, sniffing the powders and bracing in preparation of the approaching calamity.

Eleazar, arms raised on the tower, readies the people for war with a thunderous battle cry:

"If you lose your arm - show no tears! If you lose your child - show no tears! Israel has faced this war many times - we battle again for our beliefs. The giver of all life says… Israel lives!"

Eleazar signals the Jews to move to the extreme sides of the wall, away from the path of the approaching machine. The Jews race to their war positions chanting, "ISRAEL LIVES!"

The Mighty Battering Ram. Source: S18.

"Witness now the might of Rome." Tiberius turns to the Hebrew scribe. "That Ram is driven by 200 soldiers and elite Rammers. I must now tell you, this is the beginning of the end of Jerusalem."
The Roman captain raises a hand in the air, counting 1, 2, 3, then a command of <u>CHARGE</u>! The Rammers chant a chorus of 'HUP!' on the count of 4; the Rammers proceed this way, thrusting forward in unison. The guards keep the procession in line with spears leveled at their sides, as the stone ground rumbles and wavers by their unified thrust of motion; a dust storm gathers. The Captain graduates the Rammers' speed with chants:
"Gallup Speed!"
"Torpedo Speed!"
"Ramming Speed!"
The nation's delegates rise up, focused on the mounting tension, as though witnessing a chariot race coming to its conclusion.
Behind the wall there is an eerie silence. The Jews are motionless, frozen in trepidation in the far extremities away from the Ram's path. They start bouncing on the trembling ground as the rushing rumbling din nears them; utensils and foods fall crashing; the people are swaying as in an earthquake. Women are placing children in safe crevices and hands rise to the heavens in prayer.
The Roman Captain, pointing ahead:
"SMASH UP STRIKING THAT BRICK, THEN FAST MOVE AWAY!"
When the Ram head smashes into a brick, it is flung aback, the great structure bouncing all that struck it.
The ferocious Ram head breaks away. The soldiers scream in agony, arms twisted and dislodged. Tiberius races to the wall's dust filled target point to check the damage, moving his palm over the stone for indents and cracks. He scrutinizes again looking for the smallest of crack lines. He backs away in shock, gazing at the bricks in disbelief. He shouts his report from afar to Titus.
"The stone is too thick - too strong!"
Titus bangs his sword on the ground repeatedly in inconsolable fury; the soldiers back away from him.

The Jewish response comes forthwith without pause, as if they assumed such a result. Eleazar now signals with hand gestures and the Jews pass on his signals in a relay mode, shouting their Hebrew codes; he points to his foot, denoting the target points - the slingers nod. An array of fire arrows zoom out from the wall towers, their tips carrying bulbs of combustible oil; the arrows hit their target points of the Ram's bases, which upon landing explode in flames, burning the wooden platforms and wheels of the Ram's foundations; six waves of arrows follow in succession. The mighty Rams soon become engulfed in a spreading blaze. Eleazer signals the Jews at the top of the walls. The defenders now drop buckets of oil down the walls and rain continuous fire darts, igniting the oil spills. The enemy runs amok in chaos of the spreading fires; Roman soldiers lay burning and screaming on the foregrounds. Two monster sized Ram heads are burning ferociously; the Romans are backing away uncharacteristically; Titus, and the delegates on safe hill tops, watches with disbelief.

Menahem now signals to the youth on the towers. On the wall tops, Hebrew youth spin slings in ever increasing circles, focused precisely on the Roman Captains. Many Captains fall by the stone missiles, leaving their soldiers disoriented and ducking aimlessly without guidance.

The lad Boaz's sling shot travels all the way to the decorated tent of Bernice stationed outside the war zone; Eleazar gestures with a hand kiss.

The soldiers point at the burning tent. Titus leaves his post and runs to save his Bernice, lifting her in his arms to a safer place; an intended stratagem of Eleazar to have Titus in focus whenever required; he nods at the Lad Boaz. Titus sees many of his Captains struck by the Jews' devastatingly accurate sling stones, which have scored far better than the Roman war machines. Titus sees soldiers screaming with fire burns. The Rams' fires spreading; a signal is given by Tiberius for the army to pause.

The delegates from the nations rise up in hailing gestures; they are acknowledging the second round victory of the Jewish defenders.

The Jews are chanting, "Israel Lives! Israel Lives! Israel Lives!"

The somber 'Cease War' trumpet sounds as dusk falls. Titus retreats to his camp with Bernice in his arms. Josephus reads from his scroll for Tiberius.

"Rome suffered a hundred soldiers and the loss of two Ramming machines."

(68). THE WAR COUNCIL.

That night Tiberius addresses the war council.

"This is a cunning people." A Captain says. "We never expected such action from these peasant Jews - did we!?"

Tiberius moves to the war table. "Rome did not triumph by her might alone. Rome's might is based on wisdom and valor. We have to use our might wisely with the Jews, for they possess the wisdom of cunning. We must raise embankments around their walls to battle from equal levels. But first…" Tiberius unfolds a map on the war table, one made of heavy laden copper. "This is one of their Temple scrolls given us by the Hebrew scribe. See, it shows their planning works made by King Herod - our Prefects studied this writing well." He points to two sections in the scroll; it is like one that will be discovered 2,000 years later in the Dead Sea Scrolls parcel, as a new writing not known before. [1108]

"See here, these two tunnels bring water from their water pools. We need only to bore holes to direct this water supply away from their fortress. This gives us a double attack design - to starve them and to strike them… the Jews will soon be forced to surrender?"

Titus points to various sections of the scroll. "Does this scroll tell us where their treasures are hidden?"

"Yes, this is the main feature here, a real treasure map, indicating unimagined wealth also." Tiberius turns to Titus. "Your father won Londonium by such a double attack design."

"The plan is good" - a War Captain confirms; the other War Captains nod their agreement.

"Then we go with my father's design! Then draw your plans to secure every piece of that wealth!" Titus, in his rage, grasps Tiberius' coat, screaming. "But I won't be shamed by the Jews again!?"

The land of Milk and Honey. This land suffered an almost dearth of water, a most precious commodity in this region. The Romans now begin breaking the ground in two sections to cease the flow of the precious supply to the fortress, for which the Jews developed impressive works of engineering to preserve and conserve what this dry land treasured most.

Thereafter, Tiberius' war plan to implement Rome's traditional mode of attack begins the following day: to imprison the Jews behind their own impregnable wall by a Roman siege, with no water supply. The Romans expend three weeks clearing the area of its trees, building from them the fencing boards that will imprison the Jews with an enclosure of a wooden wall that surrounds the fortress. The Romans use the wood to also extend the height of their intricate embankments of beams to achieve vision and attacks over the temple wall. They raise high embankments that stand precariously on wooden stems and stairs.

After several weeks, the new embankments rise close to the height of the outermost wall and a new 120 foot high wooden fencing surrounds the entire northern frontage.

Tiberius assures a silent Titus to suppress his fury. "None can leave or enter the fortress anymore…"

Eleazar, peering through the towers, is not daunted by the Roman determination and their resolve; he calms the people who now appear braced of a terrible Roman response, one that forfeits the advantage of the high fortress walls affording the Jews protection. Focusing on the new wooden embankments of the Romans, Eleazar has a hint of a smirk. He raises his hand and signals his "GO!" code. Menahem nods, directing the Jews' actions; he smirks back at Eleazar, agreeing:

"Again they come with fresh dry wood. You were right about our oil supply"

The Jews pour down large basins of combustible hot oils; it seeps into the wood of the foundations of the Roman embankments. Eleazar again signals GO! Menahem nods, relaying the code with hand gestures. The Jews unleash swarms of firebrands; the lad Boaz secures a closer position so his slings hurl fire balls on the streams of flowing oil. The Roman embankments begin to ignite, trapping the Romans atop their tall wooden embankment structures. The oils burn the soldier's feet; screams of terror rise from trapped soldiers; many are throwing themselves down from the high embankments to escape the ascending fires; the Romans watching their flaming comrades falling wince in angst and terror.

Menahem signals success to Eleazar; songs of victory resound from behind the walls.

The delegates in the hills nod gestures of another win by the Jews.

Titus confronts Tiberius.

"Your embankments cost me seventeen days of wasted Labor! This is not the army of Hannibal - is Rome to be shamed by home-made darts of peasant Jews!?"

"How long can they last the siege? Starvation will soon bear results. Mark me by it."

The "Cease Battle" trumpet sounds again and Rome retreats the war zone to replenish. The attack stratagem of the wooden wall of embankments fails; but Tiberius' double attack plan now begins to impact; the Jews' water supply is halted.

Behind the walls, Eleazar appears daunted as he gazes at the long line of Jews standing in queues with their families holding empty pots. He is wincing; the Jews did not hearken fully to his orders concerning the water supplies; the storage pools have dropped to less than a quarter of its normal levels, with no in-coming replacement in sight. The lines of Jews are given tiny portions of two gulps of water poured into their mouths; they gaze in alarm of the measly portions; they ask for more water and are refused. The people crouch in shady crevices to avoid the searing sun.

Two Essene Priests appear before Eleazar:
"We came to save the sacred writings."

Eleazar knows this group as the strictest adherents of the Mosaic Law; one who isolated themselves on mountainous enclaves and do not mix with the mainstream Jews of the Pharisee and Sadducee Priestly rule. These are one of the Jewish groups of a Messianic belief, one who have forsaken all desire for wealth, adhering only to the strictest Mosaic codes. They have come before Eleazar to protect the sacred Hebrew writings, not the wealth of the temple treasury. Eleazar accords their petition with respect, deliberating with the Essene of their important request.

"Why not hide them in the tunnels, under the grounds where the Romans now stand?"

"Israel is commanded to guard the Torah, there is the danger of fire and flooding - and the Romans will search out all places for anything of value." The Essene responds with assuredness. "What are you fighting for - the holy writings were given us by fifty-five prophets - they are more sacred than all else we possess, even more than fine gold, even more than your war… God forbid such a loss?"

"You will be caught and they will destroy the scrolls. But I have a plan for you."

"There is only one plan…" The Essene has an unwavering determination in his stance. "We have come to remove the writings from this place!?"

Eleazar focuses on the determined unwavering gaze of the Essene. "When you see me on the tower distracting the Romans, only then will you make your exit."

"Understood." The Essene now nods his response of Eleazar's agreement with them and advises: "The scrolls are already placed in the jars. We will make prayer for you forty days. Also, we will give you an escape plan - the Romans will not find you."

"Bury them soon. The Romans will destroy this Temple if the walls fall."

"Our word is this war is not about the temple…"

"Temple or no temple, this is a war. Every nation had a reason for war with us."

Eleazar turns to see a row of large reddish-brown earthen jars standing on the ground at the entrance of a tunnel. The jars contain the scrolls and are covered with mounds of hay as a decoy. Eleazar now understands the Essenes were confident their mission will prevail. Yet the Sicarii leader appears daunted: the Essene's message aligns for the protection of Israel's most sacred writings - and the loss of the holy temple - that the Essenes infers to an existential war with a negative outcome. Eleazar appears in lone silent thoughts.

(69). A NEGOTIATION FOR SURRENDER.

Two soldiers hoist themselves on an embankment to spy behind the wall. They see long queues of the defenders; each is given a meager gulp of water and turned away. The Jews appear to move slowly and labored, appearing famished. The two soldiers race to Tiberius, giving him information of what they saw. Tiberius nods, assuring them.

"It is a good report - both of you will be recommended for your service to Rome." Tiberius nods to himself, his plan is bearing fruit.

In the following morning, the Romans make a show of bathing in view of the fortress towers, parading before the wall with basins of water. They perform a joyous orgy of bathing naked before the Jews, who appear gaunt and moving slow; the Jews watch the Roman display in torment.

"No nation withstood a Roman siege." Tiberius impresses Titus. "You can see now how my plan is working to your success."

Josephus points his finger at Titus. "Will you, a great Roman, and one destined to be emperor, let children and mothers die of thirst!?" Josephus comes forward. "What kind of glory for Rome will it be - are children accounted by Titus as a danger to mighty Rome!?"

The Roman Captains and Tiberius watch how the Jews are moving in labored pauses; they wait on Titus' response of the scribe's charges.

Titus smirks. "Rome's price for life of her enemies. The Jews must throw down their weapons over the wall and come out hands raised. They must deliver to me Eleazar and their warriors must leave Jerusalem. Let the Jews show concern of their own more than Rome. Go now - get me a chant of their surrender so all can hear it?"

As Josephus climbs an embankment, he sways his face disappointed of the terms given him. He shouts his offer to the defenders on the wall towers.

"Hear me, Israel! Judea was conquered hundred years ago. What difference to honor them with a word or a sacrifice - it is only as a gesture of respect, nothing more? You have my word before all - Rome will let you all live. It's just a word - a surrender that says no need for war - for show only, and Israel will be saved. So choose life, I beg you!?"

"Betrayer of Israel!" The Jews on the tower laugh and hoot, they ridicule, chanting back: "No surrender of our belief - Israel will not bow to Roman gods as you do!"

"Mock me not I beseech you my brethren. Rome asks nothing more of you than all other nations. Rome's ensign will stand outside the Temple, not inside, I assure you of it?"

The Jews respond defiantly. Eleazar tears off his clothes from his body, dipping it in a small basin of water; other Jews do the same. The Jews appear naked on the towers countering Rome's offer by wetting their clothes and drying them on the tops of the walls. The wet clothes sway from the wall tops like flags dripping with defiance. The nations' delegates appear amused by the Jews' ridiculing of the Roman offer. Titus opens his dress before all and pisses at the towers; he sways a Roman thumbs-down "KILL!" sign at Josephus' offer to the Jews: "Satisfied, Hebrew priest!?"

Josephus responds to Titus: "You ask too much of them - you know well the other peoples obey Rome because they have different laws and beliefs than the Jews!"

That night, alone in his tent, Titus' hand grips the handle of the sword he sleeps with. Strange visions emerge hovering over his bed:

'My son, do not weaken - do whatever you must, but give me a victory over the Jews.'

Then a challenging smirk from Eleazar appears from dark towers in the clouds:

'I shall make Jerusalem as a burden unto the Nations.'

Now bells twinkle - a decapitated donkey's head hovers above Titus - a gush of blood rains down flooding his bed. Titus jolts, screaming, hands wrestling aimlessly in the air. He sees dripping wet garments sway on the wall towers with chants of 'No Surrender?!' Titus grapples in a wrestle, his fists swiping the empty air. The appearance of Queen Bernice's face now hovers above him. He grasps his sword again, pouring in sweat from his nightmare.

"What in Jupiter's name stands on your head?!" He screams at Bernice.

"This is the crown I will wear when I stand by your side in Rome. Look! Do you see the temple's symbol in the eagle's claws - see how the mighty eagle's face is pointing to the heavens - to your father's glory - and to our glory? Only your Goddess knows your secret fears..." She whispers it seductively, swaying a face tilt: "They don't?"

Bernice removes Titus' sword, setting it on the floor. Then she tugs the bed's sheer curtains and ascends the mighty warrior.

"I will crush their walls on their heads..." Titus heaves deliriously. "The glory... the glory. Mine..."

(70). LEAPING GHOST WARRIOR. [109]

In the early dawn, on top of the wall, a lone ghost-like silhouette walks in a defiant affront of the Roman army below. In the misty dawn of the sun rising at a critical instant, the warriors of Jerusalem have acquired mastery in using knowledge of the sunlight to their advantage in battle.

Rome's soldiers shade their foreheads with their palms, maneuvering to decipher the figure on the wall; his features against the dazzling sunlight being yet indecipherable. They position their stone throwing Scorpion machine and hurl a barrage from numerous angles and vantage points at the lone Hebrew figure, but he does not run and continues to advance. The delegates rise up gazing with swaying faces of wonder at the lone Hebrew's daring.

He starts to remove his tunic, leaving him only in a brief cover over his loins; he places the folded clump of fabric over his shoulders. He pans the Roman army below from side to side, naked bodied, side-locks of hair swaying all about his face. The Romans are suspicious of what they see; the lone figure paces to and fro on the wall top in defiant strides.

"Surely one single Jew cannot dare the entire Roman army alone… it is a devious thing!" The soldiers look around for a surprise decoy attack, but they see none. They approach nearer with their attack machines.

The Hebrew now turns facing the defenders' side behind the wall. Now he receives from them a spiked boulder they hoist to him. Lifting the large stone on his shoulders, and moving directly above a Roman war machine below, he bends forward while sliding his body from under the stone snake-like, releasing the boulder. The stone comes down crashing on the Roman stone-hurling engine; the machine's head detaches from its trunk and begins to roll.

The soldiers below, in shock and not expecting such a maneuver, disperse; the machine's trunk rolls upon the army in a crushing momentum of rumbles. The army flees back in pandemonium. The log crashes and ceases its rolling.

Titus appears, aroused by the commotion; he sees the lone figure on the wall extending both arms and screaming his message in a thunder, as is way when making fiery proclamations to his men and the people…

"ISRAEL DOES NOT BOW TO ROMAN BRUTES! NO… SURRENDER!?"

Now Titus' eyes wince at the lone figure; he is first to identify him as Eleazar. He is enraged, his body is trembling, droplets of sweat stream down his sun reddened face: it is his first confrontation of one who wounded his father, destroyed a Roman legion and regained the fortress.

"Will my Legions fear one single Jew?!" He screams out. "Turn back and do battle as Romans! Turn back!?"

Eleazar pulls his tunic from his shoulders, ties its end to the wall tower, and descends in leaps down the wall and on to the detached machine's headpiece below. Titus jolts aback of Eleazar's daring to approach the army instead; the soldiers also jolt in surprise of such an action. They gaze in horror as Eleazar lifts the head of their war machine, swaying it in his arms and points it at the Romans. This action makes those soldiers now coming back to confront the Hebrew, to turn and flee again; they again run amok in a chaos of dispersal. Titus slams his sword on the ground in rage. The lad Boaz, Menahem and many Jews peer from the towers in owe of their leader - they gaze in suspense of his daring and surviving; they understand why he is their true leader.

Eleazar lifts the broken machine head in a loop of his tunic and climbs the wall with leaps, grasping the tunic dangling from the top of the wall's tower, the defenders pulling him up with the machine head he is lifting by the tunic.

"Look!" A soldier points. "He raises the head of our machine and climbs like a monkey, when we spent months erecting embankments to overcome that wall!"

The delegates from the nations rise up, pointing and jumping in astonishment what they behold, unable to contain their exuberating. The soldiers start pelting darts at the Hebrew hoisting their Scorpion machine's head piece up the vertical wall, as if it was a palm tree and he knew each notch and crevice to grip with his hands and feet. The darts skirt Eleazar's back, yet he continues his climb with measured leaps, droplets of blood now spurting from his naked body. When he reaches the top of the wall, he turns - then he throws down the scorpion head on the soldiers who are now racing back towards the centre on Titus' orders. The machine head explodes and disintegrates, causing the massacre of many and a fleeing of the Roman army again.

Eleazar gazes at Titus, waving his hand, calling on him, pointing finger to Titus and himself, offering him a solo combat between them; he taunts Titus before his legions. He spits off, then vanishes behind the wall. The Jews chant a hailing of Eleazar in a great din of reveling.

"Bless you Eleazar, Amen, Amen!"

Titus, trembling in rage, races beating the wall with his sword.

"I am Titus! I am Rome! I will prevail! This glory will be mine, mine… NOT YOURS!?"

Then Tiberius races to Titus in animated, excited gestures, imparting a new plan in his ears. Titus pauses, reflects on Tiberius' plan, then he screams. "So do it! Let no Jew shame me again!?"

The large earthen pots containing the sacred scrolls are gone. Only the hay remains on the floor. Eleazar nods; a hint of a momentary faint smile. Only Eleazar and the Essenes are aware of the significance in their saving the most precious asset the Jews possess. Then Eleazar becomes somber again, panning the famished Jews seeking water and awaiting the next strike of vengeance from the Romans. He gazes at the streaming clouds over the Temple:

"Will it never end…two thousand years of bondage… a surety of thy holy word?"

(71). ATTACK PHASE III: DOUBLE-STRIKE BATTERING RAM

Tiberius holds two sticks as he explains to the Ram Captain the new war plan.

"This time we use two sets of Rams on the same brick - each Ram will approach from a different angle and meet here at one point - like this. Both sets of Rammers will follow the same chanting order - both Rams will target only one brick - the one I will tell you. Follow?"

"Do it! End it!?" Titus gives his permission in disgust.

The next day, a great din of rumbling resounds - more than before. Now two Ram heads are rushing at one particular brick that stands at the base of the wall. The Defenders crouch in safe crevices, cupping their ears, holding on to secure positions behind the wall. There is a tremendous explosive crash as both heads smash one brick. The outer ground collapses under the soldiers' feet; many sink into its hollow.

Titus and Tiberius race to the point of impact. The wall stands. Tiberius appears fully dejected, slumping. But for the first time, chips are broken away from a massive stone brick and extending crack lines appear. Titus's eyes glisten wildly; he grasps Tiberius' throat and raises three fingers with menacing eyes. Tiberius nods, terrified of the command.

(72). ATTACK PHASE IV: TRIPLE-STRIKE BATTERING RAM.

Tiberius again confers with the Ram Captains of the new attack plan.

"All three Rams must hit on one brick. Place more Roman soldiers to guide the Arabians - steady them with spears at their sides."

Behind the wall, the Jewish Defenders gather on the towers, gazing at the Rammers assembling another new attack plan. When the Rammers assemble their three Rams and charge, the complicated maneuvers of three Rams crash into one another, causing the Triple-Strike construct to collapse. The Rammers are unable to maintain the equilibrium of aligning the three Rams construct; it fails to reach its target point. The wall stands. The Jews dance relieved.

"Resume and repeat!" Titus now takes direct control of the attack process from Tiberius; he commands the Rammers with his raging ultimatum.

"Fail me this time and you will be crucified along with the Jews! Give Rome your souls as I have given you, and Rome will give you glory in return - I swear it!"

The Triple-Rams are re-assembled again. All three Ram heads charge at one single brick. The Jews watch with suppressed apprehension; they brace again in safe crevices, cupping ears and huddling their children. Many Rammers feet give way, crushing them in the charge. When the dust storm clears, the wall stands. The Jews kiss their tassels, pointing them at the heavens.

Titus' eyes well up; he orders Tiberius to continue repeating the Ramming; then he retreats to his private camp.

Alone in his war tent, Titus is in tears before Mars, a sculpted marble figurine of Rome's deity of power sits on a small dais; he is heaving to and fro, worshiping his God of Mars in angst as the thuds of Rams resound. His eyes implore Mars; then his eyes look distant as he recalls his youth when he was the lad Titus…

He is a lad again, tested in his war school by the War Master:

"The Roman phalange battle formation prevailed over the Greek phalange. Why?"

The lad Titus, blushing red cheeks and gaping wide challenging eyes, alights on his chair, his hand suppressing down his competitors; he hoists his hand high above the others.

The War Master extends his finger, acknowledging the determined lad.

"The Greeks pressed together in one big group - they swelled themselves together, like that" - he extends his arms, swaying face comically in a ridiculing gesture. "They pressed together, allowing them no movement of attack and defense choices - bad, bad move! But the Roman phalange divided itself into smaller groups, giving it many attack and defense choices - like that - DAT! RAT! DAT!!" He smashes his fists together loudly. "The Roman phalange was superior and able to conquer Greece when no one else could. My father is Vespasian - he told it to me." He waits; the war master nods.

"We honor Titus with this sword of victory."

The lad's face glows as he accepts the golden sword handed him.

Titus heaves with both hands at his God before him; pleading in angst; banging his fist on his palm. He hears the Ramming thrust continuing its battering of the outermost wall. He screams.

Megiddo. Seated outside a shattered house by a camp fire, Simon and a wounded Ari rise up as the figure of Hillel appears before them.

"We mourn for Saul, taken from us in his youth." There is pause of silence. Then he continues. "You must know… Deborah and the Roman were both betrayed in the loss of Eleazar's family, thinking they had a peace offer from Titus." Hillel peers deeply at Simon. "Both were innocent in this matter. I bring a message from Alexis." Hillel hands a map to Ari.

"The map shows the location of their legions arriving with shiploads of armory - heading for Jerusalem."

Ari turns to Simon. "No Roman would cause such knowledge for the enemy's benefit! Its meaning… the Roman among us is not a spy!?"

"Give me your word you will not pursue Alexis or Deborah again?"

After a long pause, Simon responds reluctantly. "You have it."

"Know now this Roman is no more a stranger among us." Hillel further assures both of them, gazing deeply into them. "Something bigger is happening. The Romans… their breach failed and they lost many men and machines. Alexis made us aware of their replacement supplies. Stop them?"

(73). A WALL WAVERS.

Titus continues praying in his base camp amidst a din of the Ramming chants resounding; his teary eyes beseeching his gods for success. His father's image comes to him again.

"Fear not my son. Jupiter will send you the power of Mars. It will come…it will happen…" Titus beseeches in angst; swaying both hands in the air; his fingers cringing impatient and demanding.

"Tell Jupiteres, tell Venus, tell Apollo… I will do anything they ask, even give my life. Let me prevail now…just this, father, I beg…"

"Fear not. It will happen, it will come…" Titus' father assures his son: "It will…

As the Triple-Strike Ramming continues, a brick chosen for unceasing battering begins to waver; it moved. Stone chips fall away as fragments flying from the targeted brick. The massive brick is now clearly wavering. The high towers at the top of the wall start to sway as one massive stone begins to slide from its resting. A downpour of stone chips rain down. Tiberius' eyes are fixed fastidiously on one brick on the wall. Eleazar is focused on the wall, the tower he stands on is moving below his feet; he pans the wall, from the ground to its top. He directs the Jews aback with his arms swaying; droplets of sweat gathered on his face. The Jews flee in a panic, as if expecting an earthquake.

Another charge of the Triple-Strike Ram thunders forth in a din of thuds and chanting. The defenders on the towers look down - the Roman Rammers look up. Suddenly, there is a prolonged foreboding silence; there is no movement from the Jews and Romans.

The faces of the Jews on the towers watch in a horror as the wall starts to sway and the ground begins to waver and rumble. An enormous brick is wavering, becoming dislodged, and by its dislodging, the entire wall above it is wobbling. Two Jews fall down from the towering wall top to the stone ground. A din of screams resounds.

There is a tremendous explosion - it renders the Jews and Romans unable to hear any sounds; many cup ears in disorientation. Rows of massive stone bricks start to collapse, bringing down with it the entire section of a 110 feet high wall, along with its massive stone bricks, its towers and the defenders, descending; the enormous wall structure is smashing upon the Roman soldiers. A storm of amber dust flares all around.

As the roman soldiers look upward, a great shadow replaces the sun and a blanket of darkness covers their vision. The ground under the soldiers collapses; they disappear under the massive falling boulders. The wall crashes on the outside, creating a huge dent in the ground, killing hundreds of soldiers and Jews alike.

When the dust storm clears, a large gaping breach appears where once stood the wall; the soldiers' faces are covered in thick amber iron dust.

The Jews appear frozen, disoriented and unable to move. Their faces appear to sense a catastrophe occurred. Eleazar gazes from the second wall tower; mothers and children cling around him.

"Will we forever battle for freedom… only to die in this bondage?" Eleazar questions the catastrophe to himself, silently. "And to prove what!?" He focuses on the lad Boaz, the over enthusiastic youth who had to become a man too quickly - he stands covered in amber dust in the empty hole of the breach before the Romans. Boaz stiffens; his focus is on his younger brother who stands alone in the gaping breach.

"The Breach." Felling of the outermost wall. Source: S19.

The soldiers gaze in confusion of their first sighting behind the fortress wall. They see a Hebrew youth in the gaping hole. Now facing the formidable Roman army, their swords and spears before him, the lad slowly raises both hands above his head, standing motionless, his side-locks and tassels dangling all about him. The soldiers gaze at each other confused how to proceed.

The lad Boaz begins to flee with abandon to save his brother, but Eleazar grasps him, pinning him down; the lad Boaz struggles wildly to release himself, even throwing blows of fists at Eleazar. Eleazar locks down the lad in a firm grip between his thighs. The Jews gaze in horror at Boaz's brother standing motionless with his hands raised before the Roman legions.

In Titus' tent the vision of his father is assuring him: 'Fear not my son, weaken no more, it will come…it will…"

Tiberius enters Titus' tent screaming excitedly.

"Praise Mars! We have a breach!?"

Titus' reddened eyes open up; he rushes out his tent and approaches before the shattered wall. A menacing killer's grin forms on the warrior's face; his hand grips his sword firmly.

"My father was right…"

"Vespasian was right…" Tiberius agrees. "In his trusting of a Hebrew Priest. Victory is before us."

Behind the wall, an injured Hebrew along with his men are caught in a crevice under the destroyed wall; they hope for mercy by the sight of the lad Boaz who is standing in the wall's breach with his hands raised before Titus. "Pray the sight of the boy's raised hands will soften the brute's heart."

A Roman soldier approaches Titus. "The Hellenists desecrated this place and were conquered by a small number of Hebrews, then by Rome, never to rise again. Even the Mighty Babylon who destroyed this temple was felled by Persia. Is it not an omen for Rome?"

Boaz struggles wildly to be released from Eleazar's leg grasp as he sees Titus approaching his brother standing with raised hands in the breach.

Titus focuses on the lad with raised hands. He measures the fear on his soldiers' faces. Someone behind the shattered wall tosses a sling to the lad in the breach, but the lad does not alter his stance, his raised hands steady as Titus' gaze is fixed on him. Titus turns to his soldiers.

"No walls of stone will break me. I am Titus. I am Rome…" Suddenly, he screams at the lad. "Your own God brought me here!?" He turns to his soldiers. "Let me see no fear of superstition now…" Titus again sees images of his father flash before him:

'Fear not my son, it will happen…"

He recalls his War Master's lessons:

'No victory without the death of the enemy.'

Titus races through the gaping hole in the wall. His sword slashes the lad repeatedly; then he slays the group of twelve Hebrews caught behind a fallen stone; he slashes and disembowels the bodies in his frenzy. The Jews on the tower scream and wail. Two Sicarii warriors break away, rushing towards the breach in furious assault mode; they are stopped by Menahem.

Eleazar signals his warriors, forbidding them from engaging Titus; the Jews watch in their agony of inaction.

"Leave the Roman devil for me. Promise it…?" Eleazar makes a solemn pledge to the Lad Boaz who lies in his leg grip. The lad finally nods. Eleazar releases the lad from his leg grip.

Titus turns to the soldiers in a manic scream, his sword dripping with blood and entrails.

"We are Roman!? And Rome prevails by our valor Alone! Not by chance and good fortune - not as the meek begging of an invisible God's help! Hear me - Roman valor is our only glory… and Rome says no glory without the death of the enemy! You are all as one now… go in Phalange and go like Romans!" Titus races forth alone behind the wall, screaming. "Charge!"

"Hail Glorious Titus…" The soldiers chant. "We are with you!"

The Roman army surges ahead in their 'Tortoise' thrust. The first rows of soldiers hold their shields in front of them; the back soldiers place their shields above the first row soldiers' heads, affording optimum protection from the Jews' responses from any on-coming onslaught of slings and firebrands. They march forth as one block, as an impregnable machine covered with iron shielding and impervious to attack, as the hard shell of a tortoise. A great massacre ensues from the catastrophe of the breach. The legions, fronting shields and swords protruding, storm ahead, cutting down a great populace of the defenders.

(74). "NO SURRENDER!"

The Jews are not retreating. Instead of the anticipated fleeing, the Jews defy the rushing Roman onslaught; they fling themselves on the Roman swords, fighting back and screaming 'NO SURRENDER!' as they fall, dashing themselves on Roman swords.

The slain accumulate as mounds and hills, the soldiers having to climb over the dead while confronting streams of Jews rushing on them. The soldiers soon become exhausted from their slaughtering; the battle skilled Romans are now confused, unsure, labored and drenched in blood by the relentless willingness of the Jews to die rather than surrender. Entrails dangle from every Roman sword and mounds of dead pile the ground before them.

The Legions begin retreating, as a second assembly of soldiers immediately advances in Tortoise formation to replace the exhausted retreating front row assembly. Now Jewish youth emerge from the heap of corpses; they slither and crawl on the ground like snakes and cut down the unprotected feet of the Tortoise formation soldiers; each sway of their swords slices the feet of many soldiers as the Sicarii daggers pierce the Roman ankles, staking their feet to the ground. The screams of the Romans echo throughout the fortress; the Jews slithering on the ground advance towards the Romans crawling like a swarm of snakes. The Romans start withdrawing, fearing their armor and shields offer to protection or defense at the advancing Jews crawling on the ground determinably toward them.

Titus screams: "Rome does not retreat from the Jews!" His soldiers hold him back from charging alone.

The screams of the Romans echo - their feet sliced, their bones protruding; other soldiers scream with their foot pierced and impaled to the ground with Sicarii daggers.

A Jew tosses a Roman foot at the legions - they retreat in terror.

The Jews chant: "No Surrender!"

The Roman writer Deo Cassius reports of this first breach:

"..Though a breach was made in the wall by means of the war engines, nevertheless the capture of the place did not immediately follow even then. On the contrary, the defenders killed great numbers of Romans who tried to crowd through the opening. Nevertheless, the soldiers, because of their superstition, did not immediately rush in, but at last, under compulsion from Titus, they made their way inside. Then the Jews defended themselves much more vigorously than before, as if they had discovered a piece of rare good fortune in being able to fight near the Temple and fall in its defense."

Tiberius calms Titus: "The army will not retreat - let me govern them." He stands before the retreating soldiers, barring them, an array of soldiers with him:

"Be warned! It is my duty to remind all in Rome's army…" He orders the front rows not to retreat. "Any who abandons his position must be put to death. Retreat is assured crucifixion along with the Jews. The Arabian forces will move first. Remember the Gods are on our side - kill all who battle so the rest will fast surrender. Turn! Charge!?"

Josephus writes of the terrible plight of a Roman soldier:

"The law of the Romans was terrible, that he who left his post there, let the occasion be whatsoever it might be, he was to die for it; so that body of soldiers, preferring rather to die in fighting courageously than as a punishment for their cowardice, stood firm; and at the necessity these men were in of standing to it, many of the others that had run away, out of shame."

As the Roman army turns back to face the Jews, they pause; they know that the Jews will die killing many Romans. Titus rushes forth - his sword chops the hands of many Jews slithering on the ground. Tiberius places ten soldiers to surround Titus from attack; he orders the Arabian mercenaries to go forward; the Romans proceed behind the Arabians.

The Romans confront arrows coming out of a dark tunnel - they proceed inside, charging with a great force. Then Jews appear from their outside hideouts, throwing fire torches on the tunnel's entrance, which they previously flooded with combustible oil. A great fire seals the faith of the trapped Roman soldiers who rushed into the tunnel. The Jews hurl buckets of oil on the advancing Arabian soldiers, followed by firebrands and slings carrying fiery balls - the Romans are retreating again.

"Bastards! Bastards!" - Titus screams at the retreating Arabian and Romans; he is held back from charging forward by soldiers clinging to his arms. "I will not see such a thing - Rome never retreats! Tear their hands!"

The Arabians move forward again, hopping and dancing to dodge the swift Sicarii blades swiping and slashing on the ground, piercing the soldier's feet. Tiberius is aghast the Roman Tortoise attack is being foiled when no nation could withstand this war formation; he murmurs to himself: 'I told you these Jews will be a problem for Rome…"

The anticipated surrender is yet elusive. Instead of the anticipated fleeing, the Jews are rushing forward at the oncoming Romans, impaling themselves on the Roman swords. They burn themselves in oil, rushing on the soldiers to cause them burning also, thus they caused great terror in the Romans who again start retreating. Many elderly bearded Jews leave their safe places, jumping on the swords and piercing themselves, overwhelming the soldiers by their own armor.

But the Jews eventually become overwhelmed by the mass of the Roman numbers.

The Defenders behind the second wall watch sobbing helplessly as the Roman killing machines march forth decimating the masses, now reduced to meager numbers. Many women maidens engaged in this war are dragged away by Roman Collectors and held separately in cages; they scream, begging their comrades to kill them instead.

Eleazar pans the massacre with no emotions, signaling the remaining Jews to retreat behind the second wall. Mounds of the slaughtered appear in the forecourts between the destroyed third and second walls; an area once holding tightly mingled Jews up to a hundred thousand. Soldiers are hacking any bodies showing signs of life; jewelry and coins on the dying are ripped off.

The Jews behind the second wall chant a defiant "No surrender!" The Romans gaze exhausted and wasted; frustrated of the Jews unwavering determination. A long eerie silence holds as two battered nations gaze at each confronting and unwavering.

Tiberius announces to end the day's slaughter, preparing the army for the next day of the Roman war with the Jews:

"Clear the paths for tomorrow. Drop the dead in the lake. We attack the second wall at dawn. Leave only vigil during the night."

"I will place their Ark in Rome and break the Jews' covenant with their God." Titus declares. "I promised to respect this Arc so the queen and the Hebrew scribe will assist me in its location. Fetch me Alexis the road worker."

As the night approaches, Josephus, atop an embankment, records in his scroll.

Behind the wall, a wailing Hebrew mother approaches Eleazar.

"My sons are still children, but you use them as your warriors. Are you sure of the choices you make for us with the Romans - are you sure!?"

"Choices? We have none. Both your sons must report to Menahem for battle before sunrise."

Eleazar turns to see an Essene priest before him.

"The holy writings… saved."

"Where did you save them, you can trust me?" But the Essene has vanished. Eleazar now understands the writings will be safeguarded.

The writings were protected from the Romans who would later search out the Qumran Mountains seeking hidden treasures; they will kill this group of Essenes in its quest to destroy all Hebrew archives. Yet the writings will remain shrouded from all in the region for two thousand years, hidden deep in the crevices of the mountains north-west of Jerusalem in the region of the Dead Sea. These will be named as 'The Dead Sea Scrolls', containing the oldest and richest collection of the First Century War and of the Hebrew Scriptures.

Eleazar signals his warriors to come hear him.

"Tonight, in the dark, collect the uniforms of dead Roman soldiers. Wear them and be ready in the sunrise."

That night, the Jews are removing bloody uniforms from dead Roman soldiers. They take covert positions behind fallen bricks; they hide in crevices, many playing dead among the strewn corpses all about.

"It is the Sabbath eve this night - we can't battle!?" A new recruit lad from the Peace Party who joined the Sicarii addresses Eleazar.

"For this sacred deed you can break the Sabbath a thousand times" - An elderly Jew responds. "Otherwise you are sinning by our God's laws."

Eleazar responds to him. "We are fighting to defend the first and second laws of our God from Sinai - Israel does not bow to Roman brutes. Now we have no other laws." He pans the Jews challengingly; none respond. Eleazar turns to the elderly bearded Jew: "No Tefillin… no laws till victory is at hand." The old man nods, tears streaming down his face.

(75). THE SECOND WALL.

In the misty dawn, the Roman army, resolute and unrelenting, proceeds towards the second wall; they are transporting Battering Rams to the forecourt between the third and second walls. All is quiet in the fortress. Eleazar signals with a swaying hand, and groups of Jews, dressed in Roman soldier's attire, go forth. They mingle into the Roman army, even lifting Roman weapons, as if they are Roman soldiers performing their duties.

The Roman soldiers begin to drop screaming and dyeing, and none see where the attacks come from; they look but see no Hebrews in the distance of the second wall towers, nor do they see any attacks emanating from the defender's positions. The Sicarii daggers pierce with lightning speed then disappear; the Jews are screaming as if they are Roman soldiers being attacked, thereby escaping their discovery. There is pandemonium and confusion, the daggers at immediate close range impacting devastating losses on the Roman army. The hidden youth on the towers now drop the fleeing Romans with sling shots that hurl skull smashing rocks and fire balls.

The Roman army starts to retreat in panic and chaos; the Jews dressed in Roman uniforms run with them, mingling among them, even until the Roman bases beyond the fortress.

"Sorcery!" The fleeing soldiers are screaming. "The Jews sent ghosts upon us - they are using sorcery of their invisible God!"

Eleazar climbs via the back hidden edges of the wall; he proceeds covertly, closing in on Titus' base camp. Boaz, watching Eleazar proceeding on the wall edges, begins to follow; but Eleazar gestures he not follow him. The lad winces in pain, then retreats, watching from a distance. Eleazar pauses to swipe his blade into a poison berry, then proceeds again, gazing now at the distant target of Titus' tent, his dagger held in his jaw by its handle, clear from the poisoned blade. Boaz, gripping his sling, watches, ever ready to proceed if Eleazar fails.

Titus stands outside his tent, monitoring the war, banging his fist on his palm.

Now Eleazar comes to a stop, climbing back to the wall top. Boaz sways at the large distance between Eleazar and Titus; he loads a stone in his sling. Eleazar is measuring the distance and the wind, then, in a swift swaying of his hand he tosses two daggers at Titus' tent. One dagger just misses; the other hit reaches its target - it pierces Titus' armor, gashing into his arm:

"A present from Boaz." Eleazar screams. The lad begins a hysterical burst of tears and laughter.

Titus is screaming in terror and agony. Eleazar's stony defiant gaze engages Titus in the distance; then he blows on a ram's horn and vanishes. The Jews are chanting praises and rejoicing.

"Get that devil Jew - get him!?" Titus is carried away to Bernice's tent and placed on a table; he is tied so he cannot move or get up, as he so appeared he would do. Strong drink is poured down his throat; Bernice applies her powders on the swollen purple wound. The dislodged blade is examined - it appears razor edged on both sides, its point curled upward and serrated; green stains appear on its glistening edges.

"Poison." Bernice whispers in the doctor's ears. "His hand will never recover again. As with his father leg."

"What manner of devil is this?" Titus is delirious and shuddering as he clings to Bernice. "Shall one Jew alone cause me such humiliation before Rome, before all the nations? Shall he even shame me by my father!? Prepare for hell, devil Jews!"

"Be silent and still. You are prevailing in this war. None were able to breach the wall - you did. Do you yet not see how all your desires are being fulfilled? Enjoy this pain - it's a small price to pay for a mighty warrior."

"Yes… all my desires… small price. Only you understand me, only you - they don't."

"I know what to do in the morning." Tiberius approaches Titus. "All is ready - the bricks around the breach come down easily - it will clear the way for more than one legion attacking. If you can rise and be far from the wall tomorrow you will be pleased…"

The man in a bone tunic stands before Eleazar again.

"Now the Romans come, seeking to destroy us…. yet this war is not about Rome."

"What is it about old man, your own secret… not for those who die so freely that you say it is not about Rome?"

"This war… not about Rome." He retreats; then he vanishes.

Eleazar, on the second wall tower, removes his blood soaked Roman garment and flings it, swaying it across the wall. The Jews do the same; blood soaked Roman uniforms float and descend from the towers upon the Romans. The soldiers watch it rage and foreboding of their blood-soaked uniforms descending on them.

(76). TO LOVE THE STRANGER.

In a garden patch of Megiddo, Deborah gazes at the Moon as Alexis whispers to her.

"If everyone wants to destroy this nation, how can a Jew love the stranger?"

"I see no stranger before me." She turns to him. "And my heart is beating too much now."

He embraces her, whispering as they gaze at a golden sun setting behind the hills of Megiddo.

"Therefore you shall love this stranger…"

They fall into each other's embrace in a long held passion; rolling on the grassy meadows in an abandon. She pushes him away from her, then she grabs him again to her, grasping his hair, kicking him and kissing him. There is an abandon now, as a Hebrew maiden crossing the thresholds of a forbidden love; in the love of a stranger in a strange land.

Suddenly, abruptly, she backs away, disengaging, retreating from him; breathlessly.

"Therefore we must choose life… and it points us across the Jordan!?"

"Jerusalem is this side of the Jordan?"

"We must choose life first… and now life is on the other side of the river. I feel something terrible is coming… a darkness…I feel it…"

"I cannot stay away from Jerusalem at this time. Your brother's name is on me…" There is a long pause. "What would he do?"

"My brother would be alive if he heeded me…" She slumps now, breaking and sobbing. "Jerusalem always demands the greatest sacrifice… and I have nothing more to give. Just you. I feel the world is coming to an end now."

"Then we must never part." He takes her hand to his chest. "I placed my life in these hands. The only destruction I fear is our parting."

"We've been told it is coming… something terrible. I feel it." She begins to shudder and shake.

"I feel it too." He sways her in his arms. "And it is bigger than us. This nation's belief is being challenged by great forces."

There is a horse's neighing and Alexis jolts. The moonlight shimmers through the streaming clouds. The large figure of Florian stands before them.

"Master, Titus has again made your urgent attendance in Jerusalem. I am sent to escort you to him."

Deborah races before Alexis, hands bent back, protecting him in her defiant stance.

"If you go to Jerusalem - so will I!?"

"I made a pledge to Titus and I will abide it." Alexis turns to respond to Florian. "I will journey in the morning light to Jerusalem, but this night is my own."

"As you wish, Master. Only know that both our lives are at risk if you fail Titus." Florian bows and departs. Alexis turns to Deborah in a display of his devotion.

"Promise me you won't join with those going to Jerusalem and I will give you my word not to join this war… then I will cross the Jordan and come to you. We choose life - honorably. What say you?"

She understands his intent but she is unable to respond, her face slumped in her hands; she begins to shudder. He whispers it approaching closer to her. "It was told to Abraham, whatever Sarah tells you to do - do it.[110] You must tell me yes or no…?" He waits on her. She is unable to refute him.

"Even as the darkest omens come, whatever happens, we shall return to Jerusalem. Together. I know this in my heart. I see it… I see it!?

"Now you are my Jerusalem. I will leave at dawn."

The moon above Megiddo hides behind dark clouds as he holds her clasped in his arms. "We must never abandon each other."

(77). THE PEACE PARTY.

As the Romans prepare their war machines before the second wall, the Jewish groups behind the wall conduct a secret meeting in the midst of the Jews racing in panic to secure fortified positions in anticipation of a great forthcoming attack. Peretz, representing the Peace Party, is opposed to the Zealots and the Sicarii in the war with Rome; he confronts Menahem in the presence of Eleazar.

"How clever of Eleazar to fool the Romans with their own uniforms! Will it make the Romans go home - or are we to pray for more tricks when the Romans come back tomorrow with even greater vengeance?"

"Your party knows our position - no negotiation of our beliefs. So what is your new advice - that we worship Jupiter to please Rome - or do you prefer Mars?" Menahem responds with sarcasm.

"What belief if there is no life, no Jews, no Jerusalem?"

They pause as the thunder from a falling brick echoes. The silent and somber Eleazar plucks out the thorns from a rose stem as Perez and Menahem deliberate with venomous tongues.

"You hear it!?" Peretz is bouncing and shaking. "You hear how they come to destroy us all…?"

"The Sicarii are with the Zealots this time." Menahem warns. "You who boast of negotiating with the Romans have failed Israel - did you win us our beliefs - no!?" He sways his face. "Rome's Emperors know it from old times we are not as the nations who bow before strange gods. Rome must annul Nero's decree or face war; otherwise Rome is planning our nation's destruction with your help. Their mad emperor is dead, Rome can do away with his madness now - it is your position to tell them - why do you come to us instead?"

"There is a breech!?" Peretz screams hysterically. "Rome can do what it likes now -and Titus is more insane than Nero! The Flavians thirst for the throne and care not how they get it!?" There is a pause; another thunderous echo resounds. "We have taken advice from our teachers and our sacred writings - let us not also become brutes like them. Titus waits for any excuse to destroy us, it is his insane road to his insane glory - his name be cursed. Negotiation is our only open road left us now - do you hear me, mad man!?" Menahem turns to Eleazar, his face urging his support.

"Our only open road - or this nation's death?" Eleazar asks and answers his question. "I say…" He spits on the rose stem, then blows it clean and says ominously. "We slay those who talk of surrender and settle this now." He turns to them in a calm deathly ultimatum. "Declare both of your positions by a vow in our holy place. Slaves of Rome… or are we with the God of Israel… the only road open to us?"

Menahem throws down his dagger to the ground before Eleazar.

"In this our holy place before you both." He takes a vow; covering his eyes with his fingers with one hand raised. "I say no surrender of our beliefs." He waits on Peretz's response. A silent tension prevails. Eleazar does not turn from plucking thorns from the rose stem in his hands.

"I learnt of your disregard for Jewish life before - and we see now its result. What you say now is also not a plan." Peretz says in disdain and disgust. "It is mass suicide and destruction. I will consult with my party."

"If no vow, then the Peace Party is cut away from Israel." Eleazar storms out of the meeting. He takes a torch of fire in his hand and enters the basement grain storehouse of the Peace Party.

Two Hebrew mothers holding their children approach him beseeching and pleading.

"Stop, we beg you… will you battle for us only to destroy us by starvation… will we die by the hands of the Romans and our own people? Stop, hear the cry of a Hebrew mother - we have children?"

Eleazar pays no heed of the mothers. "We have only one law now" He torches the grain houses. The Jews scramble for spilled seeds on the ground amidst their wailing.

Now all the walls of the outermost third wall lay fallen; mounds of stone bricks lay in the open courtyard. In his tent, Titus has his wounded arm resting on a cushion. Bernice and Tiberius are at his side. A messenger arrives with news.

"There is the smell of grain burning. The Jews are destroying their food supply behind the second wall."

"They have become insane from starvation." Tiberius assures Titus.

"I don't think so." Bernice offers. "It is a sign of their defiance."

"She's right!" Titus screams. "She is always right. Get me back on the battlefield!?"

That night, the parties of the Jewish groups conduct their second meeting. "By destroying our food supply, you only assisted the Romans." Peretz addresses Eleazar with sarcasm and disdain. "Is that your answer to Israel - death by starvation… your only plan?" He pleads of Menahem: "Talk to him!?"

"It is not Eleazar who assists the enemy but the treachery is of the Peace party. You betrayers will freely bow before a golden calf - as you do now before the Roman devils!" Then he turns to Eleazar. "You have seen how my party gave you our oath, but it is your own father poisoning the people - he is with them!?"

"I will deal with my father. From this time we kill any Jews who talk of surrender - or else we battle each other now and decide. Look me eye to eye each of you… will you worship a Roman brute as your God… it is the only question before us?"

"We have already given our pledge. If Rome refuses us our beliefs, we stand with Eleazar, even against our own people, even brother against brother… as did Moses our teacher with Israel's Dathans!"

"Dathans you call us, is that what we are to you!?"

"Dathans and Korachs - enemies of God - betrayers of Israel!"

"You both speak sinfully. The first law is the sanctity of life. And too many lives are at stake. Don't you see all is negotiation with the Romans? Perchance we can…"

In a lightning jab, a Sicarri dagger slits Peretz's throat. Gushes of blood spray Eleazar and Menahem.

"Israel's beliefs cannot be negotiated - it is the only war my party has sworn to - till we achieve our freedom of belief." The demeanor of one picking out thorns from a rose stem now becomes a Sicarii warrior, his eyes reddened with a menacing. "Israel says freedom of belief or death…" Eleazar turns to Menahem. "The teacher Hillel is now with us." There is a commanding fire in his eyes. "Come, we must cleanse Israel of these Dathans…"

Eleazar and Menahem enter the Peace Party's temple quarters, Sicarii daggers in hand and in their jaws. They massacre many Jews; many other Jews join them in the slaughter of the non-combatant Peace Party Jews, and now many lay dead on the forecourt grounds before the temple.

Titus, his hand in a sling, stands with Tiberius at his side in the war room. A soldier enters with news.

"Master, the Jews are killing their own. It was seen from the top of an embankment. Many Jews lay dead by other Jews."

Titus and Tiberius race out to watch from the top of an embankment before the second wall.

Eleazar ascends atop the massive temple steps, bloody hands raised. He stands between the Temple pillars, blood soaked arms extended. He cries out in a thunderous call to the Jews.

"Let no pretend Jews appointed by our enemies teach blasphemy here! Israel worships only one God - FOREVER!?"

"Amen, amen, Eleazar!" The Jews chant.

Titus makes his own response, setting out the final phase for all out destruction.

"You all know what open heresy before the nations mean. Now I, Titus - I will erase this nation - forever!?" An agonizing determination of fury. "Forever!?" He turns to Tiberius. "All legions! Full assault phase! Let it begin!?"

The Jews are chanting:

"Amen, amen, Eleazar. Be you our savior. Israel has only one God! Forever!"

(78). ATTACK PHASE V: FULL WEAPONRY ASSAULT - LATE MAY.

Tiberius takes his position atop an embankment proclaiming Titus' order to all of the Roman legions. He raises the red banner of a final assault phase and shouts loud to the war captains:

"THE ORDER IS GIVEN. RAMMING AND FULL WEAPONRY ASSAULT! THE DAY OF ROME'S GLORY - AND YOUR OWN! THE SYRIAN LEGIONS AND THE ARABIAN MERCENARIES IN FRONT! LET IT BEGIN!"

The Captains of all divisions ready themselves with a great response of hailing; the prolonged war by the Jews has unleashed great anger on the legions, and this is now their opportunity to restore their image before the nations and their General. Now all Roman legions assemble in attack formation and a massive swarm surges ahead.

As the Jews are speedily removing their dead, the Roman army prepares its forward thrust towards the second wall. Titus' own 10th Legion provides covering fire, with the new Syrian legions storming in the front formation.

The Battering Rams are now followed by a back-up of terrifying new machines, including stone-hurling Ballista's, boulder throwing Catapults, Mantels, mobile siege towers and the Testudo method of interlocking. Formations of impenetrable swarms thrust forward, shields abreast in the front rows; protective shields covering their heads from the row behind.

Atop the second wall, Eleazar directs the Jewish defense by filling sacks with soft debris and lowering them from the wall tops before the incoming attacks of the Roman machines. When the blows from boulders and Rams hit the soft wall, they bounce back; the Rams overturn, becoming a stumbling block for the legions marching forward. The Romans fall on each other, incurring the Defenders' firebrands. The Romans are blocked by their fallen men and machines; many soldiers lay screaming in fires.

Titus and Tiberius are aghast the Roman assault appears foiled.

The nation's delegates hail as the mighty Rams bounce clumsily and collapse on the legions. A delegate at a hilltop is amazed at the Jews' ingenuity:

"They used soft wood bark to break their iron machines! If these Jews can do this, so can we?"

A broken Battering Ram is carried off in pieces past Titus.

"You bastards… again you allowed them to foil the Rammers! Re-group and resume, keep the Jews busy so the Rammers are not interrupted again! Full weaponry phase continues. Rome does not retreat!?"
Tiberius directs the focus of the legions:
"You now know the wall loses its power when breached… you saw how one fallen brick moves all the bricks on top. All Rams must attack that lowest stone… Triple Strikes as before! CHARGE GLORIOUS ROMANS!"
The rushing Rams smash on one specific brick relentlessly to and fro all day, while a host of other weapons stop the Jews from foiling the attack. Thousands of fiery boulders are catapulted on the Jews, and the deathly chants and stomping of the charging Rams fill the battle zone with plumes of amber dust. Romans in the front rows revert to the rear after each attack, replaced by the row behind, as a choreographed assembly of unceasing rotation of thrust and battering day and night, with greater accuracy and focus than with the first wall.
As the Jewish groups battle each other, a large crack line now appears around the targeted brick of the second wall. The Rammers continue their assault unceasing to and fro with a determination. The crack line on the wall is expanding. There is a tremendous crunch, followed by ear shattering explosions. The dislodged brick soon brings down the entire wall section.
At dusk, the Second Wall is breached. The Romans again confront Jews rushing to their deaths on swords; the Jews terrorize the Romans, screaming "NO SURRENDER" and blasting themselves on the on-coming killing machines. Now the massive bricks begin to fall upon the Jews - they gaze at the enormous brick swaying and toppling towards them; many are squashed and torn apart under its weight. Mounds of dead Jews pile up. A Hebrew mother embraces her fallen son in her arms; another mother screams searching for her son in the debris.
As a wave of Romans rush behind the second wall, the Jews tug a rope placed in the breached opening; the rushing soldiers stumble and fall to the ground - the Jews slay the fallen soldiers. The next rush of the Romans becomes stalled by their fallen on the ground. One Roman soldier, the same who witnessed the imprisoned Scribe read Hebrew scrolls for Vespasian, is awed by the determination of the Jews; he pauses, wincing at the bravado of the Jews sacrificing their lives. He sees six Jews approaching toward Titus who is surrounded by soldiers; he hails them pointing at a passage where Titus is unguarded.
The Jews are now throwing Sicarii daggers aimed at Titus, dropping his soldiers who buffer him. Tiberius, witnessing in panic, orders Titus to be saved; he is dragged out of the war zone, shaking and heaving, escaping barely alive. Tiberius secures Titus to a far distance from the war zone.
The Romans quickly demolish all buildings between the two walls with their Rams; leaving in its wake thousand's of corpses strewn across the newly secured clearings. The exhausted Romans thread on the mounds of slain corpses, making their movements cumbersome.
Half of the fortress is now covered with dead Jews where once stood two walled courtyards. Hebrew youth clasp arms around Eleazar, watching the destruction from the towers. Eleazar signals and the diminished Jews retreat behind the first wall. The Temple's uppermost parts now appear in the distance.
Tiberius appeals to Titus. "Let the army now retire the night, else many will die from their exhaustion?"
One final wall remains. Rome's 'Cease Battle' trumpets sound.
At dawn, atop an embankment, Josephus attempts again to persuade the Jews to cease their war before the next onslaught.
"It is only a matter of time now - only one wall remains. I can promise all of you honorable treatment at the hands of the Romans. Over 300,000 of our people lay dead. Let what is left of this nation survive, I beg you?!"
The Jews respond with a hail of sling shots. Josephus backs away, climbing down the embankment in terror. Titus sways a Roman thumb-down of "KILL!" sign at Josephus. The scribe squats on the ground, swaying in angst.
The Queen's carriage arrives where once stood the first wall; she summons the distressed scribe before her by a scepter.
"Agrippa and I went on our knees, begging for compromises from Rome. But the Jews sought to kill us as traitors. We were saved by the Romans." She looks around at the mounds of dead. "But you are causing more deaths of the Jews than even the Romans. Perhaps there is another way?"

"The people account me as a traitor. They will not forsake the temple or worship Rome's emperor in it. They see the temple as the soul of their belief in God."

"That is also their problem now. You know what happened with Babylon, the temple and half the nation perished. Israel must put the temple in here now..." She holds her hand to her heart. "Can Rome take an invisible temple?! Let the Jews surrender to Rome's depraved ones and go where the road leads for now - the road to life. How long before Rome is upon the temple - then who will be left to save?"

"Surrender the temple? This will never happen."

"Come closer and hear my plan - you don't have one. If you can convince the Jews to offer the temple as a gift to Rome, I will convince Rome to return the temple back to the Jews. Titus will hearken to his Goddess and the new queen of Rome. Do you yet not see my light, oracle giver?"

"You ask the impossible. Israel will not entrust the temple to Titus and Vespasian."

"You must entice them - as did Jeremiah warn Israel to do! [173.] You must make Israel see the light - or else she goes as with Babylon again. But if the Jews heed my plan, then they and the temple will survive. And say now, has the oracle giver forgotten who saved him from the hand of Vespasian?" Bernice exhales fumes as she departs from Josephus in her royal carriage.

(79). ENTRAPMENT.

Titus purveys the destruction thus far; he pans the mounds of slaughter, then he turns to Tiberius.

"None of their tricks will save them. And if the Jews like walls around them, that's what I will give them. Begin the entrapment. Seal them in."

The Romans begin their traditional entrapment process, one that always precedes the Roman Siege, the death knell of many nations of the empire. Josephus watches in trepidation as Tiberius ascends the stairs of an embankment and hoists a black banner. He shouts Titus' command for the captains and soldier's hearing: "ENTRAPMENT!"

The soldiers begin using debris and trees and the fallen broken bricks to build a new impromptu wall of entrapment around the final and hardiest fortress wall. Although one of poor aesthetic design and erected with a determination and haste, the impromptu Roman barricade amazes the Jews - it suffices in sealing the temple in a stranglehold. Gaunt rows of Jews watch from the towers, as a convicted prisoner in his cell watching his noose being constructed before execution. The entrapment signals the next phase of Rome's most devastating war strategy.

(80) HISTORY'S GREATEST SIEGE - JULY, 70.

The Jews are now four months in the stranglehold of the Roman siege - they have thus far survived on the most meager rations. Behind the wall a mother screams hysterically as the baby in her arms dies. Another Jew grabs her child from her arms, fleeing away.

"It is the beginning of the end." Tiberius says to Josephus. "There are reports of the Jews eating their dead." Behind the wall, armed Jewish bandits are violently taking food from the women, children and the aged; they kill any one resisting them. The Jews are searching foods on the grounds; fighting erupts over stray animals and corpses. "No choices now." A Jewish warrior. "We must keep our defenders alive... any way we can."

A Hebrew mother grasps the shirt of her husband as she lays starved and dyeing in his arms.

"No surrender... swear it?"

"*Jerusalem*" (William Blake, 1827)

(81). THE AMBUSH.

Outside the sea port of Caesarea, the new tarred highway is lined with Roman legions and heavy infantry supplies in their journey to Rome's war bases. Up ahead, in the approaching of dusk, at the top of a mountain girded by a narrow pass-way, are four Sicarii warriors. The four have ropes around their waists, pulling and dragging behind them a large, tall tree trunk. The four are pushing, wincing and dripping in sweat, rolling the enormous log to the very edge of the mount.

In the forefront of the pushers is Simon; he pushes the log with the back of his shoulders, his feet making deep indents in the ground as his face becomes distorted with raw energy. He takes a deep breath, heaves, and the tree log reels off the mountain ridge and onto the highway below.

The Roman legions on the highway screech to a halt by the great crunch of the enormous fallen log in the legion's path, their beasts of burden screaming in disarray. The Hebrew peer below the ridge. They dance around Simon.

"Bless you! The spirit of Samson stirs in your arms. The tree landed clean across the highway - it will stop the legions." Asher turns to the three. "Their war supplies will not reach Titus. And for that Roman Road Builder who gave us this map, Hillel was right - the Sicarii are in his debt now."

Simon, now a Sicarii, turns away; he ponders Asher's words in askance.

On the highway, Rome's Legions have come to a standstill; the road ahead blocked by an enormous log of tree. The four now race on horses, each lifting eight huge jars, four on either side of their saddles. They race in the darkness, parallel to the legions, and pour out the combustible liquid contents of their jars on sections of the processions. When all thirty-two jars are emptied, they lob lit torches across the procession. Great fires light up the night sky with an intense blaze soaring in the hills.

Simon, fleeing on his horse into the hills, screams in the dark night. "I know what I must do now…I KNOW!"

In Megiddo, the news spreads with a fervent urgency to safeguard the people. The town's security guard addresses the town folk.

"We must leave for Jerusalem. After news of the ambush the Romans will surely come here. Move!"

"We cannot go to Jerusalem… there is word of a Breach." Deborah remembers her promise to Alexis and declares her contrasting advice before the people. "We can cross the Jordan and return later. We must think of the children!"

"You think we don't love our children!?" The security guard is enraged of Deborah's words. "What will you do in another land while Jerusalem burns, will the Roman devils not come across the river and force you to worship their killers? Did our God command the Hebrew mothers of such betrayal?"

"We will surely go to Jerusalem!" A Hebrew mother holding her child in her arms answers Deborah. "With our children!" The Jews shout curses on Deborah and toss tree branches and dirty muddy water on her, grabbing their children from her. Deborah, in tears, starts packing her provisions in haste and fear. Then a voice calls her from behind the shrubs.

"Come with me." The Nasserite girl beckons. "Father calls you."

In Jerusalem, the lone Temple stands surrounded by one single wall, the masses of Jews that remain alive inside are tightly contracted and entrapped by a Roman siege wall; two exposed courtyards display the devastation of mounds of corpses. As Titus pans the destruction status, Josephus approaches him.

"You have now destroyed over three hundred thousand lives - many mothers and children." Josephus sways the scroll in his hand. "The rest will soon perish by your merciless siege. It is the Passover festival of the Jews - perchance they will hearken to me now!?"

"Has the scribe forgotten that Nero forbade everything Hebrew… have you forgotten, my father gave you a Roman name to protect you. Yet I show Rome's final grace for this stiff necked people. The remaining Jews will be allowed to live only if they surrender and leave Jerusalem. But the Temple and Eleazar… mine? Remember it, Hebrew scribe, your own God sent you to me?"

"Blame not God - blame falls on the hand stained with their blood. All will be held to account, as did Babylon, so will Rome. You too are tested now."

"How strange it is." Titus smirks at the Hebrew scribe. "You who came to us with word from your God - will you now have us also condemned for harkening to your God's word?"

"All are tested before God to see how we turn. You well know that Israel turns by their own God given laws, which Rome does not, nor any of the nations Rome has taken. Yet you demand of them what you know cannot do?"

"Were you not tested when you turned from your people to save your neck, Hebrew priest? Just as you claim one true God, Rome too has only one divine emperor. Let Rome judge me… not any Hebrew God who never shows his face. Go now! Tell your foolish people not to test me anymore."

So Josephus is given another attempt of negotiation with the Jews. He climbs the Roman embankment and shouts across to the Jews on the tower of the only standing wall.

"My brethren - I call on you again. I urge you to survive now by the Passover message - see there is no Moses or David sent to deliver Israel this time. And it is forbidden to rely on miracles when you have a way to survive. Israel's choice is the temple… or the nation's survival. I beseech you to consider it for you can negotiate with Rome for its return?"

Josephus is hit with a stone from a sling shot. Titus digs his thumb down on the scribe's head, mocking his attempts with the Jews.

Eleazar gazes at the devastation from a tower. Then a soft wincing appears in his eyes - the mounds of death turns to a picturesque field as he remembers cherished times. He recalls sitting against a tree in a field. His son Amos appears with home cooked food. Eleazar gives him a rose stem, no, shaving the thorns from a rose stem with his blade, making it smooth for a gentle hand with no thorns, for his mother's gentle hand. His dreaming is broken by Asher who appears before him.
"Your father fell by the hand of Menahem. You ordered him to battle the Peace Party. God's strength to you, he was your only family left."

(82). SPARKS OF LIGHT.

A pouch is on the table; the girl nods and Deborah opens it. Inside, she finds the blue sapphire which was once a heart design. It is now a blue Menorah, the symbol of the Temple. When she turns the Menorah to its other side it is again a heart as before. Deborah's teary eyes light up; she approaches the father in tears.
"You saved me and gave me refuge. Now this? Jerusalem is always in my heart."
"When you are before the Romans, turn the stone so the Menorah is hidden and facing your heart." The girl's father advises her. "One's heart is a good place for the holy temple to be facing."
"It is for your protection." The girl assures Deborah. "Come with us to Pella, the Romans are destroying Jerusalem."
Deborah clutches the blue stone and kisses it in trepidation of the girl's news of Jerusalem; the temple flashes before her. Hearing his daughter's words, the father starts a wailing; his hand grips his heart as he stumbles breathlessly. He slumps on the chair.
"Those who desecrate Jerusalem shall fall in a heap."
"Oh my God, what have I done!" Deborah appears in distant and foreboding thoughts. "I must help one who is in great danger now. The Lord forgive me for letting him go to Jerusalem."
"Abba will go to Jerusalem and he wants me to go to Pella, but I will not go without him." The girl says.
Deborah flees from the Nasserite house, storming on her horse. Alexis' words flash before her as she rides the turns in the hills she knows so well.
"Promise me you won't go to Jerusalem?"
"I will not leave you alone at such a time…" She answers to herself. "I cannot." She flees in a determination now, her mane flowing like a lioness.

Elsewhere in the hills, ascending a high ground on his own road to the Holy city, Alexis sees it in the distance. A golden hue hovers above the horizon, in its midst is a glistening white monument flashing at him. His eyes squint; he dismounts, transfixed at the sight. Suspicious sounds emerge behind him; then shadows on the ground instill his actions. His hand grasps his sword as he turns - two Romans are charging at him with raised swords.
"Death to a betrayer of Rome - one who caused his own workers' deaths!"
Alexis moves fast, positioning himself before the soldiers with his back to Jerusalem. The soldiers facing the glowing city are squinting by the temple's shining glow, their swords hovering aimlessly in the air. Alexis' sword pierces the neck of one, as he flings himself on the other soldier and rolls with him on the ground in a combat. Alexis dodges the deathly swipes of the soldier's sword, trips and knees down on his throat in a fixed thrust, till the man drops his sword and is chocking for breath. Alexis grabs the soldier's sword and smites him. His hands bloody and open, he gazes at Jerusalem, squinting in gratitude.

Deborah has arrived at a road junction showing two paths before her. She halts, deciding which road to take to the holy city, the old dirt track or the new tarred Roman highway. She ponders, looking around cautiously.

"What now… which way?" Then her horse jumps and turns towards the tarred Roman highway to Jerusalem. She tries to steady her horse; it jumps again. She soothes her horse with nudging taps; the horse is heaving, it's neck inclined toward the Roman road. She gazes at the heavens in wonder.

"I know what I must do now. I must break my word to Alexis. My Lord knows it…" She storms away in tears of abandon toward Jerusalem.

"You surely know it…" Her horse is storming away. "I do love this stranger… one you sent to me…"

As Alexis continues his own journey, he is now confronted by three Sicarii warriors - the same savage warriors who collected Simon in Megiddo. The Sicarii leader stares unflappable at Alexis; there is a long pause, then his offside warrior speaks.

"You helped us destroy the enemy's weapon supply. What brings you to Jerusalem?

"It won't save this nation. Unless…"

There is an extended silence; the Sicarii leader waits, unblinking. Finally, Alexis answers him.

"Titus."

The Sicarii look at each other, there is a nod of agreement from their leader. They put away their daggers into their garments.

Alexis makes another condition of his plan to eliminate Titus.

"I will do this alone."

The Sicarri leader stares hard and long, then blinks his approval. They move from his path; Alexis continues his journey toward Jerusalem.

As Deborah pauses for her horse to drink at a water pool, she turns and confronts Florian, Alexis' security guard. Again he holds his sword on her neck.

"You again, the cause of much danger to my Master?!" His sword holds Deborah at his mercy - he stares at her curiously, surprised to find her alone. "I head to Jerusalem to save him from you."

"I too go to Jerusalem to save him - from Rome and from my own people. You must help me save him if truth be in your heart for him."

"I should have finished you the first time - before you turned my Master's heart."

"My people also see me as a betrayer. You must believe me now. Alexis seeks the Ark to save Jerusalem, but the Jews will kill him if he even touches it… I must save him!?"

"Mad Jew, the Arc is Roman war spoils." He rests his sword on her neck with his message. "Only death waits behind the wall for your kind?"

"Death is everywhere for us. Rome has made no place as safe for Jews in our own land - I am not afraid of you!?"

"Had you not enticed my Master he would be travelling with me now to Titus - and I would have finished my service in this land. I would be with my wife, with the child I never yet saw. Better you be cut down here before you cause any more deeds of evil."

"Deeds of evil!? Then do it…" She dares him, hands held aback. "Do what Rome does well, kill me, brave Roman - woe to the conquered!?"

"If you hate Rome, why then do you pursue a Roman?" He smirks at her, the point of his sword encircling her face; she spits off at him; he smirks. "Rome has marked your nation's end for your heresy. I need not soil my hands with your blood. I spare you only for Alexis' sake… I leave you for Rome!?"

Something strange flashes in the sky; it draws away Deborah's focus from Florian and his sword on her neck. She sees a swirling light in the skies. This light appears separate from the sun, appearing from an opposite direction, and it begins to burst into a stream of sparks.

"Look! Do you see it!?" She points at the sky.

"I see nothing, mad Jew. I never saw you. Remember it." He rides away from her, smirking, swaying his face at the mad Jew.

"But I see it! I see it!?"

A stream of swirling sparks gather in the sky; they descend on Deborah, then disappearing within her. She retreats behind the bushes, crouching on the ground behind a bushel, shuddering and shaking uncontrollably.

(83). "MY FATHER SHALL ATTAIN DIVINITY."

Now Rome's most devastating siege is the most horrific that any nation encountered in all recorded history. Thus far, the Jews are withstanding devastating blows and forces, in a war they know cannot be sustained; its conclusion foreshadowed and inevitable. Imprinted with Rome's history of brute power and dominion for over a century, the Jews are equally aware Rome's acceptance of religious freedoms for conquered nations is an oxymoron for Israel; that it comes with a deathly price the Jews have never accepted in their history. For the Jews, this is a war against their most primal laws; it is of neither land nor wealth, and they are in the frontlines of its prevailing and facing an assured destruction. The Jews are again alone among the nations in a world of divine kings, fully aware this war's contestants have taken only a timeout by the night's respite, and bracing for the next round of devastation.

There is no surrender in sight, many Romans are in awe of the stiff neck resolve of the Jews, and many are secretly turning sides.

In the war room, Titus' captains are apprehensive and not eagerly forthcoming how to proceed. Josephus rises to speak before Titus and his war council.

"I put my case to you. You all have seen how the Jews are held as hostage by their foolish leaders. But now even the Peace Party has joined with them to stand against Rome. Perhaps they will even destroy the temple than surrender their beliefs."

"One thing I will say here." Tiberius offers. "I have studied this peoples' history. The Jews gave the same trouble to the Greeks and Babylonians over their beliefs - they were beaten to the ground, yet they returned unchanged… tragically for them."

"This will be seen by the nations as a shame on Rome." Josephus continues his pleadings. "How the Jews never surrendered until the last man, woman and child. But now, Rome can freely erect its ensigns where the walls were destroyed. I plead you - let Rome leave the temple standing, leave what is left of this nation…" He kneels, hand palms on his chest. "For the Jews, sacrifice to strange gods is worse than slavery and death. I beg you, cease asking only this of them!?"

"Asking…?" Titus smirks condescending. "Will this stiff neck people impose its own will on the entire Roman Empire and shame us before all? If honoring Rome is worse than death for the Jews than so be it for the Jews, but Rome's honor is what this council lives by. You, Hebrew Priest, live today only because you swore to honor Rome and my father." A menacing killer's glint: "Rome is not asking?"

As Josephus deliberates with Titus, Alexis enters. He nods at the assembly and seats himself in the war room. Titus pauses.

"Look who's here - my seeker of the Ark!"

"Eleazar's family is slain and dead - mother, wife and children, while asleep in their home. Glory to Titus."

"And Rome honors you for avenging the coward dog that tore Vespasian's leg - and who slew Aristomy and his family - while asleep in their home." Titus is responding with his own sarcasm. "Well done, road worker. You were called back to honor your second pledge to Rome."

"Let Titus now honor the pleadings before him, as he assured me he would. Jerusalem's men of war have fallen and the temple is no more a threat to Rome." Alexis pans the captains pointedly. "Only women, children and the aged remain before mighty Rome. Let your war captains decide… or have they no say anymore?"

"I thank the road builder for his advice. But the dog is still alive, there is no surrender, and this temple is now a standing affront to all the honorable Romans gathered here. Does our pretty road worker not see that, hmm?" Titus turns to the war cabinet. "The Jews are mocking us, praying, dreaming and working their sorcery to return again. Rome must not repeat the errors of the Greeks or of Babylon. Look for the Ark, Road Builder. Leave the war to the protectors of Rome."

"Will you order war commanders to kill mothers and children as a threat to Rome? Will you parade war spoils and women in the circus for your own glory - which?" Alexis asks accusingly.
"My glory is Rome's glory. And yes..." He smirks menacingly. "I will kill those who challenge Rome's glory - even treacherous mothers and their children?"
Josephus intervenes. "But what glory in parading mothers reduced to eating their dead by reason of a siege of many months? Vespasian will not see any glory here... nor the people of Rome. Titus also should not. Let Rome's warriors speak, I beg you?" Josephus turns to one of the war commanders; pleading hands opened.
"Let Titus consider it." A war commander stands up. "Spare what is left of this fallen broken people and keep the temple as a mark of Rome's glory. Why bother about a dead nation's surrender when..."
As the war captain makes his case, a panting, agonized messenger arrives; the war council pauses abruptly at his urgency.
"Our legions and war supplies... the entire cargo - all destroyed by fire. Two hundred soldiers dead... trying to save the war machines. Master, the war must be won without further supplies. The destruction was caused by four Jews. We have one of them. A strong one by the name of Simon."
"Four Jews... destroyed two Roman legions of armor carriers!?" Titus is in fury. "A crucifixion is not enough for such a devil..." Titus plunges his sword into the war table and storms out the room.
Josephus slumps, swaying his head in his hands.
"Victims of a poor history." Tiberius whispers it. "Aren't we all?"

Alexis now understands Simon has joined the Sicarii, and that Simon will account him and Deborah as enemies who caused Eleazar's family to be slain. Alexis is in a foreboding silence of Simon's capture.

At dawn, Titus approaches the battle grounds; he comes to Tiberius who is monitoring the next round of this war. The entire forecourts are covered with mounds of corpses; soldiers trample on them with their war machines as they move toward the last standing wall.
"Now you can mark this magnificent temple as your own victory." Tiberius sways his hand across the destruction. "Glory to Titus."
"My father shall attain divinity - it is the road to my glory. I will have my queen and the treasury of the Jews - all of my desires will be fulfilled. Jupiter will rise here with none to challenge Rome again. Tiberius! You shall yet see a Temple in Rome greater than this one. Plow up every cubit of Jerusalem. Place my 10TH Legion in the front - I can trust only myself now of this final deed. One wall to glory..."
"Your respect of your father cannot change, I am sure of it." Tiberius, who has heard of rumors of Titus' envy of his father, inclines his question cautiously. "Many of Rome's Emperors ascended via the act of such deeds as your honorable father."
"The glory..." The killer blue eyes glow. "Mine. Mine alone."

(84). THE FINAL WALL

Tiberius climbs an embankment to the top, where Josephus is stationed with a scroll in his hand. Tiberius turns towards the war captains.
"ONE WALL TO GLORY! CHARGE!!!"
He turns to Josephus. "See now Rome's supreme wisdom in war. See why we tarried till the Jews are starved, barely alive and much smaller in number."
Six Rams are rotating, each set behind the other in a series of Triple-Strike onslaughts on one targeted brick. The Rammers are dripping in droplets of sweat and chants of counts, with spears fixed at their sides. The ground and the towers are vibrating. Tiberius and Josephus are bouncing on their high embankment, gripping its rails for support.

"See that last wall standing…" Tiberius shows Josephus, pointing. "See how the ground it rests on shakes under our feet." Tiberius sways his hand in the air screaming, "CHARGE, GLORIOUS ROME, CHARGE! Those Ram heads are pounding one singular brick…it is my own war plan…"

"This nation challenges Rome to the very end." Josephus responds. "This too is a mark of glory, does Tiberius not see this?"

The siege starved gaunt Jews, most of their able warriors eliminated, stand on the vibrating towers directly above the smashing Rams. They watch the full might of the army approaching, and the skies marked by thousands of firebrands, arrows and boulders hurtling at them. As the noon approaches, chunks of stone chips begin to fall away. Tiberius is focused on one single brick, that it is his plan that merits this war's glory.

"Look, Hebrew scribe, how that wall… OH!? OH!? Hail great Jupiter, Hail! It's coming down! Look! The last wall is breached! Victory! It's victory!? Over! It's over!?" Tiberius leaves Josephus and descends the embankment, racing to the war front.

There is a gaping breach in the last standing wall. The Rammers burst out the hole till all the wall's bricks crumble and fall. A stampede results in the red dust storm, with the Jews abandoning their positions and fleeing towards the temple itself, now their final and only retreat.

The soldiers start to raise hands and hop on the wall tops as a signal of eminent triumph. A trumpeter blows the victory code. Titus races ahead first, his injured hand not in concert with the rest of him; the soldiers chase him to contain his bravado.

The Roman army comes to a standstill as it confronts thousands of Jews in the vast forecourts before the temple. The Romans advance with swords and shields abreast, with a back-up legion behind unleashing waves of flying arrows and boulders into the forecourt masses.

The Jews rush forth at the approaching armies. The Romans stand still again, surprised, measuring the approaching opponent. They now see the advancing Jews are of women, children and aged white bearded Jews; those kept aback from the front war zones, with no war weaponry or amour. Titus is in the front rows of the advancing soldiers.

The Jews fling themselves at the advancing Roman swords, many slaying their children and throwing themselves on the Romans.

"We will never worship your Roman kings!" - The Jews scream, rushing forth upon the Roman swords. "NO SURRENDER!?"

Titus gazes ahead at the towering structure rising before him; there is a glow of excitement in his eyes. "Search the dead - find me Eleazar! Find me their Ark!" He moves toward the Temple, then he pauses, coming to a frozen halt before the great monument, appearing awed. He moves in slow dream-like bewilderment, oblivious to the slaughter all about. He ascends the massively wide array of steps leading to the terrace where the raised temple stands, now strewn with corpses.

Titus reaches the top of the stairs and stands between two blood stained pillars where Eleazar once stood; he pauses to pan the panoramic vista of the land, now covered with death and ruins.

A woman carrying a child throws herself before a Roman's sword, screaming "NO SURRENDER!" The husband grabs a sword and slays his child, then he charges upon Titus; a host of soldiers pierce him in frenzy before he reaches his target.

SLAUGHTER AND DEFIANCE (Eim-francois, 1824)

THE TEMPLE. Titus now stands alone in a protective under part before the temple. He marvels its structure of precision and massive proportions, tracing his fingers on the outer walls of white marble, with its strange symmetries of perfectly steep angles. His gaze rises to the top of a pillar slowly, how it never ends; he appears entranced, wincing from the glows of its golden embellishments on the pillars; gold powder and flecks cover the marble pillars; they glitter.

Peering at the top, the towering monument appears tilted back, allowing the entire façade to be seen from any angle. He gazes at the unusual staggered foundations; its bottom slabs are also in layered margins and angles. He turns his face in all angles, yet the entire façade of the temple is always before him. He traces the unusual graduating foundation again. He murmurs to himself in disdain and awe of the temple's hidden secrets of construction.

"How did a small desert people get knowledge to make such perfect angles and heights from hard stone?" He asks Tiberius who approaches. "Egypt, Babylon, those I have seen… this is more than they knew. How did they get the most advanced books before nations older and mightier… how is it?"

Then a crazed smirk comes on his face; he looks around at the vast destruction - he did it - this is his moment of glory, bestowed upon him by the Roman gods. Rome is made mightier by conquering the Hebrew God; Titus is made mightier. His eyes glisten in boyish pride; he whispers it silently: "Jupiter shines on me now. The God of the Jews lays fallen before me. I did it. I am the anointed savior of Rome. I am Titus." Tiberius nods, studying the massive construction.

Alexis appears; he maneuvers covertly behind a pillar, gazing fixatedly on the demeanor of Titus before the temple. He looks around him, then he slowly moves his hand on his sword. He is about to jump Titus, but he pauses abruptly. A group of priests clasping their families pull out daggers and leap before Titus; Alexis winces as Roman soldiers rush to protect their Commander. The priests slay their children, then their wives, then throw down their weapons, dancing before the Romans, chanting "NO SURRENDER!?" Alexis sees them slaughtered in frenzy.

"Why…?" Titus whispers to himself. "Why no surrender? How so, mad Jews… don't you understand the value of the victor… why no surrender for me?"

Jews holding hands with their wives and children jump from a high terrace on to Titus, screaming "NO SURRENDER". The soldiers slash their dropped bodies. Titus is sprayed with their blood; a Jew's hand is clasped around Titus' feet.

Now Tiberius finds Alexis; he approaches him curiously. "You should be attending Titus' orders?"

"I have learnt of their works. I do this my way."

Tiberius nods at Alexis with an understanding. "This nation is ending before us - they do not see even their own God has forsaken them."

"It is surely a stiff necked people, a charge brought on them by their own God - I have read their writings." The soldiers advancing on the temple tear down the massive entrance door; gushes of dead and decapitated body parts pour out onto the forecourts. Tiberius winces in revulsion.

"Has Tiberius seen such before?" Alexis asks; his eyes focused on Titus.

"Never. This people are dying by their own hands, by their own will." Tiberius pans the mounds of corpses. "Nor did I ever imagine such. It is a strange thing, how they die so easily with no hesitation, as if in a triumph of victory?"

The blood wash now reaches the horses' shoulders. The lake, now heaped with the dead, overflows.

"Yes, as if in a victory." Alexis starts to proceed toward Titus again, but Tiberius rests his hand on Alexis' shoulder.

"Titus ordered he goes in first, alone. His glory?" Tiberius smirks nodding.

The Romans who are now agitated by the NO SURRENDER chants and the Jews' defiant sacrificing of their lives; they are hacking away in a vengeance. All movement of the Roman armies become cumbersome and labored in the onslaught; their feet wading in blood pools.

"Our soldiers are falling in exhaustion, their hands unable to lift their armor. Yet the Jews keep pushing themselves on our swords. Never have I seen anything like this. I shudder inside."

"Your feelings will remain silent with me. I too share them."

Tiberius leaves Alexis and proceeds toward Titus. He passes Roman war collectors who tear out any ornaments, sandals and valuables from corpses before the temple grounds.

Alexis, appearing dazed by the surrounding onslaught, is thankful Deborah is in Pella and far away from Jerusalem. He begins to approach again in Titus' vicinity. Alexis appears spellbound by a determination with a singular motive.

Approaching Jerusalem, Florian's horse stumbles, throwing him off and sending his horse rolling down a descending slope. His horse lies on the ground motionless. There is a rustling sound behind him.

"Stand on one leg if you wish to live?" Deborah is on her horse; she holds her sword on Florian's chest. He sees her determination, sensing her ability with her sword, her other hand rested on a dagger on the waist of her dress; he lifts one leg, raising both his hands in the air. She slashes a branch from a nearby vine and throws it to him. He totters on one foot; both his hands clasping the vine before her in a pleading stance, her sword point pressed on his chest.

"Place your weapons in my saddle bag. Hold on to this vine, both hands in front of you." Florian mounts on Deborah's horse, sitting behind her; the vine branch between them.

"I will escort you to Jerusalem to locate Alexis."

Deborah strokes her horse's neck to steady it from the extra weight; they race ahead via the back hills. The path before them appears as dark hazy amber; there is a fiery glow behind the hills. They begin to sweat profusely. Deborah rides with caution, slowing down, looking out for Romans. Trepidation mounts on her face as they ride into the reddish haze. There is a silence between them; both sense a foreboding ahead. She fondles the blue sapphire, pressing its hidden side to her lips as they approach towards Jerusalem.

At dawn in the war assembly base, a group of three hundred Roman soldiers are herded in chains before Titus. Tiberius announces their crimes.
"Betrayers. They set free many Jews and gave them their weapons. They also weakened the soldier's spirit with teachings of Hebrew sorcery and rebellion against Rome."
A bound, captive Roman soldier comes forth before Titus.
"Rome burnt Londonium… slaughtered my people, our mothers and children, and stole our lands. I fight with the Jews against Rome!?"
Titus smirks. "Nail them on crosses among the Jews where all betrayers belong."

War Spoils of the Temple of Jerusalem [Artist: Francesco Heyez] Source: S21

(85) THE SPOILS OF JUERUSALEM

Spoils of War. Tiberius is guiding rows of pallbearers lifting massive vats of war spoils. The soldiers place the precious treasury on large platforms on wooden wheels. The platforms loaded with basins of gold coins, necklaces and sacred ornaments are dragged over the mounds of the slain, stationing these on a ridge far from the battle zone and ready for its ultimate destination to a warehousing and packaging, then to

Rome. Josephus says the Menorah of gold, the most precious prize of the war spoils, was brought to Rome and carried along during the triumph of Vespasian and Titus.[IIII]

As Titus watches the securing of wealth with glowing pride, Tiberius exclaims to him.

"I never imagined such wealth existed. Tomorrow we take the inner temple which holds the Ark. It is a hellish war, a people unlike any other. But cease now for the night I beg you - let the armies recover. See, the temple is surrounded by the siege wall and the Jews have no escape?"

"The Jews will surrender - or perish forever."

"My Commander, the dead cannot surrender."

"My own legion will guard the spoils in the night." Titus nods and turns away, retreating satisfied to his tent of a successful outcome this day.

That night, sprawled on his bed, Titus is delirious of his assured glory. He lays with his goddess before him, murmuring in his delirium.

"The temple is surrounded. Only its innermost forbidden place remains. The nation of Israel lies fallen before me. And tomorrow, tomorrow… my hand shall grasp what no other has… the Ark of Moses!? This glory will rest on me. Mine…savior of Rome…even… your savior?" Titus drops, slumping into a heaving, drunken and contented sleep.

Bernice, eyes welling, grasps the handle of his blood stained sword. The eagle perched on the balcony screeches loudly - the hand retreats. The warrior snores heavily.

In the dawn, Titus is surrounded by his war captains in the war base. All three walls have fallen; all that remains is the exposed, naked temple before them and the Holy of Holies, as if defiantly awaiting the final blow.

Titus gazes out the window; he sight is affixed on the temple. The war captains await his final order in dread; all eyes are now turned and fixed on the temple from the war base window.

Alexis is again poised to rush Titus; but he is overtaken by Josephus stepping forward to address Titus and his Captains in urgency. Alexis maintains a demeanor of focusing on the war council debating, his eyes darting in askance of every move by Titus; his smile is contrived.

"Remember your father's word…this war will be concluded in three weeks!?" The Hebrew oracle giver points his finger at Titus. "Since Nero's decree, you had an elite army more than 60,000 strong - such a force never trod this land before. Then you had the Syrian back-up, then the hordes of mercenaries from Arabia, Briton and Germania." Josephus beseeches Titus, whose gaze remains fixed on the temple. "And the terrifying war machines that you brought upon Rome's smallest province." Josephus' pleadings become passionate and accusing. "But the debacle is already before Rome and her brave war commanders assembled here before us. For even as the blood covers Jerusalem's streets, you have no mark of surrender. Cease now this war of shame, stain not Mighty Rome anymore!?"

As Josephus deliberates, the war Captains pace in a dilemma. But Titus' gaze remains affixed on the strangely churning clouds above the temple; it engages his curiosity and shifts his focus from Josephus' pleadings.

"Is this your glory, how such a small group of priests, religious fanatics and mother's holding babies have reduced the greatest army to shame… who is being tested here!?"

Alexis maneuvers tracking Titus closer, securing his position of attack. He winces at Titus' guards, avoiding their suspicions.

"Where is the glory?" Josephus drops on his bent knees to get Titus' attention of his pleadings; arms raised. "Where is it, show us, when some ten thousand Roman soldiers have turned away to the other side, seeing a greater glory in perishing alongside the Jews? Cease this slaughter and grant me once more to save the holy temple - even to cease any shame on your own honor before Rome?"

(86). THE HEAVY BONDAGE OF THE JEWS

Josephus is facing a lost battle in his deliberations before Titus. His attempts of enabling a people reared on divine kings enforced for centuries to reject their allegiance of their belief and nation is akin to dissuading a mother from loving her beloved child. Like the stiff neck Jews, the Romans were long ago inculcated into their ancient beliefs. The soldiers of Rome have also faced speedy execution for any affronting of Roman laws or marrying with Jews; they have little choice in exemplifying their disdain of the Jews who reject their nation's belief as vile and detestable. It was the same the Jews faced with all divine king nations they interacted with. From early times, the Egyptian priest Manetho wrote why the Hebrew were expelled from Egypt:

"Their leader Moses gave them a way of life which differed from that of the rest of mankind."

The Egyptians, who first welcomed and cherished Joseph, the son of Israel, soon detested Joseph's people who held a variant belief from Egypt and the rest of mankind. Here, Genesis gives the first recording of an ancient disdain of the children of Israel, described with multiple clause descriptions of success, wealth, holding high positions, of great population increments and prevailing widespread across the land - which the under-privileged of their kings who knew not writings and building works as the Jews became envious:

"And the children of Israel were fruitful, and increased abundantly, and multiplied, and waxed exceeding mighty; and the land was filled with them." [Ex. 1:7]

Hence, throughout their history the Jews were accused of disrespect for the gods of other nations by their strict Monotheism, viewed with suspicion by their strange belief, and as the controllers of wealth in high places; the refinements brought by the Jews were seen with disdain. Manetho's views reflect the prevailing mindset of its period and the scenario faced by the Hebrew Israelites in Egypt, a bondage element that now rears again with Rome in the First Century.

For the Jews, this bondage became heavier by their Hebrew God's forbiddance of any images of worship, an anathema to those reared in the personal devotion expressed by the beauty of the artist's handiworks. An invisible God was regarded impersonal and not conducive of any belief tradition; and it stole the luster and pride of the divinely anointed kings. A cherished way of old, one seeped into the culture as a personal and sacred relationship of its followers, the divine appointed kings disdained the Jews' worshiping of an unseen God. And the Hebrew God allowed no crevice for confusion or reductionism, declaring in holy writ the Hebrew bible's wordiest, paragraph-length command, given in multi-clause descriptions:

"You shall have no other gods beside Me. You shall not make for yourself any graven image, or any manner of likeness, of anything that is in the heaven above, or that is in the earth beneath, or that is in the water under the earth. You shall not bow down to them, nor serve them, for I, the Lord Your God, am a zealous God, visiting the iniquity of the fathers upon the children unto the third and fourth generation." [Ex.20:3-6]

And for the Jews, their Hebrew God's command was not negotiable and sealed without any loopholes; it was further compounded with an additional law of dire warning should they seek any deflections:

"You shall not add or subtract anything from this book of laws" [Deut 13:1].

This then is how the Jews became fully entrenched and un-shakable, their destiny fixed by their Lord God's "You shall not" commands; their bondage with the nations assured and historically manifest and predicted. And the Jews carried their God's baggage alone, in strange uniforms of tassels, skull caps and beards and the strangest dietary and working conditions, with none to confer or ally with pursuant to the heavy burden of their laws; they soon learned that acquiring interest from others, like the science and philosophy sectors in the Greek and Roman nations, only further risked their plight by inciting the wrath of divine emperors and their priests. The Hebrew God's laws again led the Jews into a war, now with history's mightiest force. The disdained Jews and the people of this time yet saw no vision that would alter this paradigm. None could see that despite such unacceptable commands of their unseen hidden God, that mankind would proceed to hearken to the laws of Moses, almost exclusively so in the world's judiciary and all its institutions; that the figure of Moses would become revered as no other in human history, by period of time, by impact and with a census of the substance of three religions. [112]

At this time, the Jews were seen as different by their monotheistic adherence of 'One God' derived via Moses and initiated via Abraham, a most radical belief in the ancient world dependent on deities of the sun, moon, stars, oceans and winds for their protection, via an anointed divine emperor that represented such deities. Here, an unseen omniscient God was suspicious and an affront to all divine emperors; more so because it harbored a logical potential truth that was destabilizing of the national divine kings structures. Monotheism engulfed early humanity and the Jews in an abyss of irresolvable conflict of wrath, which the Hebrew God had predicted to the first Hebrew as a surety of bondage.

(87). THE WRATH OF THE GREEKS.

A hundred years before Rome conquered Judea, the Greek Seleucid King Antiochus IV ordered the Jews to place an idol of Zeus in their holy temple, forbidding circumcision and Sabbath observance, and demanded the sacrifice of forbidden foods dedicated to his divinity. This was not least a reaction to the fact that Monotheism was becoming attractive to many Greek minds devoted to philosophy and the sciences. The demands by Antioch were rejected by the Jews, resulting in dire consequences and it became fully ignited in the reign of Rome's Caligula's reign, culminating in the Roman war with the Jews. The war for freedom of belief was held here in Jerusalem's Temple.

It was the Greek Emperors who first forcefully transferred many Jews from Arabia to the Greek state after Persia was conquered; then the Greek Emperors forbid them to remain as Jews. It was a stratagem to negate the threatening Monotheistic beliefs that rejected the Greek king's divinity and bears a reflection of the generations of Greek Jews who emerged as secular and varied from their brethren in Judea, many hiding and camouflaging their Jewish traits and origins, many harboring an inherited mix of Greek mythological traits and a lacking of the Hebrew beliefs.

Antiochus IV, who proclaimed himself as divine, thus desired to eliminate those features of the Hebrew religion which opposed and ridiculed his divinity. Antiochus' decrees resulted in the war of the Maccabees, a most grievous war for both the contestants, and seen as a relative triumph for the outnumbered Jews - one the Greek ego never fully recovered from.

The king Antiochus sent an Athenian senator to force the Jews to abandon the practices and laws of their Hebrew beliefs. The Senator was also to display all means to profane the Jews' Temple in Jerusalem and dedicate it to Olympian Zeus. They also brought into the temple things that were forbidden, so that the altar was covered with abominable offerings prohibited by the Hebrew laws. The Jews were ordered to neither observe their Sabbath or celebrate the traditional feasts, nor even admit that he was a Jew. A decree was issued ordering the neighboring Greek cities to act in the same way against the Jews:

'Oblige them to partake of our sacrifices, and put to death those who would not consent to adopt the customs of the Greeks'.[113]

Thus, two Hebrew women who were arrested for having circumcised their children were publicly paraded about the city with their babies hanging at their breasts and then thrown down from the top of the city wall. Others, who had assembled in nearby caves to observe the Sabbath in secret, were betrayed and all burned to death. Antiochus ordered his soldiers to cut down without mercy those whom they met and to slay those who took refuge in their houses. There was a massacre of young and old, a killing of women and children, a slaughter of virgins and infants. In the space of three days, eighty thousand perished, forty thousand meeting a violent death, and the same number being sold into slavery'.

By any logical accounting, Monotheism should not have prevailed in the ancient world and should have long vanished in the Jews' confrontations among numerous powerful empires since ancient times.

Antiochus' deeds would be emulated by Rome's divine emperors and the Hebrew Monotheism would again become the # 1 enemy. Thus does the war with the Romans represent the war against freedom of belief; it will continue to afflict humanity's history - its price was greater; freedom did not come freely. And the Jews were among those who most paid its price.

(88). THE WRATH OF ROME.

The Jews now faced the wrath of Rome, and Monotheism was again on a precipice. The swords of their mightiest foe were proclaiming similar harsh decrees as Antiochus. And the Jews would again defend their beliefs in stiff-neck rebellious zeal. In the 30's of the First Century, the Roman Emperor Caligula also declared himself as divine, while his people saw him as one culminating in gross depravities for Rome. Like Nero, he too was suspected of murdering his family to ascend his path to glory; deeds he accounted as valor assisted by the Roman deities.

According to the Roman Historian Cassius Dio, who also lists impressive extravagant civic works of Caligula, he states how Caligula began appearing in public dressed as various gods and demigods such as Hercules, Mercury, Venus and Apollo; that he began referring to himself as a God when meeting with politicians and the representatives of other conquered nations. Caligula ordered his Senators to worship him as a physical living God. Then he went on to attack every religious practice of the Jews who alone rejected his commands; Rome was highly motivated by the deeds of Antiochus; The Roman Historian Tacitus writes of the same repetitious charge of the Greek kings, why Jerusalem's destruction was prudent for Rome's divine emperor realm:

'The Jews regard as profane all that we hold sacred; on the other hand, they permit all that we abhor.'

Tacitus is highlighting two factors harboring monumental historical impacts. Since Rome's appointing of Herod, a hastily converted outsider as King of Judea, the Romans and Greeks began converting to Judaism in enormous numbers; even in their millions [99]. The Romans and Greeks, lovers of royal icons and landmarks, were also attracted to Herod's grandeur of monuments, as with his lavish temple refurbishing and his palatial city atop of Masada.

Here there was also an unavoidable interaction with the Hebrew bible, when the Roman and Greek multi-deity mythical beliefs were losing credibility by its elite philosophers, and the Hebrew Monotheistic belief was seeing an upsurge like never before in its history; such was the impact of the Septuagint bible throughout the Empire. Almost the entire Roman Sennett and the elite, now knowledgeable of the Septuagint, secretly converted to Judaism. Only the later emergence of Christianity, offering salvation from the severe dietary and circumcision laws of the Hebrew God, would stem the flow of Judaism; the Septuagint created a waiting mass of ready followers.

The other impacting factor posited by Tacitus was the disdain and chagrin of the intractable Hebrew rejection of divine emperor worship: 'profaning all that they hold sacred'. Monotheism was sacred for the Jews but profanity for the Roman Emperors; it is validation that Rome's Emperors controlled all writings; Vespasian absolutely did so. It is strong reasoning why, but for the Dead Sea Scrolls secured by the Essenes by clever means, there is a total absence of other religious archives up to the first three centuries, including of anything enshrined as Scriptures from the New Testament; as well, it is the reason why many scholars become free to posit this absence as proof of such being mythical or later concocted. Thus the historical truth is made elusive by the Greek and Roman deeds.

The premise of one singular invisible God began to stir the minds of growing sectors of the people and raised the angst of Rome's divine emperors; many prominent figures desired a Republican administration and many were executed for such views by Rome's Emperors. And like all divine emperors, Vespasian and his son Titus saw the 'One God' belief as profaning and abhorring all that Rome represented as sacred; it was also the stumbling block of their own held secret desires to ascend the throne. Equally, the Jews held the same impression in adverse proportion, that brutal pagan Rome was an affront to all that the Jews held as divinely sacred. Neither of the contestants had any exit clauses from an existential battle. It was a war that had to happen. Ringside, we are approaching its final bout.

Titus dismisses Josephus:

"Your glory is not my glory. Your God is not my God."

The scribe points an admonishing finger at Titus:

"Time alone will tell… it is mightier than your sword."

"Wrong…" Titus sways his face in negation: "Time has spoken?" [114]

The Hebrew God's prophesy of bondage assured to Abraham displayed a cadence of unbroken historical credibility: no other factors can ratify the Jews' bondage to any other than with their Monotheism belief in the ancient world; no other force had any credible challenge for Mighty Rome. Throughout their history and in all their interactions with the nations, Abraham and his seed, the adherents of monotheism, saw their first and most sacred law become their greatest bondage wherever they trod. And Abraham's seed was again handed a fiery omen of things to come; in this war of the First Century it is represented by the wrath of Rome.

"Destruction" depicting Sword shaped bolt (John Martin)

(89). THE SWORD OF FIRE.

As Josephus deliberates with Titus in the war council base, they all see it; a strange lightning flashing above the temple and shaped like a Roman sword. The fiery image starts to glow and shimmer. The sword in the sky lights up the city, turning the daylight into a break-up of colors, its flashes tearing across the temple and the mounds of the dead strewn across the fortress grounds. Flashes of colored lights fall on the faces of Titus, Josephus, Tiberius, Alexis and the soldiers as they gaze at the skies in astonishment.
The sword-like image hovering above the temple is an actual historical report, now believed to be a comet.
[115]

Firebrand dislodged in the Temple. (Charbuy-francois; 1759)

(90) THE MYSTERIOUS JOURNEY OF A FIREBRAND.

In the distance ahead, one single Roman soldier is gazing at the strange sword of fire in the clouds while maneuvering on a Temple pillar. He wavers, then he trips when his foot stamps on a firebrand. The firebrand flips and tosses into the air, gliding with the wind as a bird in its own trajectory. The firebrand takes a prolonged path as it glides, ascending and descending in waves, and wavering in a direction it ought not to go, yet it would not fall to the ground or take one path. It swirls around itself curiously. [116]

Titus and the soldiers follow the firebrand's journey, their focus now shifted from Josephus' deliberations before the war council. The soldiers are pointing fingers at the firebrand, its prolonged journey in the air being a wonder. The firebrand flips in the air again and now follows another direction; it glides into one of the Temple's windows, landing perfectly on a container of oil standing tall inside - as if its direction was guided by a mysterious force.

Inside the temple, the wooden oil vat flickers with a fire on its surface. The remaining defenders' focus is fixed on the in-coming Roman onslaught; some turn, then they ignore this fire as yet too small to be a concern. The fire sweeps to the vat's wooden edges and soon one section of the burning vat crumbles, so the oil flows out onto the temple grounds, carrying with it the fiery embers, burning the curtain drapes and eaves, the rows of wooden beams, then the ornate furnishings.

The droppings of embers reach the rows of other oil vats stationed along the walls, heating the smoking pillars. A series of explosions occur inside the Temple. The torrents of fiery oils now gush like rivers in all directions, its bellowing black smoke trapping the defenders inside.

(91) THE TEMPLE IS BURNING.

The Temple is burning. S53

Alexis' gaze now turns to the great fiery explosions, as all faces are affixed on the burning Temple. The soldiers in the war zone are paused and the delegates in the distance also appear transfixed at the spectacle; all are staring at each other in amazement: the temple is burning. A surreal glow hovers over the monument, a residue of the lightning sword in the sky, its crackling flashes of colors altering the natural light of the day, extending above the outskirts of the Roman army. Tiberius removes Titus to the safe hills of Mount Scopus as the fires rise up; the eagle retreats screeching wildly.

Bernice peers from behind her tent's curtains. It had to happen; she saw it coming. The fiery sword points to her peoples' stiff-necked demise; their bondage made a divine compulsion - and the zealous and jealous Hebrew God's weapon upon the nations. The Hebrew Queen exhales fumes from a coiled pipe in her hand towards the Heavens, blowing at the Jews' One God demand as the fires grow stronger:
"The price you demanded of this nation…your sweet savoring?"

Approaching Jerusalem, Deborah's horse neighs in panic, screeching its feet, turning its neck from continuing. Florian now cautions Deborah.
"It is the smell of fires and burning. Hearken to me - you must turn away from this path. Jerusalem is no place for Jews at this time."

"Jerusalem is no place for Jews?" The defiant Deborah pauses in thought. "Who then, the Romans?" She kisses the sapphire on her neck and continues the journey to Jerusalem.

Titus on Mount Scopus. Destruction of Jerusalem. [Painting by Robert Hayes] Source: S22.

Eleazar gazes on the fires from a tunnel's opening. As he begins his final approach towards a resigned, determined battle to his own end, his son's image appears before him again.

"But father, it says... Only the soul that sins it shall pay" [Deut.24:16]. Amos is reading from a scroll, pointing to the writings with a scepter in hand, swaying his face to and fro and deliberating the written words he utters:

"My father, none can sin before being born, so how can Israel be in bondage by God's law, given to Abraham when Israel was yet not alive?"

"True my son, none can sin before being born."

Eleazar pans the dead Sicarii warriors; many lay with multiple swords pierced in their bodies. He is about to jump on the on-coming Romans when a voice hails him. He turns to see the Essene Priest waiting on him, torch in hand, hailing him with a waving hand.

"Knowledge comes from above." The Essene Priest points his finger at the skies. "And only in its due time. See, you have no answer for your son - but you will. Follow me!"

"Play no word games with me any more old man."

The Essene priest is smiling now, pointing Eleazar to a dark tunnel.

"See, our God commanded us not to take a cubit of another peoples' land, giving us cubit by cubit measure of what is ours, one smaller than all other nations."[117]

He smiles nodding at Eleazar. "Yet every nation despised our God's laws to attack us. And so it happens again. Why so, have you not considered it? Come, move now - your work has not been concluded. Come!?"

The fires encroach closer; Eleazar jolts, jumping from the fire's path.

"Better to die than be a slave to Rome…"

"Moses freed us from the bondage of slavery…" The Essene is smiling, his hand pointing to the tunnel. "Then Joshua led Israel back to our land." The Essene is hailing Eleazar to come forth. "Deborah saved us against the Canaanites…come now…Samson, Deborah and King David saved Israel from the Philistines. Come…Esther saved Israel in Babylon and we were returned…come…" [118]

"A history lesson - now!?" Eleazar shouts aghast, dodging the fiery explosions all around; yet he is weighing the Essene's words, waiting for any means of a saving as he dodges the fires.

"Judah Maccabee battled Antiochus, one who forbade us our Sabbath, one who stood Zeus in our holy places… one who desecrated this place - did they not fall? So what is our issue now in this war with the Romans - tell it if you know, for all the nations did such with us?" [119]

"Yet you said this war is not about the Romans, not about the temple, what then!?" Eleazar is darting in and out of the path of fireballs and explosions while responding to the mysterious Essene. "What then is it about, old one?"

"ONE!" The Essene is smiling, his raised index finger pointing at the sky. "That is what this war is about. And there is none to answer this call aside from Israel."

"One!?"

"One." The Essene is nodding; smiling unperturbed by the snaring flames all around. "This is the mission. To Rome and unto all else for ever more… I am the Lord…there is no other. This was our testing on this same ground of Moriah two thousand years ago with our forefathers. Come now, hurry. Complete your work… for the ONE." He points at a dark tunnel entrance.

"ONE!? Then tell me…" Eleazar is screaming in angst as the fires spread on him. "Will that impress the Romans, old man of wisdom!?"

"Yes!" The Essene is exuberant. "The God of Israel will prevail over Jupiter, as with Zeus and Baal. Belief gotten by the sword shall fall by its sword… all nations will see this. Israel will live…One God will live. Come now - tarry not, burn not!"

"Rome is not falling and Israel is burning." Eleazar appears unsure. As the fires come closer, he sees no choice left him anymore; the fires lick at his feet. Explosions from the fires burst out, forcing Eleazar to proceed into the tunnel path of the Essene's pointing finger. Eleazar enters the dark tunnel, just barely escaping the fires from overwhelming him.

Inside the tunnel, the Essene points more urgently to the left, at a path to another tunnel; one that leads South-East of Jerusalem. He hands Eleazar the torch. As Eleazar heads down the tunnel, the Essene's words are echoing.

"ONE." The Essene's voice travels forth. "The God of Israel says unto the Pharaoh in his own language… "Ano Chi". I am… you are not. It is Israel's answer to Rome." He screams joyously. "GO NOW!"

"Ano…Chi? One..?" Eleazar, confounded and perplexed, is now advancing into the dark tunnel alone, shouting the Essene's words. 'Ano Chi!? And we pay its price… this bondage, this hatred, given us even before Israel was born, it is all for your ONE … your Ano Chi!? Is that it…nothing more?" [120]
Eleazar repeats to himself as he goes deeper and deeper into the darkness:

"ANO CHI…I AM! ANO CHI…I AM! ANO CHI…YOU ARE NOT! ANO CHI…" He wonders disoriented, whether he has lost his mental faculties now from the dark smoke bellowing behind him, chasing him. He flees, panting, struggling: 'Ano….Chi…"

The Roman legions, not known to retreat, are retreating, backing away from the temple fires bursting forth and extending towards the heavens.

Deborah and Florian's faces are seared by heat gusts. As they approach what was once the Jerusalem fortress, her horse halts, kicking in a terror of the ember gushes before them. The temple is now surrounded by an encircling shaft of fires; swats of plumes rise towards the skies amidst explosions. Her horse kicks, turning its neck, screaming.

The Roman army is rushing backwards as a great wall of fire extends upon them; they panic, falling on each other, fleeing the engulfing furnace. The courtyards between the felled walls are covered with burning corpses; a deathly putrid odor permeates. Florian and Deborah dismount, gazing at the fires before them. Florian's strong grip grasps tightly the reigns of her horse, preventing it from fleeing them.

"Sorry what you see. It is a nation's burning. Escape now - it is no place for a Hebrew."

"He is there… I cannot leave. He came here to save my holy city and my people. I came to save him. Oh my God, where are you?"

"I am his security guard. Go now, I will find him and send him to you. You have my oath by Jupiter - and of my family I remember in every breath. Go… take a road the Romans will not find you." Florian approaches her from behind and lifts her; then he throws her on her horse. He screams in a thunder and slaps her horse's rump. "GO?!"

"I will wait at the Nasserite house - tell him?" She flees, shaking uncontrollably, tears streaming as the fires advance on her.

The Romans retreat to safe distances; the Jews remain and perish in the fires, many throwing themselves in the fumes, many jumping from roof tops into the flames. The Jews perish screaming and dancing without retreating.

"Look!" The Romans shout. "The Jews burn laughing!" [117]

A Roman Holocaust

Rome's retreating Legions; Jews throw themselves into the fires (Right) S50

(92) SIMON ON A CROSS.

Tiberius gazes at the burning temple from a far safe hillside. He turns to Titus.
"You did what none before you could do. You are now Rome's most glorious."
"That sword we all saw… I know now my father is divine." Titus' eyes glisten as they reflect the fires. "I will offer a thanks-giving sacrifice to Mars' victory over the Hebrew God. Let it be a special sacrifice, Mars most appreciates hearts and livers. Bring out the Jew who ambushed my legions… I want the skin torn off his body before this burning temple. Burn his living flesh with fire and open his heart - offer it to the Gods of Rome before all. DO IT?!"
Tiberius sways his face in terror.

Florian, his horse dead and Deborah gone, approaches on foot; he darts between the paths of fire seeking Alexis. He cups his hand over his nose, his eyes agape of the destruction he beholds. "The Jews are lost by their insanity… I see an unseen thing…"
Alexis is now nearing Titus again. He pauses frozen abruptly and turns when he sees Simon on a mounted cross inclined and facing the burning temple. He is nearing Simon, one who would kill him, in terror and foreboding welling tears.
The executioner presses a sword of fire on Simon's body; burning flesh tears away. Simon screams, not in agony but in a grotesque laughter in the executioner's face before all. The executioner backs away in terror of Simon's power and his eerie howls of laughter. The rest of the soldiers gaze aghast, drawing aback.
Alexis approaches Tiberius.
"Allow me to talk to this man and learn what he knows of the Arc."
"Seek also of Eleazar… it will please Titus."
Alexis approaches Simon, whose body parts display open bones with no skin. He inclines toward Simon's ear in suppressed tears and fury.
"Know it now in truth great man I am as your brother. I am no more a stranger to you… and I am in deep shame of my own nation. Also, for the loss of Eleazar's family."
"I know it… the Rav told it. You will plant a seed. Hah! Hah!??"
"What seed do you mean?" Alexis comes closer.
"And that you will climb the Mount for the Ark… to save… Hahahaha! A Roman saving Israel!! Haahhah!?!"
"Tell me now where this mount is?" Alexis inclines, whispering covertly. "Allow me only to try and save the rest if I can, I beg you… it is a cause I too will offer my life…be assured of it…tell me I beg you!?"
"Only one Mount here - the high one. Eleazar has… Hahahahh! Hah! No surrender from Israel. HAH! HAHHHH! HAHAHHHH! No surrender to Rome. NO SURRENDER! HAH! HAHHHH! HAAH! NO SURRENDAHH!?"
Simon continues his eerie screams of laughter as his words come out coughing; his eyes affixed on the burning temple before him; he points in delirious laughter. The executioner approaches again, pressing his fiery whitened sword on Simon's side. Simon's gaze is fixed on the fires of the burning temple, unflinching of the fiery sword tearing his flash away; he bellows in an ecstatic and eerie laughter of joy.
"It is a sorcerer's laughter!" The executioner backs away, throwing down his sword.
"I have never seen more power - even that you can still speak. I bow before you." Alexis holds back his tears; he shudders.
Titus now approaches, screaming in a fury.
"I will not see a Roman back away from a Jew!?" He rushes towards Simon in a rage; he dashes his sword piercing Simon relentlessly, even as Simon bellows in a fierce howling of laughter, his gaze fixed on the burning Temple, his flesh and blood spurting on Titus and Alexis.

"HAHAH! HAH! Rome knows not what glory is - HAH, HAH!?" As Titus slashes into him. "HAH! HAH! NO SURRENDER FROM ISRAEL! NO GLORY TO ROME!? SEE… NO.. SURRENDER?! HAHHHHHH… HAHH…where is your glory!?"

Titus is slashing away. Finally, after repeated piercings, the laughter is ended; the open eyes fixed on the burning temple in a challenging smirk. An eerie silence holds; the army appears frozen in a superstitious fear. The delegates in the surrounding hill tops also stand frozen at the sight they behold. All around, only the temple fires resound in bursts of explosions.

Then Alexis moves to confront Titus, who holds a sword dripping with Simon's flesh and blood. A long held anger welling in his eyes, Alexis' stance becomes that of a wild leopard about to charge its prey. But Florian emerges from behind and grips Alexis - he bear-hugs and whisks away his master amidst the fleeing pandemonium and fires erupting all around, encasing Alexis in his grip before he could reach Titus.

"Do brutes know about glory - is glory for brutes!?" Alexis screams at Titus.

Florian lifts his master off the ground, holding Alexis bear hugged from behind; Alexis struggles wildly to be free and rush on Titus, but to no avail from Florian's powerful grasp. Florian manages to steer them both away from Titus in the chaos of the war's fires, darting past the legions in disarray from the flames. In the blistering haze of the fires, all movement and vision is limited.

Titus stands blood splattered, sword in hand, as he responds before all.

"But for the oath to my father does that betrayer of Rome live."

Florian keeps dragging his master away from Titus; but Alexis is still desperately trying to free himself from Florian.

"For that Jewess…for Deborah… come with me, only trust me now my master!"

"NO! I have her word. Tell me she's not here!?"

"She is safe across the river. She saw the temple fires. I promised to make you return to her. Your work here has ended. ITS OVER! COME NOW!?"

Florian is dragging Alexis away. As they pass rows of crosses and corpses, Alexis' focus falls on a face on a cross he recognizes - it is the teacher Hillel; his neck torn open.

"Can an invisible God see?" Florian demands.

"See whose hands hold the bloody swords!?"

Florian pulls away his master. Alexis pauses again; he sees a mother on a cross, their hands are pierced onto one single beam; they dangle with their throats slit open.

"Master, that Jewess would have freely given her life for you, but I made her escape. I swore to her by my children to find you. Master, none can fight this fire… it is over. I do this now for both of you." Florian flings Alexis on Tahrah. "Go, find her - she waits for you in the house of the Nasserenes." He slaps Tahrah's hip: "GO! GO!?"

Fleeing now on Tahrah, Alexis sees in the distance Simon's burning body on a cross; his limp form and eerie smirk inclined on the temple engulfed in flames and surrounded by mounds of corpses on the grounds. The fires rush toward Alexis. Tahrah kicks; they flee, the fires licking.

Tiberius races breathless to Titus of a calamity:

"The fires have melted the gold into the temple walls and pillars. There is much gold in its inner parts - even the gate handles, the door hinges and all its fixtures are of the finest gold. Rome's Council will account us for it?"

"Tear the walls apart, overturn every cubit of Jerusalem. Let nothing stand - we have every reason to do so now. Bring out the gold from the earth's stones - it goes to Rome with me. Tear it all down - leave nothing standing of this city."

As the fires rage, amidst the dark plumes bellowing, a chanting from inside the burning temple echoes in a haunting chorus. The nations' delegates rise up pointing as the chanting reaches out the flaming temple in a roaring chorus.

"..Thou preparest a table before me in the presence of mine enemies…"[121]

"Plow up all the grounds. Leave nothing standing." Tiberius commands from atop an embankment. "Offer reward to those Jews who assist in the Ark's location and of Eleazar."

"Yea, though I walk through the valley of the shadow of death, I will fear no evil."[122] The temple chanting echoes forth.

"Great Jupiter! They sing in the fires as they perish!" Tiberius points out to Titus. "It is said they sang this way when Babylon destroyed their temple."

"He who taketh life - giveth life…"

"Rome's gods do battle for us now." Titus nods, raising his sword to the Heavens. "We need not do any more - let the Jews burn chanting! Retreat! None can dare this fire from the gods of Rome!"

"He who fashioned the eye - shall he not see?"

*"*Fools, fools!" Tiberius sways face. *"*Fool Jews who dared Mighty Rome!"

"Let none who dares Rome live to tell it." Titus turns to the silent delegates in the far hills. "Let the nations know it."

*"I shall dwell in the house of the LORD fore*ver…*"* [123]

The temple walls shatter in explosions; there is a silence of the Romans and delegates who watch from afar as dark fiery plums rise.

(93) THE HOLY OF HOLIES.

A red Moon and an amber sun rise and dip as six calamitous days of fire passes and the explosions and wailings are no more heard. Rome's armies have been stationed inactive and still, waiting far aback from the burning temple for the fires to cease. When the fires die away, Titus and Josephus approach. They come now before a cubic stone building still standing in the rear section of the burnt out fortress.

"This is their Holy of Holies!" Titus' hands are tracing the walls of the lone standing structure. "Made of hewn marble stone, raised above all else, the only place not affected by the fires… waiting for me?" His eyes glint as beholding a forbidden fruit. "Surely now this is the house of the Ark…?" His eyes challenge in a crazed fervor. "A place none must enter, where they kept hidden their most precious things. I will enter it…alone. Hebrew scribe, come closer. You will guide me, but I go inside alone … this glory is mine alone. Speak, what is this place?" The scribe sways his face in tears, unwilling to come forward.

The only figure allowed entering the Holy of Holy sanctuary, once a year on the Day of Atonement, is the High Priest. This is a set protocol commanded upon the Jews from laws given them in Sinai and described in the Mosaic Hebrew scriptures, one with a mandatory death penalty applying of its procedures failing.

The Hebrew Scriptures records that Aaron's two sons, the nephews of Moses, who were not anointed as High Priests and who entered, were consumed by a devouring fire [*Ex. 28:35*].

Josephus, who was a Priest, but not a High Priest, would not have ever entered the Holy of Holies; his knowledge of this sanctuary would be limited to the scriptures and of the "Copper Scroll" - one of the new works discovered in the Dead Sea Scrolls parcel and containing the operative service manuals of the temple, thus of special interest for the Romans. [124]

Josephus displays reluctance of Titus' demands to approach further.

"I must beg you not to enter, for it will surely come on you and upon Rome." Josephus speaks tremulously now. "This place is unlike anything seen and entry is forbidden."

"I do the orders - talk to me!" Titus grips his sword menacingly at the scribe. "The scribe will tell me what is inside, everything, numbers and counts!"

So Titus and Josephus proceed alone, without Tiberius. The soldiers approaching cease following Titus; they also pause from their killing of the Jews huddling their families in the corners. There is a silence accept for Joseph's tremulous words echoing.

"You will see no doors here…"

"No doors guarding your most precious things!? Continue." The two advance inside the Holy of Holies monument.

"No doors - for this place represents creation's heavenly pathway. It cannot be excluded from any place."
Josephus replies breathless. "So do all the inward parts appear to shine to all that approach. Its design is of
immense knowledge of the earth's elements and measurements. I shall not proceed further; this place is
forbidden to me."
"I decide that. Speak! It strengthens me."
"You see how its front is covered with fine gold to represent the everlasting luster of... Let There Be
Light." Josephus appears in a daze now as they approach closer to a lone standing inner room. "And
through it does all of its light glows outwards upon His creation."
"Never mind your everlasting light, what else is inside?"
"Inside are the Cherubim, the holy beings guarding it with their angelic wings."
"Guarding what... the Ark?"
"The Holy of Holies is ascended by twelve steps and its height and breadth are equal, each a hundred cubits.
The Ark was placed inside, behind the veil of curtains." Josephus pauses; his words failing. "The Ark
houses the two tablets of laws given to Israel via the hand of Moses, our teacher.
"This veil..." A purple glow shimmers on Titus' face as they come close to a curtain before the sacred inner
room. "How does it sparkle so strong?"
"That is the reflection of the shining veil. It is of ancient hidden knowledge, made with a sacred blue by the
snails." [125]
"Snails?" Titus is agape of the Scribe's words. "Insects made this curtain?"

In the ancient biblical period, it is believed an exquisite and sparkling color blue was extracted from
cultivated Murex snails along the region's coastline, for both ornamental and religious usage. Following a
law inscribed in the Hebrew Scriptures, the Jews utilized this blue extract in the tassels of their garments; it
glitters without sunlight. This knowledge became lost in the Jews' exile.
"So that is how the threads on your garment shine so strong." Titus points at Josephus' tassels.
"The mixture of the colors you see in this place is of a mystical design, an image of the heavenly abodes.
The scarlet signifies fire, the blue the air, the purple the sea." Josephus pauses still, unable to proceed. Titus'
soldiers who follow behind them to protect him with their bloody swords precede one step further then
cease in trepidation.
"If there be any glory here... I want it. And I don't need a Hebrew scribe any more. I will proceed on my
own. I go now as a Roman..."
Titus goes forth alone into the inner cavity shaft of marble and gold. Josephus collapses; he slumps to the
floor. Many Jews are clasping their children and are hurdled in the floor corners, the only refuge left them.
As Titus threads on corpses and disemboweled bodies strewn in his path, he pauses abruptly as he hears a
voice calling him; it echoes from behind.
"Wait! You cannot enter without my protection." Bernice races towards Titus. "First we must know that the
Shachinah has departed!"
Now disheveled and barefoot, Bernice appears unlike her glamorous and brazen self. She takes Titus' hand
and they proceed together, their feet stepping over fresh blood. They pause before the curtained entrance.
[126]

Titus gazes at a Hebrew verse on the entrance; he gestures to Bernice to explain the writing.
"Know before whom you are standing..." [127]
Titus sways open a small measure of the curtain with his sword; his head titled backwards; he peers in
cautious jerks and pauses. He gazes past the curtain alone, the whites of his eyes gaping first, anticipating a
forbidden territory the other side. Only a tottering piece of wall breaks away and falls; Titus jolts, then he
soon regains his composure. He releases Bernice's hand and alone passes through the curtain. Bernice drops
her veil to cover her face, then she follows Titus. The curtain drops behind them so they are alone inside.
There is a prolonged silence. The soldiers stationed behind, their swords and shields smeared with blood,
are poised silent and waiting, as with the Jews hurdled on the floor corners; all are still and the slaughtering
paused as a respite.
Titus emerges out again, walking backwards, his face in astonishment what he beheld. The soldiers gape at
his expression and wait what he beheld. Titus turns to his army and utters his astonishing report.

"It is… empty?" He speaks lowly first, uttering in whispers. "No God here… no Ark here… the Jews fooled us all." He hoists his sword above him, then he screams it. "Fear not anymore! There is no God here! There is NOTHING here!? Look for yourselves. A God-House without a God… it is barbaric, unseen in any nation!?" His sword tears open the curtains for all to see. "The Jews beguiled us to hide the Ark! Woe unto them - woe to the conquered! CHARGE, GLORIOUS ROMANS! Take what the God of the Jews has given Rome!?"

Titus incites an avalanche of rage as a response from the Roman soldiers and auxiliaries recruited from the empire.

"The Jews fooled us all!" The armies chant. "Their God's house is empty! No God in their God house! Even they hid away the Arc. Titus has bid us to take of the spoils!"

Tacitus, the Roman historian, describes what was found in the Holy of Holies:

"There were no representations of the gods within, but the place was empty and the secret shrine contained nothing. Only a High Priest was allowed to approach its doors, and other Jews were forbidden to cross its threshold."

A stampede results; the soldiers begin looting the temple spoils and slaughtering and destroying the hurdled Jews. Knowing their faith, the Jews rush on the soldiers' swords impaling themselves, pushing themselves onto the soldiers and screaming.

'NO SURRENDER'. A youth slays his mother and child, then he rushes on the soldiers.

Josephus, the scribe who witnessed this event writes:

"This glory escaped him. On the day the Temple fell, Titus found God's forbidden sanctum, the Holy of Holies, to be empty." [128]

Storming the Holy of Holies. S51

(94) PELLA [MOAB/JORDAN]

The people in the Nasserite House in Pella are backing away, huddling in fear as they watch a Roman on his horse approaching towards them. Then Deborah recognizes Tahrah. She races shouting in an abandon. "Alexis!? Alexis!?" They clasp each other in uncontrolled passion and tears.
"You can never forget my name… I told it long ago to you." He confronts her now. "So tell me why does a Jew risk her life in Jerusalem… to save a Roman?"
"To love the stranger, Roman fool!"
"Jewish Roman fool. Now we are even. You must never be parted again from this fool."
"Jerusalem?" There is a heavy silence.
"My eyes have seen great evils…"
"All is gone, yet you came… why, why, Roman fool?" She sways in his arms sobbing and shaking.
"To love this stranger."
"My Jewish Roman fool."

Jupiter Bust. Source: S25

(95) JUPITER ASCENDS.

The Jerusalem fortress is totally destroyed; not a cubit remains un-earthed. Mounds of the dead cover the land; burnt, smoldering parts of wooden beams sprout up from the earth. The vacuum of the new empty horizon appears as a mountain missing from the land. There is a screaming wind and dust storm; the soldiers sway in a surreal slow motion, as if the earth is rendered disheveled and wavering, fallen and weakened under their feet.

As Titus purveys his victory, a gathering of soldiers in Jerusalem's desolation distracts his attention. In the midst of the mound of corpses Arabian and Roman soldiers are scavenging, opening the torsos of the dead Jews with knives; for the corpses displayed swollen stomachs by virtue of the heavy famine sustained by the Jews and their bellies were now bursting open. Titus winces, his jowls trembling as he sees the soldiers disemboweling the torsos of the dead Jews, seeking in their entrails suspected gold; they pull out innards with their hands peering for pieces of shining metals. Titus approaches in a horror and rage; he bends over sickened, then he grips his sword in a menacing fury.

"Reports came that the Jews were swallowing their gold to escape it becoming war spoils." Tiberius attempts to calm Titus. "You ordered the soldiers to partake of the spoils given Rome…"

"Is this what Rome's glory will be reduced to!?" He looks around at the delegates; he is gritting in fury, then he staggers and squats on the ground, burying his face in his palms, nursing a throbbing ache in his head. He rises, approaching the scavengers in torment. [129]

"Has Rome not delivered to you silver swords and spears of the finest gold - what need to extract pieces from the dead Jews!? You have become barbarians, savages and beasts… lower than those dead Jews. You shame Rome, you shame me!?" He hoists his sword in the air. "I curse you - you shall not share in Rome's spoils!?" [130]

Suddenly, the attention of all is distracted:

"Hail Titus! I bring news of great glory!" A soldier storming on a horse approaches screaming in the distance. "Your father is to be crowned divine Emperor. His first command is his son must make haste and return to Rome for the celebration of Vespasian's inauguration - and of your victory over the Jews."

A stark silence holds as Titus appears speechless; he pans his captains and soldiers to determine he is not dreaming. The soldiers begin to kneel with right hands on their hearts. Titus' eyes glow agape now, as when he was handed the golden sword as a lad in a Roman war school. An eagle hovering above is screeching wildly; the sword in his hand drops away:

"Titus! Titus! Titus!" A great reveling and hailing erupts: "Glory to Titus! Glory to Rome! Glory to Jupiter!"

Those who were destroying the belief of Monotheism in Jerusalem came from the other side of the sea and from the region of Arabia; yet they will soon become fully aligned as proponents of monotheism - which Mighty Rome invested all in its power to destroy.

(96) THERE IS NO RETURN.

Titus turns to Josephus sitting forlorn on a stone, his face bent into his bosom.

"My Hebrew scribe's prophesy has come true… for my father and for me. You too have reason to rejoice… for this day will be remembered long after we are forgotten. This holy war has been decided this day…"

"This day is the holy Sabbath." Josephus' forlorn face rises from his folded palms. "This day happened before with Babylon… then too it was the Sabbath. Pray that Babylon's faith does not fall on Rome… as an omen of your deeds here."

"Oh no, my Hebrew scribe… not so? I won't allow this day of glory lessened by you. Have you not wondered what strange force compelled my father to hearken to a captured Hebrew Priest, one who should have been crucified as an enemy? It was a Goddess… my Goddess… Rome waited on her approval of your oracles. Remember it. How will you not pay honor to the hands that you live by to see this day… it comes by the words from your own mouth?"

"This nation has seen such days before and they will see it again."

Titus turns around purveying the destruction.

"Again!?" A menacing smirk appears as Titus pans the mounds of war spoils appearing as a swollen risen hill and the desolation all about; the giant Menorah of gold rests on its side on the ground in a fallen worshiping mode before Jupiter's risen statue.

"Might is right." Titus affirms. "Might is glory. Didn't your Hebrew God tell you this?" Titus sways his face at Josephus. "It's over. There is no again for Israel…" Titus nods menacingly in mocking negation. Judea Capta. No return…"

Titus approaches his war Captains who are gathered together and waiting on him of the rewards promised them.
"It is a strange and sacred thing, my fellow victors. Jupiter will have a new home here where we prevailed against the Hebrew God. Rome is neither Babylon nor Greece… Rome, not Israel, is chosen to be a light unto the world. Invisible Gods do invisible miracles, but Rome is visible before all. By great valor and by strange and mysterious happenings, I am made Rome's savior… and you all have a share in this glory. By my solemn order you all will share in what the Hebrew God has given over to Rome - all of you." There is a great hailing and rejoicing; the people lift up Titus in joyous victory.
"Laphura!?" Titus screams the Roman name for gifts of war spoils. The soldiers hail eagerly before Titus, as he races from them and pulls out a huge chest of treasures from his train of carriages. He tosses on them fistfuls of gold coins and treasures, precious stones and glittering chains of gold. The war captains prostrate, kissing Titus' feet, as he smirks at Josephus, screaming: "No Return… it is over!?"
Josephus whispers to himself:
"The Hebrew God tests all to see how they turn… so shall it be with Rome. Only time knows the victor."

(97) A REMNANT WALL.

In the breaking dawn, a new Commander is being anointed for Judea - he stands before Titus. They sway in the shrieking winds of the empty horizon that was once Jerusalem.
"You were chosen for this honor because the world fears you more than any other. Know it well Lucius Flavius Silva, I place my trust in you with all my life's glory. The power of Rome is now given into your faithful hands, one my father also trusts. I appoint you Governor and Consul of Judea, to secure Rome's war spoils and of the slave counting collection - to uphold and protect it - all is now placed in your hands. The Jews have taken six years from me, do not fail me, do not reduce my glory. I wait for news of your success."
"With my life will I protect Titus' honor." Silva kneels with his right hand on his heart. "And Rome's war spoils accounting."
"I leave Tiberius and Josephus to serve you. One more thing." Titus nears Silva's face. "Eleazar knows the Ark's location - you must find him? You must always follow him wherever he hides. Also, make good use of the road builder Alexis Matarian to seek this Ark, I demanded such a pledge from him - do not lose him to the enemy. Remember, Roman guile for Hebrew guile. Mars shine on you, as on me!"
Titus turns to purvey the desolation again. His eyes glow in the glory given him and of the news of Rome's calling to prepare for the Great Victory Celebrations. He focuses now on the remnant of a lone broken wall still standing in the empty horizon; he approaches it, tapping on the broken stones as if they were still alive and bowing before him.
"This broken wall, once so mighty, once so unconquerable, it shall be my mark to the nations. I will leave a token measure standing in the heart of Jerusalem - only a broken wall and a tower will I leave standing. It shall be a warning to those who challenge Rome again. History will remember me in tears and dread by this wall. I am Titus - a Roman. I did it."
In his farewell, Titus stands in an open top carriage, panning the devastation of a city-sized graveyard. Only a partial wall stands now in Jerusalem's desolation, and a Roman soldier stands top of a tower as a watchman. All about are only mounds of corpses and turned up heaps of the land fastidiously unearthed and plowed up cubit by cubit remains. There is an entourage of carriages awaiting the departure of Titus from Jerusalem. Titus boards his open top royal carriage with the Queen Bernice standing beside him; her face is turned away from the desolation. He waves at the wall and the end of a nation.
"It's over! Goodbye Jerusalem…"
Titus' carriage departs with a great hailing.

"TI-TUS! TI-TUS! TI-TUS!"

All his desires are fulfilled, as he imagined it on his balcony in Rome. The eagle in the streaming clouds makes its screeching and hovers following the carriage. A glowing Titus turns to his Goddess.
"What was that you said when we entered the Holy House - what has departed?"
"The Shachinah is the Holy Presence [176]. If it was not departed you would have been consumed."
"I am not consumed. It has departed - forever." He is waving an arm at the Empty Horizon. "Jerusalem is consumed. It's over."
"The Holy Spirit now dwells in that remnant wall and tower you left standing."
Titus peers at Bernice aghast.
She exhales on Titus' face: This ground is the dwelling place of this spirit forever…"
She turns away from the devastation of Jerusalem, hiding the tears none will see. [131]

(98) GHOSTS IN THE SKIES

Silva, the new Roman General, stations the war spoils base in the South-East of Jerusalem, the isolated and mountainous Judean deserts. The site afforded protection of the spoils and access to the waters of the Dead Sea. There is a resigned calm in the Roman soldiers - the war is over, the victory complete, they will go home richly rewarded. Silva addresses Josephus of his task.
"Only the spoils collection remains. Not a glorious task, but an honorable one."
As he speaks, a chanting chorus descends from the skies:
"NO SURRENDER!"
Arrows of fire rain down from the clouds, scattering the army in confusion. All faces turn to the heavens.
"The wrath of the Hebrew God has awoken!" A soldier cries, fleeing.
Josephus, facing the sky above, turns to Silva: "It's not over!"
Silva winces, slowly panning a foreboding, treacherous 1,300 feet of a near vertical mountain; its tops disappearing into the clouds. The sky is raining down firebrands; the soldiers flee, dispersing from the spreading fires.
"What is this!?" Silva turns to Josephus as fires rain down.
"Masada!"[36] Josephus takes cover in Silva's carriage. "Up there is Eleazar ben Jair, a descendent of Judah of the Sicarii tribe. He is one who deluded Vespasian and his son Titus and all of his rivals. It is he who broke Vespasian's leg and Titus' hand. It is he who persuaded the Jews never to submit to Rome. Now we have no accounting of the forces on that mount or the means how they escaped the temple destruction. It is this man who initiated the war with Rome and his challenge continues. This war is… not over!?"
Silva pans the mount's inclines in a foreboding rage. "It will be over. I swore it before Titus!"
The soldiers gaze in terror at the mount. Silva's Captains are silent, appearing frozen by the commander's decision.

(99) its NOT OVER.

That same night, Silva addresses a war weary council, one that is now resigned to return home following their triumphant victory.
"The mount is insurmountable for any army. So the enemy wants us to believe. But we will use their own weapon against them, making their own escape impossible." A gregarious and enthusiastic General addresses his war captains of a bold new plan. "We build a wall around their mountain again and siege them in - as with their temple!"
"Seven years we have not been home." A Captain responds. "How long will this new war last?"

"This is not a new war!?" Josephus warns. "This is the same people and the same war. And this mount is far more torturous than the temple you destroyed…?"

"The Hebrew is under Titus' orders to say what he knows." The war weary captain seeks more information. "Tell us of this mount and its forces?" Silva and all in the war assembly wait on Josephus.

"To build a wall around this great mountain will take two years of labors, fully ceasing Rome's victory celebrations. The Jews won't be affected by a siege wall this time - there is Herod's Palace on the top, a city in the clouds - with crops, animal farms and advanced water systems. The mount can hold a million."

[Aerial view of the Masada Fortress above the Dead Sea; and Ramp imprints.]

[Milner Moshe Photography / Government Press Office [GPO]; Israel/Wikimedia Commons] Source: 28.

Silva hears hisses and sees the faces of foreboding of his war captains; he addresses them sternly.

"If we have to climb by our nails, we will conquer this mount. It shall be just as Rome felled the Jews' unconquerable temple walls." He turns to Josephus, demanding. "And how does the Hebrew scribe account a million can climb up there - speak!?"

"The Jews know these lands, they know every cubit and turn of this mountain - they built Herod's city on Masada's top, 1300 feet high into the clouds. Herod was a Roman appointed king and a foreigner in Judea, obsessed with his own security and mistrust of the Jews. He built a city in the clouds, one that the Jews and even Rome could not infiltrate. To reach up, there are only two known pathways of ascent, the Asphaltiris and the Serpent ways. The shorter Serpent path becomes fully vertical after a small entry, so even animals cannot climb anymore… so narrow it requires to be preceded one foot a time at each hoisting, with a terror of slippage at each step." Terror grips the soldiers' faces. "And Eleazar who commands the Jews knows… no victory without Masada?"

Silva again restores order among the horrified Captains; he speaks now with contempt of Josephus's words. "We do this the Roman way. We do it with Roman ramps at secured levels. We uplift our armies and our amour and provisions on embankments."

"A ramp across such a mountain!?" An alarmed captain deliberates. "To carry heavy armor and bring the army to the top, into the clouds… many will not be returning home…"

"My order stands. It need not be one single ramp but many ramps - each beginning where the other ends. Roman wisdom, Roman valor, Captain." Silva then focuses on Josephus in disdain. "You people never learn. It will be a victory and a Hebrew scribe will write about it. The work on the ramps begins at dawn.
In the following weeks, at each dawn, Silva is monitoring his armies lifting heavy laden embankments and armory on consecutive massive ramps laid along the treacherous mount's inclines, each ramp laid to curve around the steep lines deemed insurmountable before, even as the soldier's faces are filled in dread as they work gazing up the mount.

On the mount's top, the Jews have been watching the works of the Romans - they rain down fiery arrows, boulders and boiling oil to foil the Roman plan of ascent. Many soldiers fall screaming; the Roman war machines wobble and sway in the ramps from the attacks by the Jews.

But Silva's determination has no bounds. The Jews are in astonishment of the world's greatest power displaying her supreme might; and none understand this Roman power more than Eleazar who studies the Roman works. The Jews watch in foreboding how their stronghold atop Masada, which was ever impossible to breach, is now being compromised, as was their impregnable Temple.

The seasons change. Masada's snowcapped peaks turn to torrid sunshine. Fifteen months later, in late 72, a new siege wall of wooden fences made of felled trees and debris appears around the base of the mount.

Eleazar recalls the siege of the Temple; he now directs the Jews to fill sacks with flimsy debris, as the Romans prepare their advancing ascent on the Mount of Masada.

"GIRD UP!" Silva screams, bracing his soldiers. "I swear it - any soldier ceasing to climb will burn on crosses in this land's sun! Gird you up!"

Josephus approaches Silva in his base camp.

"Allow me to speak to their leader. Let me learn his terms for surrender. I will speak to him priest to priest before all and report it to you. After all, he is also the son of a priest of Israel, as I am a priest, and we have our obligations of our priestly station?"

There are screams of fallen soldiers being carried away outside; Silva measures the Hebrew scribe's request in disdain.

"Then the Hebrew priest must hear my conditions. Let the Jews know that more legions are arriving. And that there is no escape from a Roman siege - ever! Learn for me also the power of their forces, if they be as strong as you claim. Go now."

As Josephus leaves, guards bring in Florian as Silva ordered.

"You are the security guardian of Alexis Matarian, the road builder. My good advice now is for both of you, to protect you and your loved ones. Vespasian gave you his word your family will be rewarded. It will be upheld for you - and your family. Yet you must also keep your word to Rome as its provision - you follow? Alexis too must keep his word in locating the Ark - as he pledged to Titus. That mount appears a good place to hide such an Ark - the road builder must assist in its location. Alexis must also secure for me the strength of the Jews' enemy - it appears he knows how to deal with this people - Rome is aware of it, as you also do. As you wait on Rome to keep her pledge to you, so too you shall do for Rome first. Surely you follow my meaning?" Florian bows and leaves, Silva's message made clear and without confusion should he fail.

As Florian departs, Silva addresses his War Captain in a lowered tone, as when a covert order is given.
"Two of your most trusted soldiers will follow Florian. Silently. The Road Builder's Hebrew woman - secure her. None must know of it."

Josephus shouts from atop an embankment:
"Hear me now Eleazar ben Jair. Like you, I too am a priest of Israel. The Hebrew law bids you must make a peace offer before choosing war, as did Joshua before the armies of Canaan. It is Din Torah and not yours to choose. Give now your peace offer to Rome - or you will transgress our sacred laws of Sinai before all! Also, what is the strength of your forces that you risk Israel's people so boldly? Hearken to me, Eleazar! Rome waits on your word before her most deadly assault - which you again bring on our people."
After a long pause a reply comes. Josephus explains the Jews' terms to Silva:
"One. Restore the Callegia of Caesar and annul the Heresy decrees of Caligula and Nero. Two. Let the Jews rebuild their temple which Rome destroyed, as did Cyrus the Persian grant to Israel. And three. Return the spoils stolen by Titus. The Jews say their belief is not a heresy against Rome, and say further, all due taxes will be paid as was done for 100 years. But no peace without freedom of our belief and no Roman statues in the Temple Fortress. Else know for a surety the war continues as with the temple war… and know also that our forces are greater than yours."
Silva responds in a rage, his war torn ravaged face and one broken eye erupting:
"What temple, what fortress - these do not exist anymore!? I gave them a chance to live, but they respond with the crudest defiance. Do these bandits think they can overturn everything Rome stands for, even to make a fool of me? Do they imagine I will bow to their arrogance if they hide on a mountain top - or that I will ask Rome to cease her victory celebrations? I offered the Jews life but they choose death instead. So be it?!"
Josephus slumps on the floor. Silva storms into his war room.

Florian has arrived at the Nasserite House in Pella. He stands before Alexis and Deborah with news of Silva's orders.
"Master, I caused both of you to flee Jerusalem's fires. But if you don't return now with me to Silva, great evils will fall on us and our families and loved ones. Silva orders we must not betray our pledges to Rome, so Rome will honor its pledges given us. My Master, I have family in Rome…?" Florian bends his face, hiding his pain of the news he brings.
Alexis engages his security guard's teary bent; he rests his hand on Florian's strong shoulder. Then he turns to Deborah.
"My pain is great now. You promised me your God's word is of truth. You promised we would go to Jerusalem together."
"Jerusalem is no more." Florian says. A long silence.
Then Deborah removes her necklace with trembling hands and places it around Alexis' neck. She turns the amulet's face to display a blue heart, the emblem of the Menorah she makes hidden and turned on Alexis' heart. She caresses Alexis face, assuring him.
"We will surely return to Jerusalem. Together."
Florian and Alexis are leaving. Two Roman soldiers are covertly peering from behind a rock on a hilltop; they nod, focused on Deborah.

Atop Masada's terrace, from a vantage point of its edges, Eleazar gazes down at the Roman wall surrounding the mount and the array of ramps reaching towards the top. The ramps are laden with heavy Roman armor. Beyond the soldiers lifting armor, he sees the Roman armies gathered and stationed ready for war.

In the camp of Silva, the war captain reports the status of the completion of fifteen months of labor: "The embankments are now stationed on the ramps. They reach a small distance short from the top of the Serpent pathway, as you ordered."

Silva comes out of his tent to examine the works, panning the connective ramps and the weaponry provisions. He studies the war legions ready and waiting; then he traces the mount to its top, how its treacherous curves rise vertically and disappear into the clouds.

"Captain. When you climb to the highest point, then it is by hand and foot to the top. Three thousand will cover you with flame throwers from the ground. I will head a thousand and ambush the enemy. There is also a mock diversion group on the Eastern pathway to confound the enemy. We ram down their flimsy wall of twigs, then we give the Jews fire for fire - whatever the strength of their forces. We represent Rome and I demand total victory - nothing short. Begin 'Forward Attack' phase."

Florian and Alexis have arrived at Masada. Florian proceeds to report to Silva's camp. Outside, Alexis gazes at the mount, studying its slopes and inclines. Covertly from Florian's sighting, in the confusion of the war attack phase being initiated, he uses the embankment being raised by the soldiers as a springboard, and from its top he maneuvers onto the ramps and climbs up the mount's inclines alone.

From their raised positions on embankments and now stationed at high points, the Roman soldiers catapult waves of burning fire torches toward the top of the mount. The Defender's sacks of wooden debris surrounding the rim soon catch on fire; its hollowness makes the fire spread to the mount's thick wooden forests. A mighty fire spreads on the mount; the winds are sweeping the fires upward.

Alexis, climbing on the mount, is now negotiating a treacherous incline. As the fiery gushes of the battle rise up, an eagle juts down and pecks Alexis' hand as he is about to grasp a ledge; his hand misses and his foot slips. He dangles now, hanging by a twig growth to a clear drop down the abyss. Alexis is unable to move, his ankle broken, and he is now confronting his eminent demise on a most precarious position.

Florian appears; he grasps Alexis' arm, dangerously extending his outstretched hand. He winces hard as he hoists up Alexis, who now hangs in Florian's extended arm grasp.

"Don't you need your security guard anymore - why did you flee without warning, my Master?"

"Your work here is done." Alexis looks up, his hand held now in Florian's grasp. "You need not do any more. If your arm fails let me go. I kept my word to Titus - tell it to him."

"You have honored your pledge to Rome. But I betrayed you to Vespasian when I thought I was saving you from the enemy. Forgive me."

"You were following your orders."

With a renewed burst of power to save his master, Florian succeeds in hoisting up Alexis onto a half way ledge. Florian then begins to lift up Alexis in arm to arm grasps.

"Look not down at the abyss, look only at me and my arm. Master, will you become as them… will you forsake your nation for the love of a Jew?"

"I returned. For the love of a Jew…" He faces Florian pulling him upwards, eye to eye. "And her God."

"Strange destiny yet again." Florian winces. "And I am made to go with you - whatever be this destiny." Florian's massive arm starts to shudder lifting up Alexis.

(100) A MIRACLE FOR THE JEWS.

The Romans continue catapulting firebrands from their war machines; the mount erupts in great plumes. The Jews atop the mount back off from the rim in fear of the rising fires approaching towards them. Then, suddenly, a north wind emerges, turning the fires downward upon the Romans instead. Rome's war machines start to burn. The Romans begin to retreat from their climb, descending the mount with the winds of fire sweeping upon the soldiers. The Jews return to their attack positions in the front of the terrace, hailing, pointing at the fleeing army.

(101) A MIRACLE FOR ROME.

While the Romans are in flight, a sudden change of the wind flow again occurs - it recoils abruptly in the sight of the fleeing Romans and now turns to the south, blowing strongly the opposite way. The wind carries the flames, driving it back against the wall, and rising only as it can, goes upwards to the mountain top by this new wind change.

"Look! Look!? The fire turns!" A war captain points at the winds of fire. "It rises up like a giant snake the opposite way - upwards. The fires become stronger - look! This time it will surely be over for the Jews - nothing can survive such a fire and the Jews have nowhere else to escape anymore!?"

The mountain catches on fire through its entire thickness, so the mount with its thick trees is fully aflame. The Roman army pauses it's fleeing, seeing how the fires are now rising up in its sweep all around the mount, and not at the Roman armies any more. The Jews back off from the rim of their attack positions again. Thick ferocious fires crawl up the mount.

"Move back - stay the attack!" Silva orders. "Rome has not to do anymore than witness this spectacle - this is a death by fire for the Jews. Let it be as a sweet savoring to their Hebrew God who does this."

"It is a strange thing." Josephus tells himself. "So strange, how the fires turned by itself so suddenly. It holds back the Romans - yet it attacks the Jews in their safe high place. I must witness this strange thing… I was made the royal scribe to write of it."

The up-sweeping fires now race with a mighty force, overtaking Alexis on the mount fully. Florian's arm holding his burning Master shudders violently. Above of Alexis and Florian the eagle roams; it hovers in the skies above them. Florian winces again to upload Alexis.

"Master, I sail home by the week's end, my wife waits for me with our first child I yet never saw. Call now on this invisible God's ears else we perish along with the Jews."

The eagle screeches, then it swoops down - it pecks out one of Alexis' eyes. The eagle swoops down again, pecking into his body parts and slashing away; the fires also rising on Alexis. Florian winces, lifting Alexis higher an arm length. The eagle returns in another swoop, its beak is now plunging into Florian's hand, as if knowing it will dislodge his held master. Florian's grip remains steadfast, his hand bloodied.

The eagle returns again, tearing and slashing into a limp, dangling Alexis. The eagle screeches ferociously and pecks violently as Florian continues uploading Alexis. Florian finally manages to raise his master, pushing him onto the safety of a protective crevice on a ledge of the mount. As the screeching eagle returns again, Florian, now free from upholding Alexis, grasps the attacking eagle's neck and throws a mighty fist on its head, amidst an array of the eagle's powerful beak lashings; the eagle flees, its beak broken. Florian's face is tearing open; he slumps on an open ledge, as the rising fires now overtake him fully. There is none to save Florian, Alexis being incapacitated and deprived of all consciousness as he lies still in the mount's protective crevice.

"Remind Vespasian of his pledge…" Florian's hand reaches out from the fires to his unconsciousness master. "My family… promises me…"

(102) ATOP MASADA'S TERRACE.

Eleazar gazes down as the encircling fires are racing to the top. The fires surround the entire circumference of the mount; rising upwards and allowing no escape or exit paths in sight for the Jews. As Eleazar gazes at their situation, he nods at the heavens, speaking to his God from atop the fiery mount.

"You took my family, then my father who served as a priest unto you. Then you took this nation that put all its trust in your laws. So tell me now… tell how we can believe in your laws if there is no freedom of belief, as is made on us by the Romans?" The Jews are approaching around him; they chant their pleas to him now as their only saving.

"ELEAZAR! ELEAZAR! SAVE US! BE YOU OUR SAVIOR NOW!"

"You gave Israel her name.[136.] And Israel comes to me now. They come in your name, but our unseen God does not answer them. Yet I am told this war is not about Israel and not of Rome. That this is about you, your laws!?"

"ELEAZAR! ELEAZAR! SAVE US NOW!" - The people chorus out to him.

"And see…" Eleazar is gazing at the streaming clouds above, challenging his God for answers. "Now you have none else to stand for you this day but this small broken remnant left on this burning mount… do you see it? So be it. We are ready. Again. Let thy will be done as you will."

Then Eleazar sees his son in the streaming winds of rising fires.

"My father. You gave me your truth and your love. Speak also to the people in truth and love…"

Eleazar turns to see the people; they are assembled wide eyed before him, their faces thirsting on his words. The fires now lick the top edges of the mount's circumference.

"My father, thus sayeth the Lord… I have tried thee in the furnace of affliction."

Eleazar climbs on the mount's rim and peers below; the fires are now a short distance and rising.

(103) THE SPEECH OF ELEAZAR IN THE MIDST OF FIRE.

They stand in wait before him, huddled together, women carrying children in the front rows and clinging to their men. Eleazar opens his arms to the huddled people waiting on him; behind them the winds of fire race towards the top of Masada. He begins his address, the mount now surrounded by swats of flame dancing on the rim's edges.

"See, our lot has always been a battle for our freedom. Let us not be of any contradiction now of who we are. Come, let us resolve now to declare to Rome and the rest of mankind there is only one God. For the time is now come to declare this truth in practice before the nations. Let us resolve never to be servants to the Romans, nor to any other than to our God alone. Let this be our way."

"Amen, Amen, blessed be you Eleazar." The Jews respond. "The Lord our God, blessed be his name, our God is One. There is no other."

"This… this is the bondage told to our father Abraham, as a surety to come, assured to us even before we were born… before Israel was born. We are now tested again of this same battle, as was our father Abraham when he fled his native homeland and was brought here. Now you can also be a sacred and holy people before our God, as was our forefather Abraham… it is before us?"

He pauses to study the peoples' reaction. The fire's are erupting, causing explosions; the Jews huddle closer, chanting "AMEN! AMEN!"

Now the clouds have dispersed, opening up a full vision of the mount's top. Below the mount, Josephus and six war bearers ascend in a crane box to the top of an embankment, reaching a parallel to the mount's terrace. The soldiers with Josephus leave him to seek out for Alexis. Josephus' sight is fixed on the assembly on Masada and the thick fires racing upward toward them.

Eleazar opens his arms, showing the Jews on Masada of the only saving grace left them:

"We were the first that cried for our freedom and we are the last who fight for it. And dear people, I cannot but esteem it as a grace that God has granted us to die bravely in the light of freedom… this has not been the lot of others who bow to Rome's depravity and falsehoods."

Great explosions resound as burning trees explode; the people huddle closer together.
On the ground, the Romans are affixed on the mount. Silva enquires:
Have any Jews been seen fleeing…?"
"No, my Commander. We looked but saw none fleeing down from the fires."

Atop the mount, Eleazar, arms open, welcomes the Jews closer to him.
"We are again tested this day, for we made a covenant with our God and it lives within us - in our hearts and in our souls the Holy One has written his commands. Now, we can be the first and the last to declare this truth - for there is no truth without our freedom."
The fires cross over the rim of the mount.
"It is very plain we shall be taken this day. Our enemies cannot stop this anymore - even as they are very desirous to take us alive and make us surrender. We saw how our people never surrendered in the temple fires … nor can we? For their sakes and ours… and by our God we shall not!?"
"SAVE US, ELEAZAR, BE YOU OUR SAVIOR!

(104) TITUS SCREAMS.

In a Roman ship, Titus sits on the ground in a dark corner of his bedroom. He holds his hands against his head, shuddering and screaming in an agony. Bernice moves closer to him, tracing his throbbing head with her hands. The head vibrates in her palms; there is a whizzing, buzzing sound, like that of something banging inside his head and wanting to escape. Bernice struggles to open Titus' ear with the rounded head of a knife's handle; he screams, withdrawing into the dark crevice of the room, backing away from her in his agony. Titus screams in a great angst.
Bernice peers out the ship window - dark plumes of foreboding clouds are gathering.

On Masada, the people are huddled together as Eleazar continues to tell the Jews of his plan to save them:
"It is plain to see that Herod's unconquerable fortress has not proven as a means of our deliverance… even that we have still great abundance of food and arms, even more than we need for many years."
He points to the abundance of food, the rows of farming and livestock, and the storage of weapons at the peoples' disposal. He engages the people intensely now:
"Recall well, let now your souls be opened up. What is its meaning before the nations? Recall well, for this fire, first driven upon our enemies, did not turn back and rise up the wall of its own - open now your souls and hearts to account what it means. Only our God has done it! For in our war with the Romans, we did great evils and violence in the holy places, even brother against brother did evil. My own father perished by our hands where iron and violence is forbidden us in the holy places - and we were forsaken of the holy presence. We accounted our own success more than of our God and our own people… we killed brother against brother. I tell you of my own errors in this. Now, we are left only to battle for our beliefs, even as we know not our God's own ways for us… even when this generation's last remnant is being consumed."
The peoples' faces display a foreboding now of Eleazar's words. Swats of fire swirl around the people; they advance closer to the centre of the flat terrace atop of Masada.
"This is all that is given us. Now, our answer to Rome is clear. And there can be no confusion who we are or what we must do. It is clear… there is no confusion!"
The men stand silent and motionless, considering the words emerging from Eleazar and their only hope of life; their children and wives cling to them. Eleazar pans the men intensely; their appearance is forlorn.
"Let us not receive our destiny from the Romans, but only from our God, for this will be more moderate than the other." He nods at the men assuring. "Truly, our merciful Father made for us a way of grace before our enemies. Let our wives die before they are abused and our children before any will taste Roman slavery. After we have slain them, let us bestow that glorious honor on one another, and let us preserve ourselves in our battle for freedom." Tenderly: "It is an excellent funeral for us?"
The rows of silhouette faces stand silent and still. Eleazar, the men and the entire assembly stand silent; all are silent.

Then Benjamin comes forward. "What are you saying, would you have us murder our wives and our children - is this your plan for saving our people!?"

"You are a young Rabbi." Nathan comes forward. "Still, you must know the law forbids suicide and of killing the innocent. Will you transgress both these laws of our God when also upholding the Holy One to us?"

But Eleazar sways face before them, making his response calmly.

"Suicide is forbidden. But when defending against false worship and turning from our God before many, the law says one must surrender his life."

There is again a silence. The Hebrew men and the aged ones of knowledge, who know all of their God's laws and live by them, have no answer to Eleazar. He approaches closer to the people, smiling affectionately, his eyes gleaming with love and tenderness now, which was not seen before in the warrior who led them:

"You are all now as princes and princesses of the holy spirit before us. See, the enemy of the freedom given us by our God marches against us - they advance to enslave us as cattle, to shut our spirit of freedom, to abuse us, to shame us. Let us now choose our men to direct our holy decision before heaven on the highest place we are left on. We have never been closer to our God - He waits on us. Come, let us make this a sacred place before the nations and before our God. Let us make our own sacrifice as our only redemption…"

The people stand silent and still, unable to decide; the fires are advancing closer to the people; the words of Eleazar before them.

On a Roman embankment, Josephus puts down his scroll and turns to the heavens.

"How now my God, how shall I write of such an end? Around them is only fire rising and they can devise no means of escaping anymore?" Josephus turns to the assembly on the mount - he sees their stillness and now becomes aware something is happening.

Two women break the heavy laden silence and come before Eleazar.

"If our men won't do it, we will. Beseech our God for us. Freedom from Rome - or honorable death!?"

"Amen, Amen!" Other mothers come forward, chanting. "We are as one. No surrender to Rome."

"Eleazar!" A second mother comes forward. "Let this be our answer to our God. In the name of the Hebrew women and children who have done no evil, test not our men anymore. Test instead Rome's darkness. Mark their days and not those who give their lives for our God in the fires! Sisters, are we not of the daughters of Israel - or will we ever turn from our God's laws and surrender to Rome!?"

"NO SURRENDER! NO SURRENDER!" The women chant before Eleazar.

As the fires now advance to the top of Masada's terrace, Josephus' searing eyes are wincing as he gazes amidst the haze of the sweeping fires.

On Masada, a mother holding a child in her arms approaches her husband; she embraces him, pressing her bosom into him, her hand guiding his hand on his Sicarii dagger, as her comrade's hands cover the eyes of her child. Kissing her husband, she pulls his hand firmly into her. She slumps holding onto his knees. He looks up at the heavens screaming in an agony. Then one of the Hebrew women takes his hand; she begins to chant a psalm with exuberance, honoring him and dancing around him. The other women join the chant in an ancient somber dance. The children's eyes and mouths are being bound by the women.

Josephus winces, gazing closer.

A woman brings her six children to her husband, their eyes covered up. She kisses her husband's neck, then heaves as his elbow protrudes out and then in. He kisses each of his children the same way. Likewise in this manner, women and children are embracing their men. The women start falling; the chanting diminishing; then the children begin falling.

"Let all the stars in the heavens be as witness of it…" Eleazar gazes into the skies. "We have preferred death to forsaking our freedom of our belief. We have answered the enemy of our God, those who hated our God's laws."

The men carry their provisions and their women's jewelry - they hurriedly throw these in a pile, as the raging fires sweep upon them. The men then join their shoulders on to each other, forming a revolving dance around the mound, chanting psalms in exuberance and abandon.

"Know now most sacred souls, the Romans have no surrender by us alone among the nations. And many sacred souls will emerge from here, for we made this place as our mark… never to be forgotten." Eleazar turns to the mound of women slain by their men. "Blessed are the Hebrew mothers of Israel, those that bore us." Eleazar assures the Jews: "Surely goodness and mercy shall follow you and you shall dwell in the house of the Lord forever…"

The revolving, dancing party of men diminishes, until the last man left standing is Eleazar. Now his son's words come to him again from the approaching fires.

"Father, God said to Abraham… 'Know for a surety thy seed shall be in bondage'. Then it says… 'And also that nation whom they shall serve will I judge, and afterward shall you come out with great substance. I am the Lord thy God'. My father, fear not anymore!" His son displays a joyous nodding; Eleazar sees the Essene behind his son, also joyfully nodding, his index finger pointed at the heavens.

Eleazar is now a lone figure standing on the mount before all of his people's bodies piled up in the centre of Masada's terrace. He staggers like a drunken sailor to confront his God. He kisses his dagger, then he crouches, pushing his stomach into it. He nods smirking sardonically, his eyes engaging the stars; blood streaming from his lips. The last Sicarii warrior gives his final words to his God:

"Abraham offered you one son on Mount Moriah. We gave you a thousand on Mount Masada."

The fires overflow to the top of Masada covering its terrace in the clouds and its majestic mansions of Herod the Great, its innovative agricultural works and water pool. The fires ascend towards the skies. Josephus, seen as a betrayer by his people, now has tears welling, as though he missed his place with his peoples. An understanding emerges in him, a shrouded and as yet unexplained and undisclosed message; they were as dry leaves flowing on a mighty rapid, not knowing where their road will lead or land them, when the Jews again held fastidiously in a war for their belief, and had to pay its price.

Josephus, accounted as a betrayer by his people and the only witness what really happened, is now aware of the Roman monitoring of every word he will write; he does so with a trembling hand.

"A thousand glorious souls. Yet it was as a million."

Then he blots out the line, for like his brethren he too was upon the rapid waters of history, not knowing why he came in his own situation, why his life was spared by strange words he uttered before the Romans or where his road will lead him. He glances in askance at the streaming clouds as the plumes of fire rise up to the heavens.

In Rome, Titus is screaming as the banging and knocking sounds rattles inside his head.

"Where is the glory, tell me?" Bernice smokes on her pot and ponders. "I know of no magic powders that can heal you. Perhaps…" She blows her smoke above her face. "Perhaps then… Rome is not where I belong."

Titus sways his face in terror of his Goddess' words; his face sways:

"Never say such…"

(105) ASCENDING THE MOUNT.

At the base of Masada, Silva has kept his legions of soldiers in wait and stilled seven days and nights, allowing the fires to perform the Roman's war on the Jews atop the mount. Then the rains come.

"The fires have ceased." The war captain reports to Silva. Only a howling wind and pockets of remnant embers remain. "The legions sit impatient too long for your commands - they grow weary and uncontrolled."

Silva walks out of his tent in the pouring rains. He digs his sword into the earth of the mount's base, piercing repeatedly, checking the wetness of the soil if any fires still burn in its depth.

"The order is given. We climb before the sun rises. Proceed with great caution. Remember, it is a deceitful enemy."

In a misty dark dawn, thousands of Roman soldiers are ascending the mount. They hoist heavy war equipment, including the Scorpion, Mobile Towers and huge cranes lifting soldiers and armory. Silva and his armies proceed with great caution of every stepping stone, peering every corner and crevice for any clever guise set up by the Jews.

Reaching to the top of the mount at dusk, they first encounter mounds of food storage piled up in heaps; they pause, surveying suspiciously. Nearing the center, the front soldiers see mounds of jewelry, foods and coins in a pile. As the army proceeds by the soldiers' signal, they confront a surreal scene.

The Roman army is closing in on a heap of dead bodies of men, women and children, spread out in the centre of the terrace. The first of the approaching soldiers poke swords to assure all the bodies are dead and it is not a ploy.

Silva sees burnt dead mothers clasping children, their foods and jewelry piled in a heap; a mist swirls all about the high grounds in the clouds. The soldiers nod, giving Silva a code to approach in safety. Silva turns every which way in search of a guise planned by the Jews as the dead are overturned and examined by the soldiers. [37]

"Lay down your sword." Josephus says. "You don't need it."

Silva lowers his sword and addresses the soldiers.

"This was a stiff-necked people of old. They could have won Rome's highest places - but they gave up all and took with them only a belief of an unseen God. See, we were pushed with swords behind us, but the Jews pushed themselves on our swords that were before them! Yes, I saw valor here, perhaps more than our best warriors and gladiators. Farewell Israel. It is over now."

He turns to Josephus. "Unlike us Romans, you people took this God business seriously!?"

"How will you report to Rome, a glorious victory or a glorious no surrender…?"

"That is the work for a Scribe. My war here is done. It's OVER!?"

Silva plunges his sword into the ground on Masada; it sways to and fro.

CONCLUSION

(106) ROME - 73 AD/CE.

Alexis lies in a hospital bed. Half his face and most of his body are encased in protective metal; a doctor and two nurses are administering vapors of soothing anesthetics from small burning clay pots. Alexis' breathing is labored; his demise anticipated and eminent.

Footsteps are heard. The silhouette figure of the Emperor Vespasian pauses at the entrance door. He appears unsure, reluctant to progress; a foreboding guilt of failure in his demeanor. Then he approaches limping closer to Alexis' bed. The doctor sways his face. A haunting image appears before the emperor:

"Protect my son…my only son…"

Vespasian leans forward; he kisses Alexis' forehead as tears well.

"A strange destiny moved us all." The emperor attempts to talk to Alexis. "The gods of Rome have brought you back where all our roads lead us. A son of Rome lays here, one I swore to protect. A pledge I was unable to…"

"Let the emperor know…" Josephus enters, his arms holding a covered mound with devotion. "Alexis climbed the burning mount seeking the Ark by the order of Titus. He was pulled out of the fiery mount of Masada, his body smoking and barely alive, saved by Florian, his security guard who placed him in a safe ledge. This Florian forfeited his own life to save his master - as did Alexis' father for Vespasian…"

"Yes. And I promised to reward this Florian's family. I shall."

"Now I bring a most precious gift for Alexis." Josephus lays the bundle he carries in the emperor's arms.

"Oh! Look here Alexis." Vespasian turns to Alexis. "I hold before you a gift from the gods… Jupiter's blessing to a noble Roman."

Vespasian brings the child in his arms to Alexis' face. The baby's murmur evokes Alexis; his remaining eye left unhurt by a ferocious black eagle twitches open. Alexis gazes at the child; his eye glows. He blinks at Josephus in a gesture of gratitude.

Outside the window, the clouds start to churn and swirl. As the child coils its small hands in the air, a faint voice comes to Alexis. It is a familiar enchanting voice; it is beckoning from outside the window.

"This light… it shines upon the whole earth… earth… earth…" - the voice echoes.

Alexis' face turns towards the window, focused where the voice emanates from. He winces tremulously as he sees a hand apparition of sparks of light closely outside his window. The hand is extending; beckoning. Alexis' face alights as he recognizes her voice; it comes again to him.

"Come my beloved stranger, come, ascend now to the light you alone can see…see…see… the voice you alone can hea…hear…"

Alexis' body starts to shudder as he struggles to raise his right hand, pointing to the clouds in the window; her hand of sparks is stretched out to him. He sees himself ascending out of his bed in an elevation; he is gliding outside his window into the clouds. Two forms of sparks engage each other and clasp hands.

"I was lost in a place where there was only war and death. You showed me to love the stranger."

"For the Lord had said…said…said it. Therefore the Lord loves those who love… loves… the stranger."

The doctor bends closer, examining the stillness of Alexis; then he turns to the emperor in a swaying of his face. Alexis has departed.

"I behold the mark of a noble Roman son before me, departing on the eagle's wings to Jupiter's glorious abode." The emperor nods assuring.

When Alexis' body slumps in his bed in his final breath, his shirt opens, and on his chest appears a chain with a blue talisman of a Menorah. The emperor's gaze is one of bewilderment at this sight.

"Sacred Jovis Diespiter! Whose work is this?" The emperor lays back the child on Josephus' hands and withdraws; aghast at the site of the glowing blue Menorah. He winces, jowls shuddering, looking around; he begins to retreat, walking backwards, limping awkwardly. He now remembers with a foreboding as an enemy's image comes to him: Vespasian lies bleeding and fallen on the ground; the stony gaze of Eleazar, the Sicarri warrior who tore his leg with a poisoned dagger is confronting him. Vespasian turns to Josephus.

"This was Rome's triumph - how is this enemy's sign come into my royal house? You yourself had prophesized it - your own God sent you to me!?"

He looks around for an answer; none respond. Vespasian flees the room. Josephus gazes at the clouds in the window, raising the child in his arms towards the heavens.

"As the emperor of Rome has said it - it is a seed planted here, in the heart of mighty Rome - one that God Almighty long ago assured it."

Rome's emperor staggers, limping outside in a hallway of the hospital. He finds Titus and Bernice under an archway - she gazes out the window appearing in distant thoughts. Titus is imploring her in animated gestures of pleading. They pause as the emperor approaches.

"Oh Bernice! These are a treacherous people. Even when tested by their own God."

"Are we all not tested, my great Emperor?" Her response makes Vespasian wince; he is considering its meaning.

"Hear me. Rome triumphed before your eyes - you yourself entered their God house with my son standing beside you. It was an empty house - did Bernice's eyes not see this?"

Titus covertly presses on Bernice's hand, prompting her not to engage with the emperor; but she continues in her countering of Titus father, one who wanted her more than his son did; Bernice engages Vespasian boldly.

"My eyes saw many being tested. But the Hebrew God says He alone judges Israel - and all the nations. Will not Rome also be tested?"

"A Hebrew God… will judge Mighty Rome!?" Vespasian flees Bernice's question; hands covering his ears. Then he pauses abruptly and turns, his expression now altered, formal and threatening.

"I command you now, as the Emperor of Rome. Do not to my son with your Hebrew sorcery as was done to Matarian's son. And of those Jews who remain alive, they too shall continue giving their dues into my treasury. Even from you, a betrayer of Rome, of your Emperor…" He gazes hard at his son. "And of my son!?" [132]

As the emperor departs, Titus comes closer to Bernice, holding her hand devotedly; he tells her in earnest pausing, measuring his words with devotion.

"Israel was tested, not by any God but by a stiff-necked people… they battled to the end with valor… but Rome prevailed. I kept my promise faithfully… I led you to Rome as you bid me. You have no country to go to anymore… you… you were with me…in the holy of holies you were with me… you saw Jerusalem's Temple burn… you saw there was no invisible God to save your people… You saw it - my father spoke only truth to you? Now come, you must fulfill your destiny with me… in Rome… where you belong!?"

"Now the temple is also made invisible…" She gazes out the window at the drifting clouds above.

"It can never fall again… now it is hidden here…" Her hand rests on her heart. "No, my magnificent warrior, too much innocent blood cries out. I will honor your father's command and return to my own land. To face my own destiny…"

"Oh no! No!? Without you I am just a brute with bloody hands." He opens his palms before her, tears welling, his face swaying. "You promised to be my queen, to glorify me. Stand by me now, I beg you? You are my Goddess, only you know me…" He angles his wounded hand, gesturing, pleadingly. "They don't…?" The warrior's jowls tremble, beseeching her in abject fear.

"And he separated the light from the darkness…" She continues her gazing at the drifting, streaming clouds in the skies.

"You are my light - without you there is only darkness for me. We must never separate!" [133]

Bernice bends from the waist and removes a large ruby from her toe; she closes Titus' open hand over the red stone. She blows him a kiss, moving away, walking away, seductively and languidly, the magical incense aromas drifting away with her.

"Then…" Titus confronts her, the red stone in his palm. "You lied to me?"

She pauses. "I wanted glory to save my people… you wanted glory to destroy them…"

"Then it wasn't the glory of Rome you desired… not mine or your own?"

She pauses again. "I believe…" She tells it with her back to him. "My people have paid the price asked of them, one they always had to pay… of their own glory… I saw it. It is one Rome cannot understand."

"Glory - what glory!? Your people, the nation of Israel, lay fallen. Never to rise again. What does Rome not understand - tell me!?" He screams, in fear of her rigid stance.

"What did you imagine this war was all about, my mighty glorious warrior?" His Goddess continues exiting the extended opulence of the foyer adorned with marble busts of Rome's divine emperors.

"Stay!?" He gazes long; she does not turn again.

He is alone now, forlorn as a lad berated and forsaken by his departed Goddess; only her challenging words echo, what Rome did not understand. He bangs his face on a pillar, refusing, denying like a stubborn lad, even as he rejects a certain victory hiding in what is clearly a defeat of Rome's greatest enemy. Titus staggers; he holds his hands to his temples, wincing, his demeanor trembling. He attempts now to grasp his golden sword of a Roman victory; the sword falls to the ground. A buzzing, knocking sound in his head is again emerging. He grasps at his hair, pulling at it, slumping, squatting under a Roman archway; the proud warrior is hiding any weakness being exposed. He is knocking his head against the stone wall to stop the buzzing and knocking inside his head. Titus screams; in echoes throughout the hallway adorned with statues.

Then his eyes well up as he gazes at the ruby glittering in his palm, his face dripping in sweat, a menacing smirk defying the throbbing agony in his head. He turns to the streaming clouds above; a crazed glint appearing in his eyes.

"You never showed yourself… how then can one know you?" Titus confronts an invisible God. "If this be you then…" The warrior who changed history offers himself. "Then… better an honest disagreement with my Goddess… than a dishonest agreement with an unseen God… hmm?" He grasps the ruby firmly in his hand, the killer blue eyes is now reddened in suppressed agony, his hand outstretched, offering the stone to an invisible God, begging to be freed of the pain throbbing in him:

"Take it!?" He tosses the red stone to the floor; he sways with his hands clasping his ears.

Now a wailing resounds in his head of a great slaughtering; many are dashing themselves on Roman swords; mothers are shouting "NO SURRENDER!" A great fire is ascending to the heavens. Titus screams in terror, crouching into the wall, backing away. Bernice's voice comes to him:

"Know before whom you are standing…"

He is retreating into a dark crevice, his hands grappling his temples, the left hand sagging uncontrolled.

There is a screeching cry. The warrior's face turns to confront a powerful eagle perched on the roof gazing into him. He remembers. Now he hears voices in his head. First a whisper, then it graduates to a thundering din from the Roman skies.

AUGUSTUS, TIBERIUS, CALIGULA and NERO are chanting:

"…Glory! Glory! GLORY! GLORY! GLORRREEE! GLORY FOR ROME!?"

Titus' wet face glows. He hears crowds hailing him. His eyes light up; voices are calling him urgently now, rising in a great din. He rises from his squatting position, gazing in astonishment, nodding to his imagined crowds. The pride of a warrior emerges; there is a menacing challenge. He gazes at the streaming clouds, confronting an invisible God again:

"Yet I did it - it happened? I am Titus… a Roman… and the glory…" He turns to the people calling him. "You hear them? This glory… this curse…whatever it be… it is mine… not yours…NOT YOURS!?"
His people are calling him:
"Ti-tus! Ti-tus! Ti-tus!"
"See… I… I am Rome's savior…you see it….hear it!?"

Rome's savior, in a new religion, will soon conquer Mighty Rome. One month into Titus' reign, Mount Vesuvius erupts and the Romans see Pompeii destroyed. Then a great devastating plague begins to stricken Rome. Somewhere in history there is found a legendary report of a tiny insect, a gnat, one that became embedded inside Titus' head; it buzzes, it bangs and knocks, wanting to be freed. Titus dies a young man, of a mysterious affliction within two years into his reign. [134]
The eagle is soaring in the streaming clouds; it glides slower now, as if diminishing of its power. The eagle's mighty wing span labors; the powerful eyes wincing as its head tilts south.

(107) THE EMPTY HORIZON.

The desolate empty horizon of Jerusalem, the once famed holy city and marvel of the ancient world, now appears as a city-sized graveyard. Plowed up cubit by cubit, its pillars and corpses torn in search of gold, now only the remnants of a partial broken wall and a lone standing tower of the holy city remain standing. There is a howling flow of gushing winds all about.
A Roman Sayer ascends a raised podium on the destroyed temple site of Mount Moriah, where once stood the Holy of Holies. Behind him stands Silva as the war's victory Commander. In the foreground stand the stationery processions of Jews bound and chained in six-wide rows, with containers of temple spoils hoisted on their shoulders. Further aback are enormous crowds witnessing this ceremony as in a circus passing-show.
"My fellow Romans and members of the empire…" The Sayer on the podium addresses the crowds gathered. "Be you all witness to a Roman decree this day. By order of our divine emperor, Rome declares the war with the Jews victorious. Rome, your true protector, will raise here her sacred and all protecting God Jupiter. Comrades, the heresies upon Jupiter are crushed forever - the enemy of Rome and all her people are vanquished!"
The Sayer pauses as guards approach and affix an ensign of Jupiter in the foreground with nails and hammer. The Sayer mounts the podium again, raising both hands for the peoples' attention as he proclaims it.
"The Davidic dynasty is no more. Solomon's Temple is no more." He sways his hand over the desolate empty horizon: "Jerusalem is no more!?"

(108) ENIGMATIC MAN.

A lone Enigmatic Man sitting on a stone bench is observing the ceremony from a distance, his back posture bars his face being seen, yet he is one who sees all. Before him in the foreground, the Enigmatic Man watches the Menorah hoisted on the Jews' shoulders, and further aback he can see the anointing ceremony of the Roman ensign of Jupiter being hoisted and affixed on the empty ruins of Mount Moriah.
An Arabian Sheik is approaching from the left, moving toward the lone figure on the stone bench. The Sheik slaps his thigh in amazement as he approaches closer to the Enigmatic Man.

"Aah! But where are the many nations promised of Abraham? All I see is one nation gone, and that is not many - is it?" The Sheik caresses his beard. "But this happened before, did it not? This same city was destroyed by the Mighty Babylon, was it not? Yet the mighty Babylon fell and this people were again returned." He caresses his beard. "Yes… then the same happened with the Greeks and again this people returned, true!? We can all see it, yes!?" He waits for an answer. There is no response; the Sheik slaps his thigh. "Aah! I wonder what it all means!"

(109) NAZERENES AND EBIONITES.

Two new Judean Hebrew groups, the Nazerites and the Ebionites are now enjoined to the slave processions.[135]

These are the early emerging prototype Messianic followers within Judaism. These were not spared, accounted as the same Hebrew betrayers of Rome's divine emperors; they are now thrust into the exile procession, never to rise again as a force after their displacement by a new emerging religion, one that will soon conquer Rome.

As the anointing ceremony is concluded the processions stand in wait, the handles of large chests resting on their shoulders. The streams of crowds gathered this day shout in ridicule and empathy at the Jews; they chant as witnessing a parade of the aftermath of an extended war of great destruction. The Sayer gestures; the crowds chant clapping:

"NO MORE HEBREW!" "NO MORE TEMPLE!" "NO MORE JERUSALEM!"

The Roman Sayer prompts the crowds with swaying hand gestures; more, more:

"NO MORE PRIESTS!" "NO MORE SHEKELS!" "NO MORE JUDEA!"

The procession of the Jews is of a broken people, of bloodied bodies with missing limbs and arms, a beleaguered people - a nation that will always stands alone, even when ever connected with the nations, as predicted by the only Arabian prophet in the Hebrew bible whose name was Billam:

"For from the top of the rocks I see him, and from the hills I behold him: lo, it is a people that shall dwell alone, and shall not be reckoned among the nations." (Num.23:9)

In them are the bruised faces of youth and the aged, and of fathers and mothers; faces of priests and scribes, of farmers, money changers, sages, rogues, elites; the faces of the Peace Party, the surviving Sicarii and the Zealot defenders; of Judean Jews, of the Ebionites and the Nazerites. Also in this procession are many Roman traitors who turned sides.

Deborah is one of 120,000 slaves in this beleaguered, standing procession. Now emaciated, her defiant eyes appear the only residue of her once beautiful form.

An Arabian man grabs a girl from the procession; she screams as she is hoisted away; the man hands the Roman guard a piece of silver. Menahem sways face at a Jew who jostles his chains in angst.

The crowds chant:

"JUDEA CATPA! JUDEA CAPTA!"

A man pours three pieces of silver in a Roman's hand and pulls away two adolescent girls from the exile procession, each carried in his arms. A Mother screams; she is silenced away. The Jews scream in fury, banging their chains on beams; Menahem sways face at them.

Commander Silva proceeds towards the slave procession, standing now before Menahem.

"Do you know where you go?" Silva engages the chained crimson bearded zealot commander eye to eye; Menahem makes no response.

The crowds chant:

"NO MORE SHEKELS!"

"NO MORE TEMPLE!"

"NO MORE JERUSALEM!"

Deborah shouts defiantly, raising her hand in the air: "Jerusalem will rise again when Rome becomes dust!?"

The Enigmatic Man sees Deborah is pregnant, an exiled slave with the seed she bears. Her colleagues nudge and pull at her, fearing the guards hearing her daring.

Commander Silva moves closer to Menahem, speaking lowly.

"You held your ground to the last man standing… against a superior power. I saw it. And of your strange belief of an unseen God… in this you were not conquered. I saw it."

Menahem responds cryptically, as though enlightening his opponent of a hidden victory. "What did Rome think this war was about?"

Silva's face twitches; there is a reluctant smirk of acknowledgement. "If your God is real he will remember it…?"

Menahem does not answer; his face turned in the forward direction.

(110) INAUGURATION OF PALESTINE.

The Roman war with the Jews did not end in 73. The exiled Jews battled Rome in the Diaspora, culminating in the Kitos War of 115-117. A third war occurred with the Bar Kokhba Revolt in the years 132-136, the Jews' struggle for Jerusalem continuing into the second century. In the year 135 CE, a new king rose up in Rome who knew not Israel. Publius Aelius Traianus Hadrianus Augustus, known as Emperor Hadrian, sets out on yet a final achievement of Roman glory, one following the destruction of Jerusalem and its Temple fortress.

The new divine Roman Emperor Hadrian will erase all remaining portions of the name of Israel and thereby of all things Hebrew from history - it is an ancient Egyptian custom of eternal demise by forbidding the utterance of a name, as was decreed of one Moses, removing his name from every monument and pylon. As with Egypt and pervasive in the divine king realm, this was Rome's war with Monotheism, even more so than with the Jews. And Rome considered this a holy war wherein both beliefs cannot subsist, and thus did Rome invest all her might to achieve victory - and the Jews did likewise. Both contestants of this holy war saw no alternatives and battled to the end of the final bout; nothing more could be asked of them by humanity or a God. Rome understands now, if the Jews remain than they have won; thus did Rome embark on a means to erase all memory of this nation and their laws of sorcery forever; for Mighty Rome is not like the other nations that fell away.

Again, the Sayer ascends the dais before the image of Hadrian and a huge statue of Jupiter standing on Mount Moriah, which is Mount Zion and the site of the testing of Abraham with the binding of his son, and the site wherein the Temple once stood. The Sayer proclaims Rome's new decrees:

"Thus says Hadrian, divine emperor of the Roman Empire. Judea Capta!"

An obligatory hailing: "Glory to Rome! Glory to Jupiter!"

"But Rome's emperor is not calmed and yet suspicious of this enemy." The Sayer continues. "Many Jews still live, their Hebrew sorcery still lives, and the Jews still look to an invisible God who works secretly among them to test Rome again. Hearken now to Hadrian's royal decrees to erase this greatest of Rome's enemies and their Hebrew God for ever more. Hearken to my words! Rome decrees it as Roman law." The Sayer shouts loud, commanding officially and sternly:

"The Hebrew is forbidden. Rome forbids the reading, writing or speaking in the Hebrew tongue. Circumcision and all Hebrew customs and its practices are forbidden. No Jew must be seen in Jerusalem - this city is now forbidden to Jews. This is now a Roman city honored with our divine emperor's most royal Roman name… it is Aelius Jupiteres Capitolina - Jerusalem is no more!"

The Sayer pauses as the soldiers fix the Latin banner on the dais of the Emperor Hadrian's statue; it reads: Aelius Jupiteres Capitolina!"

The Speaker continues.

"And of this rebellious province, Rome decrees your name shall no more be called Judea…" [136]

The Speaker throws both hands in the air with a music conductor's passion, swaying his index as he gives the people a one thousand year old history lesson none recognize:

"We know what was done in the past to our kin." He nods pointedly. "We know how our Philistine kin from across the sea were destroyed in Gaza by the hand of the Hebrew King David. Their pillars were broken and their sacred monument of Dagon replaced with an invisible Hebrew God. An invisible God… to beguile the people… to spread sorcery of the vilest superstitions and of their heresy against Rome's divinely anointed emperors… the protector… your protector of all the empire's peoples!?" [137]

The Sayer's finger sways in the air to and fro menacingly; the crowds nod and hearken with little understanding:

"Now, Rome returns the name of our kin to this land! By the sacred order of our divine emperor, this land is now given the name of the ancient enemies of the Jews - a fitting name… a name which will now unite us all in crushing those who seek to divide us or insult the empire again. Rome! Your one true savior!"

The people look at each other confused of the Sayer's earnest proclamations, for the people of this time were not fully instilled in reading and writing of history.

"This rebellious province shall no more be called Judea!" His hand makes a slaying action. "Judea is no more!" He screams out:

"Rome decrees this land is now… Philestina! Hail all of you, for Philestina is born again this day! Rome has resurrected you! Hail Rome! Hail Jupiteres!?" [138]

The Roman soldiers hail chants: "Long live Palestina in the glory of Rome!"

The soldiers affix a Latin banner on the dais of the statue of Jupiter. It reads: "Provincia Palestina."

"Judea is now part of our Syria Palestina!"

The Speaker raises his hand, then he turns nodding to the guards:

"Bring up their Hebrew priests and their Hebrew scrolls before the people…"

Ten Hebrew Priests, those acclaimed as possessing the greatest knowledge of their history and scriptures are hauled before the people. These are the ten elite ones who were appointed in the highest offices of Judea, the most learned and wise of all things sacred to the Jews. These are those that were an anathema for Rome's divine emperors by their monotheistic laws, those who would not forgo their belief even when death was assured them. The destroying of the most elite and knowledgeable was also the Babylonian method in 586 BCE, which killed or exiled the most elite; the Greek king Antiochus also exiled most of the elite before Rome conquered all the nations of this region. Thus did the Jews become a wondering and dispersed exiled people, disdained in the Diaspora and barred from returning to their own land.

The ten are brought out by the Roman soldiers, chained and bleeding, and paraded on a high wooden altar.

The Sayer shouts the names of the ten as he reads from a hand scroll:

"We worship the Gods of Rome. We now give unto Jupiter our thanksgiving sacrifice - of those that Jupiter sent Mars to conquer. These are their names. Rabbi Ishmael - the High Priest; Rabbi Shimon ben Gamaliel - the president of the Sanhedrin Courts; Rabbi Hanania ben Teradion - the interpreter of the laws; Rabbi Yeshevav - the secretary of the Sanhedrin; Rabbi Hanina ben Hakinai; Rabbi Huspith; Rabbi Eliezwe ben Shamua; Rabbi Yehuda ben Dama; Rabbi Yehuda ben Baba and Rabbi Akiva the Sage." [139]

The Speaker nods at the executioners. Torah scrolls are set alight and placed on the priests' heads and bound feet. To instill their silent bearing of the fires into screams, Roman soldiers pierce swords into the chests of the ten as they burn. When the priests resist screaming, the soldiers begin scaling their skins with Rome's flesh-burning fiery tools. They continue burning in their silence.

"What see you, Hanania?" The executioner taunts.

Rabbi Hanania: "I see the parchment burning and the letters of the Law soaring upward."

The executioner fans the flame, accelerating the end phase. The ten bleed and burn in a slow, agonizing death, in astonishing silence as their bodies sputter and explode. The crowds are frozen, cupping their noses, for they saw these as strange beings now. The Speaker sneers at the calm of the Priests in facing their torturous deaths and the silence of the crowds.

"They have never been guilty of false faith. In fact, before the church existed, they believed in the one true God" [140]

Now, this holy war's concluding gong is about to sound. Rome declares the war is over; the enemy vanquished. A long, foreboding set of trumpets is heralding its celebration of victory. Can you hear it…?

(111). THE EXILE.

A chilling set of trumpets pierce. The war captain releases a red piece of cloth from his hand; it drifts in the wind.
"LET IT BEGIN!" He shouts: "JEWS - MOVE!"
The exile has begun.

The Exile **"Flight" [James Tissot; Jewish Museum, NY, NY] Source: S31**

The crowds of a mixed gathering of the nations of the Empire are chanting:
"NO MORE HEBREW!"
"NO MORE TEMPLE!"
"NO MORE JERUSALEM!"

The Sayer on the dais hurls coins at the crowds, swaying his arms, compelling them to chant louder. The crowds witnessing the chained Jews hail in rhythmic clapping:
"CAPTA! CAPTA! CAPTA!"
The procession of the Jews chained to strips of wooden beams brace themselves with faces of trepidation, banging their chains to be set free. Cries of prayer and wailing rise up; there is a din of shrieks from the women blocks. Menahem hard stares at a youth sobbing, swaying to face him, gesturing; the youth ceases his tears, assuming a determined posture emulating Menahem's fixed forward stance. Other Jews emulate him, and soon the entire procession ceases from any cries, facing forward and away from Jerusalem in determined postures; for they refused to look upon their holy temple desecrated by a Roman deity.
Silva, the Roman Commander of the Masada war, moves closer toward Menahem, grasping his chained hands to incite the attention of the Hebrew warrior with final departing words.

"You will see many clowns in the Circus. I promise you won't see me there. Allow me this..." Silva steps back, dips his head in a Roman salute of honoring, right hand on his chest; an unspoken respect between enemies of war shrouded in his gaze.

Menahem turns, uttering his defiant response to Silva, whose right hand is still on his chest in a salute.

"Do you know where you go?" Menahem questions the Roman Commander.

Silva sways his face, as if respecting an omen raised by the question; he stumbles, backing away from Menahem's words, his face twitching, smirking with his own defiance. Menahem nods in mutual agreement, then he turns away, facing forward, to whatever be the destiny on the horizon across the seas.

The Sheik again approaches to deliberate with the lone figure on the stone bench:

"What destinations have you now - does any of your family remain? I am Sheik Diyalah. Friend, you cannot have a Hebrew name anymore - it is forbidden. Come in peace with me." He extends his hand in a hospitable gesture. "I have choice land. Come now...?" The Sheik's extended hand waits on the Enigmatic Man.

"FINAL WARNING!" The war captain shouts: "JEWS - MOVE NOW!?"

The Roman soldiers prod the Jews with spears on their sides to move forward; they raise spears and batons in the air as warnings. The exilic procession starts to waver, unsure and hesitant; wailings and screams erupt, as with a final departure of a loved one's coffin. The Jews are leaving behind their sacred Jerusalem. Again.

"Move and show no tears!" Menahem bellows. "None!?"

Their tears dry up; the procession of Jews begins to move forward determinedly. They begin their marching away from their holy city, now a desolate empty horizon. As the enormity of a nation-size procession heaves forward, a great din of chanting erupts from the crowds in a hailing of mocking repetitions and rhythmic hands slapping:

"CAPTA! CAPTA! CAPTA!"

The Sayer prods them; he tosses coins at the crowds.

As Deborah is being led away in the moving procession, she darts her head. She is stretching, searching to catch a final glimpse of the Enigmatic Man on a stone bench; Deborah sees the outstretched hand of the Sheik waiting on him. Now a vision comes to her; she is recalling it - the outstretched hand of a Roman traitor who turned to the other side is beckoning; waiting on her, assuring her:

"This stranger wants to know of this unseen God..."

Her eyes begin to glow.

"Wherever I look I see only you... even when I shut my eyes... all else is become ugly to me... and I know now... something has happened to me!?" His eyes are pleading of her. *"See, my life is in your hand now, if you but hear me?"*

Awareness comes to her; a joy appears on her beleaguered face.

"I know now you can never forget my name..."

Her teary eyes are agape; a delirious hopping and bouncing as with her secret friend the Moon, appears:

"Where a repentant sinner stands... even the most righteous cannot...therefore the Lord loveth the stranger...strang...ger..."

She turns to her comrades, pointing at the Enigmatic Man, assuring them:

"I see it!? I see it now!? Sisters - be not afraid anymore! I see it!?"

Her Nasserite comrades cover her delirious hopping and dancing, protecting her from the guards who are nudging the procession onward with batons and swords.

Now the Jews begin marching; a long and winding procession is departing to an unknown destiny. Each group is hoisting large wooden vats of Temple treasures. A group lifts an ancient throne; guards surround a group pushing and drawing the giant Menorah of gold on a wooden platform on wheels.

The Enigmatic Man, the sole figure not clapping in the rejoicing fervor, can see the procession moving and Deborah being jostled away. The dawn of a turning point in history opens before him. He sees all.

In Jerusalem's Empty Horizon the past and the future are mingling in the present. Multiple images are interplaying in its howling windswept gushes; a collage of history is flourishing. The images start to morph; the slaves, the Romans and the crowds begin to waver, appearing to move in elongated slow motions. The Jews lifting the temple spoils on their shoulders sway to and fro. The images flash, bend and swirl, then dissolve into each other. There is a howling wind in the desolation that is gushing into the vacuum left in Jerusalem as the procession moves forward. All is disorienting; a historical epiphany unfolding. The Enigmatic Man sees all.

There is a maiden standing defiantly in front of a teacher who is tottering on one leg.

A Hebrew priest points his finger anointing a Roman General as divine emperor.

A Roman warrior prostrates kissing the foot of a Hebrew Queen.

A rabbit explodes amidst Rome's standing legions.

Giant Rams smash at a wall.

A sword of fire is exploding in multiple tints of colors over a temple.

Jars of scrolls stand in a row covered with hay.

A temple is burning.

The statue of Jupiter ascends on Mount Moriah.

A hand grasps another hand on a mount saving it from falling to the abyss.

The Jews are dancing in abandon atop a mountain burning above the clouds.

An eagle is perched on a lone remnant wall standing in the empty horizon.

Streaming clouds are swirling.

A nation is departing hoisting war spoils.

An Arabian Sheik slaps his thigh before a lone figure on a stone bench.

History is turning…

The Enigmatic Man sees all. Can you see it?

(112) AN EMANATION.

They glide unseen to the naked eye in the streaming clouds over Jerusalem. Deborah and Alexis are emerging as incorporeal angelic beings made of sparks of light. They hover above Mount Moriah in Jerusalem's Empty Horizon, pointing at a glowing monument in an unseen realm, their voices in tremulous echoes:

"Look... do you see see it...?" Deborah points at the glowing monument in the swirling, streaming clouds.

"We return." Alexis enjoins Deborah's hand. *'Together."* He points. *"I see it."*

Can you see it? It is envisioned without vision. It is shrouded in humanity's metaphor. Ever-emanating and pulsating; ever-challenging; it is ever contested and diabolical. No such thing as an invisible God? Yet it impacted when one fled his home with a reward on his head, one who perceived an emanation thrust upon him the Greeks called as 'Monotheism'. It caused a controversy in many camps throughout history and in every nation that was intercepted by its provocative premise; it confronted all status quos. It is that same emanation that came with an assurance to one fleeing his land that his seed shall be in bondage as a surety - assured even before there was yet any seed; even before any could yet do wrong. Diabolical. And it became synonymous with holy wars and exiles throughout history unceasing. It is there where the past and the future mingle with the present, in a perfect tense of humanity's foremost battleground. It became a holy war syndrome.

"Look... do you see see it...?" Deborah points at the glowing swirling sparks forming above the empty horizon.

An emanation of invisible sparks is emitting from the streaming clouds above a small hilltop known as Mount Moriah. The sparks assemble themselves into a configuration of letters; the letters rise and dance, hovering and swirling around the mount. They form themselves above the desolate ruins of an empty horizon, becoming words and thoughts, embedding themselves into our historical psyche. They now lurk somewhere hidden where once stood a temple, one that was felled, yet never vanquished of its ever-provocative implications; one ever falling and rising as a living wave, both hidden and manifest. Monotheism was sworn here on the grounds of Mount Moriah, where a most controversial covenant was exchanged. It impacted upon Rome's Divine-Emperor beliefs, culminating in history's greatest holy war. In its aftermath, freedom of belief is ever defended against Rome's path of dominion - it is a war that will become the common denominator of all belief groups.

And Simon gazed at the burning temple in an eerie laughter of his own visions; he saw that wherever there is a perceived curse, there is also an equal blessing shrouded therein. And this falling and rising, this exile and return, it preserved safely the small and fallen one, absorbing great destruction, when many did fall yet did not rise again. Now a curse can be forgiven and negated, but not so a pledge - even by a God bound by His own truth, one declared and sworn on this mount. Mighty Rome never saw the word as God's truth; Rome saw the sword as its only truth. Here a dormant, forbidden and dead tongue, one 4,000 years old, was also resurrected to bring forth the truth of the word - that mightiest force in creation. Such never happened anywhere other than this small bloodied, battled and battered land; it is a goodly land of the word. Can you see it…?

> *'..AND I WILL GIVE UNTO THEE, AND TO THY*
> *SEED AFTER THEE, THE LAND OF THY SOJOURNING,*
> *ALL THE LAND OF CANAAN, FOR AN EVERLASTING*
> *POSSESSION; AND I WILL BE THEIR GOD.'*
> *[Genesis 17/8; The Dead Sea Scrolls.]*

(113) REBELS - OR - HEROES?

In a Roman library stands Josephus, one who turned coat with a Roman sword hovering upon him as he finishes his writing. He now confronts us; he stands amidst Mighty Rome's exquisite statues and busts of marble.

Tiberius, Caligula, Nero, Vespasian, Titus… they stand deathly silent; they appear to acknowledge the right to freedom of belief as transcendent. Herein marks the last stand of those rebel stiff-neck Jews when they defended their right of belief - and our own; it is a meriting reason to sacrifice one's life, and they did so. Mighty Rome's writers thought so; even when a sword hovered above them and many were killed for it: "And though they were but a handful fighting against a far superior force, they were not conquered until part of the Temple was set on fire. Then they met their death willingly, some throwing themselves on the swords of the Romans, some slaying one another, others taking their own lives and still others leaping into the flames. And it seemed to everybody and especially to them that so far from being destruction, it was victory and salvation and happiness to them that they perished along with the Temple.'
— [Roman Historian Deo Cassius, Epitome of Book LXV].

Josephus tosses a scroll on the table, defensively, in askance.

"And It Was So..."

(114). MODERN ROME.

Arch De Titus [Hubert Steiner] Source: S32

Can you see it? We are at the Arc De Titus stone monument in today's Modern Rome. A tour guide explains to a gathering of people a brief history of the figurines embossed under the top arch of the monument's curvature of stone - built by the Jews of Judea. He sways his finger as he explains its significance:
"Aah, yes! That was Rome's greatest prize of all!" The guide points at the Menorah lifted by exiled Hebrews sculpted on the Roman arch: "That seven-arm lamp was made from a single piece of gold in a fiery desert by the hands of the Israelites. More than 3000 years ago…"
Eastward in the Empty Horizon, two invisible figures of sparks of light are hovering. A forbidden love of two strangers glides as a residue - a 'seed'. They hover above Rome's destruction.
A subliminal faint whisper is echoing. Can you hear it…?
   "And it shall cast its light upon the whole earth…earth…wherein there are no strangers… gers… ers…"

Stone engraving etched in the Arch De Titus Monument; Rome - 95 CE. S54

[Certain historical names of similarity and certain event chronologies have been modified as enhancements. For a summary of all historical references please refer to the Index Sections.]

THE END.

■

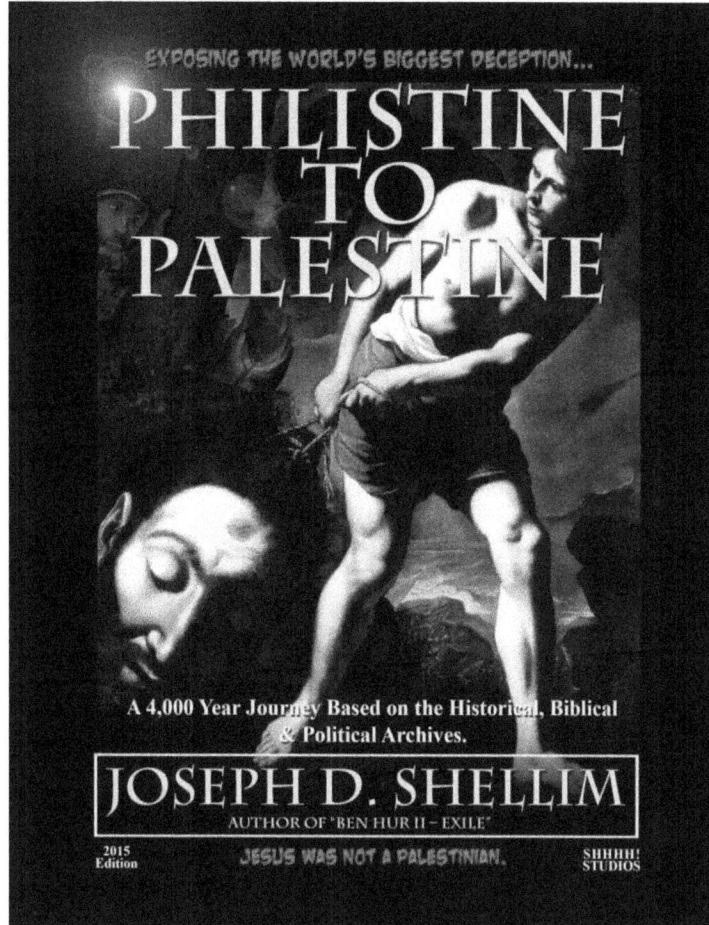

EXPOSING THE WORLD'S BIGGEST DECEPTION...

PHILISTINE TO PALESTINE

A 4,000 Year Journey Based on the Historical, Biblical & Political Archives.

JOSEPH D. SHELLIM
AUTHOR OF 'BEN HUR II – EXILE'

2015 Edition

JESUS WAS NOT A PALESTINIAN.

SHHHH! STUDIOS

Have you considered it?
Israel has never occupied another people's land in all her 4,000 year recorded history;
Israel is the world's most accused country of illegally occupying another peoples' land.
How much don't you know of the world's most controversial issue?

Prior to the 20th Century, none but the Jews were Palestinians. It was the name exclusively referred to the Jews for 2,000 years, held as their historical land, including in all official US, British, European and UN archives till the late 1960's; even the Nazis put up signs "Jews go to Palestine!"

In WW2, a battalion consisting of 26,000 Jews were enlisted in the British forces; it was called the "Jewish Palestinian Brigade". In 1951, today's Jerusalem Post media was called as 'The Palestinian Post' – issued in both English and Hebrew. All Jewish institutions were pre-fixed as Palestinian till the 1960's. Palestine was the name applied by the Roman Emperor Hadrian on Judea, the homeland of the Jews. Then, the Arabs and Britons were both recruited in the Roman Legions during the destruction of Jerusalem's Temple and Judea's name changing ceremony of 135 AD/CE.

The Question: How then did this name come to represent the antithesis of the Jews and Israel in the 20th

Century? It is not a provocative or controversial question; it is an incumbent one for humanity today and the examination premise of this book. "Philistine-To-Palestine" is a 4,000 year historical journey assessing the recorded source points of the origins of the Jews, the Arabs, the Philistines and the British role in dividing the Middle-East after the fall of the Ottoman Empire. Recent de-classified archives, six centuries of census accounts, the Palestinian Jews in the Ottoman period, incorporating interviews and quotes by a host of scholars, theologians and historical records expose the world's most intractable conflict, unfolding its controversial issues. The topics expose suppressed errors that impact today's world:

The Balfour Deception * The Refugee Deception * The West Bank Deception * The UN Deception * The "Palestinian Jesus" Deception * The Herodotus Deception * The Name Deception.

This presentation explores the impacting historical source issues: Are Arab Palestinians native to Palestine? Did the Arab race exist in King Solomon's time? Are the Jews, the Copts, the Lebanese and the Phoenicians an Arab people – or older inhabitants of this region?

How much don't you know of the world's most controversial issue?

[Release date: 2015]

"MYSTERY OF THE HEBREW"

Suddenly Emerged - Origins Unknown.

The 'word' is regarded as humanity's greatest attribute. Whether speech and writing emerged via divine intervention, evolution, superior alien interaction or from the ponderings of inspired ancient people, the origins of speech is distinctly varied from generic communication common to all life. Speech is unique to humans by a ratio of trillions of life-forms to one.

The attribute of speech and its subsequent writing remain as humanity's elusive mystery even to the foremost enthusiasts of modern evolution. One writing appears to have by-passed the thread of a gradual formation. The Hebrew is history's most isolated and forbidden language; it is not a borrowed writ for no other people spoke Hebrew. Yet it impacted more than half of humanity's belief structures for more than half of humanity's recorded history. Although a late entry in the ancient world, the Greek writers claim the Hebrew as the inventors of the alphabet; today, a growing selection of institutions accept these findings or fail to adequately explain the Hebrew origins.

It emerged suddenly and in an already advanced state; we have no written Hebrew prior to the five books of Moses. That the first Hebrew writing output, the five books of Moses (The Torah), is its most advanced writing, is its greatest mystery. It introduced new thresholds: of Origins ('In the beginning'), Creationism, Early Sciences ('a seed shall follow its own kind'), Medicine (contagious leprosy), Species (Life form groupings), Judiciary Laws, Monotheism; this writing alluded to the earth as billions of years old (the separation of water and land); the size of the universe (that the stars are unaccountable); the first recorded 'name' of a human, and deems the first words uttered in the universe as "Let there be light."

The Hebrew remains the only language that resurrected itself after 2,000 years and is the oldest active language and writing. The first translation to the Greek in 300 bce altered history and humanity as no other writing; within its peripherals lay a host of cadence that underlies the mysteries that challenge the conventional status quo. The inspiration to three religions, the Hebrew writ is a thought provoking exploration of mankind's recorded history.

[Release date: 2016; Shhhh! Studios publication]

"THE MESSIAH SYNDROME"

Was a 'Critical Factor' lost?

It emerged from biblical events and alluded verses recorded over 3,000 years ago. These ancient writings contain predictions of forthcoming events and of a divinely ordained figure appearing and an End-Times; it acquired a status of 'Biblical Prophesies'. The Jews and Christians throughout their generations referred to such a figurehead as "The Messiah" [Anointed One; Moshiach/Heb]; Deliverer; Saviour.

In the First Century the Messianic fervour intensified by the spiritual and existential crises faced by the Jews and the early prototype Christians during the Roman Empire's destructive invasion. A biblical and historical thread examines this syndrome from its inception, tracing its origins and its profound impacts on humanity. A 'Critical Factor' that was disregarded from the Messiah equation will be exposed in its accounting. A bold and challenging re-assessment says one Critical Factor cannot be dislodged from this syndrome and is incumbent, that humanity's chaos can be restored by it without loss or defacing of any belief.

[Release date: 2016; Shhhh! Studios publication]

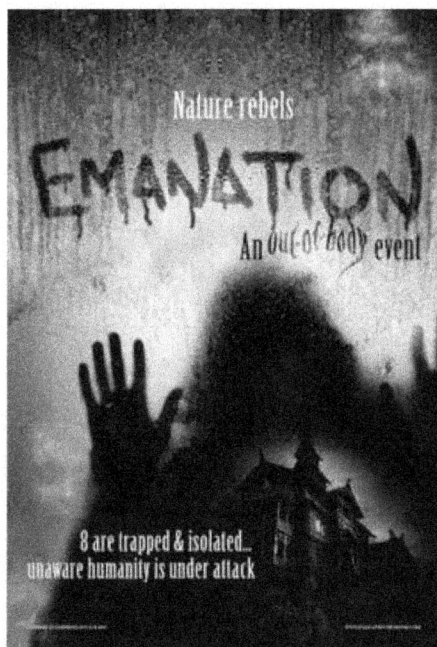

"EMANATION"
Beware of your own shadow-
It's not "you" anymore.
A New-Age Thriller. [2016]

INDEX SECTIONS

REFERENCES.

Historical Enhancements. Four modifications were adapted based on the following historical archives:
- Forbidden Love of Alexis Matarian and Deborah Hur: See Ref. 99.
- Flavius Josephus deliberations with Titus to save the Temple: See Ref. 96.
- Rabbi Hillel: See Ref. 21.
- Hadrian [135 AD/CE]-Silva [73 AD/CE] Time-Line: See Ref. 30.

1. **ABRAHAM'S FATHER TERAH'S IDOL SHOP IN UR**. [Theological/Metaphorical. A Medrash based legend on the 1st. Century sage R. Hiyya's commentary of Genesis 11:28 and Genesis 15.7] See also # 71.

2. **ARISTOTLE.** [In 200 B.C.E, the Jewish philosopher Aristobulus made the positive assertion that Jewish revelation ['In the Beginning God'] and Aristotelian philosophy ['God as A First Cause'] were identical. Jewish Encl.; Josephus "AGAINST APION/ contra Apionem," ii. 17]; Maimonades, The Jewish Religion: A Companion, *Oxford University Press].* Aristotle's Physics and Metaphysics [Joe Sachs, "The Being of Sensible Things; Metaphysics Internet, Ency.of Philosophy] Maimonades: see also # 167.]

3. **AGRIPPA** — [Agrippa II - grandson of King Herod/Virtual Jewish Libr; Wiki]

4. **"ANO CHI"** ["I Am" - The opening two words of The Ten Commandments; Exodus 34:28; Duet 1-:4]

5. **BERYLLUS** [Josephus; Antiquities 20.8.9.] See also # 93.

6. **CALIGULA.** Caligula announced his self-deification, ordered that a statue of himself should be placed in the Temple of Jerusalem and the Jews be forced to worship him; and it had not yet been carried out when Caligula was assassinated — [VRoma Org; Jewish Virtual Libr. org/Judaism/revolt.] / **Caligula** was murdered at the Palatine Games by Cassius Chaerea, tribune of the Praetorian Guard, Cornelius Sabinus, and others. Caligula's wife Caesonia and his daughter were also put to death. He was succeeded as emperor

by his uncle Claudius. [Encl. Britannica] / Caligula adorned his horse Incitatus with Jewels and servants and demanded it to be his chief Consul - [Suetonius' Lives of the Twelve Caesars; Dio Cassius]

7. **COLISEUM**. Completed in the year 80; Construction by Jews [Josephus War04].

8. **COLLEGIA**. Julius Caesar, upon his accession, vouchsafed to the Jews a writ of tolerance covering the whole empire, which thenceforth constituted the unassailable charter of their privileges. It had only one condition attached to it; namely, that they should content themselves with exercising their own rites without showing contempt for those of others — [Ency. Britannica; Josephus Antiquities 20.8.9; Ant. xix. 5, §§ 2-3] / 'These decrees show clearly that Julius César in his broad and statesmanlike manner fully recognized the rights and claims of the Jews as an important element of the Roman empire. [Caesar, Jewish Encl.]

9. **COMMAGENE AND EMESA.** — ['Auxiliaries had been sent by kingdoms on the Upper Euphrates, Commagene and Emesa; an Arabian sheik, who felt a deep hatred for the Jews, had joined the Romans with his warriors; and many adventurers - veterans Galba and Otho. [Ancient Warfare Magazine]. Vespasian found himself in command of a powerful force, consisting of the fifth, tenth, and fifteenth legions, twenty-three auxiliary cohorts, and six squadrons of horse, in addition to the troops of the native vassals, of the Jewish King Agrippa II., and of the kings of Commagene, Emesa, and Arabia. The entire Roman army mustered at least 60,000 men. Josephus Wars 03; Livius Org]

10. **CONVERSIONS** ['it is an indisputable fact that proselytes were found in large numbers in every country of the Diaspora. (Dio Cassius, xxxvii. 17). 'In Antioch a large portion of the Greek population Judaized in the time of Josephus' ("B. J." vii. 3, § 3)]

11. **COVENANT** [Genesis 17.7]

12. **CUBIT** [A cubit is 22 inches or 56.1 centimeters. Josephus; Mishnah]

13. **DEBORAH** ["Bee" - Heb] Israelite Prophetess, Canaan warrior; sole female Judge. Bk of Judges 4-5].

14. **ELEAZAR** — [The Sicarian leader, Eleazar son of Yair [Jair], relative of Menahem and Judas the Galilean; Eleazar bans Roman Sacrifices [Josephus *Antiquities* 20.409. # Two separate persons named Eleazar are featured in Josephus' writings, namely Eleazar ben Simon and Eleazar ben Ya'ir/Jair. This book's portrayal utilises one name to represent historical traits of both persons] See also # 95.

15. **ELEAZAR FORBIDS SACRIFICE FOR ROME.** [Josephus , Antiquities 20.409]

16. **ESTHER** [Heb name 'Hadassah'; Exilic orphan who rose to Queen of Persian King Ahaseuros, Savior of Israeli nation, Heb Prophetess celebrated in festival of Purim. Book of Esther]

17. **FLORUS** [Josephus, War 2.14, 4-5].

18. **GIDEON** ['Mighty Warrior'; Son of Joash, Tribe of Mennasah. Book of Judges 6-8]

19. **GNAT - TITUS DEATH**. ['Titus' Death' - Chabad Org; Jewish Ency. Legendary/Unconfirmed]

20. **GREEK-SYRIAN SACRIFICE AT CAESAREA** [Josephus War 2.14.4-6]

21. **HILLEL** [Hillel the Elder; First Century Pacifist and Spiritual Head of Israel; 60 BCE -10 CE. House of Hillel; Wiki; Chabad Org. # **Not the 'Hillel'** depicted in this Book; the historical traits of Hillel 10 CE adapted as contemporary first century culture in Judea.]

22. **HOLY OF HOLIES**: ['And let them make Me a sanctuary' - Ex Ch 5/8 ; 'As to the holy house itself, which was placed in the midst of the innermost court, that most sacred part of the temple, it was ascended to by twelve steps; etc/Josephus Wars, 5/2]**;** Titus found the Holy of Holies empty - Tacitus [32]; Cas Dio 33; Josephus]

23. **HORNED VIPER.** — [*Pseudocerastes persicus fieldi, Wiki*]

24. **HUR.** Contemporary Israelite Assistant of Moses. See also # 76.

25. *'IT IS ROMAN TO DELIGHT IN THE GIFTS OF THE GODS'.* [Wiktionary]

26. **LEAPING GHOST WARRIOR.** [Josephus Ch.4/21.]

27. **JOSEPHUS' ORACLE**. [Josephus, The Jewish War 3.8.9] See also # 70.

28. **JOSEPHUS WOUNDED** [Josephus Wars, BOOK V, CH 13,3]

29. **"JUDEA CAPTA"** — [Judaea Capta coinage/Wiki; coins relics].

30. **JUDEA RENAMING AS PALESTINE [**The Roman Emperor Hadrian renamed Judea as Palestine in the Second century [135 CE], name derived from 'Palestina'. — [Hadrian's Curse, The Freeman Center; Wiki; & Jewish History.Com.**]. # Hadrian-Silva**. These two figures were vested in the varied periods of 135 CE & 73 CE respectively; these have been featured together in the "Inauguration of Palestine" chapter as a continuation of the Roman actions in Judea, clarified in the historical thread "Philistines to Palestine.

31. **MACABEES AND ANTIOCH IV.** — [2 Maccabees 5:11-14; 6:1-11]

32. **MARCELLUS; ALIENUS** Two Roman Senators assassinated by Titus — [*Titus, Vatican Museums, Vatican City]*

33. **MARRIAGE WITH JEWS FORBIDDEN/CONCUBINE**. — [Rome forbids marriage with Jews, Jewish Ency; Grätz, "Gesch." iv. 403 *et seq.*, 702] / **CONCUBINE**: "Anyone can keep a concubine of any age unless she is less than twelve years old." — [Lefkowitz & Fant, Women's Life in Greece, John Hopkins Uni Press]

34. **MASADA** [or 'Citadel'. A mountain overlooking the Dead Sea in the Judean desert NW of Jerusalem, with a security fortress mansion, farming & water eco-systems situated on a single standing terrace plateau 1,300 feet (400 m) above steep cliffs on all sides.]

35. **MASADA MASS SUICIDE**. [Josephus, Wars of the Jews, Book 7, Ch.9. Some disputation; report is based on two escaped survivors' alleged portrayals.]

36. **MASS CONVERSION IN THE ROMAN WORLD.** [Hillel & Shammai, Jewish History Org] See also # 99.

37. **MIKVAH** [Ritual Water Emersion. 'They must purify themselves with the water on the third day and on the seventh day; then they will be clean.' Numbers 19/12.]

38. **MOUNT MORIAH** ['Then Solomon began to build the temple of the LORD in Jerusalem on Mount Moriah' — II Chronicles Chapter 3] See also # 77. **MOUNT SCOPUS**. In 70 AD Mount Scopus was used as a base to carry out a siege of the city by the 5th. 12th. and 15th Legions (the 10th. legion's position being on the Mount of Olives).The Crusaders used it as a base in 1099. [Josephus, Wars, v 81 and 82]

39. **NASSERITE [Nazarene]** — [Hebrew Bible, Numbers 6:5; Nazarene Wiki 1.3] See also # 161.

40. **'NO SURRENDER'** [Titus refused to accept wreath of victory - Philostratus; First Jewish-Roman War; The Outcome; Wiki]. See also # 62.

41. **PHILISTINES.** [The Philistines were an aggressive, warmongering people who occupied a part of southwest Canaan between the Mediterranean Sea and the Jordan River. The name "Philistine" comes from the Hebrew word *Philistia*, and the Greek rendering of the name, palaistinei, gives us the modern name "Palestine." The Philistines are first recorded in Scripture [Gen. 10:14]. It is thought that the Philistines originated in Caphtor, the Hebrew name for the island of Crete and the whole Aegean region; Amos 9:7; Jeremiah 47:4] / For unknown reasons, they migrated from that region to the Mediterranean coast near Gaza. - Got Questions Org./ The **Philistines** (Hebrew: פְּלִשְׁתִּים, *Plištim*), **Pleshet** or **Peleset**, were a people who as part of the Sea Peoples appeared in the southern coastal area of Canaan at the beginning of the Iron Age (circa 1175 BC), most probably from the Aegean region. [Wiki]. See also Palestine of Today, # 172.

42. **QUEEN BERNICE** — [Julia Berenice, 39 BC and 92 AD; Acts.Ch.25; Jewish Women's Archive.]

43. **RIGHTS ANNULLED AT CAESAREA.** — [Josephus; Antiquities 20.8.9] See also # 88.

44. **ROMAN ROAD TARRING** — ['Romans Roads' Digstar]

45. **ROMAN SWORD OF FIRE** [Josephus *Jewish War*, 6.289; Tacitus Annals, 15:47]

46. **ROMAN TAX PENALTY** [Fiscus Judaicus]

47. **ROMAN WAR RULES.** [Death Penalty for leaving war positions - Josephus War 5/4]

48. **ROYAL LIBRARY OF ALEXANDRIA.** [Or, Ancient Library of Alexandria; in Alexandria, Egypt; 3rd century BC to Roman conquest in 30 BC.] See also # 210.

49. **SABRA FRUIT** [*Opuntia, Wiki*]

50. **SAUL OF TARSUS - BERENICE**. [Acts 25:13]; Freed from Prison, Eusebius].

51. **SCAVENGERS; BARBARIC** [Titus charges Arabian and Roman soldiers as barbarians when corpses are disemboweled for gold - Josephus Wars, Book V, Ch 13, 4]

52. **SEPTUAGINT** [Greek; 'Book of the 70'; the first translation of Heb Bible; Wiki] See also # 173. **PTOLEMY REQUEST TO JEWS FOR TRANSLATION** — [Tractate Megillah, pages 9a-9b.] **SEPTUAGINT IMPACT**: The Jewish philosopher Aristobulus, in the second century B.C.E., asserts that Homer, Hesiod, Pythagoras, Socrates, and Plato were all acquainted with a translation of the Torah into Greek which had been made before the Persian conquest of Egypt (525 B.C.E.) — [Eusebius, *Praeparatio Evangelica*, 13:12, 1-16]. See also #173.

53. **TEMPLE SIZES - FORTRESS OF JERUSALEM.** [LARGEST MONUMENT: 'List of largest monoliths in the world'- Wiki; SIZES: Josephus Ant, XV, xi, 3, 5; BJ, V, v.; Antiquities 8, 95-98; War V, 220-221; War 5] The City of David: Jesus' Jerusalem | History Documentary; Tacitus (59)]; 450 ACRES; CIRCUMFERENCE = 33 FURLONGS [Josephus war 5.5.2, 192]. "It was a structure more noteworthy than any under the sun' - Josephus.] See also # 86.

54. **TAXES**. Additional tax levied on Jews [Josephus Antiquities 18.6.2; Fiscus Judaicus].

55. **TEMPLE BURNING BY TITUS.** [Sulpicius Severus; Tacitus Histories, Fr.2].

56. **TEMPLE OF JUPITER** [Tacitus: Histories, Book 4. liii]

57. **TEMPLE PILLARS** ['The pillars were of one entire stone each of them, and that stone was white marble'; WARS, CH. 5/2]

58. **TIBERIUS** - [Tiberius Julius Alexander, governor of Egypt, Jewish Ency.]/ Expels Jews from Rome in 19 AD; sends 1000's of Jews to battlefields over a conversion incident - [Dio Cassius Ivii:18; Tac Ann ii:85]

59. **TITUS WOUND** — [Dion Cassius; Josephus]

60. **TITUS-FLAVIANS REFUSED TO ACCEPT WREATH OF VICTORY** — [Philostratus; First Jewish-Roman War, The Outcome, Wiki] See also # 81.

61. **VESPASIAN/TAXES:** 'And of those Jews who remain, they shall continue giving their dues into my treasury'. [After the fall of the Temple (70), the Roman government, instead of simply abolishing a tax which had no further object, decided to impose it for the benefit of the treasury of Jupiter Capitolinus in Rome ("B. J." vii. 6, § 6; Dio Cassius, lxvi.] See also # 193.

62. **VESTAL VIRGINS** — [Tribunes and Triumphs.org/roman-gods/vestal-virgins.]

63. **WAR CAUSES**. — ['And this was the true beginning of our war with the Romans, for they rejected the sacrifice of Caesar on this account' (Josephus W 2.17.2); Religious tension between Jews & Roman government (livius/jwar04); Greek Sacrifice at Synagogue of Caesarea/Bribery - The War Begins (War 2.14.4-6); Jewish Rights Annulled at Caesarea (Josephus War 2.14.4-6)] See also # 90.

64. **WAR SPOILS DISPLAYED IN COLISEUM.** The table of shewbread, the seven-branched candlestick of gold, and the silver trumpets, which are being carried in triumph. — [Arch De Titus; Fiscus Judaicus].

65. **WAR TOLL**. Temple War: 1.1 M Jews; 270,000 were killed in surrounding towns. Masada War: 960 Jews. Deported to Rome: 97,000 Jews. [Josephus, *War of the Jews* VI.9.3] See also # 112.

66. **"WHAT IS HATEFUL TO YOU, DO NOT UNTO OTHERS."** — [Hillel the Elder; First Century Pacifist and Spiritual Head of Israel; 60 BCE -10 CE. House of Hillel; Chabad Org; Wiki]

67. *YOCHANAN BEN ZAKKAI.* — *[Wiki; Chabad Org.]*

HISTORICAL ARCHIVES AND QUOTES.

Flavius Josephus. Source S33

68. JOSEPHUS EXCELLENT HISTORIAN.

Josephus, according to ancient criteria, is an excellent historian. Authors like Lucian and Polybius of Megalopolis have published treatises on the writing of history, and Josephus lives up to the standards they set. Titus Flavius Josephus (37 - c. 100), also called Joseph ben Matityahu (Hebrew: Yosef ben Matityahu), was a first-century Romano scholar, Jewish historian and hagiographer, who was born in Jerusalem. His most important works were The Jewish War (c. 75) and Antiquities of the Jews (c. 94). The Jewish War recounts the Jewish revolt against Roman occupation (66-70). Antiquities of the Jews recount the history of the world from a Jewish perspective for an ostensibly Roman audience. Flavius Josephus fully defected to the Roman side and was granted Roman citizenship. He became an advisor and friend of Vespasian's son Titus, serving as his translator when Titus led the Siege of Jerusalem, which resulted—when the Jewish revolt did not surrender—in the city's destruction and the looting and destruction of Herod's Temple (Second Temple). — [Livius org; Wiki] See also # 105.

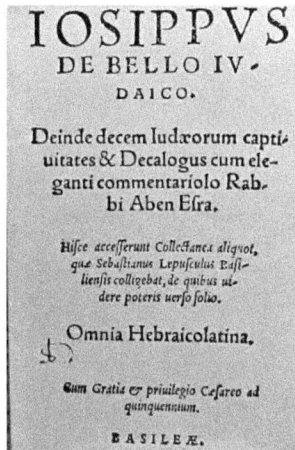

Josephus' War with the Jews; ancient Latin copy of the Aramaic Edition.

71. ABRAHAM-MONOTHEISM.

The Patriarch is recognized as the founder of Monotheism, and respected in all three primary monotheistic faiths (Judaism, Christianity and Islam). Presumed to have lived sometime in the period 2000-1700 B.C.E. — [Abraham, Jewish Virtual Libr.] JUDEA-MONOTHEISM: The Jewish lifestyle was strictly managed by their observance of monotheism. The Jews had become deeply attached to this belief system and did not take kindly to any attempts at forcing them to change. Smart rulers, like Herod tried to appease the Jews as much as possible and even adapted emperor worship so that it would not run contrary to their belief in one God. Only rulers who allowed for this religious freedom were able to maintain a quasi state of peace. — [sunburst.usd.edu Judea, Rebekah Huber]

72. **"ALL ROADS LEAD TO ROME"** The expression is generally attributed to Alain de Lille, a French theologian and poet; 1175 AD/CE. — [Wiki. answers.]

73. **THE JERUSALEM TEMPLE**. "Whoever has not seen Jerusalem in its splendour [when the temple stood] has never seen a fine city." — [Flavius Josephus Opener; Babylonian Talmud (Succah, 51b)] See also # 78-82.

74. **TEMPLE LAVISHNESS**. "The Temple was built with a lavishness and sumptuousness beyond all precedent. From the construction of the doorway and its fastenings to the door-posts and the solid nature of the lintel, it was obvious that no expense had been spared." — [The *Letter of Aristeas*/Letter to Philocrates] See also # 75

75. **TEMPLE LIGHT REFLECTIONS.** "Being covered on all sides with massive plates of gold, the sun was no sooner up than it radiated so fiery a flash that persons straining to look at it were compelled to avert their eyes, as from solar rays." — [Josephus' description of the Temple's exterior]

Artist depiction of the Ark Source: S34

76. **ARK OF THE COVENANT** The Ark construction was commanded in the camps of Sinai [Exodus 25: 22; 37:1-9] and contained the original tablets of The Ten Commandments. The Ark was built by Bezalel, son of Uri, son of Hur. — [Ark of the Covenant, Jewish Virtual Libr.]

77. **THE ARK'S WHEREABOUTS**. According to Maimonides' Laws of the Temple 4:1, King Solomon foresaw and hid the Ark. The Ark remained in the Temple until its destruction by the Babylonian Empire, led by Nebuchadnezzar; a list of war spoils did not include the Ark as found or taken by Babylon; King Josiah, aware of impending Babylon invasion hid, the Ark under the Temple Mount [A Hebrew Medrashic commentary]. Both the Ark's disappearance and location are unknown today. — [Ark of the Covenant; Jewish Virtual Libr.]

78. **TEMPLE LOCATION**. Mount Moriah is the name of the elongated north-south stretch of land lying between The Kidron Valley and the "Hagai" Valley, between Mount Zion to the west and the Mount of Olives to the east. — [Jewish Virtual Libr.]

79. **TEMPLE LOCATION**. Why Mount Moriah: 'Then Solomon began to build the house of the LORD at Jerusalem in Mount Moriah, where [the LORD] appeared unto David his father; for which provision had been made in the place of David, in the threshing floor of Ornan the Jebusite'. — [2 Chronicles Chapter 3/Theological]

80. **TEMPLE LOCATION - ISLAMIC SOURCES**: "The most authoritative Islamic sources affirm the Temple." — [Sheik Prof. Abdul Hadi Palazzi, Co-Founder Islam-Israel Fellowship; Wiki] / "The al-Aqsa Mosque was built on top of Solomon's Temple." - [Eleventh century historian Muhammad Ibn Ahmad al-Maqdisi and fourteenth century Iranian religious scholar Hamdallah al-Mustawfi] / That the Al Aqsa Mosque is located exactly where King Solomon's Temple used to exist: Abu Jafar Muhammad al-Tabari, who chronicled the seventh century Muslim conquest of Jerusalem, wrote that one day when Umar finished praying, he went to the place where "the Romans buried the Temple [*bayt al-maqdis*] at the time of the sons of Israel." - [David Barnett, writing for the Gloria Center: Global Research in International Affairs] / "You will find very clearly that the traditional commentators from the eighth and ninth century onwards have uniformly interpreted the Koran to say explicitly that *Eretz Yisrael* has been given by God to the Jewish people as a perpetual covenant. There is no Islamic counterclaim to the Land anywhere in the traditional corpus of commentary." - British-based Imam Sheikh Muhammad Al-Hussaini. Middle-East Scholar Robert Spencer cites that Hussaini bases his argument upon Qur'an 5:21 in which Moses declares: "O my people, enter the Holy Land which G-d has prescribed for you, and turn not back in your traces, to turn about losers." He then refers to classical Qur'an commentator Muhammad ibn Jarir at-Tabari (838-923), who explains that this statement is "a narrative from God concerning the saying of Moses to his community from

among the children of Israel and his order to them according to the order of God to him, ordering them to enter the holy land." — [*Rachel Avraham,* Jerusalem online]

81. **TEMPLE LOCATION**. "The Mount's identity with the site of Solomon's temple is beyond dispute." — [*A Brief Guide to the Haram al-Sharif,* written by Waqf historian Aref al Aref in 1929; Smithsonian History and Archaeology: What is Beneath the Temple Mount?]

82. **TEMPLE LOCATION**. This Temple commanded attention as it stood there on its nine foot high platform atop Mount Moriah. — [Bible Prophesy Magazine/ Theological]

THE COLISEUM.

83. **Funding**. Approximately 4,500 talents (100,000 kilograms, or tens of millions of dollars] were taken to Rome along with 97,000 prisoners. — [The Copper Scrolls - aka The Temple Scrolls; Qumran Dead Sea Scrolls parcel]

84. **Funding**. When Vespasian became emperor, the empire was in deplorable financial condition because of Nero's extravagance and the fire that devastated Rome. Construction of the Coliseum began under the rule of the Emperor Vespasian [in] around 70 AD, funded by the spoils taken from the Jewish Temple after the Siege of Jerusalem. — [Prof. Alföldy, GÉZA]

85. **Funding**. An extremely unusual inscription, one without any extant letters, points to the spoils from the Jerusalem Temple as the source of the Coliseum's funding. — [Financing the Coliseum, Louis H. Feldman BAS Libr.

86. **Temple Construction & Dimensions**. "The Romans had taken 97,000 prisoners. Thousands of them were forced to become gladiators and were killed in the arena, fighting wild animals or fellow gladiators. Some were burned alive. Others were employed at Seleucia, where they had to dig a tunnel. But most of these prisoners were brought to Rome, where they were forced to build the Forum of Peace and the Coliseum. The Menorah and the Table were exhibited in the temple of Peace. — [Josephus War04; 'Seven Wonders of the World' Livius.org]. / BRICK SIZES. The Temple Mount was originally intended to be 1600 feet wide by 900 feet broad by 110 high, with walls up to 16 feet thick. To complete it, a trench was dug around the mountain, and huge stone "bricks" were laid. Some of these weighed well over 100 tons, the largest measuring 44.6 feet by 11 feet by 16.5 feet and weighing approximately 567 to 628 tons. - [Dan Bahat: Touching the Stones of our Heritage, Israeli ministry of Religious Affairs, 2002]

87. "**The spoils** were borne in promiscuous heaps; the diversity of riches was displayed in the triumphal procession in Rome after Jerusalem was destroyed - silver and gold in masses flowing like a river. The altar and lamp stand, both made of gold, weighed no less than two talents." — [Financing the Coliseum, Alföldy] See also # 200.

88. **The Spoils** - Gold and Silver Coins. The boundless riches from the Temple treasury were used to strike coins with the legend JUDAEA CAPTA ('Judaea defeated'). Any Roman would be reminded of their emperor's victory. The Jews were forced to pay an additional tax. - [Fiscus Judaicus]

89. "Vespasian Deposited The Law…" (*nomos*), presumably the Torah Scroll of the Jews, and the purple hangings of the sanctuary of the Temple in his Palace. — [Financing the Coliseum, Louis H. Feldman]

CAUSES OF THE WAR

90. **Freedom of Belief; Monotheism**.

'The causes of this tension are to be found first and foremost in the religious-ideological conflict between the belief of the Jews and that they were forcibly subjected to the rule of an idolatrous empire which accorded divine honors to its emperors.' — [Zealots and Sicarii, Jewish Virtual Libr. Org.]. — [Zealots and Sicarii, Jewish Virtual Libr.] Greek Influence: — [Artapanus, Early Christian Writings Org; APOLOGETICS, Jewish Virtual Libr.] See also # 91 and #54.

91. **Philo of Alexandria** (Greek: Φίλων, *Philōn*; c. 20 BCE - 50 CE). 'The Temple was the most sacred place for the Jews: a statue of Caligula placed there was a sin against the Jewish faith and was bound to cause riots. The Jewish elders swore to die on the spot rather than see their temple defiled'. — [The Roman Empire in the First Century - Philo/PBS]

92. **Rights Annulled at Caesarea**. The first emperor, Julius Caesar, granted rights to Jewish communities because their ancestral laws predated Rome. Jews had legal privileges as *collegia* (defined by Roman law as religious & legal entities), giving them the right to assemble, have common meals and property, govern and tax them, and enforce their own discipline. Nero annulled these rights. — [Josephus; Antiquities. A 20.8.9

93. **Bribery**. The leaders of the Syrians in Caesarea, by offering a large bribe, prevailed on Beryllus, who was Nero's tutor …to apply for a letter from Nero annulling the grant of equal civic rights to the Jews. This letter provided the basis that led to the subsequent miseries that befell our nation. For the Jewish inhabitants of Caesarea, when they learned of Nero's letter, carried their quarrel with the Syrians further and further until at last they kindled the flames of war. — [Josephus War 6.5.4] Other Assessments - Causes of War. — [Josephus.org] [References are given in the form of Book, Chapter, and Paragraph of the Whiston edition together with the Section number of the Greek (Loeb) edition. So "Ant. 18.1.6 23" indicates Book 18, Chapter 1, Paragraph 6 in Whiston, and in the Loeb edition, Book 18, Section 23; *G. Goldberg]:*

- The involvement of Governor Albinus with criminal gangs.
- The removal of rights of Jews in Caesarea
- The pollution of the synagogue of Caesarea
- The murder of High Priests; The murder of High Priest Ananias
- The refusal to sacrifice to the Emperor
- The Fourth Philosophy that held divine assistance would come to a rebellion: "the infection which spread from them among the younger sort, who became zealous for it, brought the public to destruction."
- The criminal acts and abuse of authority on the part of governor Gessius Florus
- A conspiracy on the part of Florus
- A certain ambiguous oracle
- The issues came to a head over the large number of Gentiles who became converts, or who wanted to become converts, to Judaism. The Pharisees insisted that all converts to Judaism were joining "a new and godly commonwealth" [Baron, 1983, vol. 1, p. 181].

94. **The War Begins**. (66 CE) Greek Sacrifice at Synagogue of Caesarea:

'Now at this time it happened that the Greeks of Caesarea had obtained from Nero the government of the city, and had brought back with them the text of the decision: and now began the war, in the twelfth year of the reign of Nero, and the seventeenth of the reign of Agrippa, in the month of Artemisins [Iyar, April/May.] The Hellenes hindered the access to a synagogue in Caesarea by building shops in front of it and once, during the Sabbath services, sacrificed a bird near the entrance of the synagogue'. — [Josephus War 2.14.4-6; Josephus, War 2.14, 4-5]

ELEAZAR BEN JAIR.

95. Josephus writes: "In 66 C.E., a priest named Eleazar, incensed at Roman high-handedness, led a movement to stop offering the customary temple sacrifices on behalf of the emperor. Then in the summer of 66 CE, a very bold young man who was Captain of the Temple — Eleazar, son of the high-priest Hananiah — moved that no gift or sacrifice was to be permitted during the service of worship. And this set the foundation for the war with Rome. For, on this pretext, even the sacrifice for Nero was eliminated. Hence it came about that the war was so long protracted and the Jews drained the cup of irretrievable disaster. — [Josephus, Antiquities 20.409]

TEMPLE DESTRUCTION ORDER.

96. 'Titus favored destroying the Jerusalem Temple to help uproot and demolish both the Jewish and Christian sects' — Tacitus (56-117); *Chronica*, Sulpicius Severus (363-420).

97. 'Titus favored destroying the Jerusalem Temple to help uproot and demolish both the Jewish and Christian sects.' — Sulpicius Severus (363-420), referring in his *Chronica* to an earlier writing by Tacitus (56-117).

98. 'Now as soon as the army had no more people to slay or to plunder, because there remained none to be the objects of their fury (for they would not have spared any, had there remained any other work to be done), Titus gave orders that they should now demolish the entire city and Temple.' — [Josephus War of the Jews CHAPTER 1.]

99. ROMAN DEFECTIONS - MASS CONVERSIONS.

'Some Romans thought that the city was impregnable and went over to the other side; many gentiles came to their aid. The Jews in the Diaspora and some Samaritans, who in the past had a hostile relationship with the Jews, also joined the rebellion. The whole earth, one might almost say, was being stirred over the matter.' — [Cassius Dio *Roman history* 69.12.1-14.3; Dio Cassius, xxxvii. 17] / "The issues came to a head over the large number of Gentiles who became converts, or who wanted to become converts, to Judaism. The Pharisees insisted that all converts to Judaism were joining "a new and godly commonwealth" - [Baron - JRank, 1983, vol. 1, p. 181; Science Encyclopedia; Anti-Semitism-Overview, Roman Empire] The Jewish Population in the world at the beginning of the reign of Herod was approximately four to six million. A century later, after the destruction of the Temple, there were almost ten million Jews, representing an enormous increase. The reason was not simply related to an increased birth rate, but that hundreds of thousands - if not millions - converted to Judaism. It was a time of mass conversion in the Roman world; Roman historians wrote that approximately one out of every ten people in the Roman Empire was Jewish. The main reason is simple: Roman paganism began to break down. — [Jewish History Org; Hillel & Shammai]

THE DEAD SEA SCROLLS.

100. The Texts are written in Hebrew, Aramaic, Greek and Nabataean, mostly on Parchment but with some written on Papyrus and Bronze. The manuscripts have been dated to various ranges between 408 BCE and 318 CE. Bronze coins found on the site form a series beginning with John Hyrcanus (135-104 BCE) and continuing until the First Jewish-Roman War (66-73 CE). — [Dead Sea Scrolls, Britannica; Wiki]

101. Scholars believe Jewish scribes were trying to save their sacred texts by hiding them in the caves of Qumran. — [megaessays/viewpaper/8774.]

102. **THE ESSENES** have gained fame in modern times as a result of the discovery of an extensive group of religious documents known as the Dead Sea Scrolls, which are commonly believed to be Essenes' library — although there is no proof that the Essenes wrote them. — [Essenes, Wiki].

103. **The Location** of the site and its plan, the scrolls found in the vicinity and the simple ceramic vessels of the inhabitants bear witness in de Vaux's view, to a settlement of the Essene sect. We also know of the presence of the Essenes in the Judean Desert and near the Dead Sea from the writings of Pliny the Elder. — [Naturalis Historia V, 17; Qumran, Jewish Virtual Libr.]

104. **The Dead Sea Scrolls** were hidden by this ancient people long ago in the caves of Qumran. — [The Reluctant Messenger/Essene] / Dr. Yonathan Adler - Phylacteries. Archaeology Researcher finds tantalizing tefillin parchments from Second Temple era in Dead Sea Scrolls package. Over 25 Phylacteries, known in Judaism by the Hebrew term *tefillin,* are pairs of leather cases containing biblical passages - ["Uncovered in Jerusalem", The Times of Israel/#ixzz2w6zlusd]

105. FLAVIAN PROPAGANDA.

Vespasian gave financial rewards to ancient writers. The ancient historians of the period such as Tacitus, Suetonius, Josephus and Pliny the Elder speak suspiciously well of Vespasian while condemning the emperors that came before him. Tacitus admits that his status was elevated by Vespasian; Josephus identifies Vespasian as a patron and savior; and Pliny dedicated his Natural Histories to Vespasian and Titus. Those that spoke against Vespasian were punished. A number of stoic philosophers were accused of corrupting students with inappropriate teachings and were expelled from Rome. Helvidius Priscus [70-79 AD/CE], a pro-republic philosopher, was executed for his teachings. — [Suetonius, The Lives of Twelve Caesars, Life of Vespasian; Tacitus, Histories I.1; Pliny the Elder, Natural Histories, preface] See also # 106

106. Vespasian approved the histories written under his reign, thus ensuring biases against him were removed. — Josephus, Against Apion 9. See also # 108.

107. VESPASIAN'S DISCOURSE WITH PRISCUS. (A REPUBLICAN WHO OPPOSED ROMANISM AND WAS EXECUTED FOR HIS ANTI-EMPEROR STAND):

Vespasian: I command that you not go into the senate and speak.
Priscus: It is in your power not to allow me to be a member of the senate, but so long as I am, I must go in.
Vespasian: Well, go in then, but say nothing.
Priscus: Then do not ask my opinion, and I will be silent.
Vespasian: But I must ask your opinion.
Priscus: And I must say what I think right.
Vespasian: But if you do, I shall put you to death.
Priscus: When then did I tell you that I am immortal? You will do your part, and I will do mine: it is your part to kill; it is mine to die, but not in fear: yours to banish me; mine to depart without sorrow.
— [Epictetus, Discourses, 1.2.19-21]

108. **Helvidius Priscus** was put to death after he had repeatedly affronted the Emperor by studied insults which Vespasian had initially tried to ignore. "I will not kill a dog that barks at me" were his words on discovering Priscus's public slander. — [Vespasian, NNDB]

109. **Temple of Jupiter**. In 70 CE Vespasian ordered the restoration of the Temple of Jupiter, the Best and Greatest on the Capitoline Hill. The event was recorded by Tacitus in an account which gives some idea of the ceremonies of the state religion, and its intense conservatism. — [Tacitus Histories, Book 4. liii.]

The Triumph of Titus
[by Lawrence Alma-Tadema, Oil.] Source: S35.

110. **TITUS DEATH**. "On the last day of the games he [Titus] is said to have broken down and wept in public. His health had taken a marked downturn by then and perhaps he knew himself he was suffering from an incurable disease. Titus also had no heir." — [Illustrated History of the Roman Empire]

111. **VESPASIAN DEATH**. Vespasian's last words on his death bed: "Dammit! I think I'm becoming a god" ('Vae, puto dues fio') — [Life of Vespasian, Suetonius 23.4; Roman History 66.1 Cassius Dio]

112. **DEATH/WAR TOLL.**

HUMAN TOLL SUMMARY - ROMANS & JEWS:

• **TEMPLE WAR** [70 CE]: 30,000 Roman Soldiers; 1.1m Jewish Fighters & Civilians.

• **MASADA WAR** [73 CE]: 600 Roman Soldiers; 1,000 Jewish Fighters & Civilians.

• **KITOS WAR** [115 CE]: 4, 40,000 Roman Soldiers & Civilians; Jewish Populations destroyed in Cyprus, Cyrena & Alexandria.

• **BAR KOTCHBA WAR** [135 CE]: 580,000 Jews (Cassius Dio, History, Book 69, 12. 1-14); 400,000 Romans.

• **Crusifixions**. "Some 50,000 to 100,000 Jews were crucified by the Romans in the first century." [Joseph Telushkin, Jewish Literacy, NY: William Morrow and Co.]

113. Flavius Josephus: "There were as many as 1,100,000 slain in the destruction of Jerusalem in AD 70, along with 97,000 who were sold as slaves'. Some 270,000 were killed in surrounding towns."

114. Tacitus: "Jerusalem at the temple's final fall contained 600,000 people's dead." [# Presumably after the three walls were breached; a second Century archive.]

115. Tacitus: "Where they make a desert, they call it peace." - [Tacitus: *Agricola*, 30]

116. Augustine: "Concerning the spread of Judaism in the ancient world, "*Victi victoribus leges dederunt.*" ('The conquered have given laws to the victors.') — [Augustine, quoting the Philosopher Senegal]

"NO SURRENDER OF BELIEF"

117. NO SURRENDER. 'The populace was stationed below in the court and the elders on the steps and the priests in the Sanctuary itself. And though they were but a handful fighting against a far superior force, they were not conquered until part of the Temple was set on fire. Then they met their death willingly, some throwing themselves on the swords of the Romans, some slaying one another, others taking their own lives and still others leaping into the flames. And it seemed to everybody and especially to them that so far from being destruction, it was victory and salvation and happiness to them that they perished along with the Temple.' — [Deo Cassius, Epitome of Book LXV; History Crash Course #35: Destruction of the Temple, Aishcom] See also #118.

118. NO SURRENDER. 'Though a breach was made in the wall by means of engines, nevertheless the capture of the place did not immediately follow even then. On the contrary, the defenders killed great numbers [of Romans] who tried to crowd through the opening and they also set fire to some of the buildings nearby, hoping thus to check the further progress of the Romans. Nevertheless, the soldiers, because of their superstition, did not immediately rush in but at last, under compulsion from Titus, they made their way inside. Then the Jews defended themselves much more vigorously than before, as if they had discovered a piece of rare good fortune in being able to fight near the Temple and fall in its defense'. — [Roman Historian, Deo Cassius]

119. SICARII DAGGER [From the Latin word sica, "curved, serrated dagger"; short daggers; (mikra ziphidia), concealed in their clothing. — [Josephus, Wars, 2:254-5; Ant., 20:186-7]

120. **PHILISTINES: 'KIN OF THE GREEKS.'** Chiefly: 'The Philistines were an Aegean people - more closely related to the Greeks and with no connection ethnically, linguistically or historically with Arabia.' — [Origins of the name Palestine; Jewish Virtual Libr]

121. **MUREX SNAIL.** Murex snails were cultivated in ancient times at sites along the Mediterranean Sea, and a royal blue dye was extracted from them. This blue color was used for the priestly garments, as well as the tzitzit or threaded tassels worn by all pious Jews of the period on the corners of their garments. — [Numbers 15:38-15:39]

122. **MYSTERIOUS JOURNEY OF A FIREBRAND** 'One of the towers erected by the Romans fell down of its own accord; and how the Romans after great slaughter had been made got possession of the first wall' — [WARS BOOK 5/CHAPTER 7.]

123. **THE ROYAL LIBRARY OF ALEXANDRIA**. [Or, Ancient Library of Alexandria; Egypt, 3rd century BC until the Roman conquest in 30 BC. Initiated by Alexander the Great; conducted by successor Ptolemy. — [Norman F. Cantor's book 'Journey to the End of the earth']

124. **ESSENES - DEAD SEA SCROLLS** The scrolls are traditionally identified with the ancient Jewish sect called the Essenes; some recent views have challenged this association. — [Wiki]

Nero Claudius Caesar Augustus Germanicus; **[37 - 68 AD/CE]**

125. **Nero "Fiddled as Rome Burned."** Suetonius recounts the legend how Nero, while watching Rome burn, exclaimed how beautiful it was, and sang an epic poem about the sack of Troy while playing the lyre. — [The Twelve Letters, Suetonius]

126. **Nero's Eccentricities** continued in his personal perversions in the tradition of his predecessors in mind. According to Suetonius, Nero had one boy named Sporus castrated, and then had sex with him as though he were a woman. Suetonius quotes one Roman who lived around this time who scathingly remarked that 'The world would have been better off if Nero's father Gnaeus Domitius Ahenobarbus had married someone more like the castrated boy'. [Suetonius] / The Emperor Nero killed his mother in three attempts. Nero killed his first wife because he thought she was having an affair [wrongly]; Nero beat his second wife to death when she was pregnant - [Nero, Roman Empire Tours; Emperor Nero's Personality Profile, Miriamilani.]

127. **Nero's Suicide**. Suetonius describes Nero's suicide, and remarks that his death meant the end of the reign of the Julio-Claudians (because Nero had no heir). According to Suetonius, Nero was condemned to die by the Senate. When Nero knew that soldiers had been dispatched by the Senate to kill him, he committed suicide. [Suetonius]

128. '**Welcome as the death of Nero** had been in the first burst of joy, yet it had not only roused various emotions in Rome, among the Senators, the people, or the soldiery of the capital, it had also excited all the legions and their generals; for now had been divulged that secret of the empire, that emperors could be made elsewhere than at Rome.' — [Tacitus *Hist.1.4]*

129. **Publius (or Gaius) Cornelius Tacitus** (56 - 117 CE) was a Senator and a Historian of the Roman Empire.

Natural Disasters upon Rome.

130. '**Pompeii and Herculaneum** was engulfed by lava and red hot-ash. Yet this disaster should tarnish Titus' memory until this day, many describing the outbreak of the volcano as divine punishment for the destruction of the Great Temple in Jerusalem. But Titus' troubles were not over with the Vesuvius disaster. Whilst he was still in Campania, a fire ravaged Rome for three days and nights. But yet another catastrophe should blight Titus' reign, as one of the worst epidemics of plague on record befell the people.' — [Roman Empire/Emperors/Titus]

131. **First Century Most Impacting.** 'The destruction of Jerusalem in A.D. 70 was the greatest single event in a thousand years and religiously significant beyond anything else that ever occurred in human history.' — [J. B. Coffman in his first-century book, "Antiquities of the Jews"]

132. **First Century Most Impacting/ Most important event**: 'The war between Rome and Jerusalem deserves to be called one of the most important events in world history. If the Temple might still be standing today, the history of the world would be inconceivably different.' - [Moses Hess; "Rome and Jerusalem."] / **Grandest Battle**: "A perusal of Jewish history, a reading of Josephus, will convince the most skeptical that the grandest fight that was ever put up against an enemy was put up by the Jew. He never thought of leaving Palestine. But he was driven out. To my mind there is something prophetic in the fact that during the ages no other nation has taken over Palestine and held it in the sense of a homeland; and there is something providential in the fact that for 1,800 years it has remained in desolation as if waiting for the return of the people." - Congressman Frank Appleby N.J; U.S. House Resolution 360.

THE EVENT THAT SHAPED THE MODERN WORLD:

133. 'Judaism is a historical religion, a historical cult, in contradistinction to Paganism, which is a natural cult. When pagan Rome brought the ancient Hellenic and Jewish cultural life to an end; there arose, from the ruins of the latter, a new view of the world.' — [Rome and Jerusalem - The Last national Question. By Moses Hess.]

134. 'Certainly, the world without the Jews would have been a radically different place. Humanity might have eventually stumbled upon all the Jewish insights. But we cannot be sure.' — [Biblical Historian Paul Johnson; author of "A History of The Jews]

135. "The rabbi took the rose and moistened it with his tears, and immediately the withered rose began to bloom again in its full glory and splendor." — [The Eleventh Letter]

135A. OLDEST MANUSCRIPTS

• **Hebrew Bible** [Torah; Mosaic Five Books] - Oldest Extant copies are in the Dead Sea Scrolls. The Dead Sea Scrolls were most likely written by the Essenes during the period from about 200 B.C. to 68 C.E./A.D. [Century One Org]. Some portions are dated as: Est. 408 BCE to 318 CE [Down, David. *Unveiling the Kings of Israel*. p. 160. 2011.; Wiki].

• **Septuagint** Greek Translation of Hebrew Bible - oldest extant copy is the Codex Sinaiticus, dated 4th Century CE. **Samaritan Pentatuach** [Mosaic Bible] oldest copy is the Abisha Scroll, dated 423 BCE [Buttrick, p35] {Disputed; unconfirmed}

• **Josephus** in their original language of Greek date to the tenth and eleventh centuries. Portions of the works are also quoted in earlier manuscripts by other authors, particularly Eusebius (fourth century). There are also versions in other languages, notably a Latin translation made about the fifth century. These are all codexes, bound books, not scrolls. — [Selected Letters, Josephus Org # Manuscripts]

• **Tacitus** [Chrestianos issue; Manuscript M11] is estimated as 11 Century AD/CE - [Laurentian library, Italy] # See also 145-148.

136. THEOLOGICAL/BIBLICAL HEBREW.

> • "Whatever Sarah tells you to do - do it" [Gen. 21/12]. /
> • "Know for a surety thy seed shall be in Bondage" [Gen. 15/13] /
> • "Come, let us reason together, says the Lord." [Isaiah 1:18]

• "I shall make Jerusalem as a burden unto the nations" ['And in that day will I make Jerusalem a burdensome stone for all people: all that burden themselves with it shall be cut in pieces, though all the people of the earth be gathered together against it' [*Zechariah 12:3*]/
• "I have tried thee in the furnace of affliction." [Isaiah 48:10]
• "And also that nation, whom they shall serve, will I judge; and afterward shall they come out with great substance." [Gen. 15/14]/
• "Blessed Be The Lord my Rock, who traineth my hands for war." [King David Psalm 144; Heb Bible; N.T.]
• "Love Yea Therefore the Stranger" [Duet. 10:19].
• Not to wrong the stranger in buying or selling" [Ex. 22:20]
• "Not to wrong the stranger in speech [Ex 22:20]
• "The soul that sinneth, it shall pay. The son shall not bear the iniquity of the father; neither shall the father bear the iniquity of the son: the righteousness of the righteous shall be upon him, and the wickedness of the wicked shall be upon him. [*Ezekiel 18:20*]

• "And a stranger shalt thou not wrong, neither shalt thou oppress him; for ye were strangers in the land of Egypt. 21. Ye shall not afflict any widow, or fatherless child.
22. If thou afflict them in any wise–for if they cry at all unto Me, I will surely hear their cry" [Ex. 22:20]

Jerusalem.
• *The Land of Israel sits at the centre of the world and Jerusalem sits at the centre of the Land of Israel — Tanchuma Kedoshim 10.*
• *A snake or scorpion never injured anyone in Jerusalem — Yoma 21a*
• *In the future all the nations and kingdoms will be gathered unto Jerusalem — Avot of Rabbi Natan 35.*
• *All who pray in Jerusalem - it is as if he prayed before the throne of glory, because the gate of heaven is situated there — Pikkei de-Rabbi Eliezer 35*
• *In the merit of Jerusalem I split the sea for them - Yalkut Shimoni Isaiah 473*
• **REBECCA [RIVKA]** "And they said, we will call the damsel, and enquire at her mouth." It is the earliest known woman's marriage right prerogative. [Gen. 24:57]
• **DEBORAH** ["Bee" - Heb; Israelite Prophetess, warrior in Canaan; sole female Judge. [Book of Judges 4-5].
• **MIKVAH** [Ritual Water Emersion. 'They must purify themselves with the water on the third day and on the seventh day; then they will be clean.' [Numbers 19/12.]
• **HUR**. Contemporary Israelite Assistant of Moses, whose grandson built the Ark of the Covenant. [Ex. 17.10]
• **MENORAH**: A seven-branch candelabrum mandated in the Hebrew bible and used in the Temple, denoting 'Let there be light' [Gen. 1:3]; and 'A light unto the nations' [Isaiah 42:6].
• **MENORAH LOCATION:** Josephus claims it was taken to Rome as war spoils and deposited in the Roman Temple of Peace [Jewish War, 7.148].
• **MEZUZAH**: A case affixed on the doorstep containing a parchment inscribed with its mandated verses in the Hebrew bible [Duet. 6:4; 11:13].
• **CHERUB**. [Hebrew: כְּרוּב, pl. כְּרוּבִים; Latin *cherub [us]*, pl*cherubi[m]*. A type of spiritual being; Angelic figures hovering over the Ark. Cherubim are mentioned in the Torah — [Five books of Moses, Ezekiel, 1 Kings, 2 Kings, 1 Chronicle and 2 Chronicles, Psalms, mainly in the construction of the House of God]. There is only one mention in the New Testament, in Hebrews 9:5, referring to the mercy seat of the Ark of the Covenant /
• **ESTHER** [Heb. name 'Hadassah'; Exilic orphan who rose to Queen of Persian King Ahaseuros; Savior of the nation of Israel; Heb. Prophetess celebrated in the festival of Purim. — [Book of Esther] /
• **GIDEON** ['Mighty Warrior'; Son of Joash, Tribe of Mennasah. [Book of Judges 6-8]
• **JEREMIAH** — [2 Kings 17:13]. / Bethlehem [*Bet Lehem - Heb;* "House of Bread"].
• **JOHANAN BEN ZAKKAI.** — Hebrew law Scholar; contemporary of Vespasian; negotiated for Synagogues and study schools after temple destruction; pupil of Hillel and Shammai [Suk. 28a].

• **SHEKINAH**. (Or, Shechinah, Shechina; Hebrew: שכינה). Denotes the dwelling or settling of the divine presence of God, especially in theTemple in Jerusalem. — [WIKI]; The Kabbalistic literature has transformed the Shechina into an entity that expresses the connection between the divine and the human. - [Shalom Hartman Institute of North America; Psalm 132:5]

• **DATHAN** [Book of Numbers 16:31] And **KORACH** [Num. 16:1 - 18:32] These were two Israelites who stood in opposition of Moses. /

• **TEMPLE.** 'And let them make Me a sanctuary, that I may dwell among them'. [Ex.25:8]

• **MOSES THE LAW GIVER.** Moses is introduced in Exodus 2.1: 'And there went a man of the house of Levi' - the word 'And' denotes the verse follows as a response to the earliest recording of genocide of the Egyptian Pharaoh's decree to kill all Hebrew male first born babies. Moses became known as The Law Giver and is recorded as one who stood 'Presence to Presence' before God. The laws delivered by Moses remain ever active, almost exclusively dominating the institutions of the Judiciary; Family Law; Animal Rights Laws; Women's Rights Laws: Right of Refusal or Acceptance of Marriage/ Rebecca [Gen.24.57 & 58: "And they said: 'We will call the damsel and inquire at her mouth. 'And they called Rebecca, and said unto her: 'Wilt thou go with this man?' And she said: 'I will go.']; Woman's Property Inheriting Rights/ The Daughters of Zelophehad [Num 27:3]; Separation of State and Ruler/King [2 Samuel 12]; Monotheism and Creationism. Moses became the most revered figure in human history by period of time, impact and by worldly census accounting: 14 M Jews; 1.2 B Muslims; 2.2 B Christians.

• **HEBREW CALENDAR.** The oldest active calendar, accounting its initiation from the Birthday of Adam and spans over 5,700 years.

• **GOG MAGOG**. [Or, "War of Gog and Magog"; Gen 10:2; Eze Ch 36-37]. The Prophet Ezekiel's End of Days vision of many nations attacking Israel; it fosters an exile that will be followed by an eventual ingathering of return. Gog is the grandson of Noah via Japheth; Gog is also seen as a person, place or event symbolically coded for future times.

ARCHAEOLOGY - THE ROMAN EMPIRE AND ISRAEL.
[DISCOVERIES, DOCUMENTS & RELICS]

137. ONE MILLION BIBLICAL & HISTORICAL ARTEFACTS. Israel Relics Collection: National archaeological centre to store and showcase country's rich collection of some two million ancient artefacts, including world's largest collection of Dead Sea Scrolls. [Israel Antiquities Authority, Associated Press, Ynet/0, 7340, L-4500754, 00] / **Israel Relics Display**: The Israel Antiquities Authorities estimates that there are one million archaeological artefacts on display in Israel at present. - [Israel National News/ aspx/132808]. **JORDAN.** Other than Israel, no country has as many Biblical sites and associations as Jordan: Mount Nebo, from where Moses gazed at the Promised Land; Bethany beyond the Jordan, where John baptized Jesus; Lot's Cave, where Lot and his daughters sought refuge after the destruction of Sodom and Gomorrah; and many more. — [Biblical Archaeology Org/Biblical-artefacts/inscriptions]

BIBLICAL DISCOVERIES.

138. A ROMAN SOLDIER IN JERUSALEM OF 70 CE. Because a Roman soldier served 25 years before being released, we can deduce that this anonymous fighter was in active service as a younger man in Jerusalem in 70 CE. — [The Israel Museum]

139. TEMPLE MENORAH STAMP RELIC.

According to Syon, "This is the first time such a stamp is discovered in a controlled archaeological excavation, thus making it possible to determine its provenance and date of manufacture." — [Israel National News/ aspx 15186]

140. EXILED JEWS IN ROMAN IBERIA.

Hebrew Inscription Provides Oldest Archaeological Evidence: "It is the first instance of a Hebrew inscription found in a Roman villa in the region." — [Biblical Archaeology Inscription - E3216318]

141. COINS FROM THE LAST JEWISH REVOLT. The cache includes 120 gold, silver and bronze coins. — [Academia.edu/1201525/Coinage]

142. MILLION DOLLAR SHEKEL.

An unidentified American East Coast collector plucked down $1.1 million for an ancient Judean silver shekel coin at a New York auction. The silver coin was dated to the year 66, four years before the destruction of the Second Temple by the Romans. — [Israel National News; Aspx-153629]

143. SECOND TEMPLE ERA SEAL UNVEILED

Rare ancient seal underscores the Jewish people destroyed by the Romans in 70 CE. Archaeologist Eli Shukron of the Antiquities Authority, and Professor Ronny Reich of Haifa University, explained the significance of the coin: "This is the first time an object of this kind has been found. It is direct archaeological evidence of Jewish activity on the Temple Mount during the Second Temple era."

— [The Muslim Times/Israel national News]

144. 2,000 YEAR OLD SWORD; MENORAH 'SKETCH' Stone slab with Menorah etching, Roman era sword discovered near Temple Mount. Eli Shukrun and Ronny Reich, in charge of the digs, said that the sword "may have belonged to a Roman infantryman who was stationed in Jerusalem when the Great Rebellion broke out in 66 CE." [Israel National News; Aspx-14699]

DEAD SEA SCROLLS.

S55

145. DEAD SEA SCROLLS - HEBREW BIBLE ACCURACY.

Ancient scrolls in jars were discovered in 1947 in the Qumran Mountains South-West of Jerusalem and dated as 408 BCE and 318. / 'The texts are of great historical, religious, and linguistic significance because they include the earliest known surviving manuscripts of works later included in the Hebrew Bible canon, along with extra-biblical manuscripts which preserve evidence of the diversity of religious thought in late Second Temple Judaism of the First Century' — [Dead Sea Scrolls, Wiki]. / 'The scrolls are of vital importance for their texts from Qumran [The Dead Sea Scrolls] proved to be word-for-word identical to the Hebrew Bible in more than 95 percent of the text. They have provided textual critics with ancient manuscripts against which they can compare the accepted text for accuracy of content in the Hebrew bible and the writers of the First and Second Century CE' — [The Dead Sea Scrolls and Biblical Integrity, Brantley].

146. THE COPPER SCROLL.

A scroll in Josephus' possession, adapted from similar scrolls in the Dead Sea Scrolls package. / Unlike the others, it is not a literary work, but a list of locations at which various items of gold and silver are buried or hidden. The text is an inventory of 64 locations; 63 of which are treasures of gold and silver, which have been estimated in the tons. — [Copper Scroll, Wiki]

147. THE TEN COMMANDMENTS.

A well-preserved 2,000-year-old scroll of The Ten Commandments, which dates to between 50 B.C. and 1 A.D., was discovered in a cave near the Dead Sea in 1952.

148. A 2,600 YEAR 'PRIESTLY INSCRIPTION'.

• **The Ketef Hinnom** predates the First Temple destruction. It is a silver scroll containing 13 verses of the Temple Priestly Blessing recorded in The Book of Numbers ["The Lord bless you and keep you…"]. Discovered by Gabriel Barkay - [Christian StackExchange]

• A rare 2,000-year-old ritual vessel inscribed with 10 lines of text, discovered near the Zion Gate of the Old City of Jerusalem. 'It is an unprecedented find' according to Dr. Shimon Gibson, the archaeologist who heads the University of North Carolina team conducting the dig. - [Israel National News/aspx 132655]

149. PILATE STONE

A rare inscription attributed to Pontius Pilate, a prefect of the Roman-controlled province of Judea from 26-36 AD. It is significant as the only universally accepted archaeological find mentioning the name "Pontius Pilatus" to date. The Pilate Stone is located at the Israel Museum in Jerusalem. [Wiki]

150. FIRST RELIC MENTIONING BETHLEHEM.

2,700 year old bulla [seal] bearing inscription of "Bethlehem", mentioned in the Bible as Ephrath during the burial of Rachel (Genesis 35). Ancient Bethlehem played an important role in the life (and birth) of King David; and the Gospels as Jesus' birthplace. — [The Israel Antiquities Authority; Biblical Archaeology/ First Temple Period Bulla from City of David]

151. MEGIDDO.

Tel (mound) Megiddo Excavations has been identified as one of the most important cities of biblical times, in King Solomon's reign in the 10th century BCE; and mentioned many times in Egyptian royal inscriptions. - [1 Kings 9:15; El-Amarna, 14th century BCE, Jewish Virtual Libr.]

152. KING SOLOMON'S FORTRESS WALL.

Tel Gezer, focus of a joint archaeological expedition by New Orleans Seminary and the Israel Antiquities Authority, includes the ruins of a six-chambered gate (foreground) constructed by King Solomon. — [Bible.ca/archeology/exodus-kadesh; Bpnews-net/ID=23651]

153. FIRST HISTORICAL EVIDENCE OF KING DAVID.

Few Biblical archaeology discoveries have attracted as much attention as the Tel Dan Stele—the ninth-century B.C. inscription that furnished the first historical evidence of King David outside the Bible. — [Biblicalarchaeology.org/biblical-artifacts/the-tel-dan-inscription.]

154. KING DAVID'S PALACE.

Archaeologists claim "This is indisputable proof of the existence of a central authority in Judah during the time of King David."

— [Fox news/Science/2013-07-18; Archaeologists

155. BABYLON EXILE - Clay Seal Relic Confirmation.

Regarded as the 'Top 10 Incredible Archaeological Discoveries'. Prophecy of Book of Baruch ben Neriah, Prophetic Scribe in the Bible and relative of the prophet Jeremiah, sent to Jerusalem, acknowledging their manifold sins. [Drbo.org/chapter/30001.]

156. THE DESTRUCTION OF POMPEII, 79 AD

The ancient Roman town near modern Naples, destroyed by the cataclysmic volcanic eruption of Mount Vesuvius. The eruption was documented by a surviving contemporary Pliny's letter. - [UNESCO; World Heritage Site, Pompeii, Wiki]

157. GABRIEL'S REVELATION

A Stone dated as 4 BCE claimed as "The greatest archaeological discovery in the Middle East since the Dead Sea Scrolls." The article that made scholars around the world to reconsider links between ancient Jewish and Christian Messianism: the one meter tall stone tablet contains a collection of short prophesies that allegedly tells of a man who was killed by the Romans and resurrected in three days. — [By Ada Yardeni and Israel Knohl/Biblical Archaeology; Gabriel's Revelation]

158. "BROTHER OF JESUS" PROVED ANCIENT AND AUTHENTIC

After a 5-year trial, a new analysis and new evidence proves that the controversial "Brother of Jesus" inscription on an ancient bone box, or ossuary, is authentic, according to the July/August issue of *Biblical Archaeology Review*. - [Biblical Archaeology Org; Brother of Jesus proved ancient and authentic]

159. 'WHEN IN ROME DO AS THE ROMANS DO'

'The siesta, or afternoon's nap of Italy, my most dear and reverend Father, would not have alarmed you so much, if you had recollected, that when we are at Rome, we should do as the Romans do' ('Cum Romano Romanus eris'). *Pope Clement XIV* [a.k.a. Lorenzo Ganganelli] letter, published in 1777. *Letter XLIV* [to Prior Dom Galliard] contains the earliest version of the proverb as currently used in English. — [Phrases.org.uk/meanings.]

160. Nimrod. The first mention of Nimrod, one of the earliest recorded kings and associated with the Biblical story of 'The Tower of Babel', is in the Table of Nations, described as the great-grandson of Noah; "a mighty one on the earth" and "a mighty hunter before God". This is repeated in the First Book of Chronicles 1:10 and the "Land of Nimrod" used as a synonym for Assyria or Mesopotamia; also mentioned in the Book of Micah 5:6.

First Century Christian Jews. How many Jews became Christians in the first century? "Throughout the first century the total number of Jews in the Christian movement probably never exceeded 1000" — ["The failure of the Christian mission to the Jews", David C Sim, Biblical Theology and Hermeneutics Research project, Australian Catholic University].

161. WRITINGS; LOCATIONS; DATING.

'**Historical Evidences**' of the Biblical figureheads and events are controversial, their origin source points unproven and in constant debate and dispute, for both the Hebrew Bible and the New Testament. While King David has been evidenced, with secondary evidences of Hebrews and Israel existing 3,400 years ago, the first 400 years of both religions remain unproven; without these being disproven: "The truth of the matter today is that archaeology raises more questions about the historicity of the Hebrew Bible and even the New Testament than it provides answers, and that's very disturbing to some people." [William Dever, Professor Emeritus at the University of Arizona; Archaeology of the Hebrew Bible, PBS Org.]

"The excessive skepticism shown toward the Bible by important historical schools has been progressively discredited. Discovery after discovery has established the accuracy of innumerable details, and has brought increased recognition to the value of the Bible as a source of history." [Albright, William Foxwell. *The Archaeology of Palestine*. Pelican Books, Harmondsworth, Middlesex, England, 1960, p. 127, 128.]

EARLIEST HEBREW MANUSCRIPTS. "The original manuscripts and early copies of the Old Testament disappeared over time, because of wars, (especially the destruction of the First and Second Temples), and other intentional destructions made by enemies. As a result, the lapse of time between the original manuscripts and their surviving copies is much longer than in the case of the New Testament manuscripts." [Searching for the Original Bible, Randall Price, Harvest House Publishers, 2007, p. 45] / "**The Dead Sea Scrolls** have been dated to various ranges between 408 BCE to 318 CE." - [Doudna, Greg, "Dating the Scrolls on the Basis of Radiocarbon Analysis", in The Dead Sea Scrolls after Fifty Years, edited by Flint Peter W., and VanderKam, James C., Vol.1 (Leiden: Brill, 1998) 430-471].
ABRAHAM. "There is no independent evidence that Abraham ever lived, but Hebrew scholars assume he was born at Ur about 2000 B.C.; according to rabbinical traditions the Patriarch watched the building of the Tower of Babel, thereby dating its construction to 2000 B.C., but so conjectural is the chronology of Genesis, that the Tower, if indeed it was ever built, could have existed much earlier." - [From "God and Spacemen of the Ancient Past" by W. Raymond Drake Chapter 13 "Abraham" pg. 154]
MOSES. The existence of Moses as well as the veracity of the Exodus story are disputed. [*The Quest for the Historical Israel: Debating Archeology and the History of Early Israel*, 2007, Society of Biblical Literature, Atlanta; John Van Seters, "The life of Moses"] / "It is true that there is no evidence for Moses, the ten plagues that fell upon Egypt or the exodus 'at that time'. But there are a number of scholars who claim that a gross error in chronology has been made in calculating the dates of Egyptian history and that they should be reduced by centuries. Such a re-dating could bring the 12th dynasty down to the time of Moses, and there is plenty of circumstantial evidence in that dynasty to support the Biblical records." [Searching for Moses by David Down, Searching in Genesis Org.]

EARLIEST CHRISTIANITY MANUSCRIPT. "The earliest of the extant manuscripts [relating to Christianity], it is true, do not date back beyond the middle of the fourth century AD". - ['Catholic Encyclopedia', 1909, 'Gospels'; A glaring omission in World's oldest Bible', Vati Leaks] / "Mainstream scholarship as it has developed over the last two centuries has concluded that some of the thirteen letters attributed to Paul were not written by him." ['The First Paul" by Marcus Borg & John Crossman]

ESTIMATES FOR THE DATES when the canonical gospel accounts were written vary significantly; and the evidence for any of the dates is scanty. Because the earliest surviving complete copies of the gospels date to the 4th century and because only fragments and quotations exist before that, scholars use higher critic to propose likely ranges of dates for the original gospel autographs. [Black, David A, Rethinking the Synoptic Problem, Baker Academic; Gospel, Wiki]. /

NAZARENES, EBIONITES, ELKASITES. Ebionites: Member of an early ascetic sect of Jewish Christians. The Ebionites were one of several such sects that originated in and around Judea in the first century AD and included the Nazarenes and Elkasites. The name of the sect is from the Hebrew ebyonim, *or* ebionim ("the poor"); it was not founded, as later Christian writers stated, by a certain Ebion. They regarded Jesus of Nazareth as the Messiah while rejecting his divinity and insisted on the necessity of following Jewish Law and rites. **Ebionites on Jesus:** "He was circumcised, observed the Sabbath and celebrated the Jewish festivals, and thought all the precepts of the law should be observed" - [Eliade, Vol. 4, Eastern Christianity; Jewish Encyl.]   **Islamic View of Ebionite Jews.** 12th-century Muslim historian Muhammad al-Shahrastani mentions Ebionite Jews living in nearby Medina and Hejaz who accepted Jesus as a prophetic figure and followed traditional Judaism, rejecting mainstream Christian views. - [The Book of Religious and Philosophical Sects, William Curetonedition, Georgia Press, p.167] / Some scholars argue that they contributed to the development of the Islamic view of Jesus due to exchanges of Ebionite remnants with the first Muslims.

Nazarenes: The Nazarenes were similar to the Ebionites, in that they considered themselves Jews, maintained an adherence to the Law of Moses, rejecting all the Canonical Gospels. However, unlike half of the Ebionites, they accepted the Virgin Birth. [Encyl Britannica; Wiki; Muhammad al-Shahrastani, The Book of Religious and Philosophical Sects, William Cureton Edition, Gorgias Press. P167.] / "When people from the Nazarene church in Jerusalem arrived at his churches to try to convince the gentile converts to obey Jewish law, Paul denounced them as Judaizers" - Charles Patterson; Jewish Virtual Libr.

"The Jerusalem of the time was a place of strong religious divisions and multiple languages and a diverse economy" - [Israel Uncovers Ancient Burial Boxes dating back to the time of Jesus; Fox News; Associated Press.]   **'Christianity was born in Israel.** It seems fairly certain that the Gospels of Luke and John, the Book of Acts, the Epistles, and the Book of Revelation were originally written in Greek. The oldest known manuscripts of Matthew and Mark are in Greek. Some scholars have argued that these Gospels were originally written in Aramaic and later translated into Greek. If that is the case, no extant copies or fragments of the Aramaic text have been found. The only evidence we have is that the original text of Matthew and Mark was in Greek. Does this mean that Jesus spoke in Greek to His disciples and to the crowds He addressed in His Galilean ministry? Probably not.' - ["The Language of the Gospel" by Dr. Thomas S. McCall; Senior Theologian, Th.M. in Old Testament studies and a Th.D. in Semitic languages and Old Testament; Zola Levitt Ministries."]

The Consensus among biblical scholars is that all four canonical gospels were originally written in Greek, the Lingua Franca of the Roman Orient ['Gospel', Wiki].

162. Hebrew Bible Scriptural Alluding.

• **Ruth Conversion**: 'And Ruth said: "Entreat me not to leave thee, and to return from following after thee, for thou whither goest, I will go, and where thou lodgest, I will lodge, thy people shall be my people, and thy God my God; 17 where thou diest, will I die, and there will I be buried; the LORD do so to me, and more also, if aught but death part thee and me.' — [Book of Ruth, Ch.1, 16] / **A Moabite Foreigner**: 'Hast thou also bought of Ruth the Moabitess' — [Ch. 4/5.] / **Ruth-David-Messiah Lineage**: 'And the women her neighbors gave it a name, saying: 'There is a son born to Naomi'; and they called his name Obed; he is the father of Jesse, the father of David.' [Ch.4/17. 17]. / 'And Obed begot Jesse, and Jesse begot David'— [Book of Ruth 4/22] / **Prophetic Writing Alluding**: Hag. ii. 23 / Zech. iii. 8, VI. 12 / Ezekiel xvii. 23 / Zech. ix.

9, 10 / Jeremiah xxxiii. 15, 16 / Isaiah (ix. 1-6, xi. 1-10, xxxii. 1-5) / title of the ruling sovereign Mashiach YHWH ("God's anointed one"; I Sam. ii. 10, 35].

163. Oldest Hebrew Script. Old Hebrew script did not split off from its Phoenician predecessor until the ninth century B.C.E. The Hebrew language existed well before then; the oldest extant Hebrew language texts are recorded in Phoenician script. - [Christopher Rollston, The Oldest Hebrew Script and Language, Biblical Archaeological Society.] **William Foxwell Albright.** In 1943, he stated that "the Gezer Calendar, dated 10 Century BCE, is written in perfect classical Hebrew." — [Oldest Hebrew Script and Language; The Biblical Archaeology Society] /

• **King David.** An inscription dating from the 10th century BCE (the period of King David's reign) has been deciphered, showing that it is a Hebrew inscription. The discovery makes this the earliest known Hebrew writing, according to one scholar. Professor Gershon Galil of the Department of Biblical Studies at the University of Haifa has deciphered an inscription on a pottery shard discovered in the Elah valley dating from the 10th century BCE (the period of King David's reign), and has shown that this is a Hebrew inscription. The discovery makes this the earliest known Hebrew writing. It indicates that the Kingdom of Israel already existed in the 10th century BCE and that at least some of the biblical texts were written hundreds of years before the dates presented in current research."— ["Most ancient Hebrew biblical inscription deciphered"; ScienceDaily.]

• **Oral Transmission**. 'First we must dismiss the theory of oral transmission as the source of Genesis. It is utter nonsense to expect that a pure document could be transferred from one generation to another for hundreds of years. Even Middle Easterners, with their prodigious memories could not do it. Concentration on the role of oral tradition has led scholars to underestimate the role of written records. We will give some evidences that the Pentateuch in its entirety was written from the beginning' — [Hebrew Was First and Is the Oldest Language in Continuous Use by Dr. David Livingston] /

Aramaic was not spoken in Judea at these times: As described in 2 Kings 18:26, Hezekiah, King of Judah, negotiates with Assyrian ambassadors in Aramaic so that the common people would not understand.

• **In the Book of Esther** 3:8. In 600 BCE, Haman complained to the King that the laws of the Hebrews were 'different from those of all other people.' So the Jews had their own laws which they kept. These were the laws, no doubt, given to Moses.

• **Hebrew Was First** and is the Oldest Language in Continuous Use. - [Dr. David Livingston, Ancient Days, Hebrew].

• **The Moabite stone** [870 BCE] is incontrovertible evidence of a rich Hebrew language and culture.

• **Historical Deception.** It is truly amazing to think that, in the academic world of the past 150 years, the almost contradictory term of "Phoenician alphabet" has been established, which, in reality refers to a type of writing that has nothing to do with an alphabet. It is even more unbelievable to think that the scientific dogma that Greek came from Phoenician has been enforced. [Phoenician "Alphabet": An Historical Deception Republished from the Athenian newspaper Apogevmatini, 21 November 1999 (pages 42-43).

• **Archaeology** has clearly demonstrated the existence of a written alphabetic communication dating to the time of Abraham, and an even earlier cuneiform method. There are several theories about the development of alphabets. The early Hebrew Alphabet is nearly identical with the Phoenician Alphabet, which is dated as early as the time of Joseph. / Of Note: No proof of has yet been found.

• **Iliad Unauthentic.** The major dialogues of Plato and a dozen speeches of Cicero (including the four against Catilina) were declared unauthentic. The Iliad and Odyssey are seen as loose collections of poems by multiple authors; "Homer" was a fiction. — [German Philosopher Friedrich August Wolf; 1759-1824]. / It is currently believed that the Greeks adopted a West Semitic (from an area where Phoenician and Hebrew groups lived) version of the alphabet, perhaps between 1100 and 800 B.C., but there are other points of view [How the Greek Alphabet Developed, by N. S. Gill.]

• **Hebrew Was First** and is the oldest language in continuous active line. The alphabet was invented in Israel/Lebanon about 1700 years after the first continuous writing, and it took another 1000 years before it reached Europe's outskirts. — [Dr. David Livingston; The Schoyen Collection].

• **The Earliest Hebrew Writing** yet discovered dates around 3,000 years ago. [Israeli archaeologist Yossi Garfunkel, Oldest Hebrew Script Found, BBC News; An Introductory Grammar of Rabbinic Hebrew (Fernández & Elwolde, p.2]. /

• **The Earliest Hebrew Texts** date from the second millennium B.C.E. and evidence suggests that the Israelite tribes who invaded Canaan spoke Hebrew. — [History and Origins of the Hebrew Language By Ariela Pelaia, About.Com Judaism] /

• **The Ostracon** (pottery shard inscribed with writing in ink) comprises five lines of text divided by black lines and measures 15 x 15 cm. and was found at excavations of a 10th century B.C.E. fortress - the oldest known Judaic city. [Science daily, Nov 3, 2008]/

• **The Earliest Writing Mentioning "Israel":** Amerna Letters [14th Century BCE]; The Merneptah Stele, also known as the Israel Stele or Victory Stele of Merneptah, dated as 1213-1203 — [Wiki]. See also #175.

164. BRITON. Religious practices revolved around offerings and sacrifices, sometimes human. The bodies were often mutilated and some human finds at the bottom of pits, such as those found at Danebury. — [British Iron Age, Wiki] / Britain was one of the two most important military commands in the Roman Empire's Legions. — [Cassius Dio, Roman History 69.13.2]. In 43, Vespasian and the II Augusta participated in the Roman invasion of Britain, and he distinguished himself under the overall command of Aulus Plautius. After participating in crucial early battles on the rivers Medway and Thames, he was sent to reduce the south west, penetrating through the modern counties of Devon with the probable objectives of securing the south coast ports and harbors along with the tin mines of Cornwall and the silver and lead mines of Somerset. - [A History of Britain, Richard Dargie 2007, p. 20] See also #172.

165. The Greek King Antiochus IV Epiphanies, declaring himself as "God Manifest" was a Greek king of the Seleucid Empire. He sent an Athenian senator to force the Jews to abandon the customs of their ancestors and to live no longer by the laws of their God. — [2 Maccabees 6:1-11] / Antiochus decided to outlaw Mosaic Holy Days, Sabbaths, circumcision and traditions kept by observant Jews and by ordering the worship of Zeus as the supreme god — [2 Maccabees 6:1-12]. / This was anathema to the faithful Mosaic Pharisees and when they refused, Antiochus sent an army to enforce his decree. — [Hellenism and the Birth of Modern Rabbinic Judaism; The Shining Light].

166. ALEXANDER THE GREAT. He is mentioned by name in the Apocryphal I Macc. — [i. 1-8, vi. 2]. The only historical event connecting Alexander the Great with the Jews is his visit to Jerusalem, which is recorded by Josephus in a somewhat fantastic manner. The Jews responded to Alexander's generosity by naming their first sons after him. Alexander was a student of Aristotle and would have shared Aristotle's belief in God — [Josephus Ant. xi. 8, 4-6]. See also # 167 & #173.

167. MAIMONIDES. (1135-1204). Jewish sage and scientist, first to write code of all Jewish 613 laws, the *Mishneh Torah*; produced The *Guide to the Perplexed;* nominated 'Man of the Millennium' by Time Magazine. He writes that Aristotle's views are superior to the opinions of prophets such as Ezekiel, in matters of the sciences; the task of a prophet is to bring God to the world. - [The Jewish Religion: A Companion, *published by Oxford University Press.*]

169. THE WESTERN WALL, Wailing Wall or **Kotel** [Heb.]**,** is located in the Old City of Jerusalem at the foot of the western side of the Temple Mount. It is a remnant of the ancient wall that surrounded the Jewish Temple's courtyard, and is arguably the most sacred site recognized by the Jewish faith outside of the Temple Mount itself. — [Wiki] / When Rome destroyed the Second Temple in 70 C.E., only one outer wall remained standing — [Jewish World Libr.]

170. **THE PROMISED LAND. Biblical Limits & Conditions**, commanding Jews not to take any other lands outside of the Mosaic boundaries. [Duet. 2/4 & 2/9]: 'And command thou the people, saying: Ye are to pass through the border of your brethren the children of Esau, that dwell in Seir; and they will be afraid of you; take ye good heed unto yourselves therefore; contend not with them; for I will not give you of their land, no, not so much as for the sole of the foot to tread on; because I have given mount Seir unto Esau for a possession. And the LORD said unto me: 'Be not at enmity with Moab, neither contend with them in battle; for I will not give thee of his land for a possession'. **Hebron Name.** Cazelles, p.195, compares Amorite *ḥibrum*. Two roots are in play, *ḥbr/ḥbr*. The root has magical overtones, and develops pejorative connotations in late Biblical usage.

171. **HEBREW, NOT ARAMAIC, IN FIRST CENTURY JUDEA.** Most scholars now date the demise of Hebrew as a spoken language to the end of or about 200 CE — [Boris, Judit Targarona & Angel Saenz-Badilos, Jewish Studies at turn of the 12th Century, P3] / Hebrew was the primal spoken and written language of the Jews of Judea in the First Century until the Second Century, after the Roman Emperor Hadrian expelled the Jews from Jerusalem. Aramaic and Greek were secondary languages spoken with non-Jews and in commercial trading: 'In point of fact, at the time of the Second Temple, both languages were in common use in Palestine.'; Aramaic and Greek were absorbed by the Jews during exiles, invasions and banning of Hebrew; 'Aramaic was destined to become Israel's vernacular tongue; but before this could come about it was necessary that the national independence should be destroyed and the people removed from their own home. - [Jewish Virtual Libr.] / 'It is astonishing that the Aramaic assumption - at least as it pertains to the language of first century Judaea, still persists.' — [Brent Minge, Author of "Jesus Spoke Hebrew - Busting The Aramaic Myth; sharesong]. / 'Aramaic was considered Foreign by Ancient Hebrews. Classified as Archaic Biblical Hebrew, in about the year 300 BCE, Aramaic makes its appearance in Jewish literature. Hebrew remained the dominant tongue. — [Deborah Miller, De Anza College.] / 'Aramaic is most closely related to the Hebrew. Aramaic, nevertheless, was considered by the ancient Hebrews as a foreign tongue; and a hundred years before the Babylonian exile it was understood only by people of culture in Jerusalem.' Jacob, the grandson of Abraham, spoke Hebrew: 'In the early Hebrew literature an Aramaic expression occurs once. In the narrative of the covenant between Jacob and Laban it is stated that each of them named in his own language the stone-heap built in testimony of their amity. Jacob called it "Galeed"; Laban used the Aramaic equivalent, "Jegar sahadutha" (Gen. Xxxi. 47). - [ARAMAIC LANGUAGE AMONG THE JEWS; Jewish Virtual Libr.]

• **Aramaic was not spoken in Judea at these times**: As described in 2 Kings 18:26, Hezekiah, King of Judah, negotiates with Assyrian ambassadors in Aramaic so that the common people would not understand. **N.T:** Aramaic is nowhere mentioned in the New Testament; Paul spoke to the Jews in Hebrew — [Acts 21:40; 22:2]; Jesus spoke to Paul in Hebrew; the banner on Jesus' Cross was in Hebrew — [Acts 26:14]. / "Jesus was born a Jew, on Jewish soil. He was brought up in a Jewish family, taught from the Hebrew Bible, and his followers consisted entirely of Jewish people. He knew not Greek, Egyptian, Roman, or Persian. He spoke only Hebrew and the everyday language of the day…Aramaic. He was a Jew preaching to Jews." - [Sandra Williams; Judaic Studies Program, University of Central Florida] **Aramaic.** One of the genealogies mentions Aram among the sons of Shem as a brother of Arphaxad, one of the ancestors of the Hebrews — [Gen. X. 23]. / In another, Kemuel, a son of Nahor, the brother of Abraham, is called "The father of Aram" — (Gen. xxii. 21). / Other descendants of this brother of the Hebrew Abraham — [Gen. Xiv. 13]; are termed Arameans; as, for instance, Bethuel, Rebekah's father — [Gen. Xxv. 20, xxviii. 5]; and Laban, the father of Rachel and Leah — [Gen. Xxv. 20; xxxi. 20, 24]. / The earliest history of Israel is thus connected with the Arameans of the East, and even Jacob himself is called in one passage "a wandering Aramean" — [Deut. xxvi. 5]. During the whole period of the kings, Israel sustained relations both warlike and friendly with the Arameans of the west, whose country was later called as Syria.

171a. JUDEA, NOT PALESTINE, IN THE FIRST CENTURY.

• **Origins & Historical Thread of the Name.** The first mention of the name Philistine, one that later evolved as Palestine, is derived from the Hebrew bible and the writings of the Egyptians in the 20th Dynasty under Ramses III in the Medinet Habu Temple texts of 1,150 BCE, which refers to them as 'The Sea People' or 'Peleset' [Invaders; Migratory] — [Fahlbusch et al., 2005, p. 185]. The most copious mentions of this name appear some 250 times in the Hebrew bible. In both the latter cases, the description of non-Arabian foreign invaders applies.

• **Herodotus**. "In the 5th Century BCE the Greek writer Herodotus in The Histories used the name 'Palaistinê' as applying to a part of Syria. The descriptions referred to a foreign people, not of any Arabian group; there were no people at this time by this name. Following the Roman conquest of Greece, the Roman writers also applied the same names used by the conquered Greeks, including Tibuullus, Pomponius Mela, Pliney the Elder, Philo of Alexander and Josephus; significantly, the Jewish writers Philo and Josephus could only have referred to the Jewish kingdom and the Jews by the use of this name in the First Century." - [Pliny, Natural History, Bk.V, 66-68].

• **Hadrian.** The Name Palestine was applied to Judea by the Roman Emperor Hadrian in 135 CE, namely in the Second century; there was no country called Palestine in the First Century: "In an effort to wipe out all memory of the bond between the Jews and the land, Hadrian changed the name of the province from Iudaea ['Judea'] to Syria-Palestina, a name that became common in non-Jewish literature." — [H.H. Ben-Sasson, A History of the Jewish People, Harvard University Press, page 334] / **Hadrian-Silva**. These two figures were vested in the periods 132 CE & 73 CE respectively, and clarified in the historical thread "Philistines to Palestine"; these have been featured in the "Inauguration of Palestine" sequence as a continuation of the Roman actions in Judea.

• **Hadrian.**: "It seems clear that by choosing a seemingly neutral name - one juxtaposing that of a neighboring province with the revived name of an ancient geographical entity (Palestine), already known from the writings of Herodotus - Hadrian was intending to suppress any connection between the Jewish people and that land" — [Ariel Lewin, The archaeology of Ancient Judea and Palestine. Getty Publications, 2005 p. 33]

• **"Your name shall no more be called Judea".** "At the end of the war in 135 CE, a decision was made by Hadrian himself to change the name of the province from Judea to Palestina; never before and never after was such a drastic measure taken. Judea, derived from the name of its people (Iudaei; Judah) simply ceased to exist for the Roman government." — [Hadrian's Hard-Won Victory Romans Suffer Severe Losses in Jewish War] / Hadrian also forbade Jews from Jerusalem and all Hebrew practices. [Wiki].

• **In the New Testament**, the term Palestine is never used. The term Israel is primarily used to refer to the people of Israel, rather than the Land. However, in at least two passages, Israel is used to refer to the Land: 'Saying, Arise, and take the young child and his mother, and go into the land of Israel, for they are dead who sought the young child's life. And he arose, and took the young child and his mother, and came into the land of Israel.' [Matt.2:20-21] / 'But when they persecute you in this city, flee ye into another: for verily I say to you, Ye shall not have gone over the cities of Israel, till the Son of man shall have come.' [Matt.10:23] /

• **Rome**. 'Before 135 A.D., the Romans used the terms Judea and Galilee to refer to the Land of Israel. When Titus destroyed Jerusalem in 70 A.D., the Roman government struck a coin with the phrase "Judea Capta," meaning Judea has been captured. The term Palestine was never used in the early Roman designations'; [Namely, not as a replacement of Judea, a name coined by the Romans]. — [Zvi Rivai, Zola Levitt Ministries] /

• **Modern Christianity.** "During the last few centuries, the world, Christians included, has fallen into a bad habit. We have bought into some early Roman propaganda. We have used the name Palestine, which Roman Emperor Hadrian placed on the country of Israel in 135 A.D., for so long that it has become common usage. There is a propaganda war going on now with regard to the term "Palestine." It is specifically employed to avoid the use of the name Israel, and must be considered an anti-Israel term. In all Arab maps published in Jordan, Egypt, etc., the area west of the Jordan River is called Palestine, without any reference to Israel. Palestine is the term now used by those who want to deny the legitimate existence of

Israel as a genuine nation among the family of nations." — [Dr. Thomas McCall, the Senior Theologian of Levitt Ministry, *quoting Zola Levitt]*

• **Islamic Land Name**. "Allah Gave the Land of Israel to the Jews. I say to those who distort their Lord's book, the Koran: From where did you bring the name Palestine, you liars, you accursed, when Allah has already named it "The Holy Land" and bequeathed it to the Children of Israel until the Day of Judgment." - Sheikh Ahmad Adwan, Jordanian Muslim scholar. — [*Rachel Avraham,* Jerusalem online; Elders of Zion blog.]

• **Eretz Yisrael**. "You will find very clearly that the traditional commentators from the eighth and ninth century onwards have uniformly interpreted the Koran to say explicitly that *Eretz Yisrael* has been given by God to the Jewish people as a perpetual covenant. There is no Islamic counterclaim to the Land anywhere in the traditional corpus of commentary." - British-based imam Sheikh Muhammad Al-Hussaini; According to Robert Spencer, writing in the Middle East Forum.

• "**The al-Aqsa Mosque** was built on top of Solomon's Temple." - Eleventh century historian Muhammad Ibn Ahmad al-Maqdisi and fourteenth century Iranian religious scholar Hamdallah al-Mustawfi ["Allah Gave the Land of Israel to the Jews", JerusalemOnLine].

• "**Palestine of today**, the land we now know as Palestine was peopled by the Jews from the dawn of history until the Roman era. It is the ancestral homeland of the Jewish people. They were driven from it by force by the relentless Roman military machine and for centuries prevented from returning. [U.S. Congressional Records 1922 House of Representatives House Resolution 360 unanimously adopted].

• **Priest Martyrs**. Condemned to Death for the Law's Sake. [Jewish Ency., Ab. Zarah 17b et seq; Wiki] / "They have never been guilty of false faith. In fact, before the church existed, they believed in the one true God" - [H. Kung, 'The Church'; Jewish Virtual Libr.]

• **Briton Recruits**. Dio reports that Hadrian dispatched "his best generals" to crush the Jewish revolt. The "first of these" Generals (and the only one Dio names) was Julius Severus, who was dispatched from Britain, where he was governor and commanded the Roman troops. Britain was one of the two most important military commands in the empire. — [Cassius Dio, Roman History 69.13.2] /

• **Monotheism as Capital Crime**. A temple to the Roman gods was erected on the Temple Mount. Hadrian also renamed the country Palestine after the Biblical Philistines, though the Philistines had long since disappeared. His aim was to erase all memory of the connection between the Jews, Judea and Jerusalem. Hadrian outlawed circumcision. Like Antiochus IV during the Maccabean revolt 200 years earlier, he made the study or practice of Judaism a capital crime. The pagan world was usually pluralistic (the Romans simply added the gods of the peoples they conquered to their pantheon), and religious decrees were rare. Perhaps the rebellious nature of the Jews, the one nation that refused to accept Roman sovereignty, provoked the Romans to destroy the Jews' holy city, erase the name of their country, and eliminate their religion. — ["Jerusalem as a Roman Pagan City", Ingeborg Rennert Center for Jerusalem Studies] /

174. **Palestine - An Exclusive Reference to Jews till 20th Century.**
   • The Jerusalem Post, founded in 1932 and was called "The Palestine Post" until 1948.
   • Bank Leumi L'Israel was called the "Anglo-Palestine Bank," a Jewish Company.
   • The Jewish Agency - an arm of the Zionist movement engaged in Jewish settlement since 1929 - was called the "Jewish Agency for Palestine."
   • Today's Israel Philharmonic Orchestra, founded in 1936 by German Jewish refugees who fled Nazi Germany, was called the "Palestine Symphony Orchestra," composed of some 70 Palestinian Jews.
   • The United Jewish Appeal (UJA) was established in 1939 as a merger of the "United Palestine Appeal" and the fundraising arm of the Joint Distribution Committee.

• Princeton University professor of Semitic literature Philip Hitti (1886-1978), one of the greatest Arabic historians of the ninth century and author of 'The History of the Arabs,' testifying on behalf of the Arab cause, told the Anglo-American Committee of Inquiry on Palestine in 1946: "There is no 'Palestine' in history, absolutely not." — ['The Artificiality of the Historical Palestinian Identity' Eli E. Hertz, Myths and Facts Org]

• "There is no 'Palestine' in history, absolutely not." - Princeton University professor of Semitic literature Philip Hitti (1886-1978), one of the greatest Arabic historians of the ninth century and author of 'The History of the Arabs,' testifying on behalf of the Arab cause, told the Anglo-American Committee of Inquiry on Palestine in 1946. ['The Artificiality of the Historical Palestinian Identity' Eli E. Hertz, Myths and Facts Org]

173. THE SEPTUAGINT.

'The Septuagint Impact is a watershed in Jewish history. The first translation of the Hebrew bible into another language was in the Greek in 300 BCE. / The Septuagint Influence on Christianity. It was a source of the Old Testament for early Christianity during the first few centuries AD. Many early Christians spoke and read Greek, thus they and the New Testament writers relied on the Septuagint Translation for their understanding of the Hebrew bible. - [Septuagint; All About Truth Org] / Greeks and the Jews. "More than any other event, this translation would make the Hebrew religion into a world religion. It would otherwise have faded from memory like the infinity of Semitic religions that have been lost to us. This Greek version made the Hebrew Scriptures available to the Mediterranean world and to early Christians who were otherwise fain to regard Christianity as a religion unrelated to Judaism. Even with a Greek translation, the Hebrew Scriptures came within a hair's breadth of being tossed out of the Christian canon. From this Greek translation, the Hebrew view of God, of history, of law, and of the human condition, in all its magnificence would spread around the world. The dispersion, or Diaspora, of the Jews would involve ideas as well as people." — [Greeks and the Jews, Jewish Virtual Library; The Hebrews: A Learning Module from Washington State University, (c) Richard Hooker; The American-Israel Cooperative Enterprise]. / Thakeray. "Its Chief Value lies in the fact that it is a version of a Hebrew text earlier by about a millennium than the earliest dated Hebrew manuscript extant. It is, moreover, a pioneering work; there was probably no precedent in the world's history for a series of translations from one language into another on so extensive a scale. It was the first attempt to reproduce the Hebrew Scriptures in another tongue. It is one of the outstanding results of the breaking-down of international barriers by the conquests of Alexander the Great and the dissemination of the Greek language, which were fraught with such vital consequences for the history of religion". - H. St. J. Thakeray; The Int. Standard Bible Encycl.] See also #166.

176. 3,000-YEAR-OLD TEMPLE ARTIFACTS.

The archaeologist Yosef Garfinkel of Hebrew University says the central finds presented at a Jerusalem press conference of two model shrines, echo elements of Temple architecture as described in the Bible and strengthen his claim that the city that stood at the site 3,000 years ago was inhabited by Israelites and was part of the kingdom ruled from Jerusalem by the biblical King David. Carbon dating of olive pits found at the site show it was active between 1020 and 980 BCE. The Report is in some debate. — [3,000-year-old Temple artifacts fuel Biblical archaeology debate; The Times of Israel]

177. THE WAILING WALL.

Chotel Maarbi or Western Wall

The Kotel-Western Wall. [Rabbi Joseph Schwarz, 1850] Source: 37. The Wailing Wall [Gustav Bauernfeind, 1904] Source: 38

The Western Wall, Wailing Wall or *HaKotel/Chotel* (Heb). Located in the Old City of Jerusalem at the foot of the western side of the Temple Mount, it is a remnant of the ancient wall that surrounded the Jewish Temple's courtyard, and is arguably the most sacred site recognized by the Jewish faith outside of the Temple Mount itself. The Western Wall refers not only to the exposed section facing a large plaza in the Jewish Quarter, but also to the sections concealed behind structures running along the whole length of the Temple Mount, such as the Little Western Wall - a 25 ft (8 m) section in the Muslim Quarter. — [The Western Wall, Wiki].

179. EARLIEST KNOWN RELICS CONFIRM BIBLICAL TEXTS.

3,200 YEAR EGYPTIAN STONE TABLET & 3,400 YEAR OLD LETTERS, CIRCA MOSES AND JOSHUA PERIODS, RECORDS THE FIRST MENTION OF ISRAEL; JERUSALEM; HEBREW; CANAAN; RAMSESY; ASKELON; GAZA.

Merneptah/Israel stele [Egyptian Museum in Cairo] Source: 39.

THE MERNEPTAH STELE AND THE AMARNA LETTERS.

• **The Amarna Letters**. Letters from the Babylonian king, Kadashman-Enlil I, anchor in the time-frame of Akhenaten's reign to the mid-14th century BC. Here was also found the first mention of a Near Eastern group known as the Habiru, alluding to the battles waged by the Hebrews under Joshua: "They have seized the land of Rubute, the land of the king has fallen away to the Habiru…" [Language: Akkadian Cuneiform; Clay Tablets]

• **The Merneptah Stele** — also known as The Israel Stele, is an inscription by the Ancient Egyptian King Merneptah (reign: 1213 to 1203 BC). The writing provides the first evidence of the Hebrew tribes as active in the land and their interaction with the Pharaoh of Egypt and his armies engaged in a war. The last lines deal with a separate campaign in Canaan, then part of Egypt's imperial possessions, and include the first documented instance of the name Israel; Askelon, Urusalem; Canaan & Gaza: **"Israel** is laid waste and his seed is not.." — [Discovered by Flinders Petriein in 1896 at Thebes; Housed at Egyptian Museum in Cairo/Mernepath Stele; Bible History/Archaeology/Israel/el-amarna-letters / [Language: Ancient Egyptian hieroglyphs

• **"The Mernaptah Stele** is powerful evidence of an ancient ethnic group called the Israelites as living in Canaan what today includes Israel and Palestine" - Donald Redford; Penn. State University] / **Rameses the Great** confirms Hebrew text of this king. 'The stela is a poetic eulogy to pharaoh Merneptah, who ruled Egypt after Rameses the Great, ca. 1212-1202 BC.' - Author: Bryant G. Wood; Associates for Biblical Research; Christian Answers Network. Merneptah was the son of Ramses II. / The words relating to Israel and Hebrew are not accepted as conclusive by some scholars.

• **"Archaeology Confirms 50 Real People in the Bible."** Archaeological evidences of 22 kings, from Omri (884-873 BCE; 1 Kings 16:16) to Gadaliah (597-586; Jeremiah 38.1) as listed in the Hebrew Scriptures. - [By Lawrence Mykytiuk, Biblical Archaeology Society Review].

180. **Jerusalem - Origins of Name.** - [Kaplan, Arye (1996). "Beginnings". *Jerusalem, the Eye of the Universe*. New York: Mesorah, pp: 11-14] Held Traditions/Legend/Metaphoric.

• TIME-LINES.

Rule of Rom (230 BCE-400 CE)

230-146 B.C.E. Coming of ROME to the east Mediterranean.

142-129 B.C.E. Jewish autonomy under Hasmoneans. .

63 B.C.E. Rome (Pompey) annexes the land of Israel.

37-4 B.C.E. Heros the Great (Jewish Roman ruler of the land of Israel).

37 B.C.E. Herod captures Jerusalem, has Antigonus II executed, and marries the Hasmonean princess Mariamne I.

20 B.C.E. Herod creates Temple Mount and begins to rebuild the Termple in Jerusalem. Project continues until 72 C.E…

ca. 4 B.C.E.-ca. 30 C.E. Joshua/Jesus "the Christ."

MODERN ERA Hillel & Shammai (Jewish sages).

6 C.E. Rome establishes direct rule of prefects in Judea.

ca. 13 B.C.E.- 41 C.E. Philo Judaeus of Alexandria.

ca. 30 C.E. Jesus is crucified.

36-64 C.E. Paul "the apostle" (Jewish "Christian").

ca. 37-100 C.E. Josephus (Jewish leader, historian).

ca. 40 C.E. Gamliel/Gamaliel I (Jewish leader-scholar).

ca. 50-125 C.E. Christian Testament (NT) writings.

66-73 C.E. First Jewish Revolt against Rome.

69 C.E. Vespasian gives Yochanan Ben Zakkai permission to establish a Jewish center for study at Yavneh that will become the hub for rabbinic Judaism.

70 Destruction of Jerusalem and the second Temple.

73 Last stand of Jews at Masada.

ca. 90-100 Gamaliel II excludes sectarians (including Christians) from the Synagogues.

ca. 90-150 Writings (third and last division of Jewish Scriptures) discussed and accepted as sacred scripture.

114-117 Jewish Revolts against Rome in Cyprus, Egypt and Cyrene. The Great Synagogue and the Great Library in Alexandria are destroyed as well as the entire Jewish community of Cyprus. Afterwards, Jews were forbidden on Cyprus.

120-135 Rabbi Akiva active in consolidating Rabbinic Judaism.

132-135 Bar Kokhba rebellion (Second Jewish Revolt. Roman forces kill an estimated half a million Jews and destroy 985 villages and 50 fortresses.

136 Hadrian renames Jerusalem Aelia Capatolina and builds a Pagan temple over the site of the Second Temple. He also forbids Jews to dwell there. Judea (the southern portion of what is now called the West Bank) was renamed Palaestina in an attempt to minimize Jewish identification with the land of Israel.

138-161 Antoninus Pius, Hadrian's successor, repeals many of the previously instituted harsh policies towards Jews.

193-211 Roman emperor Lucious Septimus Severus treats Jews relatively well, allowing them to participate in public offices and be exempt from formalities contrary to Judaism. However, he did not allow the Jews to convert anyone

ca. 200 Mishna (Jewish oral law) compiled/edited under Judah the Prince.

200-254 Origen (Christian scholar, biblical interpreter).

203 Because of his health, Judah HaNasi relocates the center of Jewish learning from Beth Shearim to Sepphoris.

212 Roman Emperor Caracalla allows free Jews within the empire to become full Roman citizens.

220 Babylonian Jewish Academy founded at Sura by Rab.

220-470 Amoraim, or Mishna scholars, flourish. The Amoraim's commentary, along with the Mishna, comprises the Talmud.

222-235 Emperor Alexander Severus allowed for a revival of Jewish rights, including permission to visit Jerusalem.

240-276 Rise of Mani/Manichaean World Religion synthesis.

ca. 250 Babylonian Jews flourish (as does Manichaeism) under Persian King Shapur I

250-330 Early development of Christian monasticism in Egypt.

263-339 Eusebius (Christian author, historian)

303 Violent persecution of Christians by Emperor Diocletian.

To 311 Sporadic persecution of Christianity by Rome.

306 One of the first Christian councils, the Council of Elvira, forbids intermarriage and social interaction with Jews

312/313 Emperor Constantine embraces Christianity, announces Edict of Toleration

315 Code of Constantine limits rights of non-Christians, is Constantine's first anti-Jewish act.

368 Jerusalem Talmud compiled.

• Time-Line: Dawn of History (3800-2001 BCE)

3760 Adam & Eve created (Year 1 of Jewish calendar)

3630 Seth born

3525 Enoch born

ca. 3500 Chalcolithic Period, first settlement

3435 Kenan born

3365 Mehalalel born

3300 Yered born

3138 Enoch born

3074 Methusaleh born

2886 Lemech born

2831 Adam dies

ca. 2800 Early Dynastic period (Akkad)

2704 Noah born

ca. 2700-2400 Old Kingdom period (Egypt)

ca. 2500-2200 Ebla flourishes

ca. 2500 First houses built in Jerusalem

ca. 2300-2200 Priestess Enheduanna, first known author in the world

2203 Shem born

2150 The Flood

2100-1700 Middle Kingdom period (Egypt)

• Time-Line: Ancient Israelite Religion (2000-587 BCE)

Monotheism

2000-1750 Old Babylonian period

2000-1700 Israel's Patriarchal period

ca. 1900-1400 Old Assyrian Period

1882 Terach born

1813 Abraham born

ca. 1850/1750/1700 Abraham & Sarah, Isaac & Ishmael, famine forces Israelites to migrate to Egypt

1800 First Jerusalem city wall built

ca. 1792-1750 Hammurabi

ca. 1750-1200 Hittite empire

1765 The Tower of Babel

1743 Origin of traditions of the "Abraham covenant"

1713 Isaac born; Abraham circumcises himself; Sodom & Gomorrah destroyed

ca. 1700-1550 Hyksos in Egypt

1677 Isaac prepared as sacrifice; Sarah dies

1653 Jacob born

1638 Abraham dies

ca. 1600-1150 Kassite period (Babylonia)

1590 Isaac blesses Jacob instead of Esau.

ca. 1570-1085 New Kingdom period (Egypt)

1569 Jacob marries Leah

1565 Levi born

1562 Joseph born

1546 Joseph sold into slavery

1533 Isaac dies

1532 Joseph becomes viceroy of Egypt

1523 Jacob and his family join Joseph in Egypt

ca. 1500-1200 Ugaritic texts

1452 Joseph dies

1429 Egyptian enslavement of the Hebrews begins

ca. 1400-900 Middle Assyrian period

ca. 1400-1300 Amarna period (Egypt)

1393 Moses born.

1355 Joshua born.

1314 Moses sees the burning bush.

ca. 1300-1200 Mosaic period (Israel)

1280 Exodus from Egypt, Sinai Torah, Canaan Entry

1240 After setting up the Ark at Shiloh near Shechem (Nablus), Joshua launches foray into Jerusalem {Joshua 10:23, 15:63)

ca. 1200 Sea Peoples invade Egypt and Syro-Palestine

ca. 1200-1050/1000 Period of the Judges (Israel)

ca. 1200-1000 Jerusalem is a Canaanite city

ca. 1150-900 Middle Babylonian period:

ca. 1106 Deborah judges Israel.

ca. 1050-450 Hebrew Prophets (Samuel-Malachi)

ca. 1000-587 Monarchial Period in Israel

ca. 1030-1010 Saul (transitional king)

ca. 1010-970 David conquers the Jebusites and makes Jerusalem his capital

ca. 970-931 Solomon builds the First Temple on Mount Moriah

ca. 931 Secession of Northern Kingdom (Israel) from Southern Kingdom (Judah)

931-913 Rehoboam rules Judah

931-910 Jeroboam I rules Israel, chooses Shechem as his first capital, later moves it to Tirzah

913-911 Abijah rules Judah

911-870 Asa rules Juda

910-909 Nadab (son of Jeroboam) rules Israel

909-886 Baasha kills Nadab and rules Israel

900-612 Neo-Assyrian period

886-885 Elah, son of Baasha, rules Israel

885 Zimri kills Elah, but reigns just seven days before committing suicide, Omri chosen as King of Israel

885-880(?) War between Omri and Tibni

885-874 Omri kills Tibni, rules Israel

879 Omri moves capital of Israel from Tirzah to Samaria

874-853 Ahab, Omri's son, is killed in battle, Jezebel reigns as Queen. Athaliah, Ahab and Jezebel's daughter, marries Jehoram, crown prince of Judah

870-848 Jehoshapha rules Judah

853-851 Ahaziah, son of Ahab, rules Israel, dies in accident

750-725 Israelite Prophets Amos, Hosea, Isaiah

722/721 Northern Kingdom (Israel) destroyed by Assyrian; 10 Tribes exiled (10 lost tribes)

720 Ahaz, King of Judah dismantles Solomon's bronze vessels and places a private Syrian altar in the Temple

716 Hezekiah, King of Jerusalem, with help of God and the prophet Isaiah resists Assyrian attempt to capture Jerusalem (2 Chronicles 32). Wells and springs leading to the city are stopped

701 Assyrian ruler Sennacherib besieges Jerusalem

612-538 Neo-Babylonian ("Chaldean") period

620 Josiah (Judean King) and "Deuteronomic Reforms"

ca. 600-580 Judean Prophets Jeremiah and Ezekiel

587/586 Southern Kingdom (Judah) and First Temple destroyed-Babylonian exile

ca. 550 Judean Prophet "Second Isaiah"

541 First Jews return from Babylon in small numbers to rebuild the city and its walls. Seventy years of exile terminated. (Daniel 9, Haggai 2:18-19)

539 Persian ruler Cyrus the Great conquers Babylonian Empire

PICTORIAL IMAGES SOURCES. [S]

S1. Book Cover. [Courtesy: Frantz Kantor Productions.]

S2. Queen Bernice. [Courtesy: Frantz Kantor Productions.]

S3. Flavius Josephus [Courtesy: Frantz Kantor Productions.]

S4. Abraham's Journey from Ur to Canaan. [Oil, by Jozsef Molnár]

S5. Map Roman Empire. [Author Steerpike; Andrei Nacu. Licensed under the Creative Commons Attribution-Share Alike 3.0 Netherlands License. Wikimedea Commons]

S6. Victory O Lord. [By John Everett Millais, 1871]

S7. Beasts in the Arena ['Lions' By Jean-Léon Gérôme, 1863-1883]

S8. Nero Bust [Capitilona Museum Rome, Author: cjh1452000. Application Share-Alike 3.0 Unported CC-BY SA 3.0]

S9. Alexander in the Jerusalem Temple. [Artist Sebastiano Conca, Oil on Canvas, 1736, Prado Museum]

S10. Moses and Joshua before Ark of the Tabernacle. [By James Tissot, 1896]

S11. Trial of St. Paul. [Stained Glass Window Detail, St. Paul's Cathedral, Melbourne, St. Anselm Author]

S12. King Solomon Directing the Temple Builders. [Sketch; Artist unknown]

S13. Jerusalem - The First Sight. [Permission granted Courtesy: Artist Alex Levin. (C) Alex Levin; Web: www.artlevin.com]

S14. Jerusalem Temple - N.E. Aspect. ["Reconstruction of Jerusalem and the Temple of Herod", Opaque water color over graphite on gray wove paper by James Tissot. Location: Brooklyn Museum]

S15. Herodian Temple Fortress. [Reconstruction model of Ancient Jerusalem in Museum of David Castle. Attribution: at ru-wikipedia licensed under the Creative Commons Attribution-Share Alike 2.5 Generic 3.0 License CC-BY-SA-2.5. Russianname.]

S17. Attack Phase I - Catapulta. [By Edward Poynter, 1868]

S18. Attack Phase II - The Mighty Battering Ram.

S19. A Wall Wavers.

S20. The Tortoise Surge. [Usage Permission granted Courtesy of (C) Heritage History, WA, USA]

S21. The Spoils of Jerusalem. ["The Destruction of the Temple of Jerusalem", Oil on Canvas, by Francesco Hayez, Academia of Venice.]

S22. Destruction of Jerusalem - Mt. Scopus View. [Painting by David Roberts; 1850] S23. The Temple is Burning.

S24. Storming the Holy of Holies.

S25. Jupiter Ascends. [Jupiter Bust; Vatican Museum Alinari/Art Resource, New York]

S27. Roman Decadence Art. ["Romans during the Decadence" by French Artist Thomas Couture, 1850]

S28. The Masada Fortress. ["An aerial view of the Masada fortress above the Dead Sea." Photographer: Milner Moshe, 1993. Source: Government Press Office [GPO]; Israel. Usage: Wikimedia Commons.]

S29. Goliath - A Philistine. [By Andrea Vaccaro, Circa 1635]

S30. The Messiah Syndrome. ["Peace". Etching by Artist William Strutt, 1896.]

S31. The Exile. [Goucche on Board, 'Flight of the Prisoners, James Tissot, Jewish Museum, NY, NY. Wiki Commons]

S32A. Rebels or Heroes? [Courtesy: Frantz Kantor Productions.]

S32. Arch of Titus - Modern Rome. [Author/Photographer: Peter Gerstbach. Source: German

Wikipedia.GNU free documentation license Version 1.2]

S33. Josephus Latin Book Cover 75 CE. [First Published 75 CE, Basle. Location: Diaspora Museum, Tel Aviv - en: Beit Hatefusot.]

S34. Ark of the Covenant. [Permission Granted Courtesy of: (c) American-Israeli Cooperative Enterprise (AICE); and Jewish Virtual Library Jewish.]

S35. Titus Entering Coliseum Victory Celebrations. [Oil on Canvas, By Sir Lawrence Alma-Tadema, 1885]

S36. Dead Sea Scrolls.

S37. The Kotel - Western Wall. [Chotel Engraving. Rabbi Joseph Schwartz, Descriptive Geography and Brief Historical Sketch of Palestine.]

S38. The Wailing Wall. [Oil on Canvas. Artist Gustav Bauernfeind, 1848-1904]. 38a. Shekel of Israel [Licensed under the Creative Commons Attributioin-Share Alike 3.0 Unr3ported License. Attribition: Classical Numismatic Group, Inc.]

S39. Merneptah/Israel Stele. [Author Web scribe (JE 31408) from the Egyptian Museum in Cairo. WC. Creative Commons Attribution-Share Alike 3.0 Unported]

MAPS.

S40. The Roman Empire. [Map of the Roman Empire during 69AD. Creative Commons Attribution-Share Alike 3.0 Netherlands license. Kaart van het Romeinse Rijk in 68-69 n.Chr. het Vierkeizersjaar. De ingekleurde gebieden geven aan welke *provinciae* aan welke troonpredent loyaal waren.]

TIME-LINES.

S43. Rule of Rome. [Permission Granted Courtesy of: (c) American-Israeli Cooperative Enterprise (AICE); and Jewish Virtual Library Jewish.]

S44. Ancient Israelite Religion. [Permission Granted Courtesy of: (c) American-Israeli Cooperative Enterprise (AICE); and Jewish Virtual Library.]

S45. Post-Destruction Rabbinite Period. [Permission Granted Courtesy of: (c) American-Israeli Cooperative Enterprise (AICE); and Jewish Virtual Library.]

Endnotes

[1] "The Jews' contributions to the world's list of great names in literature, science, art, music, finance, medicine, and abstruse learning are also away out of proportion to the weakness of their numbers." - Mark Twain.

[2] Biblical Historian Paul Johnson; author of "A History of The Jews".

[3] Caligula announced his self-deification, ordered that a statue of himself should be placed in the Temple of Jerusalem and the Jews be forced to worship him; and it had not yet been carried out when Caligula was assassinated — [VRoma Org; Jewish Virtual Libr. org/Judaism/revolt.] / Caligula was murdered at the Palatine Games by Cassius Chaerea, tribune of the Praetorian Guard, Cornelius Sabinus, and others. Caligula's wife Caesonia and his daughter were also put to death. He was succeeded as emperor by his uncle Claudius. [Encl. Britannica] / Caligula adorned his horse Incitatus with Jewels and servants and demanded it to be his chief Consul - [Suetonius' Lives of the Twelve Caesars; Dio Cassius.

[4] H. Kung, "Pseudo-Theology about the Jews" in: Christian Attitudes on Jews and Judaism; 1977, 1ff.

[5] "NO SURRENDER OF BELIEF". 'And it seemed to everybody and especially to them that so far from being destruction, it was victory and salvation and happiness to them that they perished along with the Temple.' - (Deo Cassius, Epitome of Book LXV; History Crash Course #35: Destruction of the Temple, Aishcom) / 'Then the Jews defended themselves much more vigorously than before, as if they had discovered a piece of rare good fortune in being able to fight near the Temple and fall in its defense'. - (Roman Historian, Deo Cassius, Epitome of Book LXV)

[6] "NO SURRENDER OF BELIEF". 'Far from being destruction, it was victory and salvation and happiness to them that they perished along with the Temple.' - (Deo Cassius, Epitome of Book LXV; History Crash Course #35: Destruction of the Temple, Aishcom) / Act III: Holy War"

[7] 'It is astonishing that the Aramaic assumption - at least as it pertains to the language of first century Judaea, still persists.' - (Brent Minge, Author of "Jesus Spoke Hebrew - Busting The Aramaic Myth; sharesong). / # See more in "The Messiah Syndrome."

[8] "Philistine to Palestine" - A Historical Thread.

[9] SCAVENGERS; BARBARIC (Titus charges Arabian and Roman soldiers as barbarians when corpses of the Jews are disemboweled looking for suspected swallowing of gold - Josephus Wars, Book V, Ch 13, 4)

[10] TEMPLE SIZES - FORTRESS OF JERUSALEM. LARGEST MONUMENT: 'List of largest monoliths in the world' — [Josephus War04; 'Seven Wonders of the World' Livius.org]. / BRICK SIZES. Some of these weighed well over 100 tons, the largest measuring 44.6 feet by 11 feet by 16.5 feet and weighing approximately 567 to 628 tons. - (Dan Bahat: Touching the Stones of our Heritage, Israeli ministry of Religious Affairs, 2002)

[11] Josephus writes: "Then in the summer of 66 CE, a very bold young man who was Captain of the Temple — Eleazar, son of the high-priest Hananiah — moved that no gift or sacrifice was to be permitted

during the service of worship. And this set the foundation for the war with Rome. - (Josephus, Antiquities 20.409)

[12] "ALL ROADS LEAD TO ROME" The expression is generally attributed to Alain de Lille, a French theologian and poet; 1175 AD/CE. — [Wiki. answers.]

[13] First Century Most Impacting. 'The destruction of Jerusalem in A.D. 70 was the greatest single event in a thousand years and religiously significant beyond anything else that ever occurred in human history.' — [J. B. Coffman in his first-century book, "Antiquities of the Jews"]

[14] ['And in that day will I make Jerusalem a burdensome stone for all people: all that burden themselves with it shall be cut in pieces, though all the people of the earth be gathered together against it' [Zechariah 12:3]

[15] BRITON. Religious practices revolved around offerings and sacrifices, sometimes human. The bodies were often mutilated and some human finds at the bottom of pits, such as those found at Danebury. — [British Iron Age, Wiki] / Britain was one of the two most important military commands in the Roman Empire's Legions. — [Cassius Dio, Roman History 69.13.2]. In 43, Vespasian and the II Augusta participated in the Roman invasion of Britain, and he distinguished himself under the overall command of Aulus Plautius. After participating in crucial early battles on the rivers Medway and Thames, he was sent to reduce the south west, penetrating through the modern counties of Devon with the probable objectives of securing the south coast ports and harbors along with the tin mines of Cornwall and the silver and lead mines of Somerset. - [A History of Britain, Richard Dargie 2007, p. 20] Briton Recruits. Dio reports that Hadrian dispatched "his best generals" to crush the Jewish revolt. The "first of these" Generals (and the only one Dio names) was Julius Severus, who was dispatched from Britain, where he was governor and commanded the Roman troops. Britain was one of the two most important military commands in the empire. — [Cassius Dio, Roman History 69.13.2]

[16] Joseph ben Matityahu (Hebrew: Yosef ben Matityahu), was a first-century Romano scholar, Jewish historian and hagiographer, who was born in Jerusalem. His most important works were The Jewish War (c. 75) and Antiquities of the Jews (c. 94). The Jewish War recounts the Jewish revolt against Roman occupation (66-70). Antiquities of the Jews recount the history of the world from a Jewish perspective for an ostensibly Roman audience. Flavius Josephus fully defected to the Roman side and was granted Roman citizenship. He became an advisor and friend of Vespasian's son Titus, serving as his translator when Titus led the Siege of Jerusalem, which resulted-when the Jewish revolt did not surrender-in the city's destruction and the looting and destruction of Herod's Temple (Second Temple). — [Livius org; Wiki]

[17] The issues came to a head over the large number of Gentiles who became converts, or who wanted to become converts, to Judaism. The Pharisees insisted that all converts to Judaism were joining "a new and godly commonwealth" [Baron, 1983, vol. 1, p. 181].

[18] Caligula announced his self-deification, ordered that a statue of himself should be placed in the Temple of Jerusalem and the Jews be forced to worship him; and it had not yet been carried out when Caligula was assassinated — [VRoma Org; Jewish Virtual Libr. org/Judaism/revolt.] / Caligula was murdered at the Palatine Games by Cassius Chaerea, tribune of the Praetorian Guard, Cornelius Sabinus, and others. Caligula's wife Caesonia and his daughter were also put to death. He was succeeded as emperor by his uncle Claudius. [Encl. Britannica] / Caligula adorned his horse Incitatus with Jewels and servants and demanded it to be his chief Consul - [Suetonius' Lives of the Twelve Caesars; Dio Cassius]

[19] In the Book of Esther 3:8. In 600 BCE, Haman complained to the King that the laws of the Hebrews were 'different from those of all other people.' So the Jews had their own laws which they kept. These were the laws, no doubt, given to Moses.

[20] Nimrod. The 'first mention of Nimrod, one of the earliest recorded kings and associated with the Biblical story of 'The Tower of Babel', is in the Table of Nations, described as the great-grandson of Noah; "a mighty one on the earth" and "a mighty hunter before God". This is repeated in the First Book of Chronicles 1:10 and the "Land of Nimrod" used as a synonym for Assyria or Mesopotamia; also mentioned in the Book of Micah 5:6.

[21] 'Then Solomon began to build the temple of the LORD in Jerusalem on Mount Moriah' — II Chronicles Chapter 3

[22] "Know for a surety thy seed shall be in Bondage" [Gen. 15/13]

[23] Cassius Dio Roman history 69.12.1-14.3; Dio Cassius, xxxvii. 17

[24] "The Romans had taken 97,000 prisoners. Thousands of them were forced to become gladiators and were killed in the arena, fighting wild animals or fellow gladiators. Some were burned alive. Others were employed at Seleucia, where they had to dig a tunnel. But most of these prisoners were brought to Rome, where they were forced to build the Forum of Peace and the Coliseum. The Menorah and the Table were exhibited in the temple of Peace. — [Josephus War04; 'Seven Wonders of the World' Livius.org].

[25] MARCELLUS; ALIENUS Two Roman Senators assassinated by Titus — [Titus, Vatican Museums, Vatican City]

[26] QUEEN BERNICE — [Julia Berenice, 39 BC and 92 AD; Acts.Ch.25; Jewish Women's Archive; Wiki]

[27] TITUS WOUND — [Dion Cassius; Josephus]

[28] The Menorah and the Table were exhibited in the temple of Peace. — [Josephus War04; 'Seven Wonders of the World' Livius.org].

[29] "The Romans had taken 97,000 prisoners. Thousands of them were forced to become gladiators and were killed in the arena, fighting wild animals or fellow gladiators. Some were burned alive. Others were employed at Seleucia, where they had to dig a tunnel. But most of these prisoners were brought to Rome, where they were forced to build the Forum of Peace and the Coliseum. The Menorah and the Table were exhibited in the temple of Peace. — [Josephus War04; 'Seven Wonders of the World' Livius.org].

[30] NASSERITE [Nazarene] — [Hebrew Bible, Numbers 6:5; Nazarene Wiki 1.3]

[31] Mentula: Penis; Latin [Wikipedia]

[32] Nero forbade killing in circus contests. san.beck.org/AB-Chronology.

[33] TITUS-FLAVIANS REFUSED TO ACCEPT WREATH OF VICTORY — [Philostratus; First Jewish-Roman War, The Outcome, Wiki]

[34] "On the last day of the games he [Titus] is said to have broken down and wept in public. His health had taken a marked downturn by then and perhaps he knew himself he was suffering from an incurable disease. Titus also had no heir." — [Illustrated History of the Roman Empire]

[35] "ALL ROADS LEAD TO ROME" The expression is generally attributed to Alain de Lille, a French theologian and poet; 1175 AD/CE. — [Wiki. answers.]

[36] COLISEUM. Completed in the year 80; Construction by Jews [Josephus War04].

[37] MARRIAGE WITH JEWS FORBIDDEN/CONCUBINE. — [Rome forbids marriage with Jews, Jewish Ency; Grätz, "Gesch." iv. 403 et seq., 702]

[38] "The spoils were borne in promiscuous heaps; the diversity of riches was displayed in the triumphal procession in Rome after Jerusalem was destroyed - silver and gold in masses flowing like a river. The altar and lamp stand, both made of gold, weighed no less than two talents." — [Financing the Coliseum, Alföldy] The Spoils - Gold and Silver Coins. The boundless riches from the Temple treasury were used to strike coins with the legend JUDAEA CAPTA ('Judaea defeated'). Any Roman would be reminded of their emperor's victory. The Jews were forced to pay an additional tax. - [Fiscus Judaicus]

[39] Mitrash was the cult of the Roman Empire and the deity of delight, thus pleasure. Venus was the goddess of love, lust and beauty.

[40] Nero "Fiddled as Rome Burned." Suetonius recounts the legend how Nero, while watching Rome burn, exclaimed how beautiful it was, and sang an epic poem about the sack of Troy while playing the lyre. — [The Twelve Letters, Suetonius]

[41] The War Begins. (66 CE) Greek Sacrifice at Synagogue of Caesarea:

'Now at this time it happened that the Greeks of Caesarea had obtained from Nero the government of the city, and had brought back with them the text of the decision: and now began the war, in the twelfth year of the reign of Nero, and the seventeenth of the reign of Agrippa, in the month of Artemisins [Iyar, April/May.] The Hellenes hindered the access to a synagogue in Caesarea by building shops in front of it and once, during the Sabbath services, sacrificed a bird near the entrance of the synagogue'. — [Josephus War 2.14.4-6; Josephus, War 2.14, 4-5]

[42] Rights Annulled at Caesarea. The first emperor, Julius Caesar, granted rights to Jewish communities because their ancestral laws predated Rome. Jews had legal privileges as collegia (defined by Roman law as religious & legal entities), giving them the right to assemble, have common meals and property, govern and tax them, and enforce their own discipline. Nero annulled these rights. — [Josephus; Antiquities. A 20.8.9]

[43] HORNED VIPER. — [Pseudocerastes persicus fieldi, Wiki]

[44] Paul's conversion experience is discussed in Paul's Letters and in the book known by the title Acts of the Apostles, N.T.

[45] CALIGULA. Caligula announced his self-deification, ordered that a statue of himself should be placed in the Temple of Jerusalem and the Jews be forced to worship him; and it had not yet been carried out when Caligula was assassinated — [VRoma Org; Jewish Virtual Libr. org/Judaism/revolt.] / Caligula was murdered at the Palatine Games by Cassius Chaerea, tribune of the Praetorian Guard, Cornelius Sabinus, and others. Caligula's wife Caesonia and his daughter were also put to death. He was succeeded as emperor by his uncle Claudius. [Encl. Britannica] / Caligula adorned his horse Incitatus with Jewels and servants and demanded it to be his chief Consul - [Suetonius' Lives of the Twelve Caesars; Dio Cassius]

[46] COLLEGIA. Julius Caesar, upon his accession, vouchsafed to the Jews a writ of tolerance covering the whole empire, which thenceforth constituted the unassailable charter of their privileges. It had only one condition attached to it; namely, that they should content themselves with exercising their own rites without showing contempt for those of others — [Ency. Britannica; Josephus Antiquities 20.8.9; Ant. xix. 5, §§ 2-3] / 'These decrees show clearly that Julius César in his broad and statesmanlike manner fully recognized the rights and claims of the Jews as an important element of the Roman empire. [Caesar, Jewish Encl.]

[47] GOG MAGOG. [Or, "War of Gog and Magog"; Gen 10:2; Eze Ch 36-37]. The Prophet Ezekiel's End of Days vision of many nations attacking Israel; it fosters an exile that will be followed by an eventual ingathering of return. Gog is the grandson of Noah via Japheth; Gog is also seen as a person, place or event symbolically coded for future times.

[48] TAXES. Additional tax levied on Jews [Josephus Antiquities 18.6.2; Fiscus Judaicus].

[49] CALIGULA. Caligula announced his self-deification, ordered that a statue of himself should be placed in the Temple of Jerusalem and the Jews be forced to worship him; and it had not yet been carried out when Caligula was assassinated — [VRoma Org; Jewish Virtual Libr. org/Judaism/revolt.] / Caligula was murdered at the Palatine Games by Cassius Chaerea, tribune of the Praetorian Guard, Cornelius Sabinus, and others. Caligula's wife Caesonia and his daughter were also put to death. He was succeeded as emperor by his uncle Claudius. [Encl. Britannica] / Caligula adorned his horse Incitatus with Jewels and servants and demanded it to be his chief Consul - [Suetonius' Lives of the Twelve Caesars; Dio Cassius]

[50] SEPTUAGINT [Greek; 'Book of the 70'; the first translation of Heb Bible; Wiki]

[51] Nero's Eccentricities continued in his personal perversions in the tradition of his predecessors in mind. According to Suetonius, Nero had one boy named Sporus castrated, and then had sex with him as though he were a woman. Suetonius quotes one Roman who lived around this time who scathingly remarked that 'The world would have been better off if Nero's father Gnaeus Domitius Ahenobarbus had married someone more like the castrated boy'. [Suetonius] / The Emperor Nero killed his mother in three attempts. Nero killed his first wife because he thought she was having an affair [wrongly]; Nero beat his second wife to death when she was pregnant - [Nero, Roman Empire Tours; Emperor Nero's Personality Profile, Miriamilani.]

[52] Nero "Fiddled as Rome Burned." Suetonius recounts the legend how Nero, while watching Rome burn, exclaimed how beautiful it was, and sang an epic poem about the sack of Troy while playing the lyre. — [The Twelve Letters, Suetonius]

[53] COMMAGENE AND EMESA. — ['Auxiliaries had been sent by kingdoms on the Upper Euphrates, Commagene and Emesa; an Arabian sheik, who felt a deep hatred for the Jews, had joined the Romans with his warriors; and many adventurers - veterans Galba and Otho. [Ancient Warfare Magazine]. Vespasian found himself in command of a powerful force, consisting of the fifth, tenth, and fifteenth legions, twenty-three auxiliary cohorts, and six squadrons of horse, in addition to the troops of the native vassals, of the Jewish King Agrippa II., and of the kings of Commagene, Emesa, and Arabia. The entire Roman army mustered at least 60,000 men. Josephus Wars 03; Livius Org]

[54] MIKVAH [Ritual Water Emersion. 'They must purify themselves with the water on the third day and on the seventh day; then they will be clean.' Numbers 19/12.]

[55] MEZUZAH: A case affixed on the doorstep containing a parchment inscribed with its mandated verses in the Hebrew bible [Duet. 6:4; 11:13].

[56] CONCUBINE: "Anyone can keep a concubine of any age unless she is less than twelve years old." — [Lefkowitz & Fant, Women's Life in Greece, John Hopkins Uni Press]

[57] The removal of rights of Jews in Caesarea; The pollution of the synagogue of Caesarea. [Josephus, Ant. 18.1.6 23" indicates Book 18, Chapter 1, Paragraph 6 in Whiston, and in the Loeb edition, Book 18, Section 23

[58] SABRA FRUIT [Opuntia, Wiki]

[59] Josephus writes: "In 66 C.E., a priest named Eleazar, incensed at Roman high-handedness, led a movement to stop offering the customary temple sacrifices on behalf of the emperor. Then in the summer of 66 CE, a very bold young man who was Captain of the Temple — Eleazar, son of the high-priest Hananiah — moved that no gift or sacrifice was to be permitted during the service of worship. And this set the foundation for the war with Rome. For, on this pretext, even the sacrifice for Nero was eliminated. Hence it came about that the war was so long protracted and the Jews drained the cup of irretrievable disaster. — [Josephus, Antiquities 20.409]

[60] SICARII DAGGER [From the Latin word sica, "curved, serrated dagger"; short daggers; (mikra ziphidia), concealed in their clothing. — [Josephus, Wars, 2:254-5; Ant., 20:186-7]

[61] FLAVIAN PROPAGANDA.

Vespasian gave financial rewards to ancient writers. The ancient historians of the period such as Tacitus, Suetonius, Josephus and Pliny the Elder speak suspiciously well of Vespasian while condemning the emperors that came before him. Tacitus admits that his status was elevated by Vespasian, Josephus identifies Vespasian as a patron and savior, and Pliny dedicated his Natural Histories to Vespasian, Titus. Those that spoke against Vespasian were punished. A number of stoic philosophers were accused of corrupting students with inappropriate teachings and were expelled from Rome. Helvidius Priscus [70-79 AD/CE], a pro-republic philosopher, was executed for his teachings. — [Suetonius, The Lives of Twelve Caesars, Life of Vespasian; Tacitus, Histories I.1; Pliny the Elder, Natural Histories, preface]

[62] Bribery. The leaders of the Syrians in Caesarea, by offering a large bribe, prevailed on Beryllus, who was Nero's tutor …to apply for a letter from Nero annulling the grant of equal civic rights to the Jews. This letter provided the basis that led to the subsequent miseries that befell our nation. For the Jewish inhabitants of Caesarea, when they learned of Nero's letter, carried their quarrel with the Syrians further and further until at last they kindled the flames of war. — [Josephus War 6.5.4]

[63] ALEXANDER THE GREAT. He is mentioned by name in the Apocryphal I Macc. — [i. 1-8, vi. 2]. The only historical event connecting Alexander the Great with the Jews is his visit to Jerusalem, which is recorded by Josephus in a somewhat fantastic manner. The Jews responded to Alexander's generosity by naming their first sons after him. Alexander was a student of Aristotle and would have shared Aristotle's belief in God — [Josephus Ant. xi. 8, 4-6].

[64] Thakeray. "Its Chief Value lies in the fact that it is a version of a Hebrew text earlier by about a millennium than the earliest dated Hebrew manuscript extant. It is, moreover, a pioneering work; there was probably no precedent in the world's history for a series of translations from one language into another on so extensive a scale. It was the first attempt to reproduce the Hebrew Scriptures in another tongue. It is one of the outstanding results of the breaking-down of international barriers by the conquests of Alexander the

Great and the dissemination of the Greek language, which were fraught with such vital consequences for the history of religion". - H. St. J. Thakeray; The Int. Standard Bible Encycl.]

[65] Herodotus. In the 5th Century BCE the Greek writer Herodotus in The Histories used the name "Palaistinê" as applying to a part of Syria. The descriptions referred to a foreign people, not of any Arabian group; there were no people at this time by this name. Following the Roman conquest of Greece, the Roman writers also applied the same names used by the conquered Greeks, including Tibuullus, Pomponius Mela, Pliney the Elder, Philo of Alexander and Josephus; significantly, the Jewish writers Philo and Josephus could only have referred to the Jewish kingdom and the Jews by the use of this name in the First Century, mentioning those who were circumsized and followed the Sabbatical law. [Pliny, Natural History, Bk.V, 66-68].

[66] Encyclopaedia Britannica continues regarding Hebrew as the origin of today's alphabets. — [How was the Bible Written, Origins of the Bible]; Archaeology has clearly demonstrated the existence of a written alphabetic communication dating to the time of Abraham, and an even earlier cuneiform method. See more in Index section.

[67] ALEXANDER THE GREAT. He is mentioned by name in the Apocryphal I Macc. — [i. 1-8, vi. 2]. The only historical event connecting Alexander the Great with the Jews is his visit to Jerusalem, which is recorded by Josephus in a somewhat fantastic manner. The Jews responded to Alexander's generosity by naming their first sons after him. Alexander was a student of Aristotle and would have shared Aristotle's belief in God — [Josephus Ant. xi. 8, 4-6].

[68] PTOLEMY REQUEST TO JEWS FOR TRANSLATION — [Tractate Megillah, pages 9a-9b.]

[69] ARISTOTLE. [In 200 B.C.E, the Jewish philosopher Aristobulus made the positive assertion that Jewish revelation ['In the Beginning God'] and Aristotelian philosophy ['God as A First Cause'] were identical. Jewish Encl.; Josephus "AGAINST APION/ contra Apionem," ii. 17]; Maimonades, The Jewish Religion: A Companion, Oxford University Press]. Aristotle's Physics and Metaphysics [Joe Sachs, "The Being of Sensible Things; Metaphysics Internet, Ency.of Philosophy]

[70] VESPASIAN'S DISCOURSE WITH PRISCUS. (A REPUBLICAN WHO OPPOSED ROMANISM AND WAS EXECUTED FOR HIS ANTI-EMPEROR STAND): Vespasian: I command that you not go into the senate and speak. Priscus: It is in your power not to allow me to be a member of the senate, but so long as I am, I must go in. Vespasian: Well, go in then, but say nothing. Priscus: Then do not ask my opinion, and I will be silent. Vespasian: But I must ask your opinion. Priscus: And I must say what I think right. Vespasian: But if you do, I shall put you to death. Priscus: When then did I tell you that I am immortal? You will do your part, and I will do mine: it is your part to kill; it is mine to die, but not in fear: yours to banish me; mine to depart without sorrow. - (Epictetus, Discourses, 1.2.19-21)

[71] "Vespasian Deposited The Law…" (nomos), a Torah scroll he studied, and the purple hangings of the sanctuary of the Temple he kept in his Palace. — [Financing the Coliseum, Louis H. Feldman]

[72] [Josephus War 6.5.4]

[73] The Ark construction was commanded in the camps of Sinai [Exodus 25: 22; 37:1-9] and contained the original tablets of The Ten Commandments. The Ark was built by Bezalel, son of Uri, son of Hur. — [Ark of the Covenant, Jewish Virtual Libr.]

[74] 'It is astonishing that the Aramaic assumption - at least as it pertains to the language of first century Judaea, still persists.' — [Brent Minge, Author of "Jesus Spoke Hebrew - Busting The Aramaic Myth; sharesong]. / 'Aramaic was considered Foreign by Ancient Hebrews. Classified as Archaic Biblical Hebrew,

in about the year 300 BCE, Aramaic makes its appearance in Jewish literature. Hebrew remained the dominant tongue. — [Deborah Miller, De Anza College.] More in Index Section.

[75] * William Foxwell Albright. In 1943, he stated that "the Gezer Calendar, dated 10 Century BCE, is written in perfect classical Hebrew." — [Oldest Hebrew Script and Language; The Biblical Archaeology Society] / * Oldest Hebrew Script. Old Hebrew script did not split off from its Phoenician predecessor until the ninth century B.C.E. The Hebrew language existed well before then; the oldest extant Hebrew language texts are recorded in Phoenician script. - [Christopher Rollston, The Oldest Hebrew Script and Language, Biblical Archaeological Society.] * Archaeology has clearly demonstrated the existence of a written alphabetic communication dating to the time of Abraham, and an even earlier cuneiform method. There are several theories about the development of alphabets. The early Hebrew Alphabet is nearly identical with the Phoenician Alphabet, which is dated as early as the time of Joseph.

[76] The Book of Acts records Paul of Tarsus appeared before the court at Caesarea [Berenice, daughter of Herod Agrippa

[77] Because of Aristotle, Alexander was positively disposed toward the Jews. Instead of destroying and subjugating them, he made an arrangement with them. As long as they would be his loyal vassals and pay their taxes they could remain autonomous. That an enormous concession to anyone. Out of gratitude, the Jews did a few things. First, they agreed to name every child born the next year as "Alexander". That is why the name Alexander, or sender for short, became a common Jewish name even to history to this day. - Jewish History Org.

[78] The Talmud relates that the Rashbi said of the Romans, "Everything they built, they built for themselves: They built market places in order to place prostitutes there; bathhouses, in order to refresh themselves; bridges, in order to collect taxes." Rashbi was forced into hiding in a cave for 12 years after the Roman Empire heard of his statement and issued a death warrant against him.

[79] MIKVAH Ritual Water Emersion. Hebrew law: 'They must purify themselves with the water on the third day and on the seventh day; then they will be clean.' Numbers 19/12.]

[80] HEBREW CALENDAR. The oldest active calendar, accounting its initiation from the Birthday of Adam and spans over 5,700 years.

[81] DATHAN [Book of Numbers 16:31] And KORACH [Num. 16:1 - 18:32] These were two Israelites who stood in opposition of Moses.

[82] [King David Psalm 144; Heb Bible; N.T.]

[83] (Gratz, "Gesch." Iv.403 et seq., 702; Jewish Encyl.)

[84] An important Jewish sage in the era of the Second Temple, and a primary contributor to the core text of Rabbinical Judaism, the Mishnah. He is widely regarded as one of the most important Jewish figures of his time. His tomb is located in Tiberias [Wiki; Jewish Encl.]

[85] FLAVIAN PROPAGANDA.

Vespasian gave financial rewards to ancient writers. The ancient historians of the period such as Tacitus, Suetonius, Josephus and Pliny the Elder speak suspiciously well of Vespasian while condemning the emperors that came before him. Tacitus admits that his status was elevated by Vespasian, Josephus identifies Vespasian as a patron and savior, and Pliny dedicated his Natural Histories to Vespasian, Titus. Those that spoke against Vespasian were punished. A number of stoic philosophers were accused of corrupting students with inappropriate teachings and were expelled from Rome. Helvidius Priscus [70-79 AD/CE], a pro-republic philosopher, was executed for his teachings. — [Suetonius, The Lives of Twelve Caesars, Life of Vespasian; Tacitus, Histories I.1; Pliny the Elder, Natural Histories, preface] Vespasian approved the histories written under his reign, thus ensuring biases against him were removed. — Josephus, Against Apion 9.

[86] VESPASIAN'S DISCOURSE WITH PRISCUS. (A REPUBLICAN WHO OPPOSED ROMANISM AND WAS EXECUTED FOR HIS ANTI-EMPEROR STAND):

Vespasian: I command that you not go into the senate and speak.
Priscus: It is in your power not to allow me to be a member of the senate, but so long as I am, I must go in.
Vespasian: Well, go in then, but say nothing.
Priscus: Then do not ask my opinion, and I will be silent.
Vespasian: But I must ask your opinion.
Priscus: And I must say what I think right.
Vespasian: But if you do, I shall put you to death.
Priscus: When then did I tell you that I am immortal? You will do your part, and I will do mine: it is your part to kill; it is mine to die, but not in fear: yours to banish me; mine to depart without sorrow.
— [Epictetus, Discourses, 1.2.19-21]. /

Helvidius Priscus was put to death after he had repeatedly affronted the Emperor by studied insults which Vespasian had initially tried to ignore. "I will not kill a dog that barks at me" were his words on discovering Priscus's public slander. — [Vespasian, NNDB]

[87] "Love Yea Therefore the Stranger" [Duet. 10:19].

[88] FLORUS [Josephus, War 2.14, 4-5].

[89] QUEEN BERNICE — [Julia Berenice, 39 BC and 92 AD; Acts.Ch.25; Jewish Women's Archive; Wiki]

[90] "ALL ROADS LEAD TO ROME" The expression is generally attributed to Alain de Lille, a French theologian and poet; 1175 AD/CE.

[91] The N.T. does not tell us the exact time or manner of the apostle Paul's death, and secular history has yet to provide us with any definitive information. However, evidence highly suggests the apostle Paul's death occurred likely beheaded by the Romans, probably by Nero's orders.

[92] GIDEON ['Mighty Warrior'; Son of Joash, Tribe of Mennasah. Book of Judges 6-8]

[93] ['And Ruth said: 'Entreat me not to leave thee, and to return from following after thee; for whither thou goest, I will go; and where thou lodgest, I will lodge; thy people shall be my people, and thy God my God; where thou diest, will I die, and there will I be buried; the LORD do so to me, and more also, if aught but death part thee and me.' [Book of Ruth 1:16]

[94] "Where the penitent stand, even the most righteous can't stand" - [Berachos 34b]

[95] "Love Yea Therefore the Stranger" [Duet. 10:19].

[96] REBECCA (RIVKA). "And they said, we will call the damsel, and enquire at her mouth." It is the earliest known woman's marriage right prerogative. [Gen. 24:57]

[97] The date of Zoroaster, i.e., the date of composition of the Old Avestan gathas, is unknown. Classical writers such as Plutarch and Diogenes proposed dates of 358 years before Alexander, namely to 600 BCE. Nigosian, Solomon (1993),The Zoroastrian Faith, tradition, modern research. McGill-Queen's University Press, p. 15,)

[98] The Amarna Letters. Letters from the Babylonian king, Kadashman-Enlil I, anchor in the time-frame of Akhenaten's reign to the mid-14th century BC. Here was also found the first mention of a Near Eastern group known as the Habiru, alluding to the battles waged by the Hebrews under Joshua: "They have seized the land of Rubute, the land of the king has fallen away to the Habiru..." (Language: Akkadian Cuneiform; Clay Tablets). # See more in Index "The Amarna Stele".

[99] ABRAHAM'S FATHER TERAH'S IDOL SHOP IN UR. [Theological/Metaphorical. A Medrash based legend on the 1st. Century sage R. Hiyya's commentary of Genesis 11:28 and Genesis 15.7]

[100] ABRAHAM'S FATHER TERAH'S IDOL SHOP IN UR. [Theological/Metaphorical. A Medrash based legend on the 1st. Century sage R. Hiyya's commentary of Genesis 11:28 and Genesis 15.7]

[101] Temple High Priest Blessing: 'The LORD bless thee, and keep thee; The LORD make His face to shine upon thee, and be gracious unto thee;' [Num. 6:24]

[102] Jerusalem - Origins of Name. - [Kaplan, Arye (1996). "Beginnings". Jerusalem, the Eye of the Universe. New York: Mesorah, pp:11-14] Held Traditions/Legend/Metaphoric.

[103] TEMPLE LOCATION. Mount Moriah is the name of the elongated north-south stretch of land lying between The Kidron Valley and the "Hagai" Valley, between Mount Zion to the west and the Mount of Olives to the east. — [Jewish Virtual Libr.]

[104] TEMPLE LOCATION. Why Mount Moriah: 'Then Solomon began to build the house of the LORD at Jerusalem in Mount Moriah, where [the LORD] appeared unto David his father; for which provision had been made in the place of David, in the threshing floor of Ornan the Jebusite'. — [2 Chronicles Chapter 3/Theological]

[105] FLAVIAN PROPAGANDA.

Vespasian gave financial rewards to ancient writers. The ancient historians of the period such as Tacitus, Suetonius, Josephus and Pliny the Elder speak suspiciously well of Vespasian while condemning the emperors that came before him. Tacitus admits that his status was elevated by Vespasian, Josephus identifies Vespasian as a patron and savior, and Pliny dedicated his Natural Histories to Titus. Those that spoke against Vespasian were punished. A number of stoic philosophers were accused of corrupting students with inappropriate teachings and were expelled from Rome. Helvidius Priscus [70-79 AD/CE], a pro-republic philosopher, was executed for his teachings. — [Suetonius, The Lives of Twelve Caesars, Life of Vespasian; Tacitus, Histories I.1; Pliny the Elder, Natural Histories, preface]

[106] TEMPLE SIZES - FORTRESS OF JERUSALEM. [LARGEST MONUMENT: 'List of largest monoliths in the world'- Wiki; SIZES: Josephus Ant, XV, xi, 3, 5; BJ, V, v.; Antiquities 8, 95-98; War V, 220-221; War 5] The City of David: Jesus' Jerusalem | History Documentary; Tacitus (59)]; 450 ACRES;

CIRCUMFERENCE = 33 FURLONGS [Josephus war 5.5.2, 192]. "It was a structure more noteworthy than any under the sun' - Josephus.] BRICK SIZES. The Temple Mount was originally intended to be 1600 feet wide by 900 feet broad by 110 high, with walls up to 16 feet thick. To complete it, a trench was dug around the mountain, and huge stone "bricks" were laid. Some of these weighed well over 100 tons, the largest measuring 44.6 feet by 11 feet by 16.5 feet and weighing approximately 567 to 628 tons. - [Dan Bahat: Touching the Stones of our Heritage, Israeli ministry of Religious Affairs, 2002]

[107] ROMAN WAR RULES. [Death Penalty for leaving war positions - Josephus War 5/4]

[108] THE COPPER SCROLL. A scroll in Josephus' possession, adapted from similar scrolls in the Dead Sea Scrolls package. / Unlike the others, it is not a literary work, but a list of locations at which various items of gold and silver are buried or hidden. The text is an inventory of 64 locations; 63 of which are treasures of gold and silver, which have been estimated in the tons. — [Copper Scroll, Wiki]

[109] Josephus Ch.4/21

[110] * "Whatever Sarah tells you to do - do it" [Gen. 21/12].

[111] MENORAH LOCATION: Josephus claims it was taken to Rome as war spoils and deposited in the Roman Temple of Peace [Jewish War, 7.148].

[112] * MOSES THE LAW GIVER. Moses is introduced in Exodus 2.1: 'And there went a man of the house of Levi' - the verse follows as a response to the earliest recording of genocide of the Egyptian Pharaoh's decree to kill all Hebrew male first born babies. Moses became known as The Law Giver and is recorded as one who stood 'Presence to Presence' before God. The laws delivered by Moses remain ever active, almost exclusively dominating the institutions of the Judiciary; Family Law; Animal Rights Laws; Women's Rights Laws: Right of Refusal or Acceptance of Marriage/ Rebecca [Gen.24.57 & 58: "And they said: 'We will call the damsel and inquire at her mouth. 'And they called Rebecca, and said unto her: 'Wilt thou go with this man?' And she said: 'I will go.'']; Woman's Property Inheriting Rights/ The Daughters of Zelophehad [Num 27:3]; Separation of State and Ruler/King [2 Samuel 12]; Monotheism and Creationism. Moses became the most revered figure in human history by period of time, impact and by worldly census accounting: 14 M Jews; 1.2 B Muslims; 2.2 B Christians.

[113] The Greek King Antiochus IV Epiphanies, declaring himself as "God Manifest" was a Greek king of the Seleucid Empire. He sent an Athenian senator to force the Jews to abandon the customs of their ancestors and to live no longer by the laws of their God. — [2 Maccabees 6:1-11] / Antiochus decided to outlaw Mosaic Holy Days, Sabbaths, circumcision and traditions kept by observant Jews and by ordering the worship of Zeus as the supreme god — [2 Maccabees 6:1-12]. / This was anathema to the faithful Mosaic Pharisees and when they refused, Antiochus sent an army to enforce his decree. — [Hellenism and the Birth of Modern Rabbinic Judaism; The Shining Light].

[114] "Titus was appointed by his father to complete the subjugation of Judaea…he commanded three legions in Judaea itself…To these he added the twelfth from Syria and the third and twenty-second from Alexandria…amongst his allies were a band of Arabs, formidable in themselves and harboring towards the Jews the bitter animosity usually subsisting between neighboring nations." - Vol. II, Book V, The Works of Tacitus

[115] ROMAN SWORD OF FIRE [Josephus Jewish War, 6.289; Tacitus Annals, 15:47]

[116] MYSTERIOUS JOURNEY OF A FIREBRAND 'One of the towers erected by the Romans fell down of its own accord; and how the Romans after great slaughter had been made got possession of the first wall' — [WARS BOOK 5/CHAPTER 7.]

[117] THE PROMISED LAND. Biblical Limits & Conditions, commanding Jews not to take any other lands outside of the Mosaic boundaries. [Duet. 2/4 & 2/9]: 'And command thou the people, saying: Ye are to pass through the border of your brethren the children of Esau, that dwell in Seir; and they will be afraid of you; take ye good heed unto yourselves therefore; contend not with them; for I will not give you of their land, no, not so much as for the sole of the foot to tread on; because I have given mount Seir unto Esau for a possession. And the LORD said unto me: 'Be not at enmity with Moab, neither contend with them in battle; for I will not give thee of his land for a possession'.

[118] ESTHER. [Heb name 'Hadassah'; Exilic orphan who rose to Queen of Persian King Ahaseuros, Savior of Israeli nation, Heb Prophetess celebrated in festival of Purim. Book of Esther]

[119] MACABEES AND ANTIOCH IV. — [2 Maccabees 5:11-14; 6:1-11]

[120] "ANO CHI" ["I Am" - The opening two words of The Ten Commandments; Exodus 34:28; Duet 1-:4]

[121] "Thou preparest a table before me in the presence of mine enemies." [Psalms 23:5]

[122] * Psalms. "Yea, though I walk through the valley of the shadow of death, I will fear no evil, for Thou art with me." [23:4]

[123] Psalm 27:4

[124] THE COPPER SCROLL. A scroll in Josephus' possession, adapted from similar scrolls in the Dead Sea Scrolls package. / Unlike the others, it is not a literary work, but a list of locations at which various items of gold and silver are buried or hidden. The text is an inventory of 64 locations; 63 of which are treasures of gold and silver, which have been estimated in the tons. — [Copper Scroll, Wiki]

[125] MUREX SNAIL. Murex snails were cultivated in ancient times at sites along the Mediterranean Sea, and a royal blue dye was extracted from them. This blue color was used for the priestly garments, as well as the tzitzit or threaded tassels worn by all pious Jews of the period on the corners of their garments. — [Numbers 15:38-15:39]

[126] Josephus relates that Berenice sacrificed at Jerusalem with disheveled hair and bare feet.

[127] Joseph describes Berenice as a profligate, yet a heroine in the final war.

[128] Titus found the Holy of Holies empty - Tacitus [32]; Cas Dio 33; Josephus]

[129] "Titus was appointed by his father to complete the subjugation of Judaea…he commanded three legions in Judaea itself…To these he added the twelfth from Syria and the third and twenty-second from Alexandria…amongst his allies were a band of Arabs, formidable in themselves and harboring towards the Jews the bitter animosity usually subsisting between neighboring nations." - Vol. II, Book V, The Works of Tacitus

[130] SCAVENGERS; BARBARIC [Titus charges Arabian and Roman soldiers as barbarians when corpses are disemboweled for gold - Josephus Wars, Book V, Ch 13, 4]

[131] REMNANT WAILING WALL LEFT BY TITUS:

The Bene Mosheh began their letter by regretting that in their isolation they were separated forever from their coreligionists in the holy land of Palestine, and that only the western wall of the Temple remained, from which the Shekinah had not yet departed. - "If I forget thee o Jerusalem", Jewish Virtual Libr.

[132] The Temple tax was diverted by Vespasian, after the destruction of the sanctuary in 70 C.E., to the temple of Jupiter Capitolinus at Rome, the amount being two drachmas (Josephus, "B. J." vii. 6, § 6; Dion Cassius, lxvi. 7).

[133] Titus and Berenice lived on the Palatine Hill; and it was generally supposed that he would soon marry her (Suetonius, "Titus," vii.). So jealous of her was Titus that he caused the Roman general Cæcina, whom he suspected of a secret intrigue with Berenice, to be assassinated (Aurelius Victor, "Epitome," x. 7).

[134] GNAT - TITUS DEATH. ['Titus' Death' - Chabad Org; Jewish Ency. Traditional/Legendary]

[135] NASSERITE (Nazarene) - (Hebrew Bible, Numbers 6:5; "The Messiah Syndrome")

[136] Hadrian. The Name Palestine was applied to Judea by the Roman Emperor Hadrian in 135 CE, namely in the Second century; there was no country called Palestine in the First Century. Not satisfied with the destruction of Jerusalem, it's Temple and an Exile, the Roman Emperor's intention was to abolish all reference of Judaism and Christianity, namely the monotheist belief. / "In an effort to wipe out all memory of the bond between the Jews and the land, Hadrian changed the name of the province from Iudaea ['Judea'] to Syria-Palestina, a name that became common in non-Jewish literature." — [H.H. Ben-Sasson, A History of the Jewish People, Harvard University Press, page 334]. # See more in "Palestine", Index section.

[137] Samson battled with the Philistines [Judges Ch. 13]. King David finally defeated the Philistines who were absorbed into the Ten Tribes of Israel and were recruited as soldiers in David's army. [1 Chronicals 14:8:]. # See also "Philistine-to-Palestine"/Epilogue.

[138] * "Palestine of today, the land we now know as Palestine was peopled by the Jews from the dawn of history until the Roman era. It is the ancestral homeland of the Jewish people. They were driven from it by force by the relentless Roman military machine and for centuries prevented from returning. [U.S. Congressional Records 1922 House of Representatives House Resolution 360 unanimously adopted]. * Judea for the Jews. The land was mainly inhabited by Jews. Therefore, Lord Robert Cecil, acting British Foreign Secretary, was right to use the name Judea for the whole land of Palestine in his famous remark of Dec 2, 1917: "Our wish is that Arabian countries will be for the Arabs, Armenia for the Armenians, and Judea for the Jews" — ["The name Rome gave to the land of Israel", Elliot A. Green, Focus On Jerusalem] See more in "Philistine-to-Palestine"/Epilogue.

[139] Priest Martyrs. Condemned to Death for the Law's Sake. [Jewish Ency., Ab. Zarah 17b et seq; Wiki] / "They have never been guilty of false faith. In fact, before the church existed, they believed in the one true God" - [H. Kung, 'The Church'; Jewish Virtual Libr.]

[140] "They have never been guilty of false faith. In fact, before the church existed, they believed in the one true God" - [H. Kung, 'The Church'; Jewish Virtual Libr.]

[141] Louis Jacobs (1995).The Jewish Religion: a companion. Oxford University Press. p. 375.

[142] page 1, Blenkinsopp, Joseph (1992). The Pentateuch: An introduction to the first five books of the Bible. New York: Doubleday.

[143] FIRST HISTORICAL EVIDENCE OF KING DAVID.

Few Biblical archaeology discoveries have attracted as much attention as the Tel Dan Stele-the ninth-century B.C. inscription that furnished the first historical evidence of King David outside the Bible. — [Biblicalarchaeology.org/biblical-artifacts/the-tel-dan-inscription.]

[144] The Merneptah Stele - also known as The Israel Stele, is an inscription by the Ancient Egyptian King Merneptah (reign: 1213 to 1203 BC). The writing provides the first evidence of the Hebrew tribes as active in the land and their interaction with the Pharaoh of Egypt and his armies engaged in a war. The last lines deal with a separate campaign in Canaan, then part of Egypt's imperial possessions, and include the first documented instance of the name Israel; Askelon, Urusalem; Canaan & Gaza: "Israel is laid waste and his seed is not.." — [Discovered by Flinders Petriein in 1896 at Thebes; Housed at Egyptian Museum in Cairo/Merneptah Stele; Bible History/Archaeology/Israel/el-amarna-letters / [Language: Ancient Egyptian hieroglyphs]. See more in Index/Archaeology.

[145] Paleo-Hebrew alphabet; Wiki

[146] The Gezer Calendar is a small limestone tablet listing seasonal agricultural activities in seven lines of uneven letters; it dates back to the 10th century BCE at the beginning of the reign of David and Solomon. — [Hebrew Language, Wiki]. See more in Index/Archaelogy.

[147] Most specialists believe that the Phoenician alphabet was adopted for Greek during the early 8th century BC, perhaps in Euboea. - [The date of the earliest inscribed objects; A.W. Johnston, "The alphabet", in N. Stampolidis and V. Karageorghis, eds, Sea Routes from Sidon to Huelva: Interconnections in the Mediterranean 2003:263-76, summarizes the present scholarship on the dating.] / The earliest known fragmentary Greek inscriptions date from this time, 770-750 BC, and they match Phoenician letter forms of c. 800-750 BC [Pierre Swiggers, Transmission of the Phoenician Script to the West, in Daniels and Bright, The World's Writing Systems, 1996]

[148] Woodford, S. (1986). An Introduction to Greek Art. London: Duckworth, p. 12)

[149] Historical Deception. It is truly amazing to think that, in the academic world of the past 150 years, the almost contradictory term of "Phoenician alphabet" has been established, which, in reality refers to a type of writing that has nothing to do with an alphabet. It is even more unbelievable to think that the scientific dogma that Greek came from Phoenician has been enforced. [Phoenician "Alphabet": An Historical Deception Republished from the Athenian newspaper Apogevmatini, 21 November 1999 (pages 42-43).

[150] The date remains the subject of controversy, according to Glenn E. Markoe: 'The Phoenician script, a West Semitic consonantal syllabary, which was probably developed in ca. 1000 BC.[The Origin of Writing (Illinois: Open Court Publishing Company, 1986) ; Glenn E. Markoe, Bulletin of the American Schools of Oriental Research [No. 279 August 1990,13-26). p. 13; Wiki]

[151] (History of the Aleph-Bet; Jewish Virtual Libr.)

[152] The manuscripts have been dated to various ranges between 408 BCE to 318 CE. - (Doudna, Greg, "Dating the Scrolls on the Basis of Radiocarbon Analysis", in The Dead Sea Scrolls after Fifty Years, edited by Flint Peter W., and VanderKam, James C., Vol.1 (Leiden: Brill, 1998) 430-471; Wiki)

[153] N.T: Aramaic is nowhere mentioned in the New Testament; Paul spoke to the Jews in Hebrew — [Acts 21:40; 22:2]; Jesus spoke to Paul in Hebrew; the banner on Jesus' Cross was in Hebrew — [Acts 26:14]. / "Jesus was born a Jew, on Jewish soil. He was brought up in a Jewish family, taught from the

Hebrew Bible, and his followers consisted entirely of Jewish people. He knew not Greek, Egyptian, Roman, or Persian. He spoke only Hebrew and the everyday language of the day…Aramaic. He was a Jew preaching to Jews." - [Sandra Williams; Judaic Studies Program, University of Central Florida]. # See more in Index/Hebrew, Not Aramaic.

[154] THE FLAT EARTH. During the early Middle-Ages, virtually all scholars maintained the spherical viewpoint first expressed by the Ancient Greeks. From at least the 14th century, belief in a Flat Earth among the educated was almost nonexistent, despite fanciful depictions in art, such as the exterior of Hieronymus Bosch's famous triptych The Garden of Earthly of Earthly, in which a disc-shaped Earth is shown floating inside a transparent sphere. — [Myth of the Flat Earth, Wiki].

[155] "Greek Writers have proposed the Hebrew as the inventors of the alphabet / The early Hebrew alphabet, the Paleo-Hebrew alphabet could have been the source behind the Phoenician alphabet; since many agree that the Proto-Canaanite alphabet preceded the Phoenician, which was the source behind the Greek alphabet which is the source behind the alphabets in the Western world. / From the time of the Exodus, Moses in all likelihood recorded the Torah, in the Paleo-Hebrew script; this script was nearly identical with the Early Phoenician script." — [Truthnet Org. Origins of the Bible, 4. How was the Bible written?]. See more in Index Section #163.

[156] Encyclopaedia Britannica continues regarding Hebrew as the origin of today's alphabets. — [How was the Bible Written, Origins of the Bible] /* Oldest Hebrew Script. Old Hebrew script did not split off from its Phoenician predecessor until the ninth century B.C.E. The Hebrew language existed well before then; the oldest extant Hebrew language texts are recorded in Phoenician script. - [Christopher Rollston, The Oldest Hebrew Script and Language, Biblical Archaeological Society.] # See more in Index/Alphabetical Writing.

[157] / Most specialists believe that the Phoenician alphabet was adopted for Greek during the early 8th century BC, perhaps in Euboea. - [The date of the earliest inscribed objects; A.W. Johnston, "The alphabet", in N. Stampolidis and V. Karageorghis, eds, Sea Routes from Sidon to Huelva: Interconnections in the Mediterranean 2003:263-76, summarizes the present scholarship on the dating.] / The earliest known fragmentary Greek inscriptions date from this time, 770-750 BC, and they match Phoenician letter forms of c. 800-750 BC [Pierre Swiggers, Transmission of the Phoenician Script to the West, in Daniels and Bright, The World's Writing Systems, 1996]. # See more in Index/Alphabetical Writing. # See more in Index/Alphabetical Writing.

[158] The DDS manuscripts have been dated to various ranges between 408 BCE and 318 CE. Bronze coins found on the site form a series beginning with John Hyrcanus (135-104 BCE) and continuing until the First Jewish-Roman War (66-73 CE). — [Dead Sea Scrolls, Wiki]

[159] The Gilgamesh flood myth is a flood myth in the Epic of Gilgamesh. Many scholars believe that the flood myth was added to Tablet XI in the "standard version" of the Gilgamesh Epic by an editor who utilized the flood story from the Epic of Atrahasis (Tigay 1982; Wiki)

[160] King David. An inscription dating from the 10th century BCE (the period of King David's reign) has been deciphered, showing that it is a Hebrew inscription. The discovery makes this the earliest known Hebrew writing, according to one scholar. Professor Gershon Galil of the Department of Biblical Studies at the University of Haifa has deciphered an inscription on a pottery shard discovered in the Elah valley dating from the 10th century BCE (the period of King David's reign), and has shown that this is a Hebrew inscription. The discovery makes this the earliest known Hebrew writing. It indicates that the Kingdom of Israel already existed in the 10th century BCE and that at least some of the biblical texts were written hundreds of years before the dates presented in current research."- ["Most ancient Hebrew biblical inscription deciphered"; ScienceDaily.]

[161] "The early Hebrew alphabet, the Paleo-Hebrew alphabet could have been the source behind the Phoenician alphabet; since many agree that the Proto-Canaanite alphabet preceded the Phoenician, which was the source behind the Greek alphabet which is the source behind the alphabets in the Western world. / From the time of the Exodus, Moses in all likelihood recorded the Torah, in the Paleo-Hebrew script; this script was nearly identical with the Early Phoenician script. - (Truthnet Org. Origins of the Bible, 4. How was the Bible written?)

[162] Oral Transmission. 'First we must dismiss the theory of oral transmission as the source of Genesis. It is utter nonsense to expect that a pure document could be transferred from one generation to another for hundreds of years. Even Middle Easterners, with their prodigious memories could not do it. Concentration on the role of oral tradition has led scholars to underestimate the role of written records. We will give some evidences that the Pentateuch in its entirety was written from the beginning' — [Hebrew Was First and Is the Oldest Language in Continuous Use by Dr. David Livingston]

[163] Animal Rights [40 Hebrew Bible Laws]

1. Not to stand by idly when a human life is in danger (If an animal attacks; or someone ill treats an animal) (Lev. 19:16).
2. To relieve a neighbor of his burden and help to unload his beast (Ex. 23:5).
3. To assist in replacing the load upon a neighbor's beast (Deut. 22:4).
4. Not to leave a beast, that has fallen down beneath its burden, unaided [Safe environment] (Deut. 22:4)
5. Not to reap the entire field (To leave dropped produce for the poor and animals) (Lev. 19:9; Lev. 23:22).
6. Not to have intercourse with a beast (Lev. 18:23).
7. Not to castrate the male of any species; neither a man, nor a domestic or wild beast, nor a fowl (Lev. 22:24).
8. Not to eat the flesh of a beast that died of itself (Deut. 14:21).
9. To slay cattle, deer and fowl according to the laws of shechitah if their flesh is to be eaten (Deut. 12:21) ("as I have commanded" in this verse refers to the technique).
10. Not to eat a limb removed from a living beast [Health guidance] (Deut. 12:23).
11. Not to slaughter an animal and its young on the same day (Lev. 22:28).
12. Not to take the mother-bird with the young (Deut. 22:6).
13. To set the mother-bird free when taking the nest (Deut. 22:6-7).
14. Not to boil meat with milk (Ex. 23:19) (Because an animal can identify its kin by its milk).
16. Not to eat flesh with milk (Ex. 34:26)
17. Not to eat blood (Lev. 7:26)
18. To cover the blood of undomesticated animals (deer, etc.) and of fowl that have been killed (Lev. 17:13).
19. To make a parapet for your roof (Deut. 22:8) (Safe environment; Not to leave something that might cause hurt to domesticated animals and fowl.) (Deut. 22:8).
20. Not to cross-breed cattle of different species (Lev. 19:19)
21. Not to work with beasts of different species, yoked together (Deut. 22:10).
22. Not to eat the flesh of unclean beasts (Lev. 11:4).
23. To examine the marks in cattle (so as to distinguish the clean from the unclean) (Lev. 11:2).
24. Not to eat the flesh of unclean beasts (Lev. 11:4).
25. To examine the marks in locusts, so as to distinguish the clean from the unclean (Lev. 11:21).
26. To examine the marks in fishes (so as to distinguish the clean from the unclean (Lev. 11:9).
27. Not to eat unclean fish (Lev. 11:11).
28. To examine the marks in fowl, so as to distinguish the clean from the unclean (Deut. 14:11).

29. Not to eat unclean fowl. (Lev. 11:13).
30. Not to eat a worm found in fruit (Lev. 11:41).
31. Not to eat of things that creep upon the earth (Lev. 11:41-42).
32. Not to eat any vermin of the earth (Lev. 11:44).
33. Not to eat things that swarm in the water [Bacteria; virus impacting] (Lev. 11:43 and 46).
34. Not to eat of winged insects (Deut. 14:19).
35. Not to eat of the thigh-vein which shrank (Gen. 32:33).
36. Not to eat chelev (tallow-fat) (Lev. 7:23).
37. Not to eat or drink like a glutton or a drunkard (Advocating against obesity) (Lev. 19:26; Deut. 21:20).
38. Not to leave something that might cause hurt (Safe animal environment; Eco-systemization) (Deut. 22:8).
39. Not to work with beasts of different species, yoked together (Deut. 22:10).
40. Feed the animal you own before thyself. (Owner has sole onus).

[164] Thomas S. McCall, Th.D. Palestine vs. Israel as the Name of the Holy Land, Zola Levitt Ministries.

[165] The History of the Words "Palestine" and "Palestinians";

Joseph E. Katz, Middle Eastern Political and Religious History Analyst,

Brooklyn, New York.

[166] PHILISTINES. [The Philistines were an aggressive, warmongering people who occupied a part of southwest Canaan between the Mediterranean Sea and the Jordan River. The name "Philistine" comes from the Hebrew word Philistia, and the Greek rendering of the name, palaistinei, gives us the modern name "Palestine." The Philistines are first recorded in Scripture [Gen. 10:14]. It is thought that the Philistines originated in Caphtor, the Hebrew name for the island of Crete and the whole Aegean region; Amos 9:7; Jeremiah 47:4] / For unknown reasons, they migrated from that region to the Mediterranean coast near Gaza. - Got Questions Org./ The Philistines (Hebrew: פְּלִשְׁתִּים, Plištim), Pleshet or Peleset, were a people who as part of the Sea Peoples appeared in the southern coastal area of Canaan at the beginning of the Iron Age (circa 1175 BC), most probably from the Aegean region. [Wiki].

[167] In the New Testament, the term Palestine is never used. The term Israel is primarily used to refer to the people of Israel, rather than the Land. However, in at least two passages, Israel is used to refer to the Land: 'Saying, Arise, and take the young child and his mother, and go into the land of Israel, for they are dead who sought the young child's life. And he arose, and took the young child and his mother, and came into the land of Israel.' [Matt.2:20-21] / 'But when they persecute you in this city, flee ye into another: for verily I say to you, Ye shall not have gone over the cities of Israel, till the Son of man shall have come.' [Matt.10:23] / * Rome. 'Before 135 A.D., the Romans used the terms Judea and Galilee to refer to the Land of Israel. When Titus destroyed Jerusalem in 70 A.D., the Roman government struck a coin with the phrase "Judea Capta," meaning Judea has been captured. The term Palestine was never used in the early Roman designations'; [Namely, not as a replacement of Judea, a name coined by the Romans]. — [Zvi Rivai, Zola Levitt Ministries]

[168] Sheikh Ahmad Adwan, Jordanian Muslim scholar. — [Arutz Sheva; Rachel Avraham, Jerusalem online.]

[169] (US Republican presidential hopeful Newt Gingrich; ITC Interview with Steven Weiss; The Guardian)

[170] SCAVENGERS; BARBARIC [Titus charges Arabian soldiers as barbarians when corpses of Jews are disembowelled for suspected swallowed gold - Josephus Wars, Book V, Ch 13, 4]

[171] U.S. Presidents and Israel; Jewish Virtual Libr.

[172] ['Les sept view de Yasser Arafat', Biography by Christophe Boltanski and Jihan El-Tahri, 1997; Historian Said Aburish; Jewish Virtual Libr.]

[173] JKAP Publications, USA.

[174] "Palestine is the term now used by those who want to deny the legitimate existence of Israel as a genuine nation among the family of nations." — [Dr. Thomas McCall, the Senior Theologian of Levitt Ministry, quoting Zola Levitt]

[175] [Ariel Lewin, The archaeology of Ancient Judea and Palestine. Getty Publications, 2005 p. 33]

[176] - (Concerning the Origin of Peoples; Myths, Hypotheses and Facts)

[177] The Amarna Letters. Letters from the Babylonian king, Kadashman-Enlil I, anchor in the time-frame of Akhenaten's reign to the mid-14th century BC. Here was also found the first mention of a Near Eastern group known as the Habiru, alluding to the battles waged by the Hebrews under Joshua: "They have seized the land of Rubute, the land of the king has fallen away to the Habiru.." [Language: Akkadian Cuneiform; Clay Tablets]

The Merneptah Stele - also known as The Israel Stele, is an inscription by the Ancient Egyptian King Merneptah (reign: 1213 to 1203 BC). The writing provides the first evidence of the Hebrew tribes as active in the land and their interaction with the Pharaoh of Egypt and his armies engaged in a war. The last lines deal with a separate campaign in Canaan, then part of Egypt's imperial possessions, and include the first documented instance of the name Israel; Askelon, Urusalem; Canaan & Gaza: "Israel is laid waste and his seed is not.." — [Discovered by Flinders Petriein in 1896 at Thebes; Housed at Egyptian Museum in Cairo/Merneptah Stele; Bible History/Archaeology/Israel/el-amarna-letters / [Language: Ancient Egyptian hieroglyphs]

"The Mernaptah Stele is powerful evidence of an ancient ethnic group called the Israelites as living in Canaan what today includes Israel and Palestine" - Donald Redford; Penn. State University] / Rameses the Great confirms Hebrew text of this king. 'The stele is a poetic eulogy to pharaoh Merneptah, who ruled Egypt after Rameses the Great, ca. 1212-1202 BC.' - Author: Bryant G. Wood; Associates for Biblical Research; Christian Answers Network. Merneptah was the son of Ramses II. / The words relating to Israel and Hebrew are not accepted as conclusive by some scholars.

[178] Ishmael ben Fabus 15-16 (List of High Priests of Israel; Wiki)

[179] 'Therefore, the equation Arab = Ishmaelite is a myth, because Ishmael was not an Arab, nor the forefather of all Arabs' - (Origin and Identity of the Arabs; Myths, Hypotheses and Facts)

[180] 'Old Arabic seems to have remained a purely spoken language until the late fifth / early sixth centuries CE which means that no specific script was associated with it before that period.' - (Islamic Awareness org) / 'In the 6th and 5th centuries BC, north-Semitic tribes emigrated and founded a kingdom centered around Petra, Jordan. These people (now named Nabataeans from the name of one of the tribes, Naba?), probably spoke a form of Arabic. In the 2nd century CE, the first known records of the Nabataean alphabet were written, in the Aramaic language.' (History of Arabic Alphabet; Wiki)

[181] First Arab Name. "But when Sanballat the Horonite, and Tobiah the servant, the Ammonite, and Geshem the Arab' heard it, they laughed us to scorn, and despised us, and said: 'What is this thing that ye do? Will ye rebel against the king?' Then answered I them, and said unto them: 'The God of heaven, He will prosper us; therefore we His servants will arise and build; but ye have no portion, nor right, nor memorial, in Jerusalem." - [Nehemiah, 2:19; NKJV]. 'Arabian' is also used in King James Bible; many others use the name Arab.

[182] Arab - Earliest Recorded Name. Similarity of the name: "The men on camels, the scribe adds, are brought to the battle by Gindibu the 'Aribi'. This is the first known recorded reference to the Arabs as a distinct group." — ['History of the Arabs', History World; Gindibu, Wiki].

[183] ONE MILLION BIBLICAL & HISTORICAL ARTEFACTS. Israel Relics Collection: National archaeological centre to store and showcase country's rich collection of some two million ancient artefacts, including world's largest collection of Dead Sea Scrolls. [Israel Antiquities Authority, Associated Press, Ynet/0, 7340, L-4500754, 00] / Israel Relics Display: The Israel Antiquities Authorities estimates that there are one million archaeological artefacts on display in Israel at present. - [Israel National News/ aspx/132808]. JORDAN. Other than Israel, no country has as many Biblical sites and associations as Jordan: Mount Nebo, from where Moses gazed at the Promised Land; Bethany beyond the Jordan, where John baptized Jesus; Lot's Cave, where Lot and his daughters sought refuge after the destruction of Sodom and Gomorrah; and many more. — [Biblical Archaeology Org/Biblical-artefacts/inscriptions]

[184] British-based imam Sheikh Muhammad Al-Hussaini; According to Robert Spencer, writing in the Middle East Forum.

[185] "The al-Aqsa Mosque was built on top of Solomon's Temple." - Eleventh century historian Muhammad Ibn Ahmad al-Maqdisi and fourteenth century Iranian religious scholar Hamdallah al-Mustawfi ("Allah Gave the Land of Israel to the Jews", JerusalemOnLine).

[186] EARLIEST KNOWN RELICS CONFIRM BIBLICAL TEXTS. The Amarna Letters; The Merneptah Stele. 3,200 YEAR EGYPTIAN STONE TABLET & 3,400 YEAR OLD LETTERS, CIRCA MOSES AND JOSHUA PERIODS, RECORDS THE FIRST MENTION OF ISRAEL; JERUSALEM; HEBREW; CANAAN; RAMSESY; ASKELON; GAZA. # See more in Index/Archaeology.

[187] 'I will raise them up a prophet from among their brethren, like unto thee; and I will put My words in his mouth, and he shall speak unto them all that I shall command him. - (Duet 18:18)

[188] Vespasian as Messiah; Josephus' Jewish War 6.312-13 / "Alexander as Messiah"; Jewish Encyclopedia.

[190] The Gospels mention that during Tiberius' reign, Jesus of Nazareth preached and was executed by the authority of Pontius Pilate, the Roman governor of Judaea. [Tiberius is mentioned in Luke 3:1]. Tiberius banished the rest of the Jews from Rome and threatened to enslave them for life if they did not leave the city. ['Jews or Christians', Jossa, Giorgio, pp. 123-126] ; sends 1000's of Jews to battlefields over a conversion incident - [Dio Cassius Ivii:18; Tac Ann ii:85]

[191] Caligula announced his self-deification, ordered that a statue of himself should be placed in the Temple of Jerusalem and the Jews be forced to worship him; and it had not yet been carried out when Caligula was assassinated — [VRoma Org; Jewish Virtual Libr. org/Judaism/revolt.] / Caligula was murdered at the Palatine Games by Cassius Chaerea, tribune of the Praetorian Guard, Cornelius Sabinus, and others. Caligula's wife Caesonia and his daughter were also put to death. He was succeeded as emperor by his uncle Claudius. [Encl. Britannica] / Caligula adorned his horse Incitatus with Jewels and servants and demanded it to be his chief Consul - [Suetonius' Lives of the Twelve Caesars; Dio Cassius]

[192] Helvidius Priscus was put to death after he had repeatedly affronted the Emperor by studied insults which Vespasian had initially tried to ignore. "I will not kill a dog that barks at me" were his words on discovering Priscus's public slander. — [Vespasian, NNDB]

[193] "In an effort to wipe out all memory of the bond between the Jews and the land, Hadrian changed the name of the province from Iudaea ['Judea'] to Syria-Palestina, a name that became common in non-Jewish literature." — [H.H. Ben-Sasson, A History of the Jewish People, Harvard University Press, page 334]

[194] [Ramsheadpress/Messiah/Ch10].

[195] (The Roman Empire in the First Century - Philo/PBS)

[196] "NO SURRENDER OF BELIEF". 'The populace was stationed below in the court and the elders on the steps and the priests in the Sanctuary itself. And though they were but a handful fighting against a far superior force, they were not conquered until part of the Temple was set on fire. Then they met their death willingly, some throwing themselves on the swords of the Romans, some slaying one another, others taking their own lives and still others leaping into the flames. And it seemed to everybody and especially to them that so far from being destruction, it was victory and salvation and happiness to them that they perished along with the Temple.' - (Deo Cassius, Epitome of Book LXV; History Crash Course #35: Destruction of the Temple, Aishcom) / 'Though a breach was made in the wall by means of engines, nevertheless the capture of the place did not immediately follow even then. On the contrary, the defenders killed great numbers (of Romans) who tried to crowd through the opening and they also set fire to some of the buildings nearby, hoping thus to check the further progress of the Romans. Nevertheless, the soldiers, because of their superstition, did not immediately rush in but at last, under compulsion from Titus, they made their way inside. Then the Jews defended themselves much more vigorously than before, as if they had discovered a piece of rare good fortune in being able to fight near the Temple and fall in its defense'. - (Roman Historian, Deo Cassius, Epitome of Book LXV)

[197] (Hillel the Elder; First Century Pacifist and Spiritual Head of Israel; 60 BCE -10 CE. House of Hillel; Wiki; Chabad Org.)

[198] 'The Crime of Christendom: The Theological Sources of Christian Anti-Semitism Paperback'; Fred Glastone Bratton, Scb Distributors.

[199] (H. Kung, "Pseudo-Theology about the Jews" in: Christian Attitudes on Jews and Judaism; 1977, 1ff.)

[201] Pre-Catholic Times. "Before Catholicism was decreed the state religion of Rome by Constantine in the fourth century AD, the empire was pagan. They worshipped many gods, including Greek and Roman deities. Though they permitted Jews to swear oaths without calling on the gods, the Romans persecuted the believers in Jesus (both Jew and non-Jew) with zeal unknown by most today." - [Ramsheadpress/Messiah/Ch10].

[202] - ("The failure of the Christian mission to the Jews", David C Sim, Biblical Theology and Hermeneutics Research project, Australian Catholic University)

[203] - (Eliade, Vol. 4, Eastern Christianity; Jewish Encyl.)

[204] - (Schaff Philip, Ed. 1893; A Select Library of Nicene and Post-Nicene Fathers of the Christian Church: Second Series)

[205] The Dead Sea Scrolls were hidden by this ancient people long ago in the caves of Qumran. - (The Reluctant Messenger/Essene) / Dr. Yonathan Adler - Phylacteries. Archaeology Researcher finds tantalizing tefillin parchments from Second Temple era in Dead Sea Scrolls package. Over 25 Phylacteries, known in Judaism by the Hebrew term tefillin, are pairs of leather cases containing biblical passages - ("Uncovered in Jerusalem", The Times of Israel/#ixzz2w6zlusd)

[206]

DEATH/WAR TOLL.

HUMAN TOLL SUMMARY - ROMANS & JEWS:

• TEMPLE WAR (70 CE): 30,000 Roman Soldiers; 1.1m Jewish Fighters & Civilians.

• MASADA WAR (73 CE): 600 Roman Soldiers; 1,000 Jewish Fighters & Civilians.

• KITOS WAR (115 CE): 4, 40,000 Roman Soldiers & Civilians; Jewish Populations destroyed in Cyprus, Cyrena & Alexandria.

• BAR KOTCHBA WAR (135 CE):

• "Some 50,000 to 100,000 Jews were crucified by the Romans in the first century." (Joseph Telushkin, Jewish Literacy, NY: William Morrow and Co.)

[207] "Jesus spoke only Hebrew and the everyday language of the day...Aramaic. He was a Jew preaching to Jews" - (The Origins of Christian Anti-Semitism, Sandra S. Williams, Uni of Central Florida) / "The Historical Jesus (as opposed to the Jesus of the New Testament and elevated to divinity by the Christian Church) was a Jew, faithful to the law of Moses and the teachings of the prophets." / "Practically all of his sayings, including the Lord's Prayer (Math. 6: 9-13), can be found in Jewish writings before his time, the Old Testament, the Apocrypha, Rabbinical teaching, or the Essene literature." - (Fred Gladston Bratton, The Crime of Christendom, Boston: Beacon Press, 1969])/ Crucifixion of Jesus was by Romans; Jesus followed Mosaic Laws. - ("Anti-Semitism in the US", Charles Patterson, Jewish Virtual Libr.)

[208] Freedom of Belief. 'The causes of this tension are to be found first and foremost in the religious-ideological conflict between the belief of the Jews and that they were forcibly subjected to the rule of an idolatrous empire which accorded divine honors to its emperors.' — (Zealots and Sicarii, Jewish Virtual Libr. Org.)

[209] ROMAN DEFECTIONS - MASS CONVERSIONS.

"The issues came to a head over the large number of Gentiles who became converts, or who wanted to become converts, to Judaism. The Pharisees insisted that all converts to Judaism were joining "a new and godly commonwealth" - (Baron - JRank, 1983, vol. 1, p. 181; Science Encyclopedia; Anti-Semitism-Overview, Roman Empire) * 'Some Romans thought that the city was impregnable and went over to the other side; many gentiles came to their aid. The Jews in the Diaspora and some Samaritans, who in the past had a hostile relationship with the Jews, also joined the rebellion. The whole earth, one might almost say, was being stirred over the matter.' — [Cassius Dio Roman history 69.12.1-14.3; Dio Cassius, xxxvii. 17] / * The Jewish Population in the world at the beginning of the reign of Herod was approximately four to six million. A century later, after the destruction of the Temple, there were almost ten million Jews, representing an enormous increase. The reason was not simply related to an increased birth rate, but that hundreds of thousands - if not millions - converted to Judaism. It was a time of mass conversion in the Roman world; Roman historians wrote that approximately one out of every ten people in the Roman Empire was Jewish. The main reason is simple: Roman paganism began to break down. — [Jewish History Org; Hillel & Shammai]

[210] 'In 200 B.C.E, the Jewish philosopher Aristobulus made the positive assertion that Jewish revelation ('In the Beginning God') and Aristotelian philosophy ('God as A First Cause') were identical. Jewish Encl.; Josephus "AGAINST APION/ contra Apionem," ii. 17); Maimonades, The Jewish Religion: A Companion, Oxford University Press)

[211] Traktaet ueber die Juden'.

www.ingramcontent.com/pod-product-compliance
Lightning Source LLC
Chambersburg PA
CBHW081147090426
42736CB00017B/3222